Gone
Primitive

Ed Rihacek. *Gone Primitive.* Prismacolor, 40″ X 30″.
Courtesy of Somerhill Gallery.

Gone Primitive

Savage Intellects,
Modern Lives

Marianna Torgovnick

The University of Chicago Press

Chicago and London

The University of Chicago Press, Chicago 60637
The University of Chicago Press, Ltd., London

© 1990 by the University of Chicago
All rights reserved. Published 1990
Paperback edition 1991
Printed in the United States of America

99 98 97   5 4

ISBN: 0-226-80832-7 (paper)

Library of Congress Cataloging-in-Publication Data
Torgovnick, Marianna, 1949–
Gone primitive : savage intellects, modern lives / Marianna
Torgovnick.
p.   cm.
Includes bibliographical references.
1. Primitivism in art.   2. Arts. Modern—20th century.   3. Arts—
Psychological aspects.   4. Popular culture.   5. Anthropology.
I. Title.
NX456.5.P7T67   1990   89-20375
700—dc20   CIP

⊗ The paper used in this publication meets the minimum
requirements of the American National Standard for Information
Sciences—Permanence of Paper for Printed Library Materials,
ANSI Z39.48-1984.

For my parents,
Salvatore and Rose De Marco,
and parents-in-law,
Nathan and Jean Torgovnick

Contents

5
Gone Primitive

Acknowledgments

When I started writing this book, I got some advice: do not leave out the juicy things you discover along the way and, when you find yourself getting dull, pretend you are La, the barbarian priestess from the Tarzan series. Both were good pieces of advice, given by the members of my writing group, whose comembers are Jane Tompkins and Alice Kaplan. These two insisted that I write with clarity and force. They gave me a great deal of help and valuable permissions, and I thank them for both.

Two other women important in the writing of this book are my daughters Kate and Elizabeth. They helped define its scope when, as a three-year-old at breakfast, Elizabeth began to beat her chest and chant in a loud, aggressive voice, "I like bananas, coconuts, and grapes. I like bananas, coconuts, and grapes. That's why they call me Tummy-tummy-aches." She had learned this rhyme at her progressive nursery school, and the version she remembered made sense but was, of course, wrong. Before I could correct her, her five-year-old sister, speaking from the wisdom of her advanced acculturation, did it for me: "Oh, no, Lizza. Not Tummy-tummy-aches, but [you guessed it] *Tarzan* of the *Apes*." At that moment, my interest in Tarzan was born, as was my continuing concern with how soon children learn about "the primitive," and how what they learn—like our culture's general knowledge—is often just a little "off."

Numerous friends and colleagues provided information and leads, some of which eventually evolved into sections of this study. These friends helped show me how much people *care* about the primitive and have ideas about it. The tips they provided often made me feel I was in a dream. "Imagine," a voice might have said in this dream, "imagine anything you'd like about the West's relation to the primitive. Imagine and find it true." In writing this material, which is often very strong and dramatic, I have tried to achieve several balances: to write a hard-hitting critique of views dominant in the West

ix

while avoiding demonization and recognizing that Western culture is far from monolithic; to pay sympathetic attention to primitive societies while neither scanting their variety nor slipping into wanton idealization.

Virginia Dominguez, Frank Lentricchia, Julie Tetel, and Thomas Ferraro (colleagues at Duke) all read portions of the manuscript, as did John Comaroff at the University of Chicago and George Levine at Rutgers University. Audiences for talks at Duke, the University of Rochester, the Modern Language Association, and other places asked good questions and affected the directions I would take. A graduate seminar at Duke in Spring 1988 was indefatigable in providing me with information and with evidence that primitivism was everywhere present in contemporary culture. This seminar's insights and quarrels, enthusiasm and observations, helped in a real way as I wrote this book. Karl Kroeber and an anonymous reader at Chicago made tough criticisms that greatly improved the version of the book printed here.

Duke University's Research Council provided generous funds for research travel and the purchase of photographs; Duke also provided a sabbatical leave during which I was able to revise my first draft substantially. Various graduate assistants got books from area libraries, checked references, and helped me track down illustrations: Susan Poznar, Kathryn West, Stanley Blair, and Charles Paine, my thanks is greater than the meager pay you received. Marlin Price, my administrative assistant, was inventive in securing illustrations and copyright permissions, and helped assemble the finished manuscript.

I suspect I have left out more than one person, but really I cannot leave out my husband, Stuart, who has grown used to watching me become obsessed with my topic and encourages me in more ways than I can say. He is always present, as a ghost figure, in my dedications.

Finally, a book like this cannot take shape without the cooperation of numerous museums and individuals who provide illustrations and permissions. I thank here sources acknowledged more particularly below: Duke Photographers, Gerygraphics, the Museum of Modern Art, the Artists Rights Society, the Man Ray Trust, Somerhill Gallery, the Burroughs Memorial Collection, George McWhorter, Edgar Rice Burroughs Inc., the American Museum of Natural History, the Art Institute of Chicago, the Musée d'Orsay, the Bettman Archive, the Musée National d'Art Moderne, the Centre

Georges Pompidou, the Öffentliche Kunstsammlung Basel, the Musée Royal de L'Afrique Centrale, the Musée de L'Homme, the Metropolitan Museum of Art, Adrian Boot, Edmund Engelman, Ken Heyman, Frances Spalding, and the Library of Congress.

PART **1**

Going Primitive

I

Defining the Primitive / Reimagining Modernity

Imagining Them

They exist for us in a cherished series of dichotomies: by turns gentle, in tune with nature, paradisal, ideal—or violent, in need of control; what we should emulate or, alternately, what we should fear; noble savages or cannibals.[1] They exist also as a global whole—complete, knowable, definable. *La mentalité primitive, The Mind of Primitive Man, La pensée sauvage*—the "the" in these titles wrongly implies singularity, universality, a truth about primitives not only available but comprehensive.[2] They exist as well in a sexualized field. *Studies of Savages and Sex, The Sexual Life of Savages, Coming of Age in Samoa*—these are classic titles in anthropology.[3] Although part of the fabric of life, the sexual element is often separated out and designated for special study of the most intense kind, as twentieth-century ethnographers tread boldly over terrain that Sigmund Freud and Havelock Ellis had begun to explore in the West. Ethnography, especially when influenced by Freud, collaborated with other aspects of our culture in perpetuating an image of the primitive that is still with us, and still immensely powerful and seductive. This image is the subject of my book.

Listen to Bronislaw Malinowski, a Pole by birth but a leader in the development of British functionalism in the first half of this century, in his *The Sexual Life of Savages* (1929; reissued in paperback 1968 and 1987):[4]

> We shall follow several [of the villagers] in their love affairs, and in their marriage arrangements; we shall have to pry into their domestic scandals, and to take an indiscreet interest in their intimate life. For all of them were, during a long period, under ethnographic observation, and I obtained much of my material through their confidences, and especially from their mutual scandal-mongering. (14)

3

This is a remarkable, yet typical, passage which reveals some of the reasons that later anthropologists criticized Malinowski's theories and methods. Malinowski writes with substantial faith in his authority and in the power of neutral observation. He claims in the foreword to the first edition that "plain statement" about sexual matters can neither "offend" nor "be of any use to the seeker after pornography" (lxxxiii). Indeed his work, like that of ethnographers in other traditions (the historical, culture-based models of Boas and A. L. Kroeber, for example),[5] sought to overturn Victorian prudery about sexuality. Yet the structure of the passage, as of the book, is licentious.

We shall follow islanders in their lovemaking; we shall "pry" and "take an indiscreet interest in their intimate life." This is keyhole vocabulary, the vocabulary of voyeurism—nor are we given any choice about whether to join the body of voyeurs. We are Peeping Toms by virtue of reading the book. We depend on gossip—on news of scandals; we receive confidences which can become—at the twist of a phrase—scandalmongering, the confidante now feminized, censured, made to seem malicious. We are pulled through this passage until we come up against a magically powerful "I," the I of the ethnographer, the privileged part of us. That I is an observing eye, a scientific eye, but also an I who likes being powerful, who exults in having "all of them under ethnographic observation."

Malinowski's "we" refers to the populations he considers normative and empowered—European or of European ancestry, white, literate, educated, of or above the middle class. The "we" as I use it in this section basically denotes the "we" that imagines a primitive "them," a cultural "we" that often, but not always, overlaps with Malinowski's conceived audience. I use the "we" strategically, to prevent myself and my reader from backing away, too easily, from the systems of us/them thinking that structure all discourse about the civilized and the primitive. But at times—as here, for me, as a female writer suspicious of Malinowski's level of interest in primitives—that "we" is intended to produce a sense of discomfort or misfit. The "we" is necessary to expose a shared illusion: the illusion of a representative primitive "them" as opposed to a monolithic, unified, powerful "us." It is necessary to reveal the "us" as fragmented along lines of gender, national origin, class, political sympathies, race, and dozens of other categories and preferences that will determine individual readers' resistance to being part of the cultural "we."

Malinowski structures his book to reproduce what he calls "the native point of view" in a way that will make it accessible to us in the West (237). He can do so because he has lived in the Trobriands longer than ethnographers before him typically lived with the people being studied, thereby helping establish what came to be called the ethnographic method of the participant-observer. What he means is that he understands the "native point of view" so thoroughly that he is able to put its unspoken assumptions into words and to bring it into a verbal, codified order. Occasionally, Malinowski records what he has been told (myths and magic words) without attempting to fully explain and organize his materials, but this is not his usual procedure.[6] Usually, he receives gossip and transforms it into "ethnographic observation"; usually, he deals in facts (not reported facts), in scientific data wrought into what he calls an elegant "final synthesis."[7] Malinowski characteristically compares his work in ethnography to the work of the physicist (a career for which he studied), precisely because, under the functionalist model, the ethnographer explains systematically the interaction of elements within societies much as the physicist explains the interaction of forces in the physical world or the biologist the working of parts within organisms. Malinowski's method depends on piecing together in the published ethnography two (often temporally separate) roles: that of a fieldworker and an interpreter, a recorder and an analyst.[8] The seam between the two functions—as embodied in the structure and style of the ethnography itself—often reveals the exercise of power, as the cover of the Harvest paperback edition makes clear (fig. 1.1).[9]

The book's title and author's name occupy fully one-half of the cover; the white background extends even farther, for perhaps three-quarters of the page. The author's name penetrates the name of the book, a name which itself suggests penetration. If that explanation seems to go too far, the illustration at the bottom of the cover signals quite clearly the themes of sexuality and gender. It merges the biological symbols for male and female, deploying half against the white field of title and author's name, half against an illustration below. The top half of the merged symbol is male, colored gold, and displayed against the white zone that also grounds the title and author's name. The book describes social customs in which women of high rank are elevated on platforms over men and sexual positions in which males and females come together horizontally; yet the hierarchy that structures the cover design is the male-on-top order of Malinowski's culture. The male arrow points toward the title, repeating the penetration of the title by the author's name. The female

Fig. 1.1. Author's
name, male symbol, and light
background float together.
Cover, 1968 Harcourt
Brace Jovanovich edition of
*The Sexual Life
of Savages*

half of the symbol is colored bright orange and is displayed against
a gray and black picture of the jungle. Both the female symbol and
the photograph of the jungle hug the bottom of the cover—they are
marginalized, separated from the world of logic, language, words,
authority. Read symbolically, the balance of colors on the cover establishes certain linkages. "The Sexual Life of Savages," the photo
of the jungle, and the female symbol group together. The author's
name, the male symbol, and the light background float together in
Apollonian splendor.

   The Sexual Life of Savages moves from chapters on "the relations
between the sexes in tribal life," through chapters on marriage and
pregnancy customs, to sections on "customary forms of license,"
"love-making and the psychology of erotic life," and magic. The organization teases and titillates. Malinowski claims the organization
will give us a feel for how the Trobriand islander understands things:
first everyday routines; then the special customs and rituals, the
unusual events which enliven routine but are still part of normal
Trobriand life. As we move from section to section of the book, the

language of compulsion continues—we must do this or that. Malinowski takes us on a journey toward the object he posits as our desire:

> In the course of this inquiry we have been gradually approaching our main interest, and taking an increasingly detailed view of native love-making. At first we merely made a general survey of the social organization. . . . We studied their associations and their diversions. . . .
>
> Then coming nearer to our special subject we followed the typical progress of courtship, and found it leading to marriage and parenthood. . . .
>
> In this chapter it will be necessary to observe the dalliance of lovers at still closer quarters. We have to learn the nature of their love interest and of the bonds which unite them. (281)

Here we are, at last, at our "main interest," observing at close quarters "the dalliance of lovers." The copulating couple is before our eyes—in a manner of speaking, at our feet, their position(s) duly described. Am I wrong to see this narrative structure as a form of striptease, its goal (coming closer, closer) the seduction of the reader, the reader's consent to an act of voyeurism?

As someone who is not an anthropologist, I was puzzled by all those "musts." Why must we do this? Where is the compulsion? In the case of Malinowski and similar ethnographers, the answer is often "Sigmund Freud." Malinowski conceived of himself as a pioneer in the unknown territory of human sexuality, a pioneer who, like Havelock Ellis and Sigmund Freud, would tell the truth.[10] Ellis wrote the preface to the 1929 edition of *The Sexual Life of Savages*, and that seems suitable, since Malinowski paid tribute to Ellis's studies of human sexuality in his preface to the book.[11] Elsewhere, in *Sex, Culture, and Myth*, Malinowski wrote about Ellis, about James Frazer, and about Freud. This group of thinkers shared the same goal, even when they disagreed on details: they sought the universal truth about human nature and conceived of primitive societies as the testing ground, the laboratory, the key to that universal truth. Freud's explanation of the human psyche in terms of sexuality undergirded their endeavors and influenced the structure of many ethnographic inquiries at this stage of the discipline's development, even when those inquiries suggested (as they often did) modifications of Freudian paradigms, such as the Oedipus complex.[12] Other branches of anthropology (linguistics and physical anthropology, for example) would follow different directions, some of which would challenge the viability of *primitive* as a term.[13] But a genealogy of thinkers would perpetuate ideas about primitive life that would affect an entire culture's imagination of the primitive.

Ethnographers were bound to primitive societies more directly than Freud ever was: he read books and collected statues; they lived and worked in remote locations. But ethnographers like Malinowski shared Freud's larger goals. They must document the intimate life of primitive peoples so that we can learn the truth about us—safely, as observers. The conceived link between us and them often depends on evolutionist premises, on the sense that the primitive represents, in Freud's words, "a necessary stage of development through which every race has passed" (*Totem and Taboo*, 29). Many ethnographers, including Boas and Malinowski himself, intended their work to be antievolutionist in thrust. But they could not always control the way their ideas would be used by other scholars or received by the general public.[14] The evolutionist paradigm linking us and them was difficult for ethnography to discard entirely. Its assumption of an essential human nature was a useful way for ethnographers to justify their work to themselves and, very important, to obtain funding from government agencies and foundations. As Malinowski once put it, then, "the primitive mind" is "the human mind as we find it universally"; to study it is to study human nature writ large (*Sex, Culture, and Myth*, 126).[15]

To study the primitive is thus to enter an exotic world which is also a familiar world. That world is structured by sets of images and ideas that have slipped from their original metaphoric status to control perceptions of primitives—images and ideas that I call tropes.[16] Primitives are like children, the tropes say. Primitives are our untamed selves, our id forces—libidinous, irrational, violent, dangerous. Primitives are mystics, in tune with nature, part of its harmonies. Primitives are free. Primitives exist at the "lowest cultural levels"; we occupy the "highest," in the metaphors of stratification and hierarchy commonly used by Malinowski and others like him. The ensemble of these tropes—however miscellaneous and contradictory—forms the basic grammar and vocabulary of what I call primitivist discourse, a discourse fundamental to the Western sense of self and Other.[17]

Those who study or write about the primitive usually begin by defining it as different from (usually opposite to) the present. After that, reactions to the present take over. Is the present too materialistic? Primitive life is not—it is a precapitalist utopia in which only use value, never exchange value, prevails. Is the present sexually repressed? Not primitive life—primitives live life whole, without fear of the body. Is the present promiscuous and undiscriminating sexually? Then primitives teach us the inevitable limits and controls placed on sexuality and the proper subordination of sexuality to the needs of child rearing. Does the present see itself as righteously Christian? Then primitives become heathens, mired in false beliefs. Does the present include vigorous business expansion? Then primitives cease to be thought of as human and become a resource for industry, able to work mines and supply natural wealth. In each case, the needs of the present determine the value and nature of the primitive. The primitive does what we ask it to do. Voiceless, it lets us speak for it. It is our ventriloquist's dummy—or so we like to think.

This century has claimed to establish new relations with the primitive and has indeed fostered new disciplines devoted to it (ethnography, and the study of African and Oceanic sculptures as art, for example). Yet in modernism and its sequel, postmodernism, the relations are often not new enough and sometimes not really new at all. We have become accustomed to seeing modernism and postmodernism as opposed terms marking differences in tone, attitude, and forms of economic and social life between the first and second halves of the twentieth century. Yet with regard to views of the primitive, more similarities exist than we are used to acknowledging.[18] The real secret of the primitive in this century has often been the same secret as always: the primitive can be—has been, will be (?)—whatever Euro-Americans want it to be.[19] It tells us what we want it to tell us. We decide whether what we have heard is a golden confidence or a nasty bit of scandalmongering.

Judgments vary according to time, place, and circumstance. During the twenties and thirties, ideals derived from images of primitive life were used by the Right—in fascist slogans of "folk" and "blood" and "fertility," and in Nazi mass rallies and emblems like the swastika.[20] Ethnographers like Malinowski debated whether primitive societies were naturally "communistic" and "promiscuous" or "individualistic" and "monogamous."[21] The vocabulary drew upon powerful issues of the day, and the discussion linked, in a telling way, economics and sex. Especially since the sixties, versions of the primitive have been used by the Left—in antitechnological protest, as inspiration for jewelry and dress, as model for communal life. Contemporary writers, especially those on the Left, often invoke an idealized version of the primitive as a precapitalist social and economic model, sometimes ignoring the diversity of primitive life and cases in which exchange value, or something analogous to it, prevails.[22] Our usual political oppositions of left and right, liberal and conservative, socialist and capitalist, radical and reactionary fail us with regard to the primitive. As a concept, the primitive seems to be infinitely docile and malleable, as what we want shifts and changes.

Titles of books on Africa and the South Pacific—and not just the titles of the anthropology books mentioned earlier—revel in the tropes of primitivist discourse. Listen to the titles of the American journalist and explorer Henry M. Stanley: *How I Found Livingstone: Travels, Adventures, and Discoveries in Central Africa; In Darkest Africa, or the Quest, Rescue, and Retreat of Emin, Governor of Equatoria; The Congo and the Founding of Its Free State: A Story of Work and Exploration.* We have known these tropes a long time. Africa is "dark" and dangerous; its core, center, or heart counts most, even though Stanley journeyed also in the East and West. Africa is a testing ground for men, a place of adventure, of rescues from danger.[23] Then, after colonization, Africa is a place of "work." Or listen to the titles of German anthropologist Leo Frobenius: *The Childhood of Man; The Voice of Africa; The Unknown Africa; Atlantis.*[24] These tropes too are familiar: life as Frobenius found it in Africa is "childhood"—the "immature," "developing" state of human existence; the Westerner gives Africa its voice; Africa is "unknown" because Westerners do not know it. In fact, according to Frobenius, African civilization is not necessarily African at all: he thought the city of Benin was the remnant of Atlantis, a lost Western civilization. This idea of an ancient white civilization in Africa is also developed, for example, in the Tarzan novels. It is a common topos of Western writing which tries to show that the "best" of Africa is white.

The tendency to perceive primitive peoples or things through the lens of Western myths is also common: an African woman exhibited widely in nineteenth-century Europe was called the Hottentot Venus;[25] Frobenius called Benin Atlantis; Freud invented his version of the primal horde with the Oedipus story in mind.[26] Malinowski's best-known work follows a similar pattern. He called his book on Kula exchange *Argonauts of the Western Pacific,* superimposing Greek myth on his ethnographic findings; within *Argonauts,* he compares the necklaces exchanged in Kula to the crown jewels or to the gold and pearls sought by ordinary European treasure-hunters.[27] Such crossings of Western myths and primitive peoples or institutions create a never-never-land of false identities or homologies. The identities and homologies are false because the two items compared enjoy only a spurious equality.[28] Ultimately, as when Malinowski concludes that Western jewel- or gold-lust is "infinitely more complex and indirect" than the Trobriander's desire for Kula, the Western half of the comparison belittles, overwhelms, or obliterates the non-Western.[29] The tropes and categories through which we view primitive societies draw lines and establish relations of power between us and them, even as they presuppose that they mirror us.

Euro-Americans begin as controlling subject, using tropes to describe the primitive Other. But they sometimes end by adopting the tropes in their perception of self. When he wrote the first volume of his autobiography, ethnographer and art historian Michel Leiris called it *L'age d'homme—Manhood—*implicitly seeing his childhood and adolescence as a long, painful, and incomplete (indeed incompletable) initiation similar to the initiation rites accorded African youths. When D. H. Lawrence contemplated the death forces "imminent in himself," he found them prefigured in "the African way to cultural dissolution" (*Women in Love*, 330). When Jung formulated his theories of the human psyche, he did so with his journey to Africa behind him; this was, for men of his generation, the equivalent of the European Grand Tour. To Jung as to many other moderns, Africa is the quintessential locus of the primitive: it tells a tale of "the eternal beginning" and gives "the most intense sentiment of returning to the land of my youth"; it is "the immemorially known."[30] For Euro-Americans, then, to study the primitive brings us always back to ourselves, which we reveal in the act of defining the Other.

Imagining Us

My own particular versions of the primitive formed in girlhood. Steeped in Westerns but unable to identify with the cowboy, I identified frequently with the Indians; in my dreams, at least, I was an Indian princess as often as I was a schoolmarm or the rancher's daughter. In the late sixties and early seventies, I wore long braids and Indian jewelry and was amused when, in Europe, fair-skinned northerners would ask (deceived also by my Mediterranean coloring) whether I was not, in fact, an American Indian. I decorated my apartments with dashiki cloths, Mexican pottery, and Indian bedspreads. I owned clothing manufactured in India, Peru, and Central America. I read Carlos Castaneda and thought that "natural" meant "good." Without being much aware of it, I lived the sixties' version of the primitive.

My tastes in high culture also dictated—though I did not know it—that I would someday write this book. My favorite artists were Gauguin, Klee, Matisse, Brancusi, and, sometimes, Picasso—all, I now realize, among the most aggressive of twentieth-century primitivizers. I read and taught Conrad and Eliot; I wrote on Lawrence and Woolf. All these authors brought us, in their different ways, versions of the primitive.

My decision to write this book grew from the realization that I had absorbed many myths of the primitive. In the last chapter of my second book, *The Visual Arts, Pictorialism, and the Novel,* I discussed how D. H. Lawrence uses characters' reactions to African and Oceanic statues and modern art works based on them to discuss, by indirection, "taboo" sexual subjects—sado-masochism, anal intercourse, homoeroticism, subjection and domination. I knew, of course, that Lawrence's ideas about "the African way to cultural dissolution" were bizarre and unfounded, though not utterly idiosyncratic within his culture. And yet I accepted, in that chapter, Lawrence's assumption that African and Oceanic statues alluded to these sexual subjects and that the allusions were a sign of cultural dissolution. I accepted because it was not my business, I thought, to judge Lawrence's assumptions, just to explicate them, to show how they worked.

When, in late 1984, the Museum of Modern Art opened a major exhibition called "'Primitivism' in 20th-Century Art: Affinity of the Tribal and the Modern," I went to see it, aware of its relevance to my book but not, as it turned out, aware enough. MOMA (more specifically, its director, William Rubin) had done as I had done: documented how the modern West conceived the primitive. The exhibition assumed that it existed within a postmodernist, and hence postcolonialist, frame of mind; yet its assumptions everywhere raised the same kinds of political issues as colonialism itself. Only peripherally did the exhibition ask whether modernist conceptions of primitive societies matched available data; hardly at all did the exhibition consider the political and psychological cost of those conceptions. All that mattered was the Western conception of the primitive. The exhibition freely confessed in its brochure that modernism contained many "misreadings" of primitive societies or objects.[31] But it passed lightly over those "misreadings" since they were deemed necessary for the development of modern art. The exhibition made me uncomfortable, discontent, and started me on the investigations and rethinkings embodied in this book.

To speak of misreading primitive societies, as MOMA did, is to exist in a textual universe in which interpretations can be right or wrong but have consequences only within the relatively confined sphere of intellectual life. But ideas about primitive societies and, very important, the persistent Western tendency to process the third world as "primitive" have made things happen in the political world. Many events in this century would have been less possible without operative notions of how groups or societies deemed primitive become available to "higher" cultures for conquest, exploitation, or extermination: the partition of Africa, the invasion of Ethiopia, the Nazi "final solution" for Gypsies and Jews, for example. Events closer to us in time have similarly been influenced by shifting views of what is or is not primitive: Vietnam, U.S. actions in the Persian Gulf, Western backing of dictatorships in countries like Zaire, for example. Once we recognize the persistence and fluidity of primitivist discourse, Western attitudes toward and media coverage of many events can be seen as extensions of older and, to some extent, discredited, traditions.

Conditions of everyday life similarly depend on how a given era defines and values the primitive: university curricula, museum exhibitions, library and bookstore inventories, and television programming, for example. At the turn of this century, it was self-evident that primitive objects were "idols" fit only to be burned by missionaries or to teach would-be colonialists about the territories they would enter; within twenty years it became equally clear that primitive statues were beautiful objects, suitable for collectors. Before the sixties, universities rarely required or even offered courses in third world history or culture outside of anthropology departments; today such courses are commonplace, and our students are encouraged, and often required, to take them, though it is far from clear that single courses change years of cultural conditioning.

As a child I remember seeing a movie on television about the survivors of a plane crash in (no doubt) the center of Africa; I watched with suitable thrills of terror as they were picked off, one by one, by poisoned darts launched by invisible "natives." The primitive was a scary place in which Americans could find themselves stranded by plane crashes or (more traditionally) shipwrecks. A video I've seen of a film from the 1980s introduced the hero—Rider Haggard's own Allan Quartermain—to three different African

tribes. The first, he was told, would rob him; the second would de-
sert him; the third would eat him. Some views of Africans had not
changed from the fifties to the eighties. But my same television
could show me, on other nights, a documentary about Amazonian
Indians or Basil Davidson's nuanced and informative series *Africa*,
which included excellent episodes on varieties of colonialism and
their continuing effect in different parts of Africa. Our attitudes
shape representations of the primitive; those representations shape
us and our children.

But here too we reach a level of abstraction, a discourse of self and
Other which has become familiar in our books and classrooms but
which we rarely feel on our pulses. To defamiliarize that discourse,
to make us feel it in our veins, I want to tell a mysterious story that
was for me one of the ur-stories of this book. It is a story about men
and women, about the primitive as the sexual, and the primitive as
the grotesque. It is a story that ends in psychological maiming and
death. And it is a story that demonstrates how views of the primitive, as they have developed in the West, recoil against us, hit us
where it hurts.

The story comes from the life of the leading British art critic of
his day and an important member of the Bloomsbury group, Roger
Fry. During the teens and twenties, Fry wrote several influential essays on African drawings and sculpture, which were by then much
in vogue among artists and collectors. Fry repeatedly fell in love
with women who either did not fully return his love or were distinctly unstable. His wife proved insane shortly after their marriage,
and she needed life-long hospitalization. Fry fell in love with Va-
nessa Bell, but she left him for Duncan Grant. In the twenties, Fry
met a Frenchwoman named Josette Coatmellac who immediately
fell in love with him. He vacillated, he hesitated, but finally, he returned her love. Then, as Fry's biographer Frances Spalding tells it,
an African mask precipitated the denouement in their relationship:

> In Paris, in the spring of 1924, Fry showed Josette an African mask
> which he had bought and its savage expressiveness jarred on her
> nerves, leaving her frightened and alarmed. On his return to Lon-
> don Fry received a letter from Josette accusing him of taunting
> her with the sculpture, and of putting all his love and energies
> into art, leaving little or nothing for her. He replied immediately,
> urgently denying her accusations, but before the letter reached its
> destination, Josette had shot herself on the cliff at Le Havre, look-
> ing towards England. (*Fry*, 243)

Spalding's account is deadpan; she reads the incident as an instance of "the triumph of mental chaos over reason and love" (243), and she accepts as a given the "savage expressiveness" of the mask. But the incident is more mysterious and ambiguous than her account would indicate.

Spalding says Fry showed Josette the mask in Paris; Fry's last letter to Josette (written before he knew of her death) suggests instead that he sent her a plate of the mask, accompanied by a letter. She then sent him a letter that he describes as affecting him like "an earthquake," a letter that we can only reconstruct from Fry's final missive to Josette. (Josette's final letter to Fry is not included in his collected *Letters* and may not have been preserved.) In Fry's version of the story, he maintains that his earlier letter accompanying the plate of the mask meant to communicate "sympathy for [Josette's] sufferings," sympathy which she perversely found "cruel and unjust" (*Letters*, 551). Her misperception, Fry believed, hinged on her misreading of what he meant by showing her the mask:

> You speak about my having pulled your leg about a piece of Negro art—but what are you imagining? It's a beautiful thing of which I am very proud; it's one of the most beautiful pieces of sculpture and I was glad to have been able to buy it as things of that quality are usually out of my reach—they are too expensive. I only thought to please you in showing it to you. (*Letters*, 551)

Fry asks Josette to correct her misreading, to "re-read the letter that was with the plate," and alludes (incomprehensibly for me) to a box: "You believe I wanted to make you suffer by self-imposed chores for you, but nothing I do for you is a chore—I only thought of amusing you by telling you how I passed my hand several times over the box without recognising it. Perhaps it was foolish, but it was said without the least *arrière-pensée*" (551). What was in the box (or was it a decorative box given him by Josette?) I cannot tell. Nor can I tell what the *arrière-pensée* might have been. Perhaps Josette resented Fry's sensitivity to the mask but forgetfulness with regard to a "box" associated with her. Perhaps the sexual pun on "box" was one she perceived and resented. The mask clearly raised some sexual issue for them: "Won't you allow," Fry wrote, "that we may love each other tenderly, gently, affectionately, and sometimes passionately." Some issue involving money might also have been raised for Josette by Fry's purchasing the African piece; money spent on sculpture might not be available for the medical care she so persistently needed for her "nervous disorders." Elsewhere in the letter, Fry says, "I had even thought out how I should sell the old Italian pictures I have, if the treatment should prove very costly and I wanted you to have all the luxury and comfort possible" (552).

Fry ends his letter with a plea to Josette—whom he calls Jo-Jo and My Mano ("Manu" in the Tarzan novels means monkey; was the endearment meant to suggest monkeys?)[32]—once again seeing the African mask as the root of her misunderstanding:

> Ah, evidently, I am not strong enough to struggle against your wretched intuition, which discovers such extraordinary and utterly false notions as my wanting to pull your leg with a Negro object (which is now in a place of honour on the mantlepiece of my living-room, where it is admired by everyone). . . . I don't really know what I have written. I am so troubled, so tortured by your letter, by the idea that you no longer love me and by the incomprehensibility of it all. My Mano, so adorable and so delicious, what have I done? (552–53)

We cannot know whether Josette was right that Fry loved his work more than he loved her, that (in words Fry quotes from Josette's last letter) he "put all the nobility of [his] soul in [his] art and there's little left for life." Fry's last letter to her certainly provides evidence to support her accusation: Fry describes lingering before opening her letter "to find a little game in the harmony of the stamps you had put on the envelope"—an ironic delay in reading the equivalent of a suicide note. Again, when Fry remarks in the quotation above that the mask which offends Josette occupies pride of place on his mantle and is "admired by everyone," he employs a dubious rhetorical tactic, which rubs the distraught woman's nose in how wrong she has been.

Nor can we really know why Fry showed her the mask: To share with her his enthusiasm for African masks? To share with her his pleasure in acquiring a fine piece? To expose her to the "passional" forces most moderns saw in it? To expand or educate her sense of beauty? To taunt her? To invite her breakdown and suicide? To free himself from a troubling entanglement? We cannot, indeed, know whether Josette read, or misread, the statue as a sexual taunt, perhaps as an incentive to suicide. What we can know is that others in her culture thought African masks and statues "horrors" that alluded to extreme states of sexuality, suffering, and pain,[33] and that Josette's "intuitions" about and "misreading" of the mask were not purely personal. We know as well that she acted upon what she saw in the mask, acted upon what Fry calls her "wretched intuition," and that her action had the direst consequences most of all for herself but also for Fry. Josette committed suicide; Fry experienced gloom that he claimed overhung his life. After Josette's death, Fry considered the erotic segment of his life ended and he devoted himself thereafter to the service of "art" (Spalding, *Fry*, 245); he was still unaware that "art" is not necessarily a category separable from erotic life.

Fry began by writing about what he called primitive art in a cool, scholarly way; he little imagined that his attention to African masks and statues would have consequences in his personal life, as distinct from his professional life and the decor in which he lived. But the cool contemplation of the scholar will not work with this material. Like Josette and Fry, we all react to the primitive according to an accumulated set of personal and cultural "intuitions." "Primal," we call it, accurately.

Rather than valorizing a distinction between the personal and the psychological, as it might be thought to do, the incident points out the tenuousness of these terms. Everything is personal and psychological, or nothing is; everything is political, or nothing is. Our reactions to the primitive refuse to allow us to pose these as comfortable alternatives. Global, historical, political, social, communal, personal, and psychological values are simultaneously implicated in the issues which cluster around our versions of the primitive. Psychologists and imperialists, socialists and capitalists, liberals and fascists share the same assumptions, lie together in the same bed. Our sense of the primitive impinges on our sense of our selves—it is bound up with the selves who act in the "real," political world. Freud's map of the psyche placed the ego (the *Ich*, the I) at a point that mediates between the civilizing super-ego and the "primitive" libido (or id).[34] Whether his map was accurate or not is less important than its strength as a metaphor for our time. We conceive of ourselves as at a crossroads between the civilized and the savage; we are formed by our conceptions of both those terms, conceived dialectically.

What struck me most in this material about Fry—in all my material—was the way that gender issues always inhabit Western versions of the primitive. Sooner or later those familiar tropes for primitives become the tropes conventionally used for women. Global politics, the dance of colonizer and colonized, becomes sexual politics, the dance of male and female. The best commentators in the general field of Western primitivism—Said, Miller, Clifford, all

male—tend to treat in passing gender issues and related sexual issues that are enormously important and worthy of sustained attention.[35] Their quick remarks often validate connections between
women and primitives or women and death which require exami-
nation and exposure. These writers are wrong to downplay gender
and sexuality as categories of analysis, for the connections between
Western conceptions of the primitive and issues of gender and sexuality are utterly crucial. Freud's theories about sexuality, Malinowski's observations of male and female roles, and similar work
have assured that how we conceive of the primitive helps form our
conception of ourselves as sexual, gendered beings.

We imagine ourselves through the primitive in other, equally devious, ways that also challenge the border between the psychological
and the political. Especially when the conventional substitution of
females for primitives is avoided, other, often class, substitutions
may occur instead. Frequently, the working class or other subordinated segments of a population become associated or identified with
primitives—the Irish, for example, or Jews, or (more specifically)
Eastern European Jews or non-European Jews, or U.S. blacks.[36]
These Others are processed, like primitives, through a variety of
tropes which see them as a threatening horde, a faceless mass, promiscuous, breeding, inferior—at the farthest edge, exterminatable.
Ideas about the primitive sometimes intervene in anxieties about
identity as something fragile, random, subject (in Bataille's terms)
"to a thousand accidents and chances" (*Visions of Excess*, 130).
Views of the primitive become implicated in forms of Western self-
loathing, in the denunciation of the modern self as (in D. H. Lawrence's terms in "The Mozo") "a clever white monkey" whose technological tricks may yet destroy the earth. Primitive beliefs and social relationships sometimes are and sometimes are not seen as
equivalent to the "oceanic": to a dissolution of boundaries between
subject and object and between all conceived and conceivable polarities. Western thinking frequently substitutes versions of the primitive for some of its deepest obsessions—and this becomes a major
way in which the West constructs and uses the primitive for its own
ends.

Defining the "Primitive"—or Trying To

The word *primitive* first appeared in English in the fifteenth century to signify the "original or ancestor" of animals, perhaps of men.

In its dominant meanings through the eighteenth century, it referred to "the first, earliest age, period, or stage," usually of church history, later of biological tissue. It acquired specialized meanings in many fields, including art, mathematics, and grammar—the common element being that *primitive* always implied "original," "pure," "simple"—as the dictionary says, "with implications of either commendation or the reverse."[37] Its references to "aboriginals," "inhabitants of prehistoric times," "natives" in non-European lands date from the end of the eighteenth century.

In art history, *primitive* originally referred to painters before the Renaissance; then it broadened to include all early art—ancient, courtly (Chinese or Aztec, for example), and tribal. By the 1920s, the ancient and courtly had been removed from the category of the primitive, which from then on referred exclusively to "tribal" art— Native American, Eskimo, African, and Oceanic.[38] Since the twenties, the tendency to describe European prehistorical societies, the Greeks and Romans, and Chinese or other courtly cultures as primitive has markedly diminished. When we say "primitive" today, we generally designate certain social formations within relatively isolated areas of Africa, Oceania, South America, and other areas of the world—social formations characterized perhaps most clearly by the absence of tools and technology widely available elsewhere. Such societies have been the traditional objects of ethnographic research and have thus been represented in the West according to available ethnographic categories.

As early as the 1890s, but quite strongly by the teens and twenties, anthropologists like Franz Boas argued for the diversity and complexity of primitive social and mental formations (as opposed now to technological capacity), thereby cutting to the heart of the term's evolutionist connotations.[39] Like Lévi-Strauss in later decades, they claimed that primitive modes of thinking and cultures were not "simpler," just different from Western thinking and cultures.[40] The antievolutionist, cultural relativity of these views was available fairly early in the history of anthropology, and it competed with views of primitive societies as "early," "simple," and "developing" forms of human existence. But cultural relativism needed time to really take hold since it challenged so strongly Western assumptions of superiority. It required readjustments in thought that stripped away decades, even centuries, of usage which saw primitive societies not as various and complete in themselves but as developing toward Western norms. Along with the processes that led to decolonization, this adjustment in thinking put the word *primitive* in disfavor in the decades after World War II—made it go into quotation marks. Increasingly, as cultures once characterized as primitive have become actors on the world stage or come into contact with urban, technological societies, the word *primitive*—with its aura of unchangeability, voicelessness, mystery, and difference from the West—has come to be understood as problematic.

In the late twentieth century, whether one uses *primitive* with or without quotation marks often implies a political stance—liberalism or conservatism, radicalism or reaction, shame over what the West has done to non-Western societies or the absence of shame. When we put *primitive* into quotation marks, we in a sense wish away the heritage of the West's exploitation of non-Western peoples or at least wish to demonstrate that we are politically correct. But the heritage of Western domination cannot be abolished by wishing or by typography. In fact, funny things begin to happen when *primitive* goes into quotation marks. The first thing is that all other constructed terms—especially terms like *the West* and *Western*—seem to require quotation marks as well, a technique that despite its seeming sophistication ultimately relieves writers of responsibility for the words they use.[41] In the absence of such ubiquitous marks, treating *primitive* differently from abstractions such as *Western* implies that the societies traditionally so designated do not, and perhaps never did, exist—are *simply* a figment of the Euro-American imagination.

My position is very different. I would not at all deny the reality and multiplicity of the societies we have tended to call primitive, but would deny that such societies have been, or could be, represented and conceived with disinterested objectivity and accuracy. In both metaphysical and political terms, I have no objection to having the word *primitive* surrounded by quotation marks in the reader's mind's eye: I believe that it and polar terms (like *the West*) are constructed and changeable, and I share the sense of political outrage and moral guilt the quotation marks are meant to show.[42] But I omit the actual quotation marks except when the context does not in itself make clear a fact important throughout this study: for Euro-Americans the primitive as an inexact expressive whole—often with little correspondence to any specific or documented societies—has been an influential and powerful concept, capable of referring both to societies "out there" and to subordinate groups within the West.

The most persuasive definitions I have found of primitive societies note certain general tendencies, tendencies subject to widely varying manifestations. Among these are the legality of custom, the presence of traditional leadership roles, the paramount importance of kinship in social and economic organization, widespread and diffuse social and economic functions assigned each individual, the importance of ritual for individual and group expression (rituals which often include dance and the expression of ambivalence), and a relative indifference to Platonic modes of thought—in short, the condition of societies before the emergence of the modern state.[43] Additional markers, such as rudimentary technology and (frequently, though by no means always) a nomadic or village life with agrarian, herding, or hunting economies, can also be noted.[44] Such societies clearly once occupied much of the earth; today they survive in fewer and more isolated spaces and are often marked by contact, however minimal, with modern (urban and industrial) cultures.

Given the mixed history of the word *primitive*, the urge to jettison it is understandable. But before we could responsibly do that we would need a viable alternative to designate the kinds of societies it describes. Currently, we do not, since all its synonyms are either inexact or duplicate in various ways the problematics of the term *primitive* itself. And here I include savage, pre-Columbian, tribal, third world, underdeveloped, developing, archaic, traditional, exotic, "the anthropological record," non-Western, and Other. Some of these alternatives (third world, underdeveloped, exotic) blur necessary, indeed vital, distinctions between third world nations (which are often urban and industrial) and the remote, relatively primitive, societies they may still harbor. All take the West as norm and define the rest as inferior, different, deviant, subordinate, and subordinatable.[45] We simply do not have a neutral, politically acceptable vocabulary. Short of reaching the true, essential Primitive (a goal even dedicated ethnographers have disavowed), the best we can do is to uncover, from a political and cultural perspective, the kinds of work key terms like *primitive* have performed within modern and postmodern culture and the kinds of work they have evaded or shortchanged.

This study is, then, about conceptions of the primitive that drive the modern and the postmodern across a wide range of fields and levels of culture: anthropology, psychology, literature, and art—and also advertising, fashions, television series, and fads. It is about the primitive as a modern and postmodern obsession, as a bedrock or gut issue—and about the primitive as a modern and postmodern cliché, part of the ambiance and aura of our culture. What might otherwise have been the best solution to problems of terminology—

to supply geographic names to individuate primitive societies or groups, to allude to traditional Africans (or more specifically, say, to the Dogon or the Bushmen, or the Gikuyu) or to documented peoples or societies in the Trobriands, the Sepik River area, and so on—would thus often miss the point.[46] For a generalized notion of the primitive exists and has existed for a long time in our culture— a generalized notion embodied in the multiple, and often contradictory, tropes of primitivist discourse. And this generalized notion of the primitive has been as influential, and perhaps more influential, than whole bundles of detailed ethnographic studies describing the lives of individual peoples.

Our culture's generalized notion of the primitive is by nature and in effect inexact or composite: it conforms to no single social or geographical entity and, indeed, habitually and sometimes willfully confuses the attributes of different societies. Ethnographers tend to compare the societies they study to Western culture and to other societies that have been the object of ethnographic inquiries; even here a generalized primitive is often indirectly invoked as a way of understanding the special qualities of the group at hand. Less professional discourses often unabashedly and irresponsibly mix attributes and objects from widely separate geographical locales. The *jungle*, for example, is a term popularly used to describe the locale of the primitive. And yet, in a strict geographical sense, it is a term most applicable to parts of Southeast Asia—not to African savannas, plains, deserts, forests, or rain forests, not to the Amazon, not to the lands once occupied by Native Americans. The currency of jokes and cartoons about cannibalism (especially about cannibalism in Africa), as opposed to the disputed extent, nature, and function of cannibalism as described in scholarly literature, can serve as a second example: Africans and other groups have often been imaged as cannibals, and yet all scholarly research suggests that cannibalism was never a uniform (and never a simple) practice in Africa or anywhere else, and that groups which eat human flesh and groups averse to eating humans have existed side by side, in a patchwork quilt, wherever the practice has been identified.[47]

To study modern culture's image of the primitive requires that I weave in and out of generalized versions of the primitive, as reflected and promulgated in the various texts I discuss, and documentary accounts of specific peoples, institutions, and productions. I will want, at times, to correct misconceptions when I find them, by drawing to the best of my abilities upon authorities in various fields. But there is a twist and a catch here, in this book's relationship to authority, that is of central importance. With the exception of Edgar Rice Burroughs (author of the Tarzan novels, the subject of the next chapter), each of the figures I discuss possesses some claim to ethnographic authority, to making statements that deserve to be heard about primitive peoples, societies, institutions, or productions. Some of these figures (Freud, Lévi-Strauss, Bataille, Fry, Rubin) read widely and with obvious interest in available literature concerning primitive societies as they pertained to their disciplines. Others drew on the same source of ethnographic authority as fieldworkers—a sustained period of living with "exotic" peoples (Malinowski, Lévi-Strauss in the 1930s, Mead, Leiris, the Blairs, Schneebaum). All have a conceptual framework or a set of theories by which they organize their statements about what is or is not primitive.

Ethnographic authority has been a changeable concept in the twentieth century: sometimes requiring extensive reading, sometimes fieldwork, sometimes a totalizing theoretical framework, sometimes a "dialogic" inclusion of differing views, including the views of the people being studied, sometimes a combination of these possibilities (Clifford, *Predicament of Culture*, chap. 1). Whatever definition or combination of definitions we use, the figures I discuss have a variety of claims to ethnographic authority. But their ethnographic authority does not always help them and is often readily surrendered. Within each chapter, I show how specific kinds of ethnographic knowledge give way to the generalized tropes and images of the primitive described in the opening sections of this chapter. My interest is in opening the seam between "ethnographic authority" in the figures I study and a vaguer, emotional or "intuitive" response to the primitive often at odds with scientific or scholarly knowledge. Although many continuities emerge, each case is different in texture and detail; these differences prevent overgeneralizations about the West, prevent any sense that all Euro-Americans and all discourses about primitives are alike.

Traveling with Odysseus and Stanley

In literature, as in the dictionary, the history of encounters with the primitive Other goes back a long way and the beginnings mark patterns that have been hard to eradicate. In a sense, the West's history with regard to primitives is anticipated in Homer's *The Odyssey*, when Odysseus meets Polyphemus. I discuss this incident in

some detail both because it establishes patterns we shall see again
and because later Westerners who journey to remote societies
(Henry Stanley, Lawrence Blair and Lorne Blair, Tobias Schneebaum)
call their journeys "odysseys" and model themselves, often quite
self-consciously, on the intrepid Odysseus.

On his long travels home, Odysseus visits (voluntarily or not) a
variety of cultures—islands with a single inhabitant (Calypso,
Circe), primitive societies, and hypercivilized ones; his travels are
an education into the possibilities of social life. His education begins with a visit to the land of the Cyclops—his second stop on the
journey home, and a fateful stop, since it is Polyphemus, the Cyclops, who curses Odysseus and dooms him to a journey of ten
years' duration. Odysseus tells about his encounter with the Cyclops in Phaeacia, a hypercivilized land in which men have gone
"soft." Protected by the gods, provided with food as manna, magically safe on the seas, the Phaeacians "take a perennial delight [in]
the feast, the lyre, the dance, clean linen in plenty, a hot bath and
our beds." To them, Odysseus tells the tale of the Cyclops, "a fierce,
uncivilized people."

Odysseus knows as soon as he lands in the territory of the Cyclops (which has no name) that these folk are uncivilized. He knows
because the Cyclops have "no assemblies for the making of laws,
nor any settled customs, but live in hollow caverns in the mountain
heights, where each man is lawgiver to his children." Their land
"lies forever unsown and untilled"; they have "nothing like our
ships with their crimson prows," nor "merchantmen," nor "overseas
traffic." Lacking these things, the Cyclops have failed to develop a
nearby island "which would have been a fine colony for the Cyclops" (142). The process by which Odysseus decides the Cyclops
are a "fierce, uncivilized people" is obvious. They are not like "us"
in any of the categories that ethnography would later employ. The
clincher, for Odysseus, is their lack of zeal in developing colonies.

Once all this has been perceived, Odysseus' men know what to
do—they want to grab all they can and make off with it. Odysseus,
however, is curious; he wants to meet his host before he robs him
and prefers to receive "gifts" instead of booty. As Odysseus realizes
in retrospect, he made a crucial mistake. He expected the Cyclops
to follow the rules of Greek civilization—hospitality and gifts to
guests, as required by the gods. Polyphemus hears his demands, but
responds, in essence, by saying my rules are not your rules, my social contract is not like yours. Indeed, Polyphemus' rules call for

cannibalizing guests; as he says, "It would never occur to me to spare you or your men against my will for fear of Zeus" (146).

Trapped, Odysseus begins by using the weapons of civilized man: language, equivocal wording, deceit. Odysseus says his name is Nemo—a ruse that will trick the other Cyclops when Polyphemus yells for help. Odysseus gives Polyphemus wine and makes him drunk. At this point, the narrative reminds us that Polyphemus is a disgusting "savage," "monstrous" in appearance and deed: he gulps down some sailors and then vomits them up in a drunken stupor. Now Odysseus is free to descend into savagery himself. With his men's help, he heats the pointed end of a pole and

> drove its sharpened end into the Cyclops' eye, [using] weight from above to twist it home, like a man boring a ship's timber with a drill. . . . We handled our pole with its red-hot point and twisted it in his eye till the blood boiled up round the boiling wood. The fiery smoke from the blazing eyeball singed his lids and brow all round, and the very roots of his eye crackled in the heat. I was reminded of the loud hiss that comes from a great axe or adze when a smith plunges it into cold water—to temper it and to give strength to the iron. That is how the Cyclops' eye hissed round the olive stake. (149–50)

This is a long and harrowing passage, one that violates a number of psychological taboos protecting the eyes. Normally, only the villain would perform such an act (think of *King Lear*); here the hero does it, even enjoys telling about it. The narrative protects its hero in several ways: first, by making it clear that, as a "savage," Polyphemus does not deserve the protection of normal rules; second, by making Polyphemus begin the process that leads to this moment and fall liable to it through weakness for drunk; third, by having Odysseus use metaphors (the drill and axe/adze metaphors) that remind us, as we read or listen, that Polyphemus is not one of us— a sailor, a craftsman, a tool-user.

After blinding Polyphemus, Odysseus robs him, then taunts him before reaching the safety of the open sea. His taunts (which climax when he reveals his name) draw down the curse that keeps him at sea for ten years. Had Odysseus not revealed his name, Polyphemus would not have known whom to curse; Odysseus' proud assertion of his identity to the "savage" highlights the identity theme, the definition of self against Other so often involved in the dynamics of defining the primitive.[48] But the incident is not, finally, without cost for Odysseus. It hurts him almost as much as it does the "savage": a ten-year curse and many sufferings, as opposed to permanent blindness. In its rhetoric and unfolding, in its structures of action and thought, this earliest written encounter of how the West views primitives prefigures all others.

Two thousand years later, in *How I Found Livingstone* (1874), Henry M. Stanley sees in primitive societies some of the same things that Odysseus saw. Like Odysseus, Stanley has a goal that only incidentally requires encountering unfamiliar peoples: Odysseus wants to return home; Stanley wants to find Livingstone, the West's premier example of the benevolent, enlightened missionary. Although my reading highlights Stanley's encounters with Africa and Africans, Stanley's does not. To him the land and its people have geographic and ethnographic interest. But he views the land and its people chiefly as novelties and curiosities, as obstacles to or aids in his endeavor, most of all as potential resources for the West. He brings to his narration a number of familiar literary topoi: he is the intrepid explorer and a hero, like Odysseus; his goals are, like Odysseus', clear and immutable though his adventures along the way are startling and unpredictable; his men should be loyal followers but prove untrue; Livingstone is his Grail or his Penelope—the crux and meaning of his journey. Africa and its people are mere props, the stage setting for the drama starring Stanley, with a walk-on appearance by the celebrated Livingstone.

Ironically, Stanley's book about Africa and Africans helped form Euro-American attitudes toward the continent and its inhabitants. It was a best-seller, a book "no boy should be without," and it inspired other best-sellers.[49] This gender specificity should be taken seriously, for Stanley's narrative prescribes attitudes and forms, including the inevitability of hierarchies within the self and with others, that form part of our culture's sense of what it means to be manly. Edgar Rice Burroughs claimed that he wrote Tarzan with the aid of "a 50-cent Sears dictionary and Stanley's *In Darkest Africa*" (Porges, *Burroughs*, 129); his books too were best-sellers aimed especially at boys and men. Freud read Stanley avidly in his youth; writers like Gide, Conrad, and Leiris modeled their writing about Africa on Stanley's books both generically (using the journal or diary form) and conceptually.[50] The lines of influence from Stanley to modern discourse about the primitive are long and multiple. "Fact" and fiction have reinforced each other powerfully in Western perceptions of the primitive and are sometimes indistinguishable.[51] While that has become a familiar point, it is still an important point to be made and understood.

To find Livingstone, Stanley must pass through African lands rarely seen by Western eyes. When Odysseus sees the islands off the Cyclops' coast, he thinks of colonies. Stanley thinks the same way:

> At a place called Sigunga, we put in for lunch. An island at the mouth of the bay suggested to our minds that this was a beautiful spot for a mission station. . . . The island, capable of containing quite a large village, and perfectly defensible, might, for prudence' sake, contain the mission and its congregation; the land-locked bay would protect their fishery and trade vessels. (573)

Now there is a bare island; after the West's arrival, there will be a mission station, with fishery and trade vessels, on a site easy to defend from hostile Africans and foreign powers. What will be there after Western intervention always impinges on Stanley's view of what is there now.[52] His observations, made in the 1870s, reflect Victorian concerns, and he sees in Africa the two things his age valued most: opportunities for commerce and opportunities for bringing Christianity to "savages." Stanley says that the landscape satisfies the "poetic fancy," and in fact describes it often, through Western eyes, in terms of the Burkean sublime. But the land must be put to use by men like him to fulfill its destiny. Romantic "poetic fancy" gives way to the tough-mindedness of the trader in merchandise and the saver of souls.

Stanley made drawings of much that he saw, drawings that were then turned into full-scale illustrations by an unnamed artist for the published text. These drawings present Stanley as a modern Western hero. Garbed in white and wearing a European pith helmet, Stanley stands in the center of the frontispiece (fig. 1.2). He gazes modestly yet intrepidly at the viewer and holds a gun, pointed downward; he comes in peace but carries the weapon that ensures Western power. Over his shoulder, light illuminates the moody sky—the association of light with Westerner being common in the other illustrations also. To his left stands an African, bare-breasted, holding a gun that is clearly Stanley's, not his. The classic "boy," the African is here literally a child and gazes shyly off toward the ground, not toward the viewer. Stanley's back is turned slightly away from the black boy, who is invisible to him, almost beneath consideration. Beneath the caption "Stanley and Kalulu" is a single bold signature—Stanley's own, Kalulu's being neither available nor expected.[53]

STANLEY AND KALULU.

Fig. 1.2. Kalulu's signature–neither available
nor expected. Frontispiece, 1899 Scribner edition of
How I Found Livingstone.

The climactic moment of Stanley's long narrative, when he meets Livingstone, fulfills the implications of the frontispiece. This moment is iconic in Western perceptions of Africa—its key phrase, "Dr. Livingstone, I presume," a part of general culture. But although the West has favored this phrase from the book (a moment of naming, of indentity establishment, as in Odysseus' final taunting of Polyphemus), it is hardly the most significant or revealing in the incident. The event has become scripted in the popular imagination in a way that reinforces Western perceptions of Africa because Stanley works hard to make it come out that way. But the incident, as Stanley writes it in his diary, records a more complicated moment than the certainties of "Dr. Livingstone, I presume" allow. Here is the incident in full:

> Selim said to me "I see the Doctor, sir. Oh, what an old man! He has got a white beard." And I—what would I not have given for a bit of friendly wilderness, where, unseen, I might vent my joy in some mad freak, such as idiotically biting my hand, turning a somersault, or slashing at trees, in order to allay those exciting feelings that were well-nigh uncontrollable. My heart beats fast, but I must not let my face betray my emotions, lest it shall detract from the dignity of a white man appearing under such extraordinary circumstances. So I did what I thought was most dignified. . . . I would have run to him, only I was a coward in the presence of such a mob—would have embraced him, only he being an Englishman, I did not know how he would receive me; so I did what cowardice and false pride suggested was the best thing—walked deliberately to him, took off my hat, and said:
> "Dr. Livingstone, I presume?"
> "Yes," said he with a kind smile, lifting his cap slightly.
> (411–12)

This is a most peculiar passage. Although Stanley usually perceives the wilderness as something to be crossed to reach his goal, something to be civilized by the West, at this moment the wilderness would be "friendly." It would spare him the self-censorship that automatically seems necessary at this moment of "exciting feelings." In an odd way, Stanley yearns for the months that have preceded his encounter with Livingstone—away from civilization, with only Africans for his companions. He wishes for himself what has long been Livingstone's situation, the isolation from the West that Stanley has come to disrupt. It is significant that Stanley identifies his "well-nigh uncontrollable" emotions with boyishness and that he

conceives of himself, now, as a gentleman; we will do well to remember at this point that Stanley began life as an abused and des-
titute lower-class boy in Britain, rising only in adolescence to the
condition of "gentleman" after his adoption by a rich American
(Manning, *Remarkable Expedition*; Forbath, *Last Hero*).

The terms Stanley uses are conventionally used for passion—his
emotions are "well-nigh uncontrollable," and his heart "beats fast."
But Stanley feels that he "must not let [his] face betray [his] emotions, lest it shall detract from the dignity of a white man" (411).
His concern is both with Livingstone's reaction and with how he
will look to the other observers—blacks and Arabs. Before "them"
he must preserve "the dignity of the white man," even though he
knows that he opts for "dignity" from "cowardice and false pride."
His passion, his enthusiasm, his sportiveness would mar his dignity,
make him seem "boyish," not "manly"; his urge to embrace Livingstone might offend Livingstone, "he being an Englishman."[54] His
"exciting feelings" might lead to "mad freaks," "idiotic" biting of
hands; they might make him as wild as the landscape he has passed
through—childlike, irrational, dangerous, like the Africans themselves in Western conceptions of them. And so the moment is one
of curious revelation and repression. The words "Dr. Livingstone, I
presume," enshrined in our culture rather than alternative words
like "idiotically biting my hand," are forced, artificial—and Stanley
knows it.[55] In choosing to endorse the controlled formality of "Dr.
Livingstone, I presume," our culture has validated Stanley's self-
censorship. Boardroom manners pertain, even in the wilderness.
Reason must take precedence over passion.

The illustration that captures the moment (fig. 1.3) is rigidly organized in concentric circles, as though to hold in the "exciting feelings" that threaten to escape. Stanley and Livingstone stand in the
inner circle, raising their hats in greeting. Stanley stands beneath a
U.S. flag, held by a bare-chested African, the only black (except Kalulu) in the second ring. This second ring consists mainly of Arabs,
dressed in white flowing gowns or white flowing pants and shirts.
Although these Arabs are also African, their appearance and culture—as closer to that of Europeans and Americans—distinguish
them from black Africans in Stanley's mind; while he regards Arabs
as less important than Europeans, he also regards them as more important than blacks—hence their presence in the second circle. Behind Stanley, and behind his few Arab companions, blacks stand,
bare-breasted, wearing African skirts, burdened with the safari's

Fig. 1.3. Boardroom manners, even in the wilderness.

cargo. Behind Livingstone, and behind the semicircle of his Arab companions, Africans surge, spears upright. Stanley cannot see the Africans in more ways than one, and he makes a point of it:

> I turn to the Arabs, take off my hat to them in response to the saluting chorus of "Yambos" I receive, and the Doctor introduces them to me by name. Then, oblivious of the crowds, oblivious of the men who shared with me my dangers, we—Livingstone and I—turn our faces towards his tembe. (413)

"The men who shared with him his dangers"—Arab men and black men—do not count now. They merge with "more than a thousand natives . . . indulging their curiosity, and discussing the fact of two white men meeting at Ujiji" (412–13). Those are the facts which count—white men's facts, and both picture and text record the moment with a white man's sense of what is central and what is marginal.

In his classic essay "Of the Cannibals," Montaigne urges that we judge Others "by the rule of reason and not by the common report," which is likely to be tainted by the fact that "men call that barbarism which is not common to them" (71). Near the beginning of

31

How I Found Livingstone, in a passage similar in spirit to Montaigne, Stanley asserts the diversity of Africans and their equality with other men. The "white stranger about penetrating Africa," says Stanley, "begins to learn the necessity of admitting that negroes are men, like himself, though of a different colour; that they have passions and prejudices, likes and dislikes, sympathies and antipathies, tastes and feelings, in common with all human nature" (9). Even more, Stanley proclaims himself "prepared to admit any black man, possessing the attributes of true manhood, or any good qualities, to my friendship, even to a brotherhood with myself; and to respect him for such, as much as if he were of my own colour and race" (9).

Stanley thinks of himself as a liberal with regard to race: "Though I had lived some time among the negroes of our Southern States, my education was Northern, and I had met in the United States black men, whom I was proud to call friends" (9). Stanley groups together African-Americans and Africans (as did most others in his day) and assumes that he will be as fair and unprejudiced to Africans as he believes he has been to blacks in the United States. He reminds himself of his principles at the beginning of his work, but he does not, maybe cannot, live up to them. The "dignity of the white man" gets in the way; the burden of "Anglo-Saxon" greatness weighs on him. Although Stanley claims often to have "talked with my people as to my friends and equals," the very need to say so and the way he says it give him away—"*my* people," "*as to* equals and friends." He freely resorts to physical force in dealing with Africans. When he encounters a tribe, the Wagogo, that stares too boldly at him, Stanley acts by "gripping the rowdiest of them by the neck, and before he could recover from his astonishment administering a sound thrashing with my dog-whip which he little relished" (186). When the Wagogo protest, asking themselves, "Are the Wagogo to be beaten like slaves by this Musungu? A Mgogo is a Mgwana (a free man); he is not used to being beaten," Stanley "made motion, flourishing my whip, towards them, [and] these mighty braggarts found it convenient to move to respectable distances" (187). He then congratulates himself on the "manliness and show of power" he has displayed (187), and repeats it frequently.

Although Stanley makes much of having overcome his Southern past, in which he had associated blacks with slaves, at moments like these (in which the Africans protest that they are *not* slaves) it is difficult to see how he differs from the abusive overseer or contemptuous master. He holds his men's lives less dear than the things they carry, or acts that way. Once, in a moment Stanley records in a drawing (fig. 1.4), a black named Rojab began to carry Dr. Livingstone's box, containing his letters and journals, across a swollen river.

> [Stanley] caught sight of this man walking in the river with the most precious box of all on his head. Suddenly he fell into a deep hole, and the man and box went almost out of sight, while I was in an agony at the fate which threatened the dispatches. Fortunately, he recovered himself and stood up, while I shouted to him, with a loaded revolver pointed at his head, "Look out! Drop that box and I'll shoot you."
> All the men halted in their work while they gazed at their comrade who was thus imperilled by bullet and flood. (642)

This is one of many illustrations showing Stanley using guns—hunting animals, fending off hostile tribes, disciplining his men. On the left, a porter kneels as to a god, begging mercy for Rojab, whose eyes widen in terror. The other blacks adopt postures of fear and astonishment. Used to exercising control, Stanley does not think, at moments like these, of his companions as "equals and friends"; he thinks of them as beasts of burden—the function they serve, indeed, on his journey. Bearing his dog whip, aiming his gun at his potential "friends and equals," Stanley protects Livingstone's documents and his white man's mission but makes the rhetoric of friendship and equality, of liberal intentions, a hollow sham.

Fig. 1.4. Stanley with his "friends and equals."

"LOOK OUT, YOU DROP THAT BOX, I'LL SHOOT YOU."

As we near the end of the twentieth century, it would be pleasant
to think that we could judge the colonialist Victorians and moderns
and correct their errors, pleasant to think of ourselves as the bene-
factors of primitives. But there is a problem in feeling too comfortable and superior to Stanley, a problem I need now to firmly address.
Moral superiority comes along with the benefit of hindsight. Writers
like Stanley are ready targets, and it is easy to feel indignant and
superior when reading them, especially with the benefit of hindsight. Yet the repetition of Western tropes concerning primitives in
The Odyssey and in Stanley's book tells a cautionary and humbling
tale: a tale of the Western will to mastery at any cost, even at the
cost of maiming some essential part of the self; a tale of how the
desire to approach the Other with open minds and good will gives
way to something that betrays even the best intentions. Stanley's
belief that he had transcended the prejudices of the slaveholding
South is exemplary here: he believed he was beyond relations of
mastery over blacks, which he reproduced all along his path through
Africa and imitated even in his relations to his inner being.

Modernism too believed that it knew what *primitive* meant and
had established the best possible relations with primitive societies;
postmodernism sometimes makes the same mistake. This book
asks some hard questions about the relationship between the primitive and the modern as they have variously been conceived, and it
addresses both the high modernism of the years before World War II
and the postmodernism firmly in place by the sixties: Why did modernism / why do we desire the primitive? How did modernism / how
do we use the primitive to bolster our own ends? How did modernism / how do we project and seduce with versions of the primitive?
Was modernism / are we ultimately seduced by our own projections?

Gone Primitive

In 1986, the Somerhill Gallery in Durham, North Carolina, had a
show of recent drawings by Ed Rihacek. The invitation to the exhibition featured a color reproduction of a prismacolor drawing called
Gone Primitive which dramatized for me some of the dangers of my
enterprise (frontispiece). The drawing recalls photographs of artists'
studios and collectors' libraries from the twenties in which African
art stands amid Western paraphernalia. It also recalls Man Ray's fa-

mous, highly stylized photograph of a woman's head (his mistress, Kiki's) posed with an African mask, casting symmetrical shadows (fig. 1.5). But the piece belongs distinctly to the postmodern 1980s. *Gone Primitive* features a white woman in the center with primitive masks or statues in the background. The woman or someone else (the artist? her husband? lover? friend? employer?) apparently collects the masks and statues. Most are of a familiar kind—the kind sold by street vendors on West Fifty-third Street in New York, near the Museum of Modern Art—and are probably not "primitive" at all, but instead the recent product of cottage industries in the third world.

The woman wears the tribal garb of the New York art scene—loose-fitting black shirt and slacks, black shoes, sunglasses. She sits on a couch somewhat fifties in styling; fifties-revival chairs form a right angle in the foreground. On the floor is a zebra-skin rug. At one level, the drawing is about the cannibalization of different styles into "retro-chic"—the fifties (when African masks routinely appeared in bohemian living rooms) and various allusions to the primitive combine to form the eighties' sense of style.[56] The fifties evoke, for viewers like me, a sense of cultural claustrophobia, especially with regard to women. Such evocations may be part of the drawing's allusions to gender themes, which emerge quite strongly from the work's confrontation of "primitive" artifacts and postmodern ones.

The woman's arms and hands echo, but do not repeat, the arms of the massive Oceanic statue to the right, which (like the *chi wara* antelope to the left, the one not carrying its young) is male in gender. The only other piece with arms, the breasted, cycladically simple female figure to the far left, has its arms pinned rigidly to its sides, in contrast to the woman and the large statue. Out of scale and oddly positioned (it alone breaks into the foreground), this massive statue may be the chef d'oeuvre of the collection or it may be a hallucinatory presence, a presiding, perhaps mocking, spirit. The woman's eyes appear as black holes—hidden by the sunglasses which shield her eyes from us, turn her gaze inward. Like Man Ray's model, Kiki, this woman should look out at us, but does not; she is presented as a formal counterpoint to the statues or masks, not as an authentic, in-"sightful" being.

The drawing sets up a telling interplay between the woman's clothed form and the unclothed forms of the statues. As we move diagonally from the clearly female form of the statue at the far left, to the veiled white woman's form, to the bare, smooth torso of the large piece, we move from female, through neuter, to male. An

Fig. 1.5. Kiki–a formal counterpoint to the African mask.
Man Ray. *Kiki.* 1926. Gelatin-silver print, 6 3/4" x 8 7/8". Collection,
The Museum of Modern Art, New York. Gift of James Thrall Soby.
Courtesy ARS N.Y./ ADAGP, 1989, for the Man Ray Trust.
This photograph is also called *Noire et blanche.*

especially dramatic tension exists between the woman's eyes and
the eyes of the masks and statues. Our eyes are drawn to the woman's, but she cannot meet them. Where then do we look: At the
staring mask second from the left? At the hanging above her head?
At the large statue whose sightless eyes also repel ours? In its play
with the gaze, and in its allusions to gender, the drawing shows us
what is involved in "going primitive." Who owns what in this drawing? Does the woman collect the statues or do they surround her,
mock her? Does she analyze them or imitate them? Is she confident
(as her posture suggests) or sad (as her face suggests)? What do they
tell her—what does she tell them—about art, about aesthetics,
about gender, about power?

Not an example of primitivism so much as an analysis of it, the
drawing made me pause and consider. The woman's fashions were

not my fashions; I could never wear those fifties-style sunglasses, which seem to me ugly (I was born in 1949). But I wear black often, and I collect art. When I look around my living room I see posters from exhibitions of art, much of it from primitive societies or by Western primitivizers. Like the woman, I was interested in things primitive and in the idea of the primitive, as were many others at this moment of cultural history. Was I contemplating the primitive or trapped by it? Collecting examples of modernist and postmodernist primitivism or an example myself?

Gone Primitive raises many issues relevant to this study: the association of gender issues and of sexuality with primitives, the dangers of radical chic, the reciprocal modeling of the modern (or the postmodern) and the primitive, the difficulty of deciding who controls whom in that modeling. And it gives a warning. In vogue today as in the teens and twenties, ideas about the primitive are still very much with us. Are these ideas about the primitive really different in kind from Stanley's ideas, or the ideas of the twenties, or do they just tell us what we want to hear now?

Living in the Urban Jungle

The woman in *Gone Primitive* has mastered an essential fact of urban life in the last decades of the twentieth century:[57] its polyglot, syncretic nature, its hodgepodge of the indigenous and imported, the native and the foreign. In the deflationary era of postmodernism, the primitive often frankly loses any particular identity and even its sense of being "out there"; it merges into a generalized, marketable thing—a grab-bag primitive in which urban and rural, modern and traditional Africa and South America and Asia and the Middle East merge into a common locale called the third world which exports garments and accessories, music, ideologies, and styles for Western, and especially urban Western, consumption.

For every importation of traditional African, South American, Asian, or Middle Eastern objects into Western space, we can balance examples of the importation of Western objects into once primitive space: the photographer's lightbulbs on the child's blouse in figure 3.2, radio headphones or baseball caps worn in remote villages (fig. 1.6), lawsuits as the newest weapon wielded by Native Americans and by groups such as the Philippine Tasaday, a cave-dwelling society supposedly "discovered" only in the 1970s.[58] What's "primitive,"

what's "modern"? What's "savage," what's "civilized?" Increasingly
it becomes difficult to tell.

The "modern"/"primitive" circuit runs both ways now; it's complete. The primitive has in some ways always been a willful invention by the West, but the West was once much more convinced of
the illusion of Otherness it created. Now everything is mixed up,
and the Other controls some of the elements in the mix.[59] Will postmodernism end Western lust for things primitive—and for the idea
of the primitive itself—by obliterating the distinctions between
jungle and city, primitive and modern? I sense not. But the evocation
of the primitive is bound to become ever more willful, ever more
dependent upon striking a deal—based on mutual pretense—satisfactory to both partners who participate in its creation: the "them"
so much more like us now, and us, often garbed in clothing and
living amid objects that evoke "their" traditional forms of life.[60]

The first and third worlds interpenetrate now, and they do business. The Sunday New York Times Arts and Leisure section recently
ran a caveat emptor story by James Brooke about West African artifacts being sold to tourists, sometimes under the pretense that they
are antiques. Nicholas Lemann's "Fake Masks" (in Atlantic, November 1987) describes a related phenomenon: networks of "run-
ners" who smuggle both old and new African objects into the
United States and constitute a leading source for galleries and museums. In this trade, African carvers gleefully imitate the production of neighboring traditions, traditions not their own, if those
kinds of statues or masks sell to Westerners; reports have it that the
village workshops consult the "latest coffee-table books and auction
catalogues of African art" in order to keep up with shifting Western
tastes and vogues (34). "Junk" pieces successfully passed off as
"danced" in tribal rituals or, even better, as "old" will produce many
times their usual worth.

Comparable stories of how Westerners exploit non-Western artists also abound: the wholesale confiscation and sale of African and
Native American artifacts so characteristic of museum collecting
earlier in this century (German anthropologist Leo Frobenius alone
"collected" many thousands of items); grave robbers in the American West looting Native American sites and selling the artifacts for
scandalous profits (see Peterson, "Looting Tribal Sites"). The sym-
metry here is not surprising. It's what we've come to in going primitive, in being gone primitive. Brooke facetiously suggests that there
is no problem so long as everyone involved in the transactions is
happy in the game of "mental ping-pong" the trade in artifacts in-

Fig. 1.6. What's "primitive," what's "modern"? Increasingly it becomes difficult to tell. Courtesy Adrian Boot.

volves: the producer of the "fake" African antique happy with his profits, the consumer happy to believe he has purchased the real thing at a bargain price. "If the deceived and the deceiver part satisfied, who cares?" the *Times* suggests in the caption which accompanies Brooke's article. Caveat emptor (let the buyer beware), but also caveat nobody (nobody need beware): if the transactions occurring in postmodern primitivism make everyone happy, then they are cool clear rain drenching the heat of the urban jungle.

There is a common, problematic view in certain discussions of global culture, a view that energizes critics like James Clifford who argue (rightly, I think) for recognizing that the third world now includes many signs of the West, signs we should conceive of not as "cultural impurities," but as cultural facts that can lead to a number of future possibilities. The problem is one of *sprezzatura*, of carnivalesque rejoicing, of celebrating the crossing and recrossing of things, of believing that contact and polyphony are inherently liberating. Certainly I understand, and even share, the impulse to enlist in Marshall McLuhan's global village. And I'm all for having fun and for the carnivalesque moment. I agree, utterly, that traces of the West exist as part of non-Western realities and (as I suggest above) vice versa, and that this mixture will yield unpredictable (and maybe hopeful) results.

But the problem resembles the one I described earlier with reference to the juxtaposition of Western myths and primitive peoples or institutions—the processing of one as homologous to the other. The essence of the carnivalesque is that one cannot tell male from female, rich from poor, black from white: those differences, ordinarily so crucial, do not matter for the duration of the carnival. Everything is freer there, everything is possible.[61] But carnivals do not last. And the interpenetration of third and first world is not just festive. Behind the festivities are social and economic facts we should not forget.

Some facts: when the British colonized Kenya they confiscated 4.5 million acres of farmland, dividing it among one thousand families; Lord Delamere, the colonialist lord governor, owned a modest one million acres. During the same period (1902–21), famine and disease reduced the native population from 4 million to 2.5 million (Nixon, "Out of Africa"). In South African mines late in the nineteenth century, 20,000 Africans are reported to have died each day (Davidson, *Africa*). During the settlement of the Amazon, up to the mid-1960s, the indigenous Indian population dropped from 2–5 million (estimates vary) to 200,000 (Hemming, *Amazon Frontier*), and the process of converting the Amazon to modern terrain continues at a ferocious pace. As part of the postmodern festival, babies have died because the West has introduced the idea of formula feeding, so dangerous where refrigeration is unreliable, to cultures once dependent solely on breast-feeding. The politics of drought relief have been staggering. Third world nations have amassed (indeed were encouraged to amass) a debt to Western banks amounting to many trillions of dollars. Austerity measures to pay back the debt are severe and often shocking: in 1988 (according to United Nations' estimates) half a million children died in Africa and South America as a result of cutbacks in government programs. The debt crisis may yet produce political and economic collapses that will end the consumerist carnival for us all; certainly the emerging middle classes in countries like Mexico and Argentina are in a very real way threatened with economic extinction.

Isolation for third world nations and primitive groups is no longer possible or even, perhaps, desirable; these nations and groups have a future, just as they have had a past (Leiris, "L'ethnographe"). But the problem with the carnival idea, applied too uncritically, is that it ignores the real social and economic cost of the global village.[62] To count the cost is not softhearted or softheaded; it is morally imperative. It may sound a discordant note at the carnival, but that note is still heard—daily—in the ghettoes and shantytowns of the urban jungle, especially in third world cultures.

When we say "caveat nobody" and revel in the postmodern mélange of us and them, we are in danger of abjuring responsibilities every bit as grave as those evaded when early colonialists decided that land could be taken from colonized peoples, that Others should die or become the urban poor, if necessary, to make way for Western modernization. There is an arrogance in certain forms of postmodern glee every bit as dangerous as the Victorian's or modern's frequent assumption of white racial superiority. To question the carnivalesque mood is a graceless role—antisocial, overly serious, not fun. But the alternative is to participate in the postmodern carnival without understanding its rules, implications, origins, or consequences. The study which follows asks precisely that we understand the rules governing the exchange between the modern West, the postmodern West, and the versions of the primitive they have created or endorsed. It seeks to make impossible innocent reenactments of the dramas of us and them that have been staged and restaged in the modern West's encounters with primitive Others.

2

Taking Tarzan Seriously

n 1963, when one out of every thirty paperbacks sold was a Tarzan novel, magazines like *Life* and *Esquire* ran stories on the Tarzan phenomenon. *Life*'s piece was a short column by Paul Mandel cleverly called "Tarzan of the Paperbacks," which, like other pieces in the mainstream press, expressed amazement at Tarzan's renewed popularity. Tarzan, we were told, had inspired ice cream and bread products. He had hospitalized, in one day, fifteen children in Kansas City who had fallen out of trees while imitating their hero. He had sold more than thirty-five million copies and been the subject of the most lucrative and enduring film series in movie history. According to Gore Vidal in *Esquire*, he had created a generation of U.S. males who had "tried to master the victory cry of the great ape"—and he was now at work on a second generation ("Tarzan Revisited," 192).

The first of the novels, *Tarzan of the Apes*, was originally published in 1912; twenty-three novels followed, most in the teens, twenties, and thirties. The first Tarzan movie appeared in 1917, followed by roughly fifty films.[1] Although we tend to think of the novels as British—mostly because Tarzan is also Lord Greystoke, a British aristocrat—the books are American, and their Americanness urges itself upon the reader's consciousness; in fact, they share many characteristics with the Western, a genre born during the same years. In the forties, the Tarzan novels lost ground, perhaps, said Mandel, "because substantial clans of American boys had started living their own real-life jungle dramas" in the Pacific arena, in World War II (11). By 1960, only nine of the twenty-three novels remained in print.

Biographies of Burroughs and the essays by Mandel and Vidal state clearly—too clearly—the reason for Tarzan's return. Burrough's fans, the explanations go, always wanted Tarzan in paperback; Burrough's heirs, unlike Burroughs himself, became complacent in the decade after his death with regard to sales and profit.

When the fans discovered that Burroughs's heirs had sloppily allowed copyrights to lapse, they urged publishers to reprint, and the publishers did. The rest is publishing history, and history of an unusual kind in that the audience created the demand and the occasion for the reprints, not the publishing houses. This explanation of Tarzan's return by audience demand is good as far as it goes. We know that Tarzan had an audience in the sixties; what we need to know is why.

For Mandel and Vidal, the renewed life of Tarzan was a sign of escapism, and hence rather sad. As Vidal put it, "a good many people find their lives so unsatisfactory that they go right on year after year telling themselves stories in which they are able to dominate their environment in a way that is not possible in this overorganized society" (193). We cannot, these critics say, dominate our environments, but Tarzan can. The titles of the books tell us so: *Tarzan Triumphant, Tarzan the Invincible, Tarzan the Untamed, Tarzan Lord of the Jungle.* Tarzan has freedom and strength and power; we read him to reclaim a little of our own. This motivation for the Tarzan books was, presumably, already present in the teens and twenties; if we believe the critics, however, it had deepened and become more acute and pitiful by the sixties. The man in the lion skin was a fantasy-projection of the man in the pinstripe suit or on the assembly line, caught in a system he had not created and could not control.

Other critics from the sixties and seventies shared this head-shaking sense that Burroughs's Tarzan books reflect "waking and sleeping fantasies that he [Burroughs] obviously held in common with his readers" (Seelye, "Tarzan," 35). In fact, when respectable critics treated Tarzan, they tended to look down on him, to assume that "fantasy" has little positive connection to social "reality," and that they knew more than the duped and bedazzled Tarzan fans possibly could. It seems likely in retrospect that critics were reading Tarzan through assumptions about heroes—and antiheroes—appropriate to their time but less fully appropriate to the original novels.

The novels most often published, sold, and reviewed in the sixties and those (increasingly) being taught from the sixties in our colleges and universities—novels by Updike, Bellow, and Cheever, for example—certainly project a different image of man in relation to society from that in the Tarzan novels. Academically respected best-sellers from the sixties frequently focus on middle-class, middle-aged businessmen and tell, repeatedly, the story of the individual's limited power within and against the establishment (Ohmann,

"Shaping of a Canon"). It is thus not surprising that mainstream critics belittled Tarzan as the fantastic antithesis of fictional characters by writers like Updike, Bellow, and Cheever, characters the critics saw as more representative of their time. But mainstream critics of the sixties and seventies reacted to Tarzan quite differently from the way early reviewers did, and from the way "fans" continue to react.

The original advertisements for and reviews of the Tarzan novels promised a *re-creation* of the modern world, not an escape from it.[2] Tarzan's aristocratic ancestry was widely emphasized, as was the role of "the intelligence of his civilized ancestors" (Heins, *Bibliography*, 34, 314). Much was made of the process by which, under the influence of Jane's love, he "tries to learn the ways of civilization" (314). Burroughs, too, makes much of factors like heredity in Tarzan's history—factors that make him spend years learning to read English (before he encounters it as a spoken language), refrain from cannibalism, organize the apes into political factions, and kiss Jane's hand when he first meets her. Tarzan is a maker and a shaker, less effete (we are repeatedly told) than the "Lord Greystoke" who rules in Britain in his stead. The reader, far from escaping into a passive fog, shares in the energy and vigor of Tarzan's enterprise and is constantly invited by the books to compare Tarzan's world to the reader's own. The novels do not evade the drabness of modernity: they repeatedly compare Tarzan's robust table manners with such customs as finger bowls, comment on the difference between the warning given by a lion's roar and an automobile's horn, and contrast the exhilaration of swinging through the upper terraces of the forest with the boredom of hanging from a strap in a subway car. In the first two novels, Tarzan samples "civilization" and dislikes its stink; he both emulates Western customs (in an attempt to please Jane) and selectively revitalizes them in African contexts.

The several popular biographies of Burroughs published in the sixties and seventies identify with this spirit of heroic force and with the potential to make things anew. They tend to cast Burroughs himself as Tarzan and to tell his life as an adventure story.[3] Some of the events in that life—Burroughs was in the cavalry, and loved fast cars and planes—fit this mold readily. But every event, even the most mundane, becomes in these biographies a challenge to Burroughs's fortitude and resourcefulness. Even downbeat events that fit the sixties' sense of the little guy's powerlessness against the establishment (like Burroughs having to sell his vast Tarzana estate to suburban subdividers or surviving two divorces) are narrated in a vocabulary of drama, challenge, and heroic endeavor. Burroughs may have had experiences similar to those of Updike's or Cheever's characters, but his biographers do not tell them that way. He is not portrayed as demoralized or defeated or in midlife crisis; like Tarzan, he is always out there swinging.

I found it tempting to sneer at the upbeat, heroic tone of Burroughs's biographies: their brand of buoyant, macho optimism does not come naturally. But these biographies serve a purpose beyond telling us about Burroughs's life and creations: they help us re-create the sense of wonder and potential that originally surrounded the Tarzan materials, the sense of power and of "making things anew" recorded in the early advertisements and reviews. Recapturing this sense can help us take Tarzan seriously as an attempt to imagine the primitive as a source of empowerment—as a locus *for* making things anew, to preserve what is worth preserving and change what deserves to be changed.

In the Tarzan series, the primitive has multiple meanings: Tarzan himself is the "personification of primitive man," but the apes' social systems, the Africans in the novels, and some of the lost civilizations Tarzan encounters are also presented as primitive. Burroughs works with no specific ethnographic model in mind, but he does repeatedly address ethnographic categories like the nature of the primitive mind (logical or prelogical?), the status of primitive beliefs (superstitions or religions?), and the nature of language, gender relations, and leadership patterns within different societies.[4] It is possible that Burroughs read anthropology—he did, we know, research plant and animal life in Africa (Porges, *Burroughs*). But it seems more likely that Burroughs assimilated ethnographic categories by osmosis and hearsay, especially given the popularization of anthropological studies in his lifetime. At any rate, despite his attention to ethnographic categories, Burroughs's primitive is a composite, free-floating creation; it shares many attributes with prehistoric Pellucidar and with Mars, the settings for Burroughs's two other major fictional cycles, both science fiction. The primitive as Burroughs uses it in the Tarzan novels in fact intermittently performs some of the functions of science fiction, including commentary on the author's society and projections of alternative possibilities interpolated into the basic plots of adventure. In this use of the primitive for social commentary and the projection of alternative possibilities, the Tarzan novels are not just an epiphenomenon of primitivism. They are in many ways the best place to begin to understand what modernity had at stake in its encounters with the primitive.

A fundamental basis of Western interest in the primitive depends on archaic and evolutionist meanings of the word as the "original" or "natural" state of things. Within these meanings, explorations or representations of the primitive could be seen as explorations of origins and the marking of patterns that could reveal the truth about human nature and social organization. As we have seen, this fundamental conception undergirds many well-known ethnographies, especially those with a psychological orientation. The belief that primitive societies reveal origins or natural order depends on an ethnocentric sense of existing primitive societies as outside of linear time, and on a corresponding assumption that primitive societies exist in an eternal present which mirrors the past of Western civilization (Fabian, *Time and the Other*). This temporal illusion has been among the most persistent aspects of primitivism in the West—both in high culture and in popular culture, like the Tarzan novels.

Explorations of the primitive could thus potentially make us change our ideas about ourselves and change our social forms. Or they could support traditional values and arrest changes found threatening in contemporary culture. Through the power invested in original, "natural" systems, definitions of the primitive could comment on and affect social change. They could alter or affirm existing hierarchies, especially during times when the stability of those hierarchies experienced stress—as they did (especially in matters of race and gender) in the twenties and sixties, at the respective peaks of Tarzan's power. This is one reason anthropologists such as Margaret Mead and Claude Lévi-Strauss have sometimes been treated as gurus by American culture: their knowledge of other societies has been considered a firm basis for prognostications about our own.[5]

The Tarzan materials perform by turns all these functions. As the series develops, it increasingly affirms existing hierarchies, including the hierarchy of male over female, white over black, West over rest. But, especially in the opening volumes of the series (and intermittently thereafter), the Tarzan materials also expose the shaky basis of these hierarchies by showing how far from "natural" they seem to Tarzan as a boy and young man and how subject they are to cultural variation. In fact, the Tarzan story begins with scenes that dramatize confusion and contradiction about black-white relations, about maleness, and about men's treatment of women.

The books assume that males are, biologically and hence "naturally," more violent than females: *Tarzan of the Apes*, in fact, begins with parallel scenes of male violence in the human and animal worlds—a murderous mutiny aboard the ship carrying the Greystokes to Africa, a male ape going berserk and killing a female ape's (Kala's) baby. But within the limits established by this assumption of male violence, possibilities for social relations remain open. Kala, for example, faces down the male apes' hostility to the infant Tarzan and asserts her desire and right to adopt him as her own: "Those of the apes who attempted to examine Kala's strange baby were repulsed with bared fangs and low menacing growls" (33). Since "Kala was a fine clean limbed young female," valuable to her tribe, "they did not wish to lose her," and so the males reluctantly agree to Kala's demands and acknowledge her power to keep and protect her adopted son.

Other incidents in Tarzan's youth confirm this sense of open possibilities and of norms as a function of individual societies. Raised in the jungle by apes, Tarzan quite simply does not know who or what he is. The early books repeatedly develop scenes in which Tarzan shares the apes' standards of beauty—the only standards he has ever known. When he first sees himself reflected in a pool, in an obvious inversion of the Narcissus motif, Tarzan feels authentically inferior:

Tarzan was appalled. It had been bad enough to be hairless, but to own such a countenance! He wondered that the other apes could look at him at all. That tiny slit of a mouth and those puny white teeth! How they looked beside the mighty lips and powerful fangs of his more fortunate brothers! (*Tarzan of the Apes*, 36)

His fellow apes agree with Tarzan's assessment, and "persecution . . . followed him remorselessly for twelve of his [first] thirteen years of life" (*Tarzan of the Apes*, 52). Tarzan's first rival in love, for example, an ape named Taug, gloats over Tarzan's dismal appearance:

How could one compare his beautiful coat with the smooth and naked hideousness of Tarzan's bare hide? Who could see beauty in the stingy nose of the Tarmangani after looking at Taug's broad nostrils? And Tarzan's eyes! Hideous things, showing white about them, and entirely unrimmed with red! (*Jungle Tales*, 16)

Incidents like these suggest that communal norms control values and dictate the kinds of questions that can be asked. The question Tarzan has asked himself, with shame and confusion, is, therefore, "why don't I look like the other apes?"

At moments like these, the Tarzan novels imply that norms and any sense of self and Other are culturally defined.[6] When they do, they defamiliarize axiomatic Western norms and raise the possibility of their radical restructuring. But such radical, relativistic moments are counterbalanced and finally overcome by others, in which the self is increasingly defined, in ways that yield security and satisfaction, by comparisons with Others. Of these encounters between self and Other, the first few between Tarzan and blacks, Tarzan and Euro-Americans, Tarzan and females count most. In fact, Tarzan's encounters with blacks and with females teach him who he is. Perhaps because it begins with confusion and insecurity, the assertion of identity in the Tarzan novels is always stronger and more definite than it need be. "Tarzan is a man. He goes alone," Tarzan says, desperately trying to clarify things for himself. But Tarzan is not alone for long in Africa.[7] Various villains and lost Europeans drop in. And the Africans and the "woman question" are there practically from the beginnings of Tarzan's story.

Tarzan meets black Africans in the first of the novels, *Tarzan of the Apes*, before he has seen any people of European descent. The meeting occurs at a point when he fears that his human features may be a singular aberration. Kulonga, prince of an African tribe that has recently fled Belgian colonialism and resettled in Tarzan's territory, has killed Kala, Tarzan's mother among the anthropoid apes. As a prepubescent youth, as a child who has lost the only mother he has ever known, Tarzan is vulnerable. Indeed, "his grief and anger were unbounded. . . . He beat upon his chest with his clenched fists, and then he fell upon the body of Kala and sobbed out the pitiful sorrowings of his lonely heart. To lose the only creature in all his world who ever had cared for him was the greatest tragedy he had ever known"(67). The apes tell Tarzan that "a strange, hairless, black ape with feathers growing on its head" has slain Kala. Tarzan tracks the "ape," but finds that Kala's killer makes "footprints such as he alone in all the jungle had ever made" (68). Tarzan now feels curiosity and excitement as well as the desire for revenge: "Could it be that he was trailing a MAN—one of his own race?" (68). When he finds Kulonga, he discovers that he *was* tracking a man, though, significantly, not a man of his own race:

> Tarzan looked with wonder upon the strange creature beneath him—so like him in form and yet so different in face and color. His books had portrayed the *Negro*, but how different had been the dull, dead print to this sleek thing of ebony, pulsing with life.
>
> As the man stood there with taut drawn bow, Tarzan recognized him not so much as the *Negro* as the *Archer* of his picture book—A stands for *Archer*.
>
> How wonderful! Tarzan almost betrayed his presence in the deep excitement of his discovery. (68)

The passage asks us to imagine Tarzan's shock at the sight of Kulonga. He has never seen a human, white or black, save for his own reflection. He has taught himself to read from children's books that his dead parents brought with them to Africa, which he has found in their abandoned shack.[8] These books have taught him the words *man, boy, Negro,* and *archer.* Now the reality represented by those words stands before him. He must have suspected at times that the books told fairy tales, even lies. Now he knows they told the truth— how wonderful! But he immediately worries about whether they have told him the whole truth. Specifically, Tarzan needs to know the relationship between himself—a "tarmangani," a "white ape"— and the "Negro archer" before him.

Intrigued, Tarzan follows Kulonga, studying him, imitating and memorizing his actions, and teasing him by stealing his weapons. He kills Kulonga only at the moment that the African is about to reenter his tribe's village and escape Tarzan's revenge on the man who has killed Kala, Tarzan's mother among the apes. Tarzan then examines the body, removes its ornamentation, and realizes that he ought now to eat the body of his "kill," since he is hungry. Like other creatures, according to Burroughs, Tarzan shrinks from eating his own kind, "but who was Kulonga that he might not be eaten as fairly as Horta, the boar, or Bara, the deer?" Still, "a strange doubt stayed his hand. Had not his books taught him that he was a man? And was not The Archer a man, also? Did men eat men? . . . All he knew was that he could not eat the flesh of this black man." "And thus," Burroughs insists, "hereditary instinct, ages old, usurped the functions of his untaught mind and saved him from transgressing a worldwide law of whose very existence he was ignorant" (72).

Tarzan recognizes that both he and Kulonga are "men"; indeed Kulonga's existence has proved to him that he is not the sole specimen of "man." But he also recognizes racial difference: Kulonga is a "Negro," a "black man," in the books' specialized vocabulary, a "gomangani" (Burroughs uniformly avoids the term "colored," common in his time, preferring "black" or "gomangani" for Africans and "Negro" for the occasional African-American in his stories). Like many in his day, Burroughs believed that race implied culture and mores, which could be transmitted genetically.[9] Accordingly, as the son of Europeans, Tarzan "instinctively" knows he cannot eat a fellow man. Kulonga, on the other hand, has "sharpened teeth"; he belongs, in fact, to a cannibal tribe—shades of Polyphemus and Montaigne, and of the West's obsession with cannibalism.[10] Kulonga's cannibal status belies the "worldwide law" against cannibalism which Burroughs invokes above; on this detail, as on others, Burroughs felt little need to be consistent. The really important thing to notice, though, is how unresolved matters are for Tarzan. His first meeting with a black results in murder. And he has yet to understand how far he and Kulonga are related.

Tarzan's views on racial matters never do become unambiguous. As in this first encounter with blacks, the series moves rapidly between racist and antiracist positions. Kulonga's tribe consists, we are told, of "savage cannibals," "low and bestial" in appearance (64); they viciously torture captives, then eat them, as they are about to do to Tarzan's friend and mentor, the Frenchman D'Arnot, before Tarzan rescues him. Yet Kulonga's tribe has fled Belgian colonialism, and the books in no way mute the horrors of Belgian rule. In fact, we are told that "the fiendishness of [the tribe's] cruel savagery" is spurred by "the poignant memory of still crueler barbarities practiced upon them and theirs by the white officers of that arch hypocrite, Leopold II of Belgium, because of whose atrocities they had fled the Congo Free State—a pitiful remnant of what had once been a mighty tribe" (175). Even that "pitiful remnant" will be annihilated, in *Tarzan of the Apes*, by D'Arnot's comrades in a battle scene rendered so as to give full weight to the terrors inflicted on blacks by better-armed whites: "the revolvers, rifles and cutlasses of the Frenchmen crumpled the native spearmen and struck down the black archers with their bows halfdrawn"; children are spared, and some women, but the affair is a "grim massacre" after which all that is left of Kulonga's village is "the wailing of the native women for their dead" (184). In his early history, Tarzan murders several Africans after he has killed Kulonga. His usual motive is to frighten the villagers or to steal weapons. But the novels are uneasy about having Tarzan act as wantonly as the French and Belgian colonialists do.

Indeed, one of Jane's first official acts in the series is to make Tarzan promise that he will kill no one—white or black—except in self-defense.[11]

Jane enters Tarzan's life under dramatic circumstances which, like the encounter with Kulonga, cause Tarzan both bliss and confusion. Jane has been abducted by Terkoz, a rebel ape ostracized by his (also Tarzan's) tribe. In search of females to form a new tribe, Terkoz comes upon Jane and her black servant, Esmeralda, who are lost in the jungle.[12] Esmeralda, true to "her manner under stress of emergency which required presence of mind, swooned"; she is a stereotyped black servant, overweight, cowardly, and given to malapropisms. Jane bears the brunt of the ape's attentions, and we experience the terror of the moment through her eyes:

> Jane did not once lose consciousness. It is true that that awful face, pressing close to hers, and the stench of the foul breath beating upon her nostrils, paralyzed her with terror; but her brain was clear, and she comprehended all that transpired . . . She could not have known it, but she was being borne farther and farther into the impenetrable jungle. (*Tarzan of the Apes*, 153)

Abduction always carries with it the double meanings of kidnapping and rape, and both meanings pertain here. The jungle may be impenetrable, but Jane is not. Face to face, her body in his arms, Jane experiences fear and disgust toward Terkoz. When Tarzan arrives in pursuit, Terkoz feels he will have a "double revenge" against Tarzan—he will kill the "tarmangani," the white ape he has long hated, and he will then enjoy what he assumes must be "Tarzan's woman."

Tarzan, Burroughs tells us, is "the personification of primitive man"; at this moment, Jane becomes the personification of primitive woman, and she watches the combat between Tarzan and Terkoz in suitably primordial style:

> Jane—her lithe, young form flattened against the trunk of a great tree, her hands pressed against her rising and falling bosom, and her eyes wide with mingled horror, fascination, fear, and admiration—watched the primordial ape battle with the primeval man for possession of a woman—for her. [Then,] when the long knife drank deep a dozen times of Terkoz' heart's blood . . . it was a primeval woman who sprang forward with outstretched arms toward the primeval man who had fought for her and won her. And Tarzan? He did what no red-blooded man needs lessons in doing. He took his woman in his arms and smothered her upturned, panting lips with kisses. (155–56)

"Primeval ... primordial ... primitive ... red-blooded"—the moment, in a chapter titled "The Call of the Primitive," encapsulates the "natural" relations of the sexes. Man is woman's protector; without him she is subject to privation, abduction, rape, and death. Woman can be won by strength and daring—and she knows it. Only Tarzan is confused:

> He discovered himself speculating upon the fate which would have fallen to the girl had he not rescued her from Terkoz. He knew why the ape had not killed her, and he commenced to compare his intentions with those of Terkoz. True, it was the order of the jungle for the male to take his mate by force; but could Tarzan be guided by the laws of the beasts? Was not Tarzan a Man? But what did men do? He was puzzled; for he did not know. (163)

Almost immediately after he wins Jane, Tarzan feels confusion about "what a man does." First Kulonga causes this confusion, then Terkoz and Jane do.

Tarzan thinks of asking Jane "what men do," but he only reads English and cannot speak it. His recollections of mother love suggest a course of action, and Tarzan "stroked her soft hair and tried to comfort and quiet her as Kala had him" (165). Then he decides he will "act as he imagined the men in the books [he has read] would have acted were they in his place" (166). He surrenders his knife, his best weapon, to Jane, hilt first. All this works amazingly well. By the end of the afternoon, Jane is very much in love with Tarzan. In turn, the afternoon leaves "a very different Tarzan from the one on whom the morning's sun had risen. ... He had not in one swift transition become a polished gentleman from a savage ape-man, but at last the instincts of the former predominated, and over all was the desire to please the woman he loved, and to appear well in her eyes" (169).

Burroughs's prose invites us to take Tarzan's rescue of Jane first as a paradigm of primordial man's winning of primordial woman and then as a paradigm of how white women arouse "hereditary instincts" of chivalry in white men. But other things are going on here as well, at the margins of perception. This abduction scene is not unique in the novels. White Euro-American women are repeatedly abducted—three abductions per novel per woman being a typical allotment. When the triple abduction occurs, the first abductor is usually a renegade European, the second either an Arab or an African, the third an ape. The last kind of abduction was the climax, the payoff of the abduction motif, and was featured on the covers of some versions of the Tarzan story. What was its special appeal?

When Terkoz abducts Jane, he leaves Esmeralda behind, indeed does not seem to notice her. And this is typical of the novels, in which black women are bypassed as erotic objects, but white women invariably incite lust in villainous hearts. When we remember, as the books repeatedly remind us, that Burroughs believed blacks to be a midway stage of evolution from ape to white humans, the scene's meaning and appeal become clear. The scene encodes not just the "natural" in male-female relations but also encodes the "unnatural," the threat of miscegenation, disguised as a species difference.[13] Both the text and available illustrations point in this direction. On the cover of an early comic book retelling of the novel (fig. 2.1), Jane is blond and wearing modern dress: light-colored sheath skirt, low neckline, bare arms, high heels dangling pathetically. She is rigidly upright, as is Terkoz, the "man-like beast" whose black coloring contrasts vividly with Jane's lightness. We see Terkoz's face: broad-nostriled, white-fanged, with large eyes and whites rolling (even though Burroughs repeatedly says the apes have no whites in their eyes—a key difference from Tarzan). Tarzan wears an animal skin and is dark-haired, his colors combining those of Jane and ape. His white hand reaches out to arrest Terkoz's huge paw, which grips Jane's flanks.

The abduction scene teases and titillates, bringing together the racial and gender subtexts so frequently involved in Western treatment of the primitive—subthemes that make it important to take Tarzan seriously. Everyone involved in it—Terkoz, Tarzan, Jane, the reader—anticipates Jane's violation, referred to, discreetly, only as "Terkoz' intentions." Tarzan compares his own intentions to Terkoz's and rejects the similarities; Jane knows, simply by looking at him, that she can trust Tarzan. Scenes like this suggest certain rules: qualities like lust belong to animals and blacks, not to Euro-Americans, except when they are renegade, outcast; flirtations with miscegenation are allowed, but miscegenation, especially between white females and nonwhite males, must never occur.

The threat of miscegenation is most directly invoked in volume six of the series, *Jungle Tales of Tarzan*, in an incident that forms a natural companion to the two incidents just examined. It too dramatizes a moment of Tarzan's confusion over who or what he is. In a story called "Tarzan's First Love," set shortly after he has killed

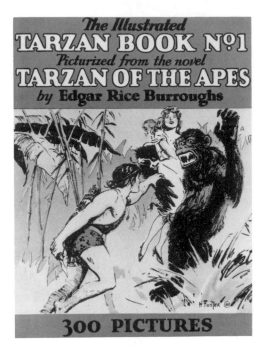

Fig. 2.1.
The threat of miscegenation,
disguised as a species
difference. Cover, *The
Illustrated Tarzan Book #1*.
Courtesy Burroughs
Memorial Collection.

Kulonga, Tarzan feels the need for a mate. He as yet knows no Euro-American women, Jane's arrival being several years in the future. Although in "Tarzan and the Black Boy," in the same volume, Tarzan tries to adopt a black child, he never considers mating with a black woman—and the omission is conspicuous. In this regard, the novels selectively reflect the realities of their culture. A cultural outsider would never guess, from the novels, that white men in Burroughs's United States could have access to black women, though one would guess that access in the other direction—black males to white females—was a vivid cultural taboo.

As a mate, Tarzan chooses Teeka, a handsome young ape, who "outstretched at luxurious ease in the shade of the tropical forest presented, unquestionably, a most alluring picture of young, feminine loveliness" (7). To win her, Tarzan fights a rival ape named Taug. He has to win her since, as we have already seen, for none of the parties in this triangle is Tarzan obviously more attractive than Taug. Having won Teeka, Tarzan begins the courtship which should lead to mating. The moment is, once again, a flirtation with miscegenation, disguised as a species difference:

[Teeka] came quite close and snuggled against him, and Tarzan, Lord Greystoke, put his arm around her. As he did so he noticed, with a start, the strange incongruity of that smooth, brown arm against the black and hairy coat of his lady-love. He recalled the paw of Sheeta's mate across Sheeta's face—no incongruity there. . . . The males and females differed, it was true; but not with such differences as existed between Tarzan and Teeka. (20–21)

He immediately gives Teeka to Taug in a moment that articulates, as fully as the books are willing to articulate it, the fascination yet "horror" of miscegenation: "For the Gomangani (black) there is another Gomangani. . . . For Numa, the lion, there is Sabor, the lioness; for Bara, the deer, for Manu, the monkey. . . . Taug is an ape. Teeka is an ape. Go back to Teeka. Tarzan is a man. He will go alone" (23).

We are back, then, at that utterly simple formulation, "Tarzan is a man, he will go alone." But we can appreciate now that the formulation is not so simple, that it masks a host of anxieties, uncertainties, displacements, and repressions caused by Tarzan's encounters with apes and with the human Others in the jungle—blacks and females, sometimes separately, sometimes in conjunction. Tarzan has defined himself as a "man" by his difference from the apes, from blacks, and from females, in a process that replicates the process of white male self-definition in our culture with unusual clarity. He needs now to preserve his "manliness," his aloneness, figuratively, if not literally. He does this through establishing power hierarchies in which all others—and especially blacks and women—are subordinate to him. I now trace in some detail the processes by which Tarzan establishes himself as the head of various hierarchies, for they are the processes by which the books' potentially utopian uses of the primitive surrender to uses of the primitive that bolster existing power relations.

———

Tarzan always rises to the top of hierarchies. In the first two volumes of the series, Tarzan twice becomes a king. In *Tarzan of the Apes*, he survives jungle combat to become king of the anthropoids by using technology to compensate for his smaller size. Then, in *The Return of Tarzan*, Tarzan becomes king of the Waziri, an elite tribe which adopts Tarzan and stays with him for most of his adventures. Self-possessed, dignified, and omnicompetent as askaris or warriors, the Waziri contrast with the only other tribe Tarzan has known to this point—Kulonga's people. They were cannibals; the Waziri are not. They had "the flat noses and thick lips of the typical west coast savage"; the Waziri do not.[14] Tarzan hates Kulonga's people and finds them "in most ways lower in the scale than the beasts." But the Waziri are "as much higher in the scale of evolution as were the west coast blacks above the apes" (*Tarzan and the Golden Lion*, 84). Within Burroughs's generally evolutionist way of thinking, Tarzan's development from king of the apes to king of the Waziri is a natural development and proof of his Greystoke genes.

When Tarzan meets the Waziri, they mediate for him between the ape society no longer his and the white society not really his either. At the end of *Tarzan of the Apes* and beginning of *The Return of Tarzan*, the hero visits the United States, London, and Paris and finds them sinks of corruption—less honest and more dangerous than the jungle, an expression of "the urban jungle" theme that has persisted in our time. When he is accidentally stranded in Africa, he is overjoyed. In a chapter called "Back to the Primitive," Tarzan exults: "Now he was living. Now, indeed, was the happiness of true freedom his. Who would go back to the stifling, wicked cities of civilized man when the mighty reaches of the great jungle offered peace and liberty? Not he" (*Return of Tarzan*, 119). Enter the Waziri—human companionship free of the Western "stink of civilization."

Initially, Tarzan follows Waziri ways and exults in their "savage" customs. At the ceremony that makes him king,

> the ape-man sprang to his feet and joined in the wild ceremony. In the center of the circle of glittering black bodies he leaped and roared and shook his heavy spear in the same mad abandon that enthralled his fellow savages. The last remnant of his civilization was forgotten—he was a primitive man to the fullest now; reveling in the freedom of the fierce, wild life he loved, gloating in his kingship among these wild blacks. (*Return of Tarzan*, 149)

At that coronation, Tarzan takes the traditional title "Waziri, King of the Waziri." By the fifth book in the series, *The Jewels of Opar*, however, and increasingly as the series progresses, the Waziri have been domesticated and brought into a feudal, not tribal, mode of existence. They live with Tarzan on the African estate he creates for his life with Jane, a feudal paradise separate from both the jungle and from European settlements. They put loyalty to Tarzan and his lady above all. They cook, they clean, they tend Jane's rose garden. Their changed relationship to Tarzan has a linguistic marker. Now they address Tarzan not by the title of "Waziri, King of the Waziri" but by the more colonial "Big Bwana." In turn, Tarzan calls the Waziri "my children" in the later novels.

In his handling of Tarzan's evolving relationship to the Waziri, Burroughs means to illustrate how Tarzan "slowly but surely was ... following the evolution of his ancestors" and taking the Waziri with him (Return of Tarzan, 149). The reference is to cultural and economic norms as well as to a process of mental evolution: Tarzan and the Waziri develop from tribalism to feudalism to (in the late novels) a form of capitalism. In fact, the relationship of Tarzan and the Waziri exemplifies, in miniature, certain versions of imperialism and liberal neocolonialism. It enacts a fantasy of Western superiority being voluntarily recognized and rewarded by "natives" that is typical of Western writing about Africa.[15] The Waziri adopt Tarzan as a lonely outsider. He establishes first his fellowship, then his kingship (on the prevailing first-among-equals model), and then his benign mastery. As benign master, Tarzan teaches his "children" skills he deems useful—from gardening and serving to fighting battles according to Western strategies.[16] He then pays them according to their skills, becoming "boss" as well as "master." "Progress" has, however, the inevitable price tag: a magnificent group of Africans, who have fled Arab slavers, serve as kitchen servants and as porters on Tarzan's safaris. What begins as an association of fellows very quickly becomes one of leader and followers, and soon becomes that of master and servant, employer and employee.

After The Return of Tarzan, we are not really expected to think much about the Waziri. They are there when Tarzan needs them, dropped from the novels when he does not. The novels do not ask us to think much about the Waziri and the relationship Tarzan establishes with them, but it is important to do so. For we have already seen that when the West confronts the primitive, power and sex— geo-politics and gender politics—almost immediately come into play.

As American books published mostly in the teens and twenties, the Tarzan novels could afford to condemn colonialism in Africa and brutality toward African peoples, especially in Belgian and Portuguese territories—after all, the United States had no African colonies. And, as we have seen, they do condemn colonialism, in unequivocal terms, exempting only British colonialism, the colonialism of fellow Anglo-Saxons, represented by Tarzan's father, John

Clayton, a benevolent man who was on his way to aid Africans he regarded as "British subjects" when he was stranded and died.

It would be wrong, though, to assume that because the United States had no African colonies it had no stake in colonialism and in the host of issues associated with it. The United States had done to Native Americans and Mexicans what countries in Europe were doing to Africans. It had recently embarked on imperialist adventures in Cuba, Hawaii, and the Philippines. The ancestors of its black population came from Africa and came here unwillingly, as slaves. Slavery constituted the great shame of America's past and conditioned all racial attitudes. Set in Africa, the Tarzan novels have to be about race and to address American curiosity about the origins of African-Americans: the ease with which we saw Stanley (one of Burroughs's acknowledged sources) move between the categories of African and American blacks provides evidence of this association. And as Western documents on the "primitive," the novels also have to be about slavery, imperialism, and economic exploitation, all facts of life in the West's relations with Africans. Like British and U.S. law, the Tarzan novels do not tolerate the idea that blacks should be slaves, now, in the modern world. But the novels have a strange fascination for slavery in displaced settings and contexts. In this, the topic of slavery resembles that of miscegenation: it is most frequently addressed by displacement.

Tarzan the Terrible, reminiscent of Swift's *Gulliver's Travels,* is one of a series of novels written during the twenties in which Tarzan encounters a variety of odd civilizations, often with humanlike, rather than human, inhabitants, and often prehistoric in animal life. In it, Tarzan addresses the issue of race and slavery by displacement out of recent times and nearby places and into the remote past. In Pal-ul-don, one of the many isolated civilizations Tarzan finds in remote Africa, Tarzan encounters two races similar in form to humans, except for the possession of primeval tails. The races, the Waz-don and the Ho-don, both have "unlooked-for civilization in creatures possessing so many of the physical attributes of beasts" (21), but they have, nonetheless, differing appearances and modes of life. The Ho-don live in a mighty city, A-lur, city of light; the Waz-don live "in the trees of the forest and the caves of the hill" (21). The Ho-don have smooth, hairless skins, the Waz-don hairy ones. The Ho-don are light complexioned, the Waz-don dark. The Ho-don keep slaves; the Waz-don do not. While the Ho-don and Waz-don might distinguish between themselves on the basis of dwelling place or hairiness, to them their difference in color seems paramount and controls other differences:

> "The Waz-don have no cities [said Ta-den the Ho-don] . . . is it not so, *black man*? . . ."
> "Yes," replied Om-at, "We Waz-don are free—only the Ho-don imprison themselves in cities. I would not be a white man." (21)

Although the black does not seem to feel inferior, the white feels superior, and Tarzan knows this:

> Tarzan smiled. Even here was the racial distinction between white man and black man—Ho-don and Waz-don. Not even the fact that they appeared to be equals in the matter of intelligence made any difference—one was white and one was black, and it was easy to see that the white considered himself superior to the other—one could see it in his quiet smile. (22)

While it might suggest the ridiculousness of racial pride, appearing as it does in tailed creatures, the passage does not really work that way. Tarzan smiles; Ta-den the Ho-don smiles. Both their names begin with *Ta*; Tarzan meets and befriends the Ho-don before he meets and befriends the Waz-don. Although Tarzan likes and admires both Om-at and Ta-den, the similarity of name, skin, and smile allies Tarzan most with the "white man."

In many of the books dealing with invented civilizations, the kind of slavery common in the ancient world and independent of race prevails: conquered or captured or unlucky peoples become slaves, a norm quite different from that of the European slave trade in modern times. Even Tarzan becomes a slave, though he invariably never stays one for long and sometimes organizes slave rebellions. Blacks, we are told, are subservient by tradition, not nature, and strike back when they can against abusive masters.[17] The commonness of slavery in the novels reinforces the idea that slavery is "natural" among civilized people, but does not function in a racist way. It remains true and striking, however, that blacks are the only people *always* liable to enslavement on the basis of sheer biology (a partial exception being white women, always ripe in these novels for the harem). Almost all the books touch, at least in passing, on the idea that blacks are slaves—and not as the prizes of conquest. The references have, I think, a cumulative effect, similar to that produced when blacks occupy almost all the service positions in a given community. It is not that Burroughs endorses slavery, especially black slavery, any more than most whites consciously endorse the idea that blacks should fill service positions. But the acceptance of the situation, almost without notice, makes it seem both familiar and natural.

"Familiar and natural" ideas that are also racist surface almost unthinkingly in the Tarzan series, often as the by-product of standard elements in the plot. One such standard plot element is the hero's encounter with a lost, white civilization, long established and geographically isolated in Africa. This motif is profoundly political in the way it draws on historical events, especially the discovery of the ruins of Zimbabwe in the late nineteenth century. Until recently, these ruins were attributed to a lost colony of Phoenicians or to other non-African sources rather than (as is now recognized) to an indigenous African civilization. The misattribution supported colonialist views that Africa included no "states" which could be "invaded," no people worth considering, just territories available to any European who got there first. Since cities like Zimbabwe were tangible proof of both "culture" and "history," they could not be recognized as black by the colonialist mentality.[18]

Africanists have testified to the liberating effect of giving Africa a "history" by uncovering its great peoples and cities and its contributions to civilizations such as Egypt; some Africanists even consider the ground-breaking work of Davidson and others in this area a turning point in Africans' conceptions of themselves.[19] The Tarzan novels gave enduring cultural life to the idea that civilizations in Africa were of white origin. They helped shape popular (mis)conceptions of Africa and its (non)past. In using the motif of the lost, white civilization, Burroughs inscribed and reinscribed a trope central to the imperialist enterprise he was in so many ways critical of.

Like Egypt, India, and Eastern civilizations in the Western imagination, these white civilizations are often a midway stage between the primitive and the civilized. Sometimes their inhabitants have "degenerated" by mating with apes. Typically, they are slaveholding societies. The most prominent of these lost, white civilizations is Opar, a colony established by Atlantis for the mining of gold and jewels in central Africa, and left stranded when its parent city sank into the sea. As a lost colony of Atlantis, Opar echoes Frobenius's misidentification of Benin as Atlantis itself.[20] Opar figures in several of the novels, beginning with the second in the series, *The Return of Tarzan*. Initially, "the ape-man and his companions stood gazing in varying degrees of wonderment at this ancient city in the midst of savage Africa" (162). But after a while, Tarzan is no longer even surprised to see such sights. Joining Opar in the category of lost, ancient, white civilization, there are more than twelve such civilizations in the twenty-three novels.[21]

Some of Tarzan's lost civilizations are sheer fantasy and invention—by which I mean simply that they are unknown in previous Western tradition. But some, like Haggard's invented Kukuanaland in *King Solomon's Mines*, occupy a middle ground between fact and fantasy, and serve as the "actualization," in fiction, of European legends and of discoveries like the "lost" city of Zimbabwe. Men have "heard tell" of King Solomon's fabulous lost mines in the Haggard novel, though few have ever dared to approach them. Similarly, after finding Opar, "Tarzan recalled something that he had read in the library at Paris of a lost race of white men that native legend described as living in the heart of Africa" (*Return of Tarzan*, 162). It is significant and fully in accord with dominant primitivist tropes that these legends invoke the unknown "heart" or "center" of Africa, even when the African site that is the source is really in the east or south. The coreness implies both geographical isolation and typicality, the quintessence of Africa, with riches or knowledge, or both, being the "bribe" for penetrating the hazardous African terrain. The masculine sexual metaphors of penetrating closed dark spaces no doubt help account for the West's attachment to the trope of the center, heart, or core of Africa. African landscape is to be entered, conquered; its riches are to be reaped, enjoyed. The phallic semiology accompanies the imperialist topoi, a conjunction based on the assumption that if explorers (like Stanley and Tarzan) are "manly," then what they explore must be female.[22]

Lost civilizations must (once again like women) be laden, ornamented, worth "penetrating," raping and plundering. These cities are of gold and ivory, their inhabitants' garb encrusted with jewels. Their cellars and storehouses are loaded with gold or gems viewed as simply ornamental by the inhabitants but known to be fabulously valuable by the Europeans. In this regard, the "ancient" whites often mirror Africans and Native Americans, who were celebrated, and often scorned, by the Europeans for favoring "beads and trinkets" over gold or currency.

The motif of the rich, lost civilization assumes that Africa means, and has always meant, plunder to the West—that this is its "natural," its inevitable, meaning. In the "history" of Opar, Atlantis wanted gold; therefore it sent administrators, impressed blacks as slaves, and set to work to get it. Belgium did pretty much the same in the Congo, Britain in South Africa. Tarzan wants gold, and he is, in turn, free to take it from the later Oparians, who have mated with apes and hence "degenerated" from their original whiteness, even forgotten the value of gold. The resources of the continent are "useless" to the inhabitants (Africans, Oparians), though very useful and valuable to others. Tarzan views these civilizations as Odysseus viewed the Cyclops' cave, as Livingstone viewed Sigunga, as Western civilization traditionally views "primitive" land and culture—as treasure trove, as the observers' rightful possession. Indeed, Tarzan funds himself (after losing the Greystoke inheritance in business scams) exclusively by raiding gold and jewels from the lost city of Opar. Tarzan thus replicates the actions of colonialism, without ever approving of colonialism itself. In this, Tarzan resembles many of his readers in the West, even when their beliefs and politics are humane or anti-imperialist. His prosperity, our prosperity, depends—seemingly inevitably—on the poverty of others.

What are we to make of the books' contradictory and conflicting views on race, colonialism, and imperialism? I believe we must perceive and stress the conflicts themselves. The Tarzan materials have often been dismissed as "racist," as the product of a colonialist era; within current critical trends, readings of the Tarzan novels as imperialist fantasies are sure to come.[23] But the words *racist* and *imperialist* do not tell us clearly enough how the stories work. Tarzan recognizes the blacks' humanity and resents any violation of it. Yet he feels himself distinctly different from blacks and enforces superiority in his relations with African tribes. The books condemn slavery and yet represent it as a constant in human cultures. The books loathe colonialism and imperialism, and yet they valorize ideas that made (and make) Euro-American colonialism and imperialism possible. With regard to race and related issues, the books are as contradictory and double as our culture is, as confused as Tarzan himself is: Are nonwhites so very different from whites? And if they are not so different, why have whites exploited them? Enslaved them? Killed them? The books do not, finally, find it necessary to decide. Tarzan can take blacks, or leave them. They help him define his manliness but do not really threaten it. Women, on the other hand, Tarzan cannot do without.

———

At the moment Tarzan first kisses Jane, he finds the woman he will marry and love faithfully for the next forty years. She will be the mother of his son; she will be the meaning of his life. They will enjoy good health, prosperity, and common interests. They will rarely quarrel, scarcely age, and never tire of each other. It sounds like an enactment of what happens *after* the classic happy ending. Still, there is a problem that might be summarized in the opposition between the formulation "Tarzan is a man. He will go alone" and the image of Tarzan winning Jane in the jungle. After this moment, Jane fundamentally changes Tarzan's life. True, she goes with him to live in Africa, but (as is typical of these novels when a cross-cultural marriage occurs) the couple by and large conforms to the woman's "tribal" customs, setting up a Western estate rather than actually living in the jungle. For the first dozen or more years of their married lives (as we learn in *The Son of Tarzan*) Tarzan even lives in England, withholding from the couple's son any knowledge of his father's past life. Only after the son, Korak, befriends a captured ape in England and spontaneously returns with the ape to Africa does Jane allow Tarzan renewed access to the jungle he loves (his mission: to find his son).[24]

What results, in practical terms, is Burroughs's need—also Tarzan's need—to find good reasons to leave Jane and return to the jungle. Jane's abduction into the jungle is one good reason; the need to raid Opar for funds is another. And Burroughs repeats these plot elements many times in the early novels in order to get Tarzan back into the trees. Ultimately, in midseries, Burroughs banishes Jane from the novels for a ten-year period (a period which, not so coincidentally, corresponds to his own marital troubles), freeing Tarzan to be in the jungle simply as a given of the plot. When Jane returns, in *Tarzan's Quest* (1935–36), her aversion to the jungle has been forgotten, and Tarzan has automatic permission for any excursion he wishes to make, for any reason. In terms of the bourgeois family structure, the little woman has been "whupped." There are any number of ideas, useful for patriarchal cultures, embedded in the history of Tarzan and Jane.

In nature ("naturally") Jane depends on Tarzan for survival, and his mastery is unchallenged. Only within the domestic sphere does the woman exercise control, and her role is to tame, reduce, and finally betray her man's true character. To get to the quintessential Tarzan material—jungle adventure—Jane must be removed from the domestic sphere or Tarzan must. Woman thus "civilizes" man, but also represses his vital nature. Woman is loved, but also resented. The novels express this resentment by trotting out all the familiar stereotypes about women. Whether they are European or

African, modern or primeval, women share, in the novels, a common propensity for gossip, for jealousy, for vanity, and for love above
all things; to say "for she was a woman" is, for Burroughs, to say all
these things. The men in the novels—Tarzan himself, the various
male friends who share Tarzan's adventures, the Africans, the villains—know "woman's nature." The novels repeatedly assert the
image of woman as monolithic, despite individual or cultural differences. Their shared image of women often facilitates bonding between Tarzan and the various white and black men with whom he
becomes friends and pursues adventures.

And yet, despite their resentment of women, the novels seem to
need a heroine, and not just a hero. When Tarzan is removed from
Jane's domesticating influence, the novels frequently supply an alternative heroine. Sometimes she is the love interest for a stray
American or European. More often she is the female ruler of one of
the many lost, white civilizations Tarzan encounters—and she is in
love with Tarzan. La, priestess and ruler of Opar, is the most frequent alternative heroine, and initially she seems very different
from Jane—a femme fatale to offset Jane's goodness.

When Tarzan first meets La—if one can call it a meeting—she is
the priestess assigned to make him into a human sacrifice by piercing his heart. She seems friendly, even enchanting—she rescues him
from unfriendly gorillas, dances around him, sings in a "soft and
musical voice." Then she places a rope around his neck and leads
him to a blood-stained altar, "transformed by the fanatical zeal of
religious ecstasy into a wild-eyed and bloodthirsty executioner,
who, with dripping knife, would be the first to drink her victim's
red, warm blood from the little golden cup that stood upon the altar"
(*Return of Tarzan*, 168). Always cool in distress, Tarzan still notes,
appreciatively, her getup:

> Her bare arms and legs were almost concealed by the massive,
> bejeweled ornaments which covered them, while her single leop-
> ard skin was supported by a close-fitting girdle of golden rings set
> in strange designs. . . . In the girdle she carried a long, jeweled
> knife, and in her hand a slender wand. (168)

Part primitive ruler, part S and M queen, La and characters like her
adorn several of the Tarzan covers, sometimes caught in the moment of raising their long knives, sometimes surrounded by dead
men or animals or by skulls (see figs. 2.2 and 2.3).

I especially want to call attention to the Tarzan-like iconography
associated with La and characters like her. Knives (like spears) are

Tarzan's weapons. The covers love to show him, knife raised, about to kill lions and other creatures. These women are rulers—priestesses and queens. They are powerful and therefore, iconographically, masculine despite their voluptuous beauty. These women who are not dependent on men, who are in fact rulers of men, are murderous, usurping male postures and male prerogatives, bearing conspicuously the knife elsewhere associated with Tarzan. Here indeed is a challenge to Tarzan's power, to Tarzan's manliness—and he meets it.

Tarzan saves La's life (quite absurdly he cannot resist "the call of the woman in danger," even when the woman was about to kill him). He then steals La's knife, wins her love, and ultimately becomes the kingmaker in Opar. In the later novels, La rules her people only on Tarzan's sufferance and by virtue of Tarzan's physical strength. From murderous femme fatale, La becomes Tarzan's platonically protected friend and ally. She remains in love with Tarzan for many years, to the Ape Man's consternation. In other volumes, less redeemable female rulers (like Nemone, a crazed, murderous Caligula-like figure in *Tarzan and the City of Gold*) are killed or kill themselves by the novel's end. In *Tarzan and the City of Gold*, Nemone turns her Tarzan-like weapon against herself (fig. 2.4); she who lives by the knife does herself in, and her power passes to men.[25]

Through figures like La, the Tarzan materials show a strong interest in matriarchal social organizations—or perhaps we should say a deep hostility. Both the interest and the hostility reflect potential threats to the social hierarchy which places white Euro-American males at the pinnacle, including (in Burroughs's time) women's successful drive for suffrage and increasing influence outside the home. An interest in matriarchy is not uncommon in fantasy literature, though it is not always handled with so thorough a reordering of the matriarchal order as exists in the Tarzan stories.[26]

Tarzan's hostility toward matriarchy is writ large in *Tarzan and the Ant Men* (1924), published during the period of Jane's disappearance from the series. One-half the book concerns Tarzan's adventures with the Alali, primitive whites of gigantic stature; the second half, which gives the book its title, concerns Tarzan's adventures among a group of highly civilized, white lilliputians. In Alali society, "women regarded all men as less than slaves" to be captured and used for breeding purposes only; hence, there may be some carryover between the "ant men's" physical stature and the social subordination of the Alali men. Life among the Alali is rendered as primeval,

Fig. 2.2. (Above) Tarzan with his
favorite weapon; in the background, La—
surrounded by skulls. J. St. Allen John.
Tarzan and the Jewels of Opar.
Courtesy Burroughs Memorial Collection
and Edgar Rice Burroughs, Inc.

Fig. 2.3. (Above right) Nemone—like La,
part primitive ruler, part S and M queen.
J. St. Allen John. *Tarzan and the City
of Gold.* Courtesy Burroughs
Memorial Collection and Edgar Rice
Burroughs, Inc.

Fig. 2.4. (Right) She who lives by
the knife does herself in. Advertisement
for *Tarzan and the City of Gold,*
Publisher's Weekly, 1933.

archetypal, even allegorical, with the women called simply "The First Woman," "The Second Woman," and so on. Socially, Alali society is a loveless dystopia, marred by "jealousy, greed, the hazards of the hunt, the contingencies of intertribal wars" (27). Burroughs knows the cause and is willing to tell his readers:

> The hideous life of the Alalus was the natural result of the unnatural reversal of sex dominance. It is the province of the male to initiate love and by his masterfulness to inspire first respect, then admiration in the breast of the female he seeks to attract. Love itself developed after these other emotions . . . Having no love for her mate and having become a more powerful brute, the savage Alalus woman soon came to treat members of the opposite sex with contempt and brutality with the result that the power, or at least the desire, to initiate love ceased to exist in the heart of the male . . . and so he fled into the forests and the jungles and there the dominant females hunted him lest their race perish from the earth.(27)

This essayistic passage (rather atypical of the Tarzan novels) is slick and more than a little suspect: note the ease with which Burroughs distinguishes the "natural" from the "unnatural"; note too that Alali men have lost only the "desire" and not the "power" to initiate sex. Published in 1924, during the period of Burroughs's marital problems and Jane's disappearance from the novels (Porges, *Burroughs*), the book seems to address, indirectly, Burroughs's own problems at home. More, it seems designed as a cautionary tale in the wake of suffrage for U.S. women.

In the land of the Alali, if not in his own life or in the modern United States, Burroughs could guarantee what in his terms was a happy outcome. The Alali men transform the social order and empower themselves with weapons they get from Tarzan:

> Now each male had a woman cooking for him—at least one, and some of them—the stronger—had more than one. To entertain Tarzan and to show him what great strides civilization had taken—the son of The First Woman seized a female by the hair and dragging her to him struck her heavily about the head and face with his clenched fist, and the woman fell upon her knees and fondled his legs, looking wistfully into his face, her own glowing with love and admiration. (178)

Here and only here in the Tarzan novels does one find the full clarity of gender order implied in the tag phrase "Me Tarzan, you Jane." The man is the boss, absolutely, and the woman loves it and feels no desire for power of her own. But the implications of this scene are more than a little pornographic. How to entertain Tarzan? Push some woman around a bit. Get her on her knees, caressing your legs, looking up and begging for more. Scenes like this tally uneasily with gentler images of male-female relations near the beginning of the series—like Tarzan stroking Jane's hair to comfort her as he remembered his mother, Kala, stroking his, or Tarzan wistfully wondering how a man is supposed to act. By this point in the series the utopian possibilities of re-creating Euro-American male-female relations have largely dissipated. Tarzan by now *is* a man in all the negative ways that men are often men in our culture. *This* Tarzan cannot remember his confused youth and his first encounters with Jane. The question What does a man do? has been answered—but not by Jane (the first person Tarzan thinks of asking) and not with any subtlety. As a severe and persistent threat to a man's power (using his love, Delilah-like, to undo his manhood), woman must be controlled and subordinated. What a man does *is* to control and subordinate others, though the definition is narrower and less appealing than earlier definitions Tarzan considers.

Although they appear to occupy the top of the social hierarchy along with Euro-American males, within the structure of the Tarzan series women really parallel the Africans and the African landscape.[27] The books want women to be invisible, ignorable, like the Africans—but they just are not. As the song says, "Man must have his mate," and Tarzan needs Jane. Resenting that need, the books make women always vulnerable, always in danger. Like blacks, women are always subject to slavery—in the harems of Arab raiders. Rape is a constant threat—from renegade Europeans, Arabs, Africans, and apes (the series's own descending hierarchy). Indeed, many of the plots turn on the need to rescue women from potential rapists. While rape is always forestalled, its imminence serves to emphasize the vulnerability of women and their need to be rescued by strong (white) men. Like the African landscape, women are there to be entered, conquered, mastered, made useful and productive to males.[28]

In some novels, as in the Alali beatings discussed above, women are subject to worse treatment than blacks. For distasteful as it is, this exercise of power is intended to be amusing, even good-natured. Burroughs would never have used an equivalent scene involving black men. Indeed, whites who beat blacks in the novels are labeled "fiends" and are uniformly villains, while the Alali men are supposed to seem rather cute. Power exerted over females is, most often in the Tarzan books, the occasion for smugness or humor, which compensates for the sense that women (like Jane) gain too much power over the men who love them. Occasionally, though, as in the Alali beatings, the ugly side of such domination glares through.

It does as well in the plots of other late Tarzan novels. In *Tarzan's Quest*, for example, Jane returns to the series after her unexplained absence during the troubled end of Burroughs's first marriage. Her return occurs in a novel whose major plot involves a tribe whose dress and village seem African, despite their having white skin. The tribe lures young women to their territories by hypnotic power, but not for the expected purposes of procreation. Rather the tribe consists of celibates who have achieved immortality by drinking a potion brewed from the glands of young women. In the last Tarzan book, *Tarzan and the Foreign Legion*, Burroughs jokingly explains Tarzan's persistent youthfulness as the result of his having drunk some of the potion. The joke seems to me less stable than Burroughs thought, for the motif brings out the latent misogyny of some of the Tarzan materials, despite their overt respect for ideals of feminine beauty and purity.[29]

———

In any remaking of social orders and power relations, there must be two stages: first, the telling of stories (the creation of myths) that make it possible to think new things, and then the painstaking transferral of the thoughts into actions. At some point in the process a certain key question arises: who will gain and who will lose power in the projected restructuring? The Tarzan stories offer us fleeting images of significantly altered relations between whites and blacks, men and women: Tarzan joining the Waziri in *their* dance and functioning within *their* societal norms, and Tarzan stroking Jane's hair and imitating the nurturing "maternal" role are two key examples. But the power implications of making these moments last, of using them as the basis for a new social order, are clear enough: white men must yield the hegemonic power they have enjoyed in traditional Western culture; white men will lose some forms of the power they have traditionally exercised over women and blacks, though they may gain less tangible forms of power, including the power to express their emotions freely (as Tarzan does at Kala's death), and to enjoy reciprocal rather than power-driven relations with others. The trade-offs were not likely to be attractive to Burroughs's primary audience.

Everything about the Tarzan series' history suggests that its *primary* audience was (and by and large continues to be) English-speaking Western males, despite a widespread network of secondary circulation.[30] The first Tarzan stories were serialized in U.S. men's and boys' magazines, and, shortly after Tarzan's first appearance, Burroughs organized a series of boys' clubs (called "tribes") centered on Tarzan as hero. In U.S. bookstores today, the Tarzan materials are displayed and sold alongside Westerns and other genres aimed mainly at men; Burroughs and Louis L'Amour in fact dominate the bookstore sections devoted to what we might call male romance. Commentators from the sixties—including Mandel, Vidal, and Seelye—confirm the gender specificity of Tarzan's readership and popularity. An informal survey of my contemporaries also yielded a strong gender linkage. Men frequently said they had read the Tarzan materials, though they usually hastened to add that they had done so "long ago," when they were kids; they often added, perhaps somewhat nervously, that the Tarzan materials were "racist" (though, it is significant, they never said "sexist"). Women usually had not read the Tarzan books, in fact usually did not know anything more than the bare facts of Tarzan's story. The rare exceptions among the women who had read the Tarzan books usually attributed their reading to older brothers or to a rebellious, tomboy past. Had the Tarzan materials been addressed to or received by a larger female and/or third world audience, their development might well have been different (Burroughs was usually willing to give audiences what they wanted). But the Tarzan books developed within, and in their turn helped to form, Anglo-American male systems of socialization—so much so that the macho tone and male bonding embodied in biographies of Burroughs are hardly surprising.

The Tarzan I like best is the doubt-filled Tarzan, willing to learn from blacks and women, willing to ask and examine the question What does a man do? That preference would probably be shared by most female readers today, and by many men. But while my preference may arise from reading the Tarzan novels through contemporary feminist perspectives, it also—and this is important—corresponds to impulses found in the original Tarzan materials but gradually suppressed, both in the novels and in popular abstractions of a chest-pounding, "Me Tarzan, you Jane" Tarzan who lords it over Africans. For while Tarzan ends by affirming Western hierarchies in his seemingly irresistible urge to rise to the top, he begins by needing to learn what hierarchies exist in the human world and by suppressing his doubts about their inevitability and basis.

The implications of Western primitivism as I describe it will often be unappealing and oppressive, sometimes even repulsive. But primitivism need not be either repulsive or oppressive. Rare, fugitive examples of more attractive forms of primitivism exist, and one of the best is, not surprisingly, a version of the Tarzan story. The 1984 film *Greystoke: The Story of Tarzan* alters Burroughs's narrative extensively and yet recaptures some of its original potential to consider radical change.[31] The most remarkable part of the movie is its opening—long sequences without language that show Tarzan being raised by apes and entering into intimate, loving relations with them. This Tarzan, on screen for long periods of time, acts completely within ape norms. He believes apes worthy of respect, love, fear, and consideration (as we all believe "our kind" worthy). And his early patterns reassert themselves even after he has learned English speech and customs and assumed his role as heir to the Greystoke fortune.

The movie's turning point (borrowed, perhaps, from a similar scene in *The Son of Tarzan*) comes when Tarzan finds his stepfather among the apes brutalized in scientific experiments and helps him to escape.[32] When the ape is killed by policemen, Tarzan's commitment to English culture vanishes; knowing this, Jane releases him back to Africa, and we last see him reentering the forest to rejoin the apes among whom he was reared. This Tarzan has learned the only serious lesson Burroughs was ever willing to draw from his Tarzan series: the lesson that man alone among living creatures kills wantonly and that comparisons between men and beasts often insult the latter.[33]

The film's animal sequences stress what has always been an essential component of the Tarzan stories—ultimate harmony between humans and animals, humans and nature, without troubling relations of hierarchy and Otherness. In these sequences (as at moments in the Tarzan series) Tarzan talks to the animals and has friends among them. Like the animals, he lives by clear-cut rules. Wanton killing is unknown, except when male apes go berserk, as they occasionally do. Males and females know their places and the duties appropriate to their gender; species keep their distance. But the sequences need to amplify on what is actually found in the texts of the Tarzan novels. For, as we have seen, oneness with animals and with nature is only brief and intermittent in the Tarzan stories and does not drive their plots as his relations with Europeans, Africans, women, and various Others do. In the novels, Tarzan does return to the apes or go off into nature alone several times, but always to

realize that he cannot go home again, especially not after his commitment to Jane: the fall into humanity that occurs roughly one-
third of the way into *Tarzan of the Apes* implies a permanent fall
into the need to master human Others. The film is useful in pointing out alternative possibilities in the Tarzan story, possibilities that
the novels themselves were unable or unwilling to fully explore.
The harmony the film's animal sequences invoke is a vision of
seamless unities very much a part of postmodernism's mélange of
views and desires concerning the primitive—a seamless unity we
sometimes project onto primitive life but have difficulty either finding, or documenting, or preserving within our own culture. If the
film is true to its utopian impulses, this film (unlike earlier Tarzan
films) will have no sequel, for Tarzan will have passed through and
beyond the social systems humans have made.

Making Primitive Objects High Art

3

"But Is It *Art?*"

*Nothing seems to me so like a
whorehouse as a museum.*
—MICHEL LEIRIS

t the turn of the century, museums displaying primitive objects resembled department stores during clearance sales: items were displayed en masse, in no special order; they were on view, but not exhibited lavishly or enticingly.[1] We can capture the feel of such museums through photographs and by recollecting museums we have visited, perhaps in childhood. In such museums, primitive artifacts are displayed in a semblance of context, as functional pieces. They are situated in models of village life, or placed in diagrams showing where they were found, or grouped with similar objects labeled "stools" or "spoons." Function receives emphasis rather than form or beauty, though the element of display always implies an aesthetic dimension.[2] This is the ethnographic approach.

For example, in the installation of Congolese objects at the Exposition Universelle, in Brussels in 1897 (fig. 3.1), a lifelike tableau of statues occupies the center.[3] A black warrior, spear in hand, confronts defiantly an Arab who points imperiously downward. For a moment, distracted by the overfilled background, the eye misses the drama here. Then we see it. Sprawled languorously below, her body naked and tipped toward the viewer, is an African woman with shaved head, but otherwise rendered as a European beauty. The Arab is, presumably, demanding the woman, and the African man resisting. The tableau, which resembles many in the Tarzan novels, represents the exotic (the Arab) confronting the primitive; the observer is distinct from both these Others, who enact a sexual drama for voyeuristic eyes.

Surrounding the central tableau is a clutter of objects—spears and knives on the wall to the right, a hut (out of proportion to the figures) to the left, a cased mummy in the foreground.[4] The miscellany testifies to the casualness of museum displays of African objects toward the end of the nineteenth century. But the room's

Fig. 3.1. The exotic confronting the primitive. Installation of Congolese objects at the Exposition Universelle, Brussels, 1897. Courtesy of the Musée Royal de L'Afrique Centrale, Tervuren, Belgium.

overall message is not so casual, suggesting as it does that African life was messy, chaotic, in need of Western order.

The most calculated elements in the room are probably the murals which decorate the walls and comment on the room's contents much in the way that settings comment on dramas or backgrounds on the main action of nineteenth-century narrative paintings. Reading the contents of the room against the background would have been an established habit of mind for the nineteenth-century observer.[5] To the left and labeled "Arabes" is a frieze easy to read in the reproduction: armed Arab men, in flowing white gowns, march several black men into slavery. To the right, there is a village scene hard to read in the reproduction. Some Africans (women?) sit behind forms that appear to be baskets but might be drums. Some of the seated figures grasp their heads in gestures that look despairing. In fact, this frieze may continue the other and show the reactions of the villagers to their men's enslavement. Taken as a whole, this room in the exhibition probably communicated a calculated message to its Belgian audiences, a message that made Belgian intervention in the Congo more palatable than it might otherwise have been. These poor savages, the display suggests, have no saving order in their lives. They are preyed upon, victimized by the Arabs, who rape their women and sell their men into slavery. Compared to this, how mild and benign seems Belgian rule! The same circle of imperialist name-calling that we saw in the Tarzan novels operates here, though for the Belgians the villains are the Arabs and not themselves.

In France, the packed, ethnographic approach also had political motivations. "The most conspicuous effect of the Exposition Universelle of 1878," according to Jean-Louis Paudrat, was "the strengthening in public opinion of the idea of France's colonial destiny in Africa." When the Musée Africain was founded, its sponsors "hoped to convince public opinion of the continuity they thought should exist between the sciences and their applications in the conquest of new territories." During this era, many of the sciences—zoology, botany, and ethnography—were conceived as useful because they "could help provide better information about countries to be taken over, the dangers they concealed, the resources they offered, and any customs of their inhabitants that would be useful to know in order to subject them to the plans of the colonial power." Even the most famous of French ethnographic museums, the Musée d'Ethnographie, "responded to this didactic purpose," which motivated much early collecting ("From Africa," 128).

The ethnographic approach still survives in many museums. As a child, visiting the Brooklyn Museum and the American Museum of Natural History, I saw those ethnographic displays; most New York children never forget the canoe in the main hall at the Museum of Natural History, filled with realistic looking Indians and surrounded by their objects. Realistic statues of primitive peoples and displays of their objects function in the same way as the dioramas of African animal and plant life still so striking a part of this famous museum. Their function is "educational"—they preserve for Western eyes vanishing curiosities. We are not supposed to ask, as my children did when I took them to see the dioramas, "did they have to kill the animals to bring them here?" That is a given, the price of progress, of education—or so I said to my children when asked. But my young children had grasped an essential point. These "life-like" displays bespeak the death of animals, and the death of cultures. Their existence can be justified by their ability to "salvage" vanishing forms of life and by their educational value; but their ideological basis and their origins in conquest, killing, and appropriation remain suspect.

Today, it may cost us little to admit the shocking origins and suspect ideologies of the great ethnographic collections. Assembled in the nineteenth and early twentieth centuries, they can be seen as the fruit of colonialism—a fruit whose bitter taste we want to place in the past. Their ethos may seem as distant from us as the aesthetics of the statue of Teddy Roosevelt, mounted on horseback, which guards the Museum of Natural History's entrance on Central Park West. Now, we want to believe, attitudes toward primitive peoples, and toward the things they have made, are better and purer than in the days when Teddy Roosevelt rode roughly. And our museums and galleries help us believe this.

Today, museums and galleries of what we have agreed to call primitive art resemble jewelry stores.[6] Objects are displayed, singly or in groups, in glass cases. Dramatic spotlights isolate the objects, from each other and from us. We peer at them, sometimes walk around them, but with the glass marking a distance between us and them. Walls are a modernist white or a uniform, mysterious darkness—either way the walls ground the objects against a solid, neutral background, conducive to the contemplation of form. The displays aestheticize the objects and present them as the valuable, jewel-like things they have become. Floating in cases, spotlighted against light or dark, the objects cast a mysterious spell, invoke images of "unknown," "mysterious" places. These stark spaces work in two ways: they create a nude formalism which is somehow sensuous and erotic, even as it is primarily hermetic and cold.

For me, odd details often jar the purity of the display. Sometimes, when objects sit outside of cases, a discreet sign informs me that the object is "electronically protected"; to touch it would, presumably, be shocking in more ways than one, though the temptation is strong. Sometimes the objects cut off by the glass case invite touch, were in fact made to be touched; they were once used as game pieces or fortune-telling pieces, and note cards tell me that they were worn smooth "by frequent use." Sometimes, tucked into a corner of the case is a temperature graph—protecting the object, like a medieval painting, from radical fluctuations; how odd that seems, for objects born in the heat of the tropics or in the arctic zones of the Eskimos. At other times, the display forces the observer into an uncanny, unnatural relation to the objects observed. At a recent exhibition of objects from the Staatliches Museum of Art in Munich,[7] a display case held three mirrored figures once used to ward off evil. The face of one figure, with staring red eyes above a mirrored body, impressed me and seemed indeed to ward off the eyes I directed toward it; the other figures similarly deflected the gaze—returned it via the mirrors—so that their function might have been guessed without the explanatory notes. Yet the display forced me to confront these objects head-on, even when a superstitious nature (like my own) might have rather viewed the objects obliquely or from behind, preferring not to risk being the person receiving the reflected evil. The display refused to acknowledge the physical power of the objects except in *words*, which said that *primitives* thought them powerful. The words are our words and thus safely place and contain what primitive hands and imaginations have wrought.

At the Margaret Mead Hall of the American Museum of Natural History, a hybrid of the ethnographic and aesthetic approaches, a case testifies to what it mildly calls "culture contact." My eye was caught by a photograph of what is identified as a "native girl," smiling broadly at the camera in the classic welcoming "aloha" way (fig. 3.2).[8] The pubescent girl wears flash bulbs she has received (the caption tells us) "as payment for collection," so that the camera has become part of what it photographs. The girl holds in each hand the tips of palm fronds—this is perhaps a photograph meant to evoke a fertility or initiatory ritual. Other individual fronds, stripped from the trees, form the girl's elaborate necklace/breastpiece/blouse. From the tip of each frond in the breastpiece dangles one of the photographer's light bulbs. The photograph is shown as an example of "culture contact"—of indigenous peoples incorporating Western materials into their dress, rituals, and art. But the bulbs function here as a kind of visual pun, exploiting the visual image's power to say things by juxtaposition that would be unacceptable to put into words. They suggest, on the young girl, the forms of the breasts she does not yet have, replace them in a metonymy both verbal (bulbs/boobs) and visual. The bulbs may have come—probably did come—from the camera taking the picture. Is this "culture contact" or "cultural hegemony," "sexual politics," even, at the most extreme view, "child porn"? The photograph suggests an uneasy crossing of all four.

I have said that behind the West's rhetoric about the primitive there is often an interest in power—economic, sexual, and psychological power. The aestheticism of today's displays of primitive objects may seem to belie that statement. The photograph of the "native girl" restores its truth. Just below the surface of some modernist and postmodernist writing about and displays of primitive objects as art lurk the issues of sex, money, and power. Examining these materials is like turning over stones, revealing the insects beneath. Unturned the stone looks simple, cold, and solid—pure fact or pure form; once turned the stone reveals a mass of swarming life—instinctual, irrational, out of control. Western tropes encourage us to identify the "lower," the "irrational," the "instinctual," the "swarming" with the primitive. But instead, I want to identify what we find beneath the turned stone with a certain doubleness in the work of many moderns and postmoderns who write about primitive objects as "art," who see primitive objects with biases and obsessions they will not, maybe cannot, acknowledge—biases that cut to the very heart of "the modern" and "the postmodern" as they have been narrated in this century.

Part Two examines in turn three major theorists of primitive objects as art: Roger Fry, Michel Leiris, and William Rubin. These theorists typify and indeed helped bring about the change in our

Fig. 3.2. A visual pun—on the young girl, the forms of breasts. "Culture Contact," Negative No. 336443. Courtesy Department of Library Services, American Museum of Natural History, New York.

attitude toward primitive objects. Together, they cover a range of possible relations between Western observer and primitive artifact, from the ethnographically charged to the aesthetically committed, and cover a time span from 1910 to the present. Fry was one of the first art historians to write, in the teens and twenties, about the formal qualities of African drawings and sculptures. Leiris represents a midcentury revised ethnographic approach to African masks, sculptures, and decorative techniques: he possesses a knowledge of place and culture quite beyond Fry's reach and is highly relative in his theories of culture; more, he views African masks, sculptures, and decorative patterns with the formal appreciation Fry helped to create. Rubin's work and writing represent the full postmodern apotheosis of primitive objects into art, a stage by which the "status" of primitive objects as formal icons and high art important in the West is too often unquestioned and treated as unproblematic.

The tension between the designations "art" and "functional object" permeates the politics of art theory and museum exhibitions when they pertain to primitive societies. In turn, that tension forms part of this century's most characteristic intellectual debates between contextual and formal approaches, between differentiating via historical and cultural backgrounds and universalizing via the study of deep structures and continuing forms.[9] Our dominant narrative about the West's relation to primitive masks and sculptures—produced in part by the history of our museum exhibitions—runs as follows: first there were ethnographic approaches, followed by "better," "purer" aesthetic ones. Sometimes the narrative is complicated by a subplot that calls for combining ethnographic and aesthetic approaches, since the aesthetic, isolated unto itself, may distort the meaning of primitive objects. But we need to complicate that narrative further.

The chronological separation of "aesthetic" and "ethnographic" approaches is not, for example, entirely accurate: writing about primitive art that is *either* aesthetic *or* ethnographic appears as early as the teens and sometimes continues into the present.[10] Some studies, especially since the sixties, have programmatically combined the two approaches.[11] But the gesture is often marked by the assertion of power, as each side claims to be giving the "better" or "truer" picture. Even today, some art historians (like Rubin) remain indifferent to ethnographic contexts or employ them superficially. Ethnographers almost always mention art history, grateful perhaps for the widespread interest it has created in their subject. But ethnographers often betray some contempt for art historians, as when Willett maintains that only someone who has done work in the field (something relatively few art historians have done) is in a position to make fully meaningful statements (*African Art*, 40).[12]

Within the dominant narrative as told by art historians, the "elevation" of primitive objects into art is often implicitly seen as the aesthetic equivalent of decolonization, as bringing Others into the "mainstream" in a way that ethnographic studies, by their very nature, could not. Yet that "elevation" in a sense reproduces, in the aesthetic realm, the dynamics of colonialism, since Western standards control the flow of the "mainstream" and can bestow or withhold the label "art." The imperial tendency entered the art world quite early in its attention to primitive objects. "You don't need the masterpiece to get the idea," Picasso is reported to have said after his first visits to the Musée d'Ethnographie at the Trocadéro in Paris; the Westerner could enter a cluttered display and cleverly pick out its "best" and "worst" pieces. As we saw in chapter 1, Roger Fry could afford to buy an African piece that he described as "one of the most beautiful pieces of sculpture," and "was glad to have been able to buy it as [Western] things of that quality are usually out of my reach—they are too expensive." Then as now, the attribution of "best" and "worst" implies a price tag, as the objects primitives create become objects of desire for Western connoisseurs and enter an elaborate network of sale and resale quite different from their original conditions of production and circulation.

I do not want to underestimate the change that has occurred in the processing of primitive objects in Western art theory and museums. We have recently seen several instances in which major museums have returned pieces to their groups of origin, acknowledging cultural over monetary or scientific value; such considerations would have seemed laughable to many in past decades.[13] At the end of the Second World War, Margaret Trowell could write that no full-scale survey of African sculpture existed in English and that volumes in French and German were for specialists only; today numerous studies have been published for specialist and amateur alike. Toward the beginning of this century, expensive installations of African and Oceanic pieces as art, like that in the Rockefeller Wing of the Metropolitan Museum, would have been unthinkable, as would the new National Museum of African Art on the Mall in Washington.[14] Now a solely ethnographic approach, with pieces from Africa or Oceania grouped together in functional displays would also be unthinkable. A great deal has, indeed, changed. But it is far from clear whether we have really faced the inconsistencies in the West's double attitude toward primitive masks and sculptures as both artifacts and art.

When the ethnographic approach to primitive objects as artifacts survives in museums today (as in portions of the American Museum of Natural History), it generally exists nearby or as a supplement to the jewelry-store display of primitive objects as high art, often in halls that seem to be awaiting renovation. Within the same museum, the two kinds of display send very different messages: here, amid a jumble of similar items, sit primitive objects; there, amid stark walls and lighted cases, stands art. The fact that context controls the message "art" or "non-art" indicates one of the many continuing problematics in using the very term *primitive art* and the need to pay more attention to it.[15]

At one level, the term *art* is desirable when discussing primitive objects as a corrective to patterns of thought that made colonialism possible. For many Western thinkers, the production of "art" is a basic element of "culture"; to others (Fry, for example) both "art" and a guiding "aesthetics" are required for a society to be a "culture." The attribution of "art" or "aesthetics" to a particular group is thus often connected, whether rightly or not, to political identity and hence to the problematic dynamics of the word *primitive* itself (see chap. 1). A group without an "art" and "aesthetics" can be thought to lack "culture" and "political integrity"; it can then be "discovered" and "developed" by "superior" groups, that is, those who possess both "art" and "culture." Any challenge to the designation of "art" for African, Oceanic, and Native American pieces thus flirts dangerously with modes of thought that made the appropriation of land from primitive peoples possible and contributes to their continuing economic exploitation.

Yet, at another level, to call primitive objects "art" brings to bear conceptions that may once have been foreign to their contexts of origin, especially for work completed before the first half of this century:[16] "the artist," "the marketplace," "masterpiece," "abstract versus naturalistic," "realistic versus expressionistic," and "form versus function," for example. In asking Eurocentric questions about primitive masks and sculptures, we miss important opportunities: the opportunity to preserve alternative value systems, and the opportunity to reevaluate basic Western conceptions from the viewpoint of systems of thought outside of or aslant from those in the West.

Despite a century of intense work and attention, modern and

postmodern ways of treating primitive sculpture, drawing, and artifacts often turn out not to be new enough. In fact, even quite recent
discussions sometimes share the tropes that governed the 1897
Brussels Exposition and the colonialist modes of thought it represents. Can we escape the implications of the Exposition Universelle,
with its prurient interests and assumption of Western power? Can
we forge new relations with the work of primitive Others? To answer
these questions we must first examine some of the stages by which
primitive objects became high art, and something of what was going
on behind the scenes for writers like Fry, Leiris, and Rubin. Then, at
the end of part two, we return to the issue of primitive objects in
their contexts of origin and in the West in order to suggest that the
debate between ethnographic and formal approaches to primitive
masks and sculptures, as it has often been staged, may evade some
important and far-reaching questions, questions as basic as What is
Art? and How should we treat it?

4

The Politics of Roger Fry's
Vision and Design

n 1910, Roger Fry organized the famous exhibition "Manet and the Post-Impressionists," which introduced Impressionist and Post-Impressionist art to England more than thirty years after their appearance in France. The show caused a public scandal, with visits to hoot and jeer at the art commonplace.[1] Even thirty years after the fact, England was, apparently, not ready for the "modern" in art, and Fry's role as the organizer of the exhibit was controversial and embattled. Though the exhibition is usually read as the dawn of the modern, it will help to see it as, simultaneously, the English debut of the primitive in high culture.

Everything about the exhibition sent the signals: "Modern!" and "Primitive!" The exhibition poster showed one of Gauguin's paintings from his Tahitian phase, with a "native" woman posed next to a Tahitian statue (fig. 4.1). Gauguin was a wise choice for the poster, his relatively realistic works the only ones the public liked. Other artists—especially Picasso and Matisse, whose shown works were less naturalistic than Gauguin's—shocked the viewers, though only two years later they dominated the second Post-Impressionist exhibition, also organized by Fry. In fact, three of the most famous artists at the 1910 show—Gauguin, Matisse, and Picasso—were heavily invested in primitivism as a mode in modern art. Only Manet and Cézanne, among the featured artists, were not primitivists; even van Gogh, by virtue of his troubled biography, occupied a zone always allied with the primitive in the tropes of primitivist discourse—the zone of madmen, the zone of the insane as cultural Other (Gilman, *Difference and Pathology*).

In the same year as the first Post-Impressionist exhibition, 1910, Fry published a little essay, "The Art of the Bushman," in *Atheneum*. Fry's interest in Bushman drawings went hand in hand with his interest in Post-Impressionist art and produced similar reactions in the British public. Referring to the 1910 exhibition, Virginia Woolf said that "in or about December, 1910, human character

Fig. 4.1.
"Modern!" and "Primitive!"
Poster for 1910 exhibition
"Manet and the Post-
Impressionists." Courtesy
Frances Spalding.

changed" ("Modern Fiction," 320). Paraphrasing Woolf, we can say that in or about December 1910—and also through the agency of Roger Fry—primitive objects became, in England, high art.

Fry's essay "The Art of the Bushman" provoked bafflement and scorn. As one drawing master put it, "I say, don't you think Fry might find something more interesting to write about than Bushmen, Bushmen!" (Spalding, *Fry*, 129). But Fry could not find something more interesting to write about because for him, as for other art theorists of the teens and twenties, primitive drawings and sculpture represented the future of modern art. Like others in the art world, he thought primitive and modern art twin phenomena—and scripted both as attempts to rescue art from the morass of photographic representation and narrative. In 1920, once again in *Athenaeum*, Fry published a second essay on African art called "Negro Sculpture." He then collected the "Bushman" and "Negro Sculpture" pieces with other essays in his major volume *Vision and Design*, which is considered of "immense importance" in the development of modern art.[2]

Though Fry was in many ways a dabbler in African and other non-Western art, with no ethnographic or special training, he was the premier art theorist in Britain, and his work on African art has weight and importance greater than the eighteen-page length of the essays would suggest. *Vision and Design* was the volume that made primitive objects, in England, high art and made them the occasion for an emerging modernist aesthetics.

——

Fry uses African art in *Vision and Design* as an important test case for his larger aesthetic theories. The volume begins with several essays on general aesthetics, each promulgating Fry's key ideas: the importance of form over content in works of art, the need to educate the eye in the perception of form, and the universality of form as a medium of vision. If these ideas sound familiar today, they should, for they are the basis of formalism in the twentieth century and passed, via Fry's association with Bloomsbury, into literature, art, and philosophy in modern Britain. The volume then moves, in its middle section, to the essays on Bushman and African art, and to related essays entitled "Ancient American [Aztec] Art" and "Mohammedan [Islamic] Art." Next come essays on figures of varying, yet canonical status in the Western tradition—Giotto, Dürer, El Greco, and Blake. The volume ends with essays on artists that Fry was urging upon the British public as major—Renoir, Cézanne, and other Post-Impressionists.

The organization of the volume in itself tells us that Fry conceived of his aesthetic theories as educating the eye to appreciate masterpieces wherever it finds them—in museums and galleries, in the ateliers of neglected artists, or in African villages. He begins his close analyses with primitive works because of their shock value. If these works by ordinary Africans (not really "artists" in the Western sense) have an aesthetic claim upon us because of their formal power—as Fry insists they do—then we must pay attention to derided works within the modern tradition, ridiculed for their rejection of narrative and representation, the cornerstones of post-Renaissance art until the modern era. *Vision and Design* uses African art to establish its argument and to dramatize its case for the universality of form as a criterion for evaluating art.

The essay "Negro Sculpture" opens with an invocation of past cultural parochialism and glories in a sense of expanding the canon:

What a comfortable mental furniture the generalisations of a century ago must have afforded! What a right little, tight little, round
little world it was when . . . Greek art, even in Roman copies, was
the only indisputable art, except for some Renaissance repeti-
tions! . . . And now, in the last sixty years, knowledge and perception have poured upon us so fast that the whole well-ordered system has been blown away, and we stand bare to the blast, scarcely
able to snatch a hasty generalisation or two to cover our nakedness for a moment. (99)

Confronted by the work of the Other, Westerners are "bare to the
blast," "naked" like those producing primitive sculptures. African
pieces leave us especially "naked," as Fry suggests when he compares the typical Englishman's reactions to Africans with those to
Indians. "If to our ancestors the poor Indian had 'an untutored
mind,' the Congolese's ignorance and savagery must have seemed
too abstract for discussion," Fry says; "one would like to know what
Dr. Johnson would have said to anyone who had offered him a negro
idol for several hundred pounds. It would have seemed then sheer
lunacy to listen to what a negro savage had to tell us of his emotions
about the human form" (99–100). Fry is aware of the irony in using,
as he does repeatedly, terms like "savage" to describe the producers
of what he will argue is high art. In fact, that tension underlies the
entire essay.

At times, Fry recognizes and attacks contemporary prejudices and
the colonialism they support; note in the comment above, for example, how Fry puts into quotation marks certain received ideas
about Indians. At other times, he speaks from within those prejudices and uses rhetoric typical of colonialism. Fry cannot be accused
in any simple way of racism or of supporting the colonial system. A
member of Bloomsbury, Fry would have tended to share, or at least
hear, progressive and socialist political opinions, though articulated,
to be sure, from within privileged social classes. He would have seen
himself as a Victorian (he was older than the typical denizen of
Bloomsbury) defiantly emerging into modernity. His life was void of
any significant political involvement beyond a refusal to serve in
World War I—an act motivated by his Quaker background but also
by resistance to the jingoism of the times (Spalding, *Fry*, 196). Yet,
as was the case for Livingstone and for Burroughs, revisionist, liberal
impulses with regard to Africans cannot, it seems, sustain themselves. Fry's discussions of African pieces vacillate and waver, and
remain fundamentally ambivalent about the value of things African.
His statements in praise of African drawing and sculpture undercut

themselves in ways he seems unable to control. Reading Fry with regard to the primitive is like witnessing a tug of war: on one side, and almost winning, is the innovative Fry, free of contemporary prejudices; on the other side, and finally dragging his opponent through the mud, is a Fry who thinks and speaks in the rhetoric of colonialism.

When Fry notes, for example, that the number of Bushmen "is now nothing but a remnant," he seems to recognize the cost to African peoples of Western intervention. But then he goes on, blandly falling back to colonialist patterns of thinking:

> The race itself . . . is now nothing but a remnant. The treatment that they have received at the hands of the white settlers does not seem to have been conspicuously more sympathetic or intelligent than that meted out to them by negro conquerors, and thus the opportunity of solving some of the most interesting problems of human development has been forever lost. (98).

This statement undercuts—and yet airs—the idea that white settlers would treat conquered peoples better than rival blacks would. Africans are the objects of European racism and yet racists themselves: "the South African Bushmen are regarded by the other native races in much the same way that we look upon negroes"(94). The formulation suggests a circle of erroneous racial thinking but also accepts "the way that we look upon negroes" as a view shared by the writer and reader. In the statement about the near extinction of the Bushman, Fry seems to lament a lost opportunity for anthropological and developmental study more than he does the fate of a people. Viewed least charitably, Fry may be said "to value as art what is now a ruin," as "an imaginary resolution of a real contradiction" (Foster, " 'Primitive' Unconscious," 61). The elevation of primitive objects to high art becomes a compensation for the spoliation of cultures, becomes, for the primitives, a booby prize.

Perhaps the guiding paradox in Fry's essays on Bushman drawings and African sculpture is his avowed purpose—to assert their greatness as art—and the resistance some part of his mind or, more likely, background, makes to that purpose. Fry notes that since "we have the habit of thinking that the power to create expressive plastic form is one of the greatest of human achievements . . . it seems unfair to be forced to admit that certain nameless savages have possessed this power not only in a higher degree than we at this moment, but than we as a nation have ever possessed it." ("Negro Sculpture," 100). It seems unfair—not quite cricket, not good form—that these "nameless savages" should excel us in one of the greatest areas of human achievement. Fry groups the artists in question as "nameless savages"; the term "savages" speaks for itself, the implications of wildness tallying oddly with the sensitivity attributed to the artist. The "nameless" functions equally insidiously: it makes the artist part of a group—the fearsome black horde—dissolving his individuality because, being nameless, he seems to have taken no precautions to preserve that individuality.[3] The Western tradition, of course, as Fry well knew, covers such namelessness by naming the artist by the work (the Aurora Painter, the Beowulf Poet) or by omitting the artist's name while giving the work a descriptive title. In no sense does it confuse the state of anonymity with that of being nameless, or being nameless with being savage. "Namelessness" resembles "nakedness": it is a category always brought to bear by the Westerner on the "primitive" and yet a phony category insofar as the namelessness and nakedness exist only from the Euro-American point of view.

Overcoming his reluctance to pronounce African sculpture great art, Fry declares: "And yet that is where I find myself." But he immediately hedges the firmness of his declaration by two telltale comparisons between Western and African art. First, Fry notes that the ability to "conceive form in three dimensions," equivalent to "complete plastic freedom,"

> with us seems only to come at the end of a long period, when the art has attained a high degree of representational skill and when it is generally already decadent from the point of view of imaginative significance. Now, the strange thing about these African sculptures is that they bear, as far as I can see, no trace of this process. Without ever attaining anything like representational accuracy they have complete freedom. (100–101).

This passage comes replete with a rhetoric of "us" and "them," and with biased rhetorical linkages ("us" with "attainment," "them" with "complete freedom"). In it, Fry sees no evidence of "process" in the development of African carving. Today, art historians agree that most of the African masks and sculptures available to us date from the late nineteenth and early twentieth centuries, although some African works (the Tassili cave drawings, and sculptures from Ife and Benin, for example) were completed much earlier. In part, the preponderance of objects from the last two centuries is due to the simple fact that most African sculpture was made of perishable substances and that no effort was made by the producing cultures to preserve it. But the dating, the lack of a "process," of a "tradition," can also be ascribed to the arrival of Western eyes only in the nineteenth and twentieth centuries.[4] Very simply, we cannot know what came much earlier and must leave open the idea of past traditions or developments in African art; recent evidence suggests, in fact, that certain African traditions can be traced hundreds of years and show as much evidence of change as Western art during a comparable period.[5]

More radically, we must question the assumption that traditions must "progress" or that "progress" means the same thing in African traditions that it does in the West. In Fry's time, much African sculpture was, erroneously, thought to be ancient, hence the equivalence of the terms "primitive" and "Pre-Columbian." Fry's statement that African art shows no development was understandable, but also displays a certain arrogance, the sort of arrogance that nourished the common colonialist belief that colonized people were incapable of internal order or change. Yet that point, while accurate, masks a still larger one: Fry's terms, and others like them (including "art" and "artist"), imply values like "evolution" and "progress" and "development"—values I want to resist because they impose Western ideals (some would say fictions) on non-Western societies.

A similar, unacknowledged racism inhabits some of Fry's other assertions of the greatness of African sculpture. Comparing African to Western pieces, Fry sees the emphasis as "utterly different":

> Our emphasis has always been affected by our preferences for certain forms which appeared to us to mark the nobility of man. Thus we shrink from giving the head its full development; we like to lengthen the legs and generally to force the form into a particular type. These preferences seem to be dictated not by a plastic bias, but by our reading of the physical symbols of certain inner qualities which we admire in our kind, such, for instance, as agility, a commanding presence, or a pensive brow. The negro, it seems, either has no such preferences, or his preferences happen to coincide more nearly with what his feeling for pure plastic design would dictate. (101)

In one sense, the passage is a masterpiece of tact and cultural relativity: note the "forms which appeared to us," and the frequent use of "seems" rather than a more definite rendering of fact. But note as well how Fry insidiously, and probably without even realizing it, manages to endow even the failings of Western art with virtue: "we" fail in certain sculptural attempts because "we" value a noble image as "they" do not seem to do. Significantly, "we" add "pensive brows" while they (less rational, ultimately less intelligent, as our colonialist psychology will have it) do not seem to value, even understand, the demands of rationality or intelligence. Indeed, they have not so much "preferences" as "feelings."

Perhaps the most basic failings in this statement involve its inability to raise, with regard to primitive art, issues that form the cornerstone of Fry's career as a critic: first, that ideals of representation can and do shift (the basis of Fry's championing of Impressionism); and, second, that perceptions and conceptions can be, often are, culturally conditioned.[6] To see African masks and sculptures as unconcerned with "nobility" (or to see only the conventions of one's own culture as conferring "nobility") ignores the high relativity of that term.

Here an example will be helpful. Figure 4.2 shows a mask of the *mwaash a mboy* type from what is now Zaire, dated from the late nineteenth, early twentieth century. The mask was used in initiation rites and represents Woot, a mythic god who originated royalty, the political structure, and most of the art and crafts (Willett, *African Art*, 190); according to Bascom (*African Art in Cultural Perspective*), he also married his sister. The mask looks, to Western eyes, peculiar. It uses hyena and baboon fur and an elaborate, stylized design of cowrie shells—intricate and lovely. Most oddly to Westerners, the mask crosses human with animal attributes—not just the fur but the stylized outgrowth like an elephant's trunk in form (though ending in an outburst of orange, perhaps suggestive of breath), a likeness reinforced, indeed confirmed, by the tusklike projections beneath it. To the artist producing the mask and to his audience, the mask must have suggested the size, strength, and stature of the hero and the ancestors being honored during the initiation rites. A representation falsified to enhance human nobility? Surely so, though hardly in the mode of Greek sculpture. African sculptures, artifacts, and masks repeatedly draw on animal attributes, creating an artistic idiom for representing the dignified, impressive, and powerful, an idiom vastly different from the West's in imagery but not so dissimilar in intention and effect on the audience. Fry's inability to understand African art in its own terms results in partial, insensitive readings.

For Fry, the factor that perhaps above all else differentiates African from Western art, and from much non-Western art (Islamic, Aztec, Chinese, and Japanese, for example), is that it was the product of peoples but not of cultures. Fry insists on this point:

Fig. 4.2. An idiom to suggest the size, strength, and stature of ancestors. *Mukyeem Mask.* Kasai, Mweka, Kuba; Zaire. Wood, beads, feathers, hair, shell fiber; 27 1/2" h. Courtesy of the Art Institute of Chicago, Laura T. Magnuson Fund, 1982.1504.

It is curious that a people who produced such great artists did not produce also a culture in our sense of the word. This shows that two factors are necessary to produce the cultures which distinguish civilised peoples. There must be, of course, the creative artist, but there must also be the power of conscious critical appreciation and comparison. (103).

No simple racist or even ethnocentric Englishman, Fry then compares the societies that produced African sculptures with the one that produced Chinese art—a literate and courtly society which, for Fry, is thus less than fully Other:

If we imagined such an apparatus of critical appreciation as the Chinese have possessed from the earliest times applied to this negro art, we should have no difficulty in recognising its singular beauty. We should never have been tempted to regard it as savage or unrefined. It is for want of a conscious critical sense and the intellectual powers of comparison and classification that the negro has failed to create one of the great cultures of the world, and

93

not from any lack of the creative aesthetic impulse, nor from lack
of the most exquisite sensibility and the finest taste. (103)

Here, in full dress, Fry rehearses a view of the primitive natural
and useful in an imperialist culture. Many in our time still inter-
nalize this view, despite intellectually rejecting it. Fry trades in the
idea of "the primitive mind" high in intuitive powers. He allows
"the primitive mind" harmony with nature and access to the spirit
world. He further grants it high creativity and evocative power. But
he denies "the primitive mind" rational ability, analytic power, the
"self-consciousness" that "distinguishes" (and the diction is not accidental) "our" culture from the primitive. He proposes to supply
the aesthetics which Africa has "failed" to provide for itself. He becomes the voice of Africa. He also irresistibly elevates the art critic's, that is, his own, role in creating "cultures": the Africans have
the "artists"; what they lack, according to Fry, are the Frys of this
world.[7]

Despite Fry's Quakerish honesty and openness of mind, despite
his liberal intentions, the essays on Bushman and African art—a
mere eighteen pages in print—contain a virtual encyclopedia of colonialist stereotypes about the African. One of the more extensive
entries in that encyclopedia is a long discussion of Bushman drawing in relationship to children's art.[8] As we have already seen several
times in different contexts, Fry's rhetorical habit is to dismiss the
pejorative association of the primitive with the childlike and yet,
somehow, to valorize it by airing it once again. "The Art of the Bushman" begins by raising the analogy between children's drawings and
those of Bushmen:

> The primitive drawing of our own race is singularly like that of
> children. Its most striking peculiarity is the extent to which it is
> dominated by the concept of language. . . . The symbols for con-
> cepts gradually take on more and more of the likeness to appear-
> ances, but the mode of approach remains even in comparatively
> advanced periods the same. (85–86)

After several pages elaborating traditional comparisons of Bushman
to children's art, comes Fry's repudiation:

> Such, in brief outline, are some of the main principles of drawing
> both among primitive peoples and among our own children. It is
> not a little surprising then to find . . . that the principles are more
> often contradicted than exemplified. (87–88)

Renderings of animals by Bushmen show the ability to capture "complicated poses" and "momentary actions with photographic verisimilitude" in a way unavailable to Western eyes until the invention of photography. In describing figure 4.3, for example, Fry notes that "the gesture is seen by us to be true only because our slow and imperfect vision has been helped out by the instantaneous photograph" (91). All in all, the essay concludes, "Those who have taught drawing to children will know with what infinite pains civilised man arrives at this power" (92).

The essay goes on to compare Bushman to Western Archaic art (Paleolithic, Assyrian, Greek), speculating that the relatively high quality of vision expressed in Bushman drawing may in fact account for the Bushman's lack of change as a people: "It would seem not impossible that the very perfection of vision, and presumably of the other senses . . . fitted them so perfectly to their surroundings that there was no necessity to develop the mechanical arts beyond the elementary instruments of the chase" (94–95). We see here, once again, a compliment to Bushman drawing concealing a pejorative sense that Bushman culture, while—perhaps because—capable of vision, exemplifies most fully the primitive incapacity to reason and to progress without Western intervention. If we read it harshly, the passage can be said to provide a rationale for the extinction of primitive peoples.

Fig. 4.3. "Momentary actions . . . photographic verisimilitude." Bushman drawing reproduced in 1920 Brentano's edition of Roger Fry, *Vision and Design.*

The rhetorical effect of this long section, which forms, in fact, the bulk of the Bushman essay, is curious. The analogy between Bushman art and childish art is rejected, but its persistence shows its power and suggests its truth. Indeed, many readers will retain the fact of the comparison rather than its discrediting. The effect reminds me of that made on Othello by Iago's repeated warnings that he should not be jealous—the prohibition inflames the proscribed emotion. Freud noted a similar psychological mechanism when patients would recount, for example, a dream in which they seduced an unknown woman and would respond, when asked the woman's identity, "I don't know, but it wasn't my mother." One might object that, in the patient's case, the denial anticipates the analyst's "script." This would, however, prove my point, that repetition can give fictions or hypotheses the status of truths. Derogatory Western tropes seem to dominate discourse about primitives, even when the Westerner attempts to speak in favor of primitives, as Fry clearly did.

"Negro Sculpture" ends on a crucial point. Bushman drawing and African sculpture are, clearly, admired by Fry and offered to the West as models for what art can be and what art can do when allied to vision rendered in design. But at the end of "Negro Sculpture," Fry briefly, and half facetiously, imagines how Africans would respond to Western art in its most slavishly representational modes. Repeating his view that African sculpture depends on instinct and vision, without thought or concept, Fry speculates that the lack of concept, the lack of an articulated aesthetic, "leaves the artist much more at the mercy of any outside influence." Thus, "It is likely enough that the negro artist, although capable of such profound imaginative understanding of form, would accept our cheapest illusionist art with humble enthusiasm." (103).

These are frightening images: black velvet paintings adorning huts in Africa; swans swimming on placid rivers displayed with pride in museums near the Congo. In the images rest, of course, the lasting tragedy of the colonial experience, the full display of cultural hegemony established after conquest. Implicit in them as well is the "beads and trinkets" view of "natives" so common in the West. Fry means here, unless I misread him, a little joke. The tragedy in the display is outside the circle of Fry's attention, though not, I think, properly outside ours. Coming at the end of "Negro Sculpture," the remark undercuts the celebratory thrust of the essay. The last-minute regression confirms that making primitive objects high art is a European game with high cultural stakes, a game in which primitives are pawns, unable to grasp the rules and unable to win.

———

With their emphasis on form and design as expressive of universal vision, Fry's theories clearly count among the powerful formal theories of art so characteristic of the twentieth century. Like many theories of what Fry's followers called "significant form," they do not, of course, "embrace the wider social issues that cluster around art"; for Fry, "the question of where and when a work was produced had only subsidiary interest and did not affect the aesthetic emotion aroused" (Spalding, *Fry*, vii). In the case of Fry's essays on African art, the potential limitations of this approach are realized.

Quite strikingly, Fry makes no attempt to distinguish between different parts and different peoples in Africa. Hundreds of distinctions must be made; Fry makes only two—Bushman and "Negro"—the breadth of the second category creating an overlap. More important, Fry shows no recognition that the objects discussed as museum pieces were often functional items, and sometimes sacred objects, in the daily life or special rituals of a people. As we have seen, African objects were in Fry's day typically the preserve of ethnographers and anthropologists. Even today, many art historians would approve of Fry's noncontextual approach; we need to return to this issue later, in contexts closer to us historically. But even if we grant the validity of sometimes giving aesthetic considerations priority over ethnographic ones, the latter do not lose all relevance. Fry's discussion of African objects is analogous to a discussion of medieval chalices and reliquaries that proceeds without reference to Christianity or to the organization of the medieval church, indeed which neither knows nor cares that such things existed.

In describing Fry as an amateur with regard to primitive societies, and an amateur with a formalist bias, I may seem to imply that others writing about primitive objects as art in his day were able to do better. In fact, while some did *better*, Fry's mistakes are entirely typical. Most early writers on primitive masks and sculptures—beginning a tradition which has continued among art historians up to our day—discussed primitive masks and sculptures only in the contexts of modern art; they were seen as interesting only because or insofar as they influenced modern artists.[9] Even when this common mindset was missing, when the focus was exclusively on the African, the works were often blind in ways that Fry's work is blind. Consider, for example, the case of Georges Hardy—geographer, director of L'Ecole coloniale, and author of *L'art nègre: L'art animiste des noirs d'Afrique* (*Negro Art: The Animistic Art of Black*

Africans), one of the first book-length treatments of African objects as art.

Expert in his field, Hardy knows only too well the scope and complexity of his topic. He begins by posing the inevitable flaws in any survey of African art and by asking outright "Does the Negro exist?" He wants to protest against the generalizations his large topic will force upon him: "We speak easily of a Negro art, a Negro religion, a Negro language: yet wouldn't we find it an abuse of generalization to speak of white art, white religion, a white language?"[10]

To avoid overgeneralization, Hardy spends the first portion of his book detailing the social structures within which Africans created their masks and sculptures and the third portion characterizing the art of three broadly conceived regions: the savanna, the forest, and the art of Benin. But in between these two sections, at the very heart of his book, comes a series of generalizations about what Hardy calls "the negro soul" that seems at odds with his original suspicions about encompassing a continent's many peoples in a single word.

Even more surprisingly, given his chosen subject, Hardy seems preoccupied with the *limitations* of what he calls African art; even as he studies it, it seems to him lacking what his Western education has led him to consider necessary for great art. It seems odd to him, indeed damning, that Africans emphasize small-scale sculpture rather than painting or architecture.[11] He worries over African art's lack of a "tradition" and aspiration for permanence. He misses most of all the free-spirited figure of the artist, Byronic in his ability to stand alone and to renovate conventions. As in Fry's study, African art cannot really win; it is, paradoxically, both not "traditional" enough and not "innovative" enough. The chapter titles of the book tell a tale of African limitations. According to these titles, African art is bound by "The Tyranny of Natural Forces," "The Tyranny of History," "The Tyranny of the Social Group," and "The Sterility of Isolation."

While Hardy's expertise spares him some of the embarrassments Fry falls into—as a historian and ethnographer, Hardy knows Africa has a history, and he knows its diversity—ultimately Fry and Hardy write out of similarly racist assumptions. "The Negro soul has remained immobile, or nearly so," writes Hardy; "It is lost when left free, but capable of great and beautiful actions when it finds the master it needs" (83). Though found within a book about art, these statements clearly serve as apologia for colonialism. For Hardy as for Fry, African art lacks aesthetics: "among Africans, aesthetic concerns remain narrowly subordinate to social and religious concerns"

(112). It is inconceivable to him that these close ties between art and society *might in themselves* constitute the equivalent of Western "aesthetics," albeit in terms different from those in the West.[12] For Hardy as for Fry, African art is a "problem" that can best be solved in the West, a region that (tellingly) becomes equivalent, in some of Hardy's sentences, to what he calls "universal life."

Linguists and anthropologists have, by and large, rejected or modified the ideas of the simple "primitive mind" promulgated during the colonialist period in which Fry and Hardy wrote. Historians have performed a similar function by showing that Africa has a rich and diverse history. Literary scholars have begun the same task. Art historians and aestheticians have been slower, caught up in other concerns, bemused perhaps by the pretense that aesthetic theory is above and beyond mere politics. As a theorist and aesthetician, Fry also thought that aesthetic theory could and should be above mundane political realities; that, indeed, was a central theme in some of Fry's work and that of his followers, such as Clive Bell.[13]

But the essays in *Vision and Design* have distinct and uncomfortable political implications. They helped reinforce a chain of ideas vital to the colonialist enterprise, a chain whose links were often familiar Western tropes for the primitive. First was the idea that primitives were like children—intuitive, spontaneous, and irrational. Second, the idea that primitives needed guidance in order to emerge into modernity, the cultural equivalent of adulthood. Third, expanding the opening premise, came the idea that primitives were sexually volatile and, by a further extension, naturally violent. Fourth, a vital and quickly forged link, was the belief that primitives were incapable of responding to the gentle guidance of the West, and required severe control. Fifth, and inevitably, came the belief that whites were destined, indeed obliged, to control and dominate primitive peoples and their territories.

Fry's essays do not—I must note in fairness—make all these connections. But the culture receiving *Vision and Design* was accustomed to moving from the first two stages to the third, after which conquest and control would follow. Continuing and expanding an older tradition of including blacks as signs of sensuality, paintings of the modern movement like Manet's *Olympia* and Picasso's *Les demoiselles d'Avignon* had used blacks and African masks in connection with debased sexuality, especially the depiction of prostitution and brothel life. Is it an accident that these two paintings—linking nonwhites, women, and sex for sale—have become icons of modern art?

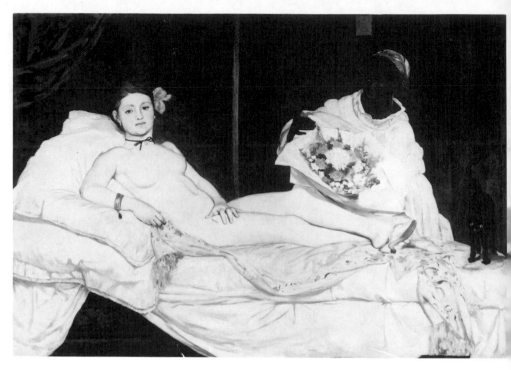

Fig. 4.4. An icon
of modern art.
Edouard Manet. *Olympia*.
Courtesy Musée
d'Orsay, Paris.

Fig. 4.5. The black cat—a stand-in for Olympia's
genitals and her black maid. A nineteenth-century
parody of *Olympia* which appeared in *Cham*.

Fig. 4.6. The black maid, stripped. Pablo Picasso. *Parody of Manet's "Olympia."* Copyright 1989, ARS N.Y./SPADEM.

Fig. 4.7. To change one color is to change them all. Larry Rivers. *I Like Olympia in Black Face.* Collection, Musée National d'Art Moderne, Centre Georges Pompidou, Paris. Courtesy ARS N.Y.

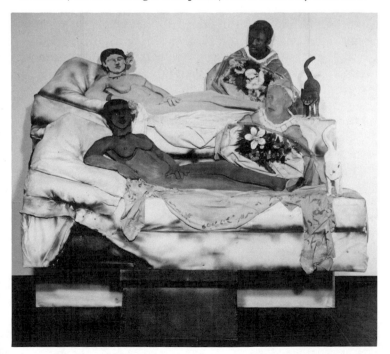

Manet's *Olympia* (fig. 4.4) scandalized Paris and prompted numerous parodies (see fig. 4.5), many of which exploited the black cat's potential as a sexual symbol, as a stand-in for Olympia's genitals and for her clothed black maid, who proffers a basket of flowers, itself a symbol for the female genitals Olympia hides. In Picasso's parodic sketch (fig. 4.6), the substitutions are made more directly. Now the black maid, stripped, replaces Manet's white Olympia. Her body is fuller, lusher, more frankly sexualized than the original Olympia's, with a special emphasis on breasts and thighs. The black cat is replaced by white pets since a black cat ("pussy") is no longer needed in the picture—the black Olympia's pubic hair being frankly on view, not hidden as in the original. Two white males (customers—one a self-portrait of Picasso) surround Olympia, one offering her a bouquet. The men's eyes and hands point very directly at Olympia's sexual parts—breasts and genitals. In Larry Rivers's *I Like Olympia in Blackface* (fig. 4.7) the same economy prevails. To change one color is to change them all: when, in the foreground, Olympia becomes black, her maid and cat become, as if by magic, bleached white. Blackness equals sex for sale, equals eroticism—and more directly than white can.

Modern artists typically valued primitive statues' allusions to conception, gestation, and birth. But they often interpreted these allusions to the reproductive cycle as displays of stark sexuality, reading the generative as the pornographic. This swerve to the pornographic appears widely in Surrealism and Expressionism.[14] The Expressionist artist Kirschner, for example, began by photographing black circus performers in costume, doing their circus acts, but he ended by having them pose naked for a series of erotic lithographs (Gordon, "German Expressionism," 371–72). The Surrealists' interest in the primitive was often colored by an interest in violence and by a misogyny that finds fullest expression in the opening sequence of *Le chien Andalu*, in which a young man fantasizes (and the audience seems to witness) the slitting of a young woman's eyeball by a razor blade. Dadaist and Surrealist works almost obsessively superimpose or juxtapose the white female with primitive masks, often creating a collage of white female body against African head, or white head against black; the absence or substitution of heads seems of special interest (see, for examples, Man Ray's *Kiki*, also called *Noire et blanche*, fig. 1.5; Hannah Hoch's *Monument to Vanity II*; Max Ernst's *Elephant of the Celebes*).

In an early sketch for *Les demoiselles d'Avignon* (fig. 4.8), Picasso included a sailor, smoking a cigarette in the center of the group of

Fig. 4.8.
A memento mori and
exercise in syphilophobia.
Pablo Picasso. *Study for
"Les demoiselles d'Avignon."*
Courtesy of Öffentliche
Kunstsammlung
Kuperstichkabinett, Basel.
Copyright 1989
ARS N.Y./SPADEM.

Fig. 4.9. The working girls of Avignon. Pablo Picasso.
Les demoiselles d'Avignon, Oil on canvas, 8' x 7'8" 1907.
Collection, The Museum of Modern Art, New York.
Acquired through the Lillie P. Bliss Bequest.
Copyright 1989 ARS N.Y./SPADEM.

whores, and a male doctor, holding a book and a skull to the far left: the painting was to be, thematically, a memento mori, an exercise in syphilophobia (Vallentin, *Picasso*; Gilman, "Black Bodies, White Bodies"). In the finished version (fig. 4.9), the sailor and doctor have been removed, with the viewer of the painting now the only one gazing at the whores, the "working girls of Avignon." But the syphilophobia and thanatophobia remain, encoded in Western readings of the African masks added to the painting after the men were removed. Respectable medical theory ventured the opinion, around this time, that syphilis originated in Africa and that black skin was "caused" by syphilitic sores. The adjectives *horrible* and *deathlike* were often used in the early part of this century to describe primitive statues (see chap. 1).

Our own culture by and large rejects the association of blackness with rampant sexuality and irrationality, with decadence and corruption, with disease and death—but not entirely. Its nonintellectual life—its popular images, its pornography, its fantasies—still trades freely in the link between blackness and sexuality, especially dangerous, death-dealing sexuality. The report that AIDS is of African origins (and the Africans' correct inference that this fact was a political as well as a medical issue) serves as a reminder. So do often-made distinctions on how AIDS appeared in the 1980s: "here" largely a disease of homosexual men and of drug users; "there" a disease often passed in heterosexual intercourse.

We may seem to have moved very far, very fast: from African masks and sculptures and their formal properties, to sex, prostitution, disease, and death. But these moves have been freely and frequently made in our culture. In Fry's time and in ours, these "intuitive," reflex associations are not politically and experientially neutral. We have already seen, in chapter 1, how an African mask precipitated the suicide of Fry's lover, Josette Coatmellac, during the years he wrote on African drawings and sculpture—how she saw Fry's showing her a photograph of an African mask as a sexual taunt and an invitation to suicide. Fry glossed Josette's reading as a "wretched intuition," but it was an intuition widely shared in her culture. We shall see again the linkage of Africans, sex, and "horrors" that is apparent in the suicide of Josette Coatmellac. Though the incident in Fry's life seems unlucky and bizarre, chance has nothing to do with it, and the incident illustrates one typical form of Western reactions to the primitive.

5

The Many Obsessions of
Michel Leiris

ichel Leiris is a French novelist, poet, and man of letters,
but also, and by profession, an ethnographer who has written a massive and important book on African art. Intellectually, he has traveled with his culture, moving from Surrealism in the twenties and thirties, to Existentialism after World
War II, to, most recently, a poststructuralist concern with language.
He has been the intellectual bridesmaid of figures better known in
this country, like Georges Bataille and Jean-Paul Sartre. In prefaces
later attached to his early writings, he interprets and reinterprets
intention and meaning in the terms that interest him at the point
the prefaces were written. Those terms enact a dialectic between
ahistorical and historical points of view, and between obsession and
observation.

The prefaces to *L'Afrique fantôme* provide a good example of
Leiris's tendency to rewrite himself by rewriting his relationship to
Africa. First published in 1934, *L'Afrique fantôme* is a diary of the
Mission Dakar-Djibouti of 1931–33, Leiris's baptismal mission as
an ethnographer, which was funded by the government to collect
African art for French museums.[1] Hallucinatory and dreamlike, the
diary records at once external facts and Leiris's state of mind. Implicitly, though not explicitly, the juxtaposition between documentary data and subjective impressions mounts an attack on the
traditional assumptions of ethnography: who is to say that the daydreams are not as valid as the ethnographic observations, the diary
seems to ask. At this point in his career, however, in the 1930s,
Michel Leiris was unwilling to answer that question or even to pose
it explicitly.

In a preface to *L'Afrique fantôme* written in 1950, Leiris rejects
what he sees in the postwar era as his earlier fear of Africa, a fear
that made him concerned (in the 1930s) more with himself than
with the cultures he studied. He rejects not only colonialism but
cultural contact "by which entire peoples find themselves alienated

from themselves" (9; my translation). Leiris refers to the colonized as "alienated" here, but he may be projecting outward, in Existentialist terms, his own condition onto the Africans. That projection would repeat, in a different form, the equation between his confused impressions in Africa and the nature of Africa (L'Afrique fantôme) in the work itself.

This preface of 1950 coincides with other documents from the same period in which Leiris foregrounds, quite explicitly now, his doubts about traditional ethnographic assumptions of scientific disinterest. He published in the same year "L'ethnographe devant le colonialisme," an analysis of the ethnographer's changing role in the coming era of decolonization, during which, Leiris correctly notes, the colonized would begin to "speak back" to the once monologic West. Leiris admirably maintains that the ethnographer's role should be that of facilitating the future that the formerly colonized imagine for themselves. His analysis of ethnography's past failures and present responsibilities makes him, for some recent ethnographers, an intellectual hero (see Marcus, Cultural Critique, and Clifford, Predicament of Culture).[2] But with Michel Leiris, which texts we read makes a radical difference. And texts both before and after "L'ethnographe devant le colonialisme" make it difficult to endorse absolutely recent views of Leiris as a postmodern ethnographic hero.

In a later preface, written for the 1981 edition of L'Afrique fantôme, Leiris reads the history of his prefaces to the volume as a history of lability itself. He traces the stages by which he established first a self-interested relation with Africa, then an ethnographic one, then (in the 1950s) an anticolonialist one, and then, "tristement," a neocolonialist relation. He is suspicious of his book, but trusts that it will still interest those "who speak French and are not analphabetic" (5; my translation). One senses behind each of the prefaces the changing terms of his intellectual life: Existentialism in the 1950s with its political commitments prior to the era of decolonization; the poststructuralist drama of language and its unreliability (now sometimes severed from politics) in later years. Leiris's intellectual life is the focus of the drama; Africa and things African are mere settings and props.

Contemporary literary critics have followed Leiris's lead, reading his early works in the light of his late ones. In the best-known work in English on Leiris, a special issue of SubStance edited by Jean-Jacques Thomas, and in much of the work published in French, Leiris is presented as a saint and martyr of language. His entire endeavor—as autobiographer, poet, ethnographer, novelist, and critic—is seen by Thomas as an

> effort at comprehension . . . exercised in a super-coding which respects the givens of the code considered but restitutes them in its own terms. This explains, in the texts of Michel Leiris, the incessant play of verbal *destructions*, of truncations, of homophonic chains inside which one can read the words of vehicular language, appearing in the form of constellations and different regroupings ("brisées" or "fibrilles") opening up a new, multiple universe of signification. (33)

In the same spirit, though using Leiris's own vocabulary rather than Thomas's semiotic one, Mary Ann Caws celebrates Leiris's metaphor of writing as bullfight:

> For the phoenix to be reborn from the flame, the poem from the dagger of the word stabbing the page, the cry, whether of a man or of a beast, a passage must be effected through the blood—a source as vital as it is voluminous. . . . The savage liquid breathed forth not by the beast's entrails only, but by ours also, in the enforced act of confrontation, marks our enclosure for the act of gestation and slaughter. (114)

Caws does not pause here, or elsewhere, to confront the content of the style and aesthetics she praises; indeed, she tries to imitate the style of her subject, even when the imitation lands her (a female critic) in the middle of misogynist sentences in which the feminine becomes "a nightmare of wounds" and "the beast inside" (114).

Reversing the procedure of most of his critics, I would like to read a late work by Leiris, *African Art* (1967), in light of an early one, *Manhood* (1939). Read together, these books make utterly explicit the spillage between sexuality and Western interest in African art—a spillage we too often take for granted, and take for granted to our shame. They raise serious questions about the implications of the ethnographic approach to African objects as art, questions as serious as those we have seen in the formalist approach. In fact, they suggest some surprising points of convergence.

———

Manhood was written during the late thirties, when Leiris was thirty-four. It followed a nervous breakdown in 1929, extensive psychoanalysis, and a career change in the early thirties (this was when

Leiris became an ethnographer). Two years before beginning *Man-hood*, Leiris had journeyed to equatorial Africa on the Dakar-Djibouti expedition, and the book gives the background and after-math of that journey. About a year before beginning to write, he had attempted suicide. The book is a Surrealist autobiography, intent on self-exposure; it is "fictional" in tone and perhaps in construction. Critics like Thomas and Caws would be inclined to emphasize its literary quality and to downplay what it reveals about the autobio-graphical self on that basis. I assume, on the contrary, that the terms Leiris chooses for his exposure of self should be taken seriously and count as facts about his brand of primitivism, even if they are "in-vented" or "constructed" facts (e.g., "fictions").

During the twenties and thirties, Leiris was a crony of Georges Bataille, who wanted to arrange a human sacrifice in Paris as a way of "loosing the sacred" and paving the way for a revolution which would flood the streets of the city with blood. Although the plan was secret at the time, Roger Caillois revealed its existence many years later.[3] Human sacrifice was Bataille's special version of the primitive, centered on the Aztecs and based in part on D. H. Law-rence's *The Plumed Serpent*. Bataille's scheme had the modern twist that the victim was to sign a presacrificial agreement absolving his murderers of legal responsibility. The legal considerations finally thwarted the plan, even though Bataille had apparently found a will-ing victim, and they constitute a peculiarly twentieth-century slant on the primitive. In a similar way, *Manhood*, a Surrealist text writ-ten under the influence of psychoanalysis, and recounting the years during which Leiris became an ethnographer, can be seen as a con-fluence of the idea of the primitive with certain modern notions of the self and sexuality.

The book is, to put it mildly, disturbing. It takes as its inspiring icon a diptych by Cranach, of Lucrece and Judith—whose figures and actions Leiris finds "particularly arousing" (fig. 5.1). His reading of the paintings brings together a number of Leiris's obsessions which ultimately join his obsession with the primitive: sex and blood, disfigurement, pain as the source of pleasure, death as the price for sexual consummation, betrayal as the reward of trust. To give you a feeling for Leiris's sensibility, I cannot do better than to give you Leiris's gloss on these paintings:

> the first, Lucrece, pressing to the center of her white chest, be-tween two marvelously hard, round breasts (whose nipples seem as rigid as the stones decorating a gorget or cuirass at the same

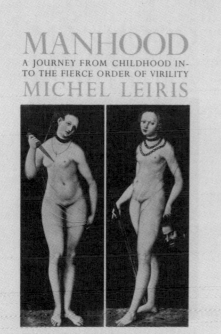

Fig. 5.1.
"Particularly arousing"
figures and actions. Cover,
Michel Leiris's *Manhood,*
with Lucas Cranach's
Lucrece and *Judith.*

place), the narrow blade of a dagger whose tip is already beaded, like the most intimate gift appearing at the end of the male member, with a few drops of blood, and about to annihilate the effect of the rape she has suffered by a similar gesture: one that will thrust into a warm sheath of flesh, and for a bloody death, the weapon at its maximum degree of stiffness, like the rapist's inexorable virility when it enters by force the orifice already gaping between her thighs, the gentle pink wound that soon after returned the libation in full measure, just as the wound—deeper, wickeder too, but perhaps even more intoxicating—made by the dagger will release, from Lucrece's very heart as she faints or fails, a torrent of blood;

the second, Judith, in her right hand a sword naked as herself, its point piercing the ground close to her slender toes and its firm broad blade having just severed Holofernes' head, which hangs, sinister trophy, from the heroine's left hand, fingers and hair mingled in hideous union—Judith, wearing a necklace as heavy as a convict's chain, whose coldness around her voluptuous neck recalls that of the sword close to her feet—Judith, placid and already seeming to ignore the bearded ball she holds like a phallic glans she could have sundered merely by pressing her legs together when Holofernes' floodgates opened; or which, an ogress at the height of her madness, she might have cut from the powerful member of the drunken (and perhaps vomiting) man with a sudden snap of her teeth. (94)

The passage insists on a number of substitutions which sexualize objects and actions with pornographic violence: Tarquin's penis for Lucrece's knife, rape for suicide, semen or vaginal discharge for blood, wound for female genitals, bondage chain for Judith's necklace, phallic glans for Holofernes' head, Judith's legs or teeth for Judith's sword. Other passages extend the substitutions: suicide attracts because it obliterates the subject/object division; Leiris sometimes identifies himself with the male characters in the stories behind these paintings (Holofernes) and sometimes with the females (Judith). The passage repels most, perhaps, by its suggestion that Lucrece enjoyed (must have enjoyed) her rape and repeats that voluptuous satisfaction in suicide, and its parallel suggestion that Judith castrates Holofernes to punish him for his sexuality, rather than kills him as a political act.

The autobiography details the chance associations which made the gruesome substitutions of this passage inevitable for Leiris. His first erection was stimulated by the sight of barefoot children climbing a tree, their soles painfully bruised (14). He played in childhood a game called "eyes put out" in which he would plunge a finger into an egg cup filled with moistened bread crumbs, a game that came, for Leiris, to signify penetrating "the female organ as something dirty or as a wound" (46). He received a cut requiring stitches "shortly after [he] had learned from a school friend the true nature of sexual intercourse" (87). He experienced a tonsillectomy as having his "throat cut" and then found his throat pleasured with cool sherbets (64). He remembers being chosen as the "scapegoat" in childish games and being "tied to the stake, scalped" by Indians (21). He chronicles repeated episodes of masturbation in youth and impotence in manhood. All his life, he sets his own experiences against mythic ones: male/female love against the image of Judith or of Cleopatra, after Antony, hurling her lovers to their death; Electra, Salome, Carmen. His book is a disturbing reminder of how this linking of sex and violence, and especially the sense of woman as either dangerous or victimized, pervades Western culture and provides a psyche like Leiris's with ready simulacra.

As we have seen, Leiris wrote *Manhood* after he became an eth-nographer and journeyed to Africa under the sign of his work as an ethnographer, which he tells us "is quite in accord with my tastes" (5). On what does this vocational bliss depend? *Manhood* suggests that Leiris came to ethnography via sensual associations very much like those which attract him to Cranach's Lucrece and Judith. He remembers from childhood, at the circus, "a North African woman naked to the waist, so that I could stare my fill at her nipples and navel, which I had never been able to do with any other woman, save in a fragmentary and stealthy manner" (60): the African woman is available to the gaze, her parts on view, much as his African objects of study would be later. Her nipples presage Lucrece's nipples, her navel the "bleeding navel . . . the secret wound" Leiris discovers, in a dream, and identifies with his lover's vagina (145). In a memorable sentence, Leiris says that "nothing seems more like a whorehouse to me than a museum" (30). The erotic potential of the gaze, its potential to violate its object and to arouse the self, opens to Leiris via the North African woman and remains part of what pleasures him in ethnography and in his study of African art.

Leiris tells us that *Manhood* was conditioned by "the period when I spent most of my nights in Montmartre . . . preferring the Negro bars to all the rest," a period epitomized in "a jazz tune that was suitably melancholy or blues sung by a colored woman whose throat seemed to have been pecked by a bird" (131). There are other fateful associations with blackness. After World War I, his genera-tion, says Leiris, experienced "an abandonment to the animal joy of experiencing the influence of a modern rhythm. . . . In jazz, too, came the first public appearances of *Negroes*, the manifestation and the myth of black Edens which were to lead me to Africa and, be-yond Africa, to ethnography. Under this vibrant sign of jazz—whose frivolity masked a secret nostalgia—occurred my union with Kay, the first woman I authentically 'knew'" (109). For Leiris (and, he claims, for his generation, the generation that made Josephine Baker a star) Africa is "Edenic," a place of "ritual intoxication." Leiris tries to reproduce its qualities through drink and through jazz, and these partial replications lead him to Africa, and "beyond Africa, to eth-nography." Blackness figures, inexorably, in Leiris's first sexual en-counters, and sex remains part of his associations with his objects of professional study.

Leiris wrote *Manhood* following a year of psychoanalysis, begun after an episode of "all-night debauchery after which, having been unable to achieve my purpose with a little American Negro dancer,

I appeared at a friend's house around five in the morning and asked to borrow his razor with the—more or less sham—intention of castrating myself" (137). A failed Lucrece/Judith, he fled Paris for Africa where he fell in love "with an Ethiopian woman who corresponded physically and morally to my double image of Lucrece and Judith" (140). A syphilitic, "her clitoris extirpated, like all the women of her race," the woman never became Leiris's lover; but he "had various chance encounters with Somali girls," often, we learn in *L'Afrique fantôme*, whores, who left him "with an impression of Paradise" (140). Before he goes to Africa, the primitive exists as a place of fantastic satisfactions; the real thing, not surprisingly, fits his images of it, and the site of "Paradise" becomes the body of the African woman.

Leiris reads all his experiences, reads the world, in terms of the drama of subject and object, a drama he associates, again from childhood, with the difference between male and female:

> always beneath or above concrete events, I remain a prisoner of this alternative: the world as a real object which dominates and devours me (like Judith) in suffering and in fear, or else the world as a pure fantasy which dissolves in my hands, which I destroy (like Lucrece thrusting home the dagger) without ever succeeding in possessing it. Perhaps, above all, the question for me is to escape this dilemma by finding a way in which the world and myself—object and subject—confront each other on an equal footing, as the matador stands before the bull. (141)

Everything in Leiris's *Manhood* becomes implicated in everything else, and one might say worlds about his obsession with bullfights and animal sacrifice—not to mention the spurious "equality" of matador and bull, a relationship that is another version of the deathly images that haunt him. But let us simply say, for now, that things African, black, primitive mesh thoroughly with Leiris's fixation on subject/object relations and with the sexualized nexus of pain/pleasure/wounds/decapitation/death which he sees everywhere he looks.

African Art was published in 1967 as part of the Arts of Mankind series edited by André Malraux. It was translated and published in English in 1969 in a large, handsome volume with a lavish 450 illustrations. The book is divided into three separate parts: "Towards a

Definition of African Art" and "The Visual Arts," written by Leiris; and "Art and People," an overview of the history of each major region of Africa, written by Jacqueline Lelange, which is not included in my discussion. Following a typology proposed by Marcel Griaule, Leiris divides the visual arts into "arts of the body" and "environmental art," as well as "autonomous figure arts" (sculpture). The book combines formal analysis with ethnographic information, and seems to strike a balance between these two major approaches to African art. Leiris adds to Fry's formal appreciation of African art a sense of its geographic and cultural specificity and of its cultural functions—he seems authoritative where Fry seems amateurish.

But when we read *African Art* with a knowledge of *Manhood*, strange things begin to happen. How do we connect the mind and sensibility that wrote *Manhood* with the following prose, from the "Arts of the Body" chapter of *African Art:*

> Scarification and tattooing, whether on the face or on some other part of the body (for example round the navel in the case of women) are usually tribal marks or indications of social rank.
>
> As a general rule, these different markings are conferred on an individual at various crucial moments in his life: at the time of his initiation from adolescence to manhood, his marriage, promotion to elder of the community, and so on. Scarification causing indentation of the skin . . . or which stands out in relief . . . or which causes evenly raised bumps . . . is much more common than actual tattooing. The appearance of the markings, in relief or indented, depends both on the peculiar susceptibility of the African's skin to scar tissue, and on the kind of treatments to which the 'patient' is subjected. . . . These markings . . . identify the wearer as a member of a definite ethnic group and designate his position in the social hierarchy. This is the reason for the great care that is taken in African sculpture to reproduce the subject's markings exactly. Yet these scarifications, although fundamentally symbolic, also have an aesthetic purpose. . . .
>
> The most widespread form of physical mutilation practised in Africa is circumcision, or in the case of girls, excision, first of the clitoris and eventually of the *labia maiora*. Usually a village practices these rites every three to four years, most often calling on the services of the blacksmith to perform the operation. The boys, all of the same age group, submit to this when they reach the age of puberty and will remain henceforth united by a common bond of solidarity. Circumcision is the first, painful step towards attaining manhood, and is at the same time an initiation and a test of fortitude. (120–22)

On the one hand, connections are easy. The passage shares with passages in *Manhood* a fascination with transitions from one stage of life to another, with initiations, with wounds, scars, with bleeding navels, with the metaphor of "doctor" and patient (recall his tonsillectomy), with pain as the threshold of manhood. The passage moves from "scarification and tattooing" in general to circumcision and clitoral extirpation—and we know, from *Manhood*, how the first would be, for Leiris, always the superficial sign of the second.

On the other hand, the connections between *African Art* and *Manhood* are hidden: the narrative voice of *African Art* is cold, dispassionate, factual, giving the facts because they are the facts. In *Manhood*, similar facts would lead to reveries, to fantasies and actions of the most bizarre and disturbing kind. In *African Art*, the reveries and fantasies have been deleted, censored, perhaps banished as something Leiris considers behind him and "cured." An ethnographic style has left only traces of Surrealist fantasy.

But the traces are important. In fact, Leiris's case reveals most clearly what we might call the prophylactic effect of the ethnographic approach to the primitive—a prophylactic effect also typical of formal theories of art, and of the jewelry-store approach to photographing and exhibiting primitive art. The analytic ideal of the ethnographer or formalist seems to solve the problem of subject and object, to remove Leiris—ostensibly at least—from the obsessive tangle of associations which makes the world a devouring subject, devouring him, or makes himself into that subject, reducing everything outside him to "pure fantasy." Both ethnography and the formal approach posit the stable reality of analytic subject and object of analysis; they posit further the equality of subject and object, though that equality is as spurious as the equality Leiris imagines between matador and bull. Michel Leiris the ethnographer and art historian is as free to gaze on the woman in figure 5.2, which appears in *African Art*, as he was, in boyhood, to gaze at the naked North African woman at the circus. The woman in this photograph and the statues in many of the other illustrations make no demands of the viewer—their nipples and scarified navels lie open to his gaze and do not talk back. They are object; he is subject. He is in control, empowered, unthreatened.

The experience of art and the role of the ethnographer have their advantages over other kinds of experiences: gazing at a live woman (or a woman who was not the object of study) might prompt expectations of sexual performance, might occasion one of the instances of impotence which haunts *Manhood*. The ethnographic gaze

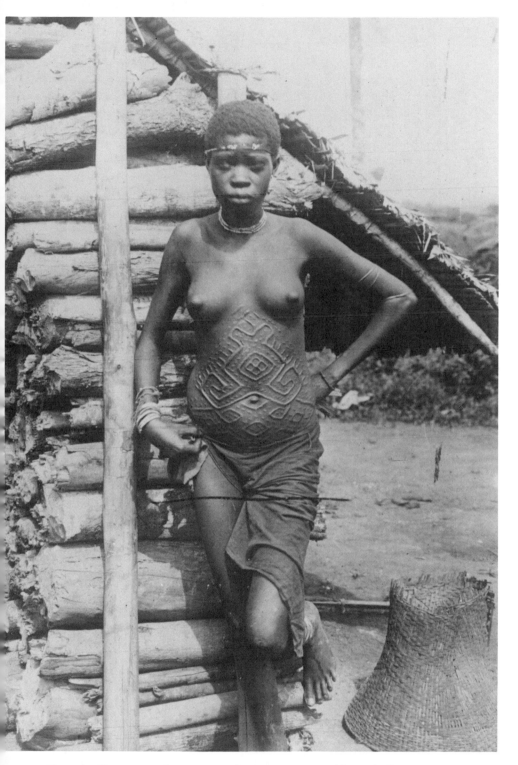

Fig. 5.2. The woman lies open to the gaze. "Tattooed [scarified] Woman."
Yombe, Mayombe; Zaire. Courtesy Musée Royal de L'Afrique
Centrale, Tervuren, Belgium.

arouses no expectations in the woman beheld; the art object cannot even have such expectations. Modernist formal theories of art insist that the object of contemplation cannot excite the observer to more than an aesthetic emotion; art cannot be, formalism insists, pornographic. In this, the formal approach also resembles certain strands of ethnography—remember Malinowski's claim that his observations on "the sexual life of savages" could neither "offend" nor "be of any use to the seeker after pornography." Yet I cannot believe these claims of neutrality, of coolness, of stable subject and object with regard to the primitive. Leiris seems to me the perfect example of how these claims must be false.

The gift of *Manhood* is that it alters familiar perceptions. It makes me wonder more than ever whether our jewelry-store conventions for photographing and exhibiting primitive art do not have hidden meanings, send hidden messages, like the 1897 Brussels Exposition. The head of Holofernes obsesses Leiris. Page after page in *African Art* displays African masks and sculptures which are disembodied heads, floating against neutral colored backgrounds, like art in the museum as jewelry store. Many of the photos, many of the statues feature scarification or metalwork around the neck, emphasizing the metaphor of "decapitation." How are we to react to the revelation of decapitation, itself the image of castration, in such contexts—so unfamiliar and shocking and yet, really, always present?

As many ethnographers attest, the masks would not be disembodied in their cultural contexts. They would be worn by men, in full costume, in dances—a wholeness our photographs and exhibits only rarely convey. The female masks, sometimes accompanied by false breasts, would also have been worn by men, as in figure 5.3, which appears in Leiris's *African Art*. From a Western perspective, this is cross-dressing; but that is a category that would make little sense in most African cultures, where few of the social formations that use masks are open to women.[4] As in periods when women were barred from the Western stage, female roles must be performed by men in almost all African dances and rituals. The masquerade here is not "transvestite" in the usual sense of the term. But the masks and costumes, and the dances in which they appeared, may well accommodate an interest in the opposite sex and, hence, a host of curiosities and ambivalences that have needed to find other outlets in our society, including the outlets suggested by Leiris's poses and prose in *Manhood*.

In the West, the hermaphroditic potential of the cross-dressed dance (in Africa or among South Pacific groups like the Iatmul) or

Fig. 5.3. Cross-dressing? "Man Wearing Mask of Young Woman."
Collection, Musée de L'Homme, Paris. Photo M. Griaule.

the double-sexed implications of some primitive objects (like Nigerian Ekoi masks) suggest crossings and connections taboo within our society. In the West, they suggest violating the rigid sexual roles the West has created as norms and provide, perhaps, a flirtation with homoerotic desires. We have, of course, no reason to assume that primitive cultures have any cure for sexual difference or any magical formula for sexual harmony; in fact, available studies suggest extremely wide variations in sex roles in societies we call primitive.[5] But the crossing between male and female was, for some moderns and postmoderns, a significant lure of African art.

Did it enable Leiris to play Holofernes and Judith, Tarquin and Lucrece, to fantasize an escape from the subject/object split which sexual differences encoded for him? Was it part of their attraction to African sculpture for Freud, D. H. Lawrence, and other moderns whose written work expresses curiosity about the origin and effect of sexual difference?[6] Because of his honesty and confessional mode in *Manhood*, Leiris brings into the open some surprising underpinnings of the modern fetishization of primitive masks and sculptures.[7] Can we say, with absolute confidence, that his obsessions are his alone and not more widely shared, even if at less perverse levels, among us? Even when they are not the formalist connoisseur's objects of desire, primitive works sometimes remain objects of more obscure desires—desires implicit in Leiris's metaphor of the museum as whorehouse.

6

William Rubin and the Dynamics of Primitivism

William Rubin helps control today's perceptions of primitive objects as art. From 1973–1988 he was director of painting and sculpture at the Museum of Modern Art in New York; he currently holds the title of director emeritus, having been succeeded as director in 1988 by Kirk Varnedoe. In 1984 he organized the "'Primitivism' in 20th-Century Art: Affinity of the Tribal and the Modern" exhibition at the Museum of Modern Art, a project that occupied six years of his professional energies, galvanized public interest in its topic, and generated intense controversy.[1] He also edited the massive two-volume catalogue for the show, which is likely to be the definitive source on its topic for years to come. This catalogue includes essays by noted scholars, including two essays by Varnedoe and two by Rubin himself, one an introduction to "Modernist Primitivism," the other on Picasso, and especially on *Les demoiselles d'Avignon*.

If we had to choose a single painting that exemplifies modernism in art, it would probably be Picasso's *Les demoiselles d'Avignon* (1907), his rendering of a brothel in a landmark work of Cubism. Not coincidentally, *Les demoiselles* is a centerpiece of MOMA's collection and was a featured work at the "'Primitivism'" show because of its use of forms that resemble African masks. Its only rival as a modernist icon (chosen by certain cognoscenti) would be Manet's *Olympia*, which, as we have seen, has similar subject matter: it portrays a whore accompanied by a black servant who is the sexualizing equivalent of the African masks in Picasso's piece. As an officer at the Museum of Modern Art and organizer of the "'Primitivism'" exhibition, Rubin had a clear interest in how we perceive this painting and its similarities to primitive masks. And, perhaps inevitably, Rubin's use of the painting exemplified much of the controversy surrounding the "'Primitivism'" show.

The MOMA exhibition included modern art by Max Ernst, Paul Klee, Henri Matisse, Gauguin, the Fauves, Braque, Brancusi, the

Dadaists, Surrealists, Modigliani, Giacometti, Calder, Moore, and others; "tribal" works came from the Zunis in New Mexico, the Eskimos of the Northwest, the Dogon, Baule/Yuro/Guro, Dan, Yoruba, Fang, Kota, Kongo/Vili/Wogo, and other peoples of Africa, and Oceanic peoples, especially those of what is now Indonesia and New Guinea. Bringing together an astonishing variety of works, the exhibition proved that primitive objects exerted great power in the imagination of modern artists and that their forms, themes, and media coincided in interesting ways or were inspirational to one of the great flowerings of the visual arts in Western civilization. The exhibition's demonstration of how modernism absorbed the primitive was broad, dramatic, stirring—a revelation even to those who knew that such things had been.

The exhibition coincided with a vogue for primitive motifs or primitivizing elements within contemporary art and included a section on these phenomena. It was part of a wider revival of interest in primitive objects, marked by a symposium and exhibition at the Israel Museum in 1985, the opening of the Michael C. Rockefeller Wing of the Metropolitan Museum of Art, the creation of a new Center for African Art in New York, and improved facilities for the National Museum of African Art in Washington, D.C. There were also numerous local exhibits in this country, including (from my random, firsthand experience) shows at the Brooklyn Museum, the Ackland Museum (Chapel Hill, North Carolina), and the Nelson-Atkins Museum of Art (Kansas City). But the MOMA exhibition was *the* primitivism exhibition, and it excited an unusual level of controversy.

Everything about the exhibition was controversial. It revealed fissures and cracks, power struggles within the modern art scene, and provided an opening for those who would challenge the hegemony of modernist aesthetics or alter the prevailing hierarchy in modern art—MOMA's hierarchy—in which abstract works in the line of Picasso, Brancusi, and Matisse occupy the pinnacle. Ultimately, in the replacing of Rubin by Varnedoe, the controversy struck a blow for certain forms of postwar art, since Varnedoe is closely associated with postmodern art and with "popular" art forms and pledged to mount exhibitions of them, even as Rubin is closely associated with the high modernism of the Picasso era (Glueck, "Modern Prepares for Twenty-first Century"). In *October*, Hal Foster roasted the show's political implications along lines I have been arguing here, but with the apparent subgoal of elevating Surrealist art, part of the tradition in which he saw himself and certain fellow members of the New Left. Hilton Kramer in the neoconservative *New Criterion* saw the exhibition's quotation-marked title as unnecessarily apologetic for the West's relation to the primitive. He wanted his primitivism without quotation marks and wanted the show to stress expressionism, not abstraction. The objects in MOMA's show not only engaged aesthetic emotions, but also revealed bedrock levels of political disagreement.

Much of the criticism focused on what the exhibition said or did not say about the primitive objects displayed as art. Many observed that the choice to exhibit primitive sources or "affinity-pieces" side by side with Western works jarred and offended. It implied some timeless realm in which the primitive and the modern speak to each other as equals, a timeless, ahistorical realm as eternal as modernism itself—and this at a time when modernism was a much beleaguered concept. The strategy revealed (though it tried to conceal) the fictiveness of the idea that art is eternal and "above" mere politics: "Here is the primitive instance; here is the masterwork, with the primitive absorbed and transcended," the exhibition seemed to say. For me the side-by-side exhibition also dramatized the different ways we label primitive and Western pieces and the oddity of the difference when they are exhibited together. The exhibit paid fetishistic attention to the dating of Western objects—sometimes down to the month or week of composition; the primitive objects were labeled by centuries.[2] Some observers found that, despite its declared interest in the influence of primitive works on modern art, the exhibition functioned to protect some movements, like analytical cubism, "as the very crux of MOMAism . . . from outside influence" (Foster, " 'Primitive' Unconscious," 56). If this was indeed one goal of the exhibition, it was an unspoken and perhaps unconscious, though profoundly political one. At the very least, the emphasis on refuting direct influence in some cases (most notably Picasso's *Les demoiselles d'Avignon*) was extreme and confusing within the context of the exhibition.

In its brochure and notes, the exhibition announced its goal, quite clearly, as to examine "the influence of tribal art on modern art, the affinities they share, and the nature of modernist 'primitivism' as a force in Western art over the last century." The exhibition said nothing about the political consequences of modernism's absorption of African and Oceanic pieces and was, indeed, uninterested in how the contact of cultures left traces, impurities, even creative mutations of third world traditions (Clifford, *Predicament of Culture*, chap. 9). Whenever colonialism was mentioned in the notes, it was only in terms of whether or not certain tribal objects were accessible to the West by the time a given Western work was completed (Foster, "'Primitive' Unconscious," 62). Thus, in a way typical of the Western tradition, the exhibition reenacted the dynamics of colonialism by positing the importance of primitive productions solely in terms of their relationship to modern art. Such a maneuver takes objects reflecting wholly different modes of social, economic, and religious experience and neutralizes them by making them a part of Western cultural history (53–55). This is what happens when we lose interest in objects as African—in their independent history, functions, and traditions—to focus instead on how they affected Western artists.

The omission of political and ethnographic concerns from the MOMA exhibit was quite deliberate. In his introduction to the two-volume catalogue, Rubin says that "the ethnologists' primary concern [the history, function, and significance of objects in their contexts of origin] is irrelevant to my topic, except insofar as these facts might have been known to the modern artists in question" (*"Primitivism,"* 1). The brochure available for each visitor at the show similarly noted that

> the term "primitivism" does not refer to tribal art itself, but only to modern Western interest in it. Our exhibition thus focuses not on the origins and intrinsic meanings of tribal objects themselves, but on the ways these objects were understood and appreciated by modern artists. The artists who first recognized the power of tribal art generally did not know its sources or purposes. They sensed meanings through intuitive response to the objects, often with a "creative misunderstanding" of their forms and functions.

Obviously the writers of that statement recognized but sidestepped some of the political problems inherent in the exhibition. But I don't think their disclaimers let the exhibitors off the hook. The term "intuitive responses" is incredibly naïve—surely our "intuitive responses" to "primitive" objects come to us culturally, not neurologically. In the same way, it seems facile to say, as MOMA did, that although "the word 'primitive' may still have negative associations for some readers," for the modern artist it was "a term of praise," used in a "wholly positive sense." Western idealization of the primitive has been as damaging as any other Western version and often conceals more pejorative views.

Although he was severely attacked for ignoring political and ethnographic questions in the exhibition, Rubin has not repented. For a recent exhibition called "Perspectives: Angles on African Art," the Center for African Art published a catalogue in which noted figures (mostly American) commented on some favorite pieces from Africa. Rubin was one of the commentators. The photograph that accompanies his commentary summarizes his interests nicely. Rubin sits in the middle ground of the photo, wearing casual yet professional dress—open-necked shirt, chinos, casual shoes, dark jacket, pipe-in-hand. In the background hangs a Léger, with a characteristic mixture of organic and machinelike forms, entangling a woman typical of his art. On the table in the foreground rests an African *chi wara*, a Bambara antelope that is among the most popular African genres in the West and exists in a variety of styles from the naturalistic to the highly stylized. The one Rubin chose is abstract and stylized, formally balanced, like most of the objects Rubin selected for his section of *Perspectives*. Rubin sits between the modern and the primitive, though the accent is modern. He surveys the primitive with the modern looking over his shoulder, controlling his eye.

His prose, like his pose, makes us trust him—it is friendly, colloquial, less magisterial than one expects from someone in his high position. "These guys [African sculptors] have to be as good as Picasso or Brancusi or they don't interest me," says Rubin (*Perspectives* 51–52). He confesses frankly that he is "obviously only interested in them for something they have that by definition transcends their origins." He has Picasso's authority for feeling this way: "Picasso once said to me that he never read anything about African art; he said 'everything I need to know about Africa is in those pieces.'" This kind of talk, quite typical of Rubin—in which Picasso, Matisse, and other moderns become the touchstone for what we should and should not know about primitive cultures—made James Clifford quip in critiquing the "'Primitivism'" show that "what was good enough for Picasso is good enough for the Museum of Modern Art" (*Predicament of Culture*, 200).

In this 1987 interview in *Perspectives*, Rubin returns quite explicitly to the controversial positions he took in 1984:

> What I'm really trying to insist on is that the choices are not between a total contextual reconstruction—which is a mythic pursuit—and a pure aesthetic response, whatever that is. We don't respond to art objects with one particular set of responses that are isolatable as aesthetic. We respond to them with our total humanity. We are moved in areas which I don't think any physiologist or psychologist would call aesthetic. What makes art ART is that the work is invested with an expressiveness that is not

particularized, and that it expresses feeling through the structural relationship of forms, and says things that you can't say any other way. (50)

Rubin nods here toward the idea that we cannot define (as Fry thought we could) a "purely aesthetic response"; we respond to art, he says, with our "total humanity." Yet by the end of the quotation, the purity of the formal definition of art is intact: art is formal icon, unparaphrasable, devoid of context. By eliminating ethnographic concerns, Rubin limits severely (though he does not seem to realize it) the terms of "our total humanity." His position and attitude, though they look logical and open-minded, suggest that he could never really understand what bothered many observers of the "'Primitivism'" show. It might have been acceptable for the show to declare certain questions off limits (after all, how can one show do everything?), but observers rightly sensed that ethnographic and political questions were omitted not for spatial economy but for a political economy that declared them "irrelevant."

Consider the last sentence in the free, widely circulated brochure distributed at the "'Primitivism'" exhibition, read by far more people than the expensive catalogue. In that sentence, 1984 repeats 1910 and 1920:

Nothing in Western (or Eastern) art prepared modern artists for the otherness of tribal art. Yet they were moved by it, and we are too, precisely because we see something of ourselves in it—a part of ourselves that Western culture had been unwilling to admit, not to say image, before the twentieth century.

There is much unspoken here that Fry, with his greater innocence about the dangers of ethnocentricity, speaks clearly. Note, for example, the unselfconscious use of the term "otherness" in a context that goes on to assert universality. Note too that Eastern art, also "Other" culturally, is distinguished from "tribal" art, presumably on the same bases that Fry distinguished Bushman drawings and African sculpture from Aztec and Islamic art, though not so crudely put (the latter being created by courtly societies which produced cultures recognizable in the West). What we see in "tribal" art, that "something of ourselves" suppressed by Western culture before the twentieth century, suggests, though it may not intend to do so, the encoding of taboo unconscious urges, the violence and sexuality repressed by the Victorians but projected onto the primitive by moderns like Leiris. In the context of the larger *Primitivism* volume, from which it is excerpted, it is clear that the sentence does not make these kinds of allusions. But most of those attending the exhibition would have seen only the brochure, not the catalogue—which cost $40 in paperback, $75 in hardcover.

The catalogue contained useful correctives to the exhibition, including three essays on the way the West acquired primitive art. But the brochure and the exhibition echoed typically colonialist ways of thinking, despite their marked awareness of the dangers of colonialism. And this is one reason so many viewers, even while impressed by the exhibition, were depressed by it, or even angered.

In both the *"Primitivism"* and *Perspectives* volumes, Rubin takes the absorption of the primitive by the modern as a given, and as a benevolent, cost-free given at that. But was it really cost-free for the primitives? Of course not. Possession of tribal objects in French, German, and British museums and homes resulted from—was the spoils of—the disruption and subjection of tribal cultures. Contemporary documents often listed, quite literally, body counts of dead Africans alongside of catalogues of "objects" acquired for exhibition and sale (Paudrat, "From Africa"). Why should we put aside the images of bloodshed and suffering, of economic dependency and exploitation implicit in colonialism, whether direct or economic? Why should we pretend that the contemplation of tribal art by European artists, aestheticians, and audiences was politically neutral? Conditioned by control and condescension, fear and contempt, such relationships were not coolly or purely aesthetic, even when occurring far from tribal territories, in settings seemingly void of political implications (though actually rich in such implications), like museums, galleries, and homes.[3]

To some extent, our entire notion of primitive art is a fiction, generated by the network of collecting and sales. We know that tribes sometimes created works to meet Western demands (and expectations) and sometimes reserved truly sacred objects or misrepresented their uses (Paudrat, "From Africa"). Primitive artifacts in a sense lost their authenticity as soon as the West got access to them. Rubin must know all this; in his *"Primitivism"* catalogue he includes essays exploring the colonial contexts under which the West acquired primitive art. But he persistently filters out this information in his own narratives about primitive art, creating a story in which Picasso and the modernists are unblemished heroes and in which primitives should be happy and willing to become part of Western art history.

If, clearly, the process by which primitive artifacts became high art was not cost-free for the primitives, was it cost-free for

Westerners? One of my central contentions is that it was not. Reading primitive objects in terms of private and cultural obsessions or in ignorance of ethnographic contexts has its costs, like those in the psyche of Michel Leiris or in the death of Josette Coatmellac, who committed suicide because she "intuitively" perceived a sexual taunt in the African mask Fry showed her.

━━━━

There are many ironies in Rubin's choosing to present the West's relation to primitive art as a cost-free given, for he should know better. In the introduction to *"Primitivism,"* Rubin writes unequivocally and at length against what he calls the expressionist misreading of primitive art, a misreading he describes as all too common in the West:

> Of all the modernist misreadings of tribal works, the most common one interprets the sometimes rigid, frontal, symmetrical, and often awkward poses of many African figures as examples of Expressionism—as in Read's previously mentioned association of them to *angst.* . . .
> Conventions . . . that encourage . . . misreadings are very common in African art, indeed, in tribal art in general. . . . There are, of course, many tribal works which (if, indeed, we do not misread them) deal with ferocity, horror, or fright, and express a certain violence. . . . But unlike modern Expressionist works, in which such sentiments are generally identified with the psychic states of the figures represented, tribal expressions of this order appear outer-directed, in the sense that they are aimed at intimidating evil spirits and protecting reliquaries. (35–38)

Indeed, as Rubin says, "placidity . . . is more typical of African art" than anger, fright, or violence (38).

Since by now we may well question Rubin's ability to make credible statements about African art, it is worth pointing out that his assertion is shared, emphatically, by other experts. Willett, for example, notes that "Western writers are very prone to look for expressions of horror and terror in African masks which in their own society may be intended merely to amuse" (*African Art,* 152); Fagg and Laude agree that what Westerners find "horrible and frightening" is often intended to be comic, so that "our interpretation of African art could [from African viewpoints] subject us to every kind of mockery" (Laude, *Arts of Black Africa,* 177). With regard to the sexuality Westerners often perceive in African Art, Laude points out that "insistence on sexual functions is an aspect of African art limited to few groups. Nudity in Africa is perfectly innocent; there is no other art that has been more indifferent to sexuality," as opposed, that is, to a concern for fertility, which is something quite different (179). Indeed, relatively few African traditions explicitly deal with sexuality in and of itself, and the forms most discussed by experts (the Ibo *mbari* house, for example) accompany limited periods of excess that contrast with the community's normal mores (Brain, *Art and Society in Africa*, 252–58).

The expert's testimony has, then, been quite clear, though it has also been controlled by the need to *overturn* the widespread and persistent perception of primitive (and especially African) statues and masks as violent and sexualized.[4] The interesting question, it seems to me, is why violence and horror and sexuality have been so strongly and so uniformly seen in primitive statues and masks by those who rely or fall back on "intuition"—why this should be the preferred twentieth-century misreading. So many other things might have been seen instead—respect for the ancestor, semiscientific attempts to understand and control nature, ideals of physical beauty and strength, a religious emotion. But placidity is not what Western observers have chosen to see in African statues and masks. Rather, Westerners, including many of the artists in MOMA's " 'Primitivism' " exhibition, did not—in the words of MOMA's brochure—"know [tribal art's] sources or purposes." Instead, Westerners "sensed meanings through intuitive response to the objects, often with a 'creative misunderstanding' of their forms and functions." In this formulation, "intuitive response" is equivalent to "creative misunderstanding." But which intuitions can we trust? More, which "intuitions" are truly "creative," and what do they create? Surely Rubin does not mean to celebrate the common "intuitions" of horror, sex, and violence, which fit absolutely colonialist ideas about primitive peoples and which—one is forced to conclude—say more about "us" than about "them."

Rubin claims that "it little matters, of course, if artists misinterpreted the objects in question if that misreading was of use to them" (*"Primitivism,"* 35). My central purpose in discussing Rubin is to defamiliarize that "of course" and to maintain that such misreadings are consequential—psychologically and culturally, experientially and politically. Once we accept as a matter "of course" that Westerners see violence and sexuality in African masks and sculptures, it becomes all too easy to suggest that violence and sexuality are what the objects typically "must" represent, and "must" characterize the people producing them. After this, the rhythms of control, domination, and exploitation develop freely. Rubin himself entertains the opening suggestions, thus triggering a dangerous dynamics.

We have already seen that, near the beginning of the *"Primitivism" in 20th-Century Art* volumes, Rubin denounces the expressionist misreading of African art so typical in the West and asserts that tranquillity is common in African art. Several hundred pages later, in an essay on Picasso and the primitive, Rubin seems to have forgotten his own principle. Twice, Rubin describes Picasso's discovery of forms suggestive of African masks in *Les demoiselles d'Avignon* as designed to convey the artist's discovery of the same horrors that Kurtz and Marlow had found in the heart of darkness:

> We sense the thanatophobia in the primordial horror evoked by the monstrously distorted heads of the two whores on the right of the picture. . . . One can hardly imagine the fear, shock, and awe these heads must have imparted in 1907, given the vividness with which we still experience them. These "African" faces express more, I believe, than just the "barbaric" character of pure sexuality. . . . They finally conjure something that transcends our sense of civilized experience, something ominous and monstrous such as Conrad's Kurtz discovered in the heart of darkness. ("Picasso," in *"Primitivism,"* 254)

Rubin's use of quotation marks does not protect him. In this passage, the "primitive," the primordial, is a "horror" revealing the "barbaric character of pure sexuality." The primitive, the whorish, the deathlike travel together in this rhetoric. Rubin oddly and irrationally takes Conrad's fiction as a baseline for facts about Africa, and incorrectly locates "the horror" *out there* rather than within Kurtz.

Nor is the allusion to Conrad incidental. Rubin returns to Conrad five pages further into his analysis of *Demoiselles:*

> The archetypal "night journey" of the soul recounted in *Heart of Darkness* by means of the metaphor of Kurtz's voyage to the interior of the Congo seems to me close in spirit to Picasso's descent into his psyche during the elaboration of the *Demoiselles.* Indeed, Picasso's radical primitivizing of the *Demoiselles* might well be considered a pictorial rendering of Conrad's words, "The mind of man is capable of everything—because everything is in it, all the past as well as all the future." Certainly the "African" figures on the right of Picasso's painting were meant to express something alien, menacing, and virtually unutterable about "the

primitive" such as Kurtz discovered in the recesses of his own unconscious when, in the heart of the Congo, he released himself from the constraints of "civilization"—something he could express at the moment of his death only as "the horror" of it. (259)

I have little doubt that Rubin means for his extensive quotation marks to distance the perceptions from his own, to show his skepticism about concepts like "civilization," to cast such concepts off, perhaps, onto Kurtz or Picasso. But the statements function in the way that we have seen some of Fry's statements function. The Westerner's "intuitive" response interferes with the revisionary impetus, with the desire to appraise the work of the Other coolly and objectively. The old stereotypes, the old, damaging colonialist tropes slip in when we're not looking.

William Rubin has spent much of his professional life inside the white cube that is MOMA.[5] Yet in passages like the two just quoted comparing Picasso and Kurtz, Rubin evokes the psychic space suggested by the 1897 Universal Exposition in Brussels, discussed in chapter 3. Here we are again, looking at the African man protecting his woman, her naked body tipped toward us amid a profusion of objects that constitute the West's "intuitive" version of the primitive. Here we are again, caught in a voyeuristic trap and in colonialist modes of thinking. Despite the lines we have become accustomed to draw (in part correctly) between modernism and postmodernism in terms of tone, style, and objects of attention, 1984 is not so different, after all, from the benighted thinking of 1910, 1920, and 1938. With regard to the primitive, there are more continuities between modernism and postmodernism than we like to think—even though, in 1984, attitudes like Rubin's could arouse public outrage.

How can we escape the trap? Both the formalist and ethnographic approaches have tried, unsatisfactorily, to give answers. Formal approaches to primitive objects as art imply a utopian end point in which the primitive and the modern or postmodern speak to each other in a timeless dialogue of line, form, vision, and design. Ethnographic approaches project a different utopian end point: the full and accurate re-creation of an Other's point of view. But there is no psychic space that fully corresponds to the neutrality and purity desired by the formal approach; even devoted formalists like Fry and Rubin cannot help but slip from their aesthetic ideals into their

culture's emotionally charged image of the primitive. There is also
no guarantee that ethnographic knowledge can ever reproduce an
Other's viewpoint or that even the fullest ethnographic knowledge
will fully overcome cultural conditioning or psychological imperatives—Leiris shows that, as does Rubin's refusal to *use* the ethnographic knowledge available at points in the *"Primitivism"* volume
he edited. Still, traditional African and other forms of what we call
primitive art may offer potentials behind and between the formal
and ethnographic approaches, potentials that have only recently begun to be pursued. To reach these potentials, Westerners need to
allow what we call primitive art to interrogate the bases of our own
art. We also need to resist the persistent temptation to translate differences into similarities.

If there is some truth in Leiris's metaphor of the museum as
whorehouse—and I think there is—such an interrogation can show
us some alternatives to the debased cash relations and exploitative
gaze that the metaphor implies. One way to get beyond Leiris's metaphor of the museum as whorehouse is to respect other ways that
art can be created, circulated, displayed, and received—to use ethnography as what George Marcus calls "cultural critique," here specifically a critique of Western aesthetics and art systems. That is one
real potential of what we call primitive art, a potential too many
discussions thus far have failed to pursue.

In its 1987 volume and exhibition, "Perspectives: Angles on African Art," the Center for African Art attempted to answer the question But what *is* art? from various points of view, both Western and
non-Western. Rubin was one of several Americans with interests or
expertise in African sculpture invited to select and comment on
some favorite pieces. Non-Western commentators were mostly Africans raised or educated in European traditions. But the volume included a section by Baule carvers living in what is described as "a
traditional Baule milieu in the Yamoussoukro area of the Ivory
Coast" (Lela, *Perspectives*, 146).[6] In its attempt to record the viewpoint of sculptors still functioning in traditional milieus, the *Perspectives* volume was one of several recent efforts to interview traditional African carvers and to present their perceptions in terms
Westerners could understand; such attempts are of special interest,
since they are the closest we are likely to come to understanding
the motivations for what we call primitive art. I want to probe the
Baule sculptors' comments and compare them with William Rubin's as a way of highlighting some important differences in the way
Western art historians and traditional African carvers view "art."

Fig. 6.1.
A dance of rejoicing.
Helmet Mask (Dye sacred
mask). Baule, Ivory Coast.
Woodwork-sculpture,
19th-20th c. Courtesy the
Metropolitan Museum of Art,
Michael C. Rockefeller
Memorial Collection. Gift of
Adrian Pascal LaGamma,
1973.

Here, for example, are the Baule carvers' comments on a Dye sacred mask (fig. 6.1):

This is the Dye sacred mask. The Dye god is a dance of rejoicing for us men. So when I see the mask, my heart is filled with joy. I like it because of the horns and the eyes. The horns curve nicely, and I like the placement of the eyes and ears. In addition, it executes very interesting and graceful dance steps. I never saw one with those things beside the nose. This is a sacred mask danced in our village. It makes us happy when we see it. There are days when we want to look at it. At that time, we take it out and contemplate it a while. (159)

Quite decidedly, the Baule carvers perceive the mask as part of a dance and as part of cultural life. The mask has no importance in and of itself: it merges with recollections of the dance, of the dancer who wore it, and with the music and audience response which enveloped it.[7] Grammatically, their syntax does not conform to Western norms: the mask "is danced in our village," and "it executes very interesting and graceful dance steps." The mask is not an object cut off from action and isolated for display; it *is* action. It is also, very clearly, emotion—the emotion of joy, which it creates whenever the viewers choose to take it out and look at it.

The "joy" the mask inspires surely corresponds to a Western aesthetic emotion; the Africans' "looking at" the mask on certain days corresponds to Western contemplation of art objects. But the African terms are not fully translatable into the Western: the periods when the men choose to look at the mask are, for example, prescribed by ritual or dictated by impulse, not by available gallery space or an exhibition's calendar. And the experience of the mask is collective ("for us men"), not private, and its ownership is (as is true for many African masks) collective as well.

The Baule carvers' emotional involvement with the mask and "ethnographic" placing of it in cultural contexts do not diminish the aesthetic pleasure the mask affords. The Africans intersperse comments about function and feeling with comments on form: "the horns curve nicely"; "I never saw one with those things beside the nose." For these Africans, the work exists as unique (they have never before seen "those things beside the nose") but also as one with other masks of the Dye god.[8] For the Baule sculptors, to like this one mask does not imply not liking the others—negative evaluation simply does not enter into the commentary.

This refusal of negative evaluation tallies with other evidence that Africans in traditional societies are often "unwilling to criticize each other's work" (Fernandez, "Principles"; Willett, *African Art*, 220).[9] When evaluation does occur, it tends to be based on factors other than the object's inherent value as a formal icon. Pieces acquire value not through abstract standards of beauty or through the price they fetch in the marketplace but rather through their place in the consecrating rituals of the group involved. Unconsecrated pieces may be discarded; even consecrated pieces will often be discarded and then replaced if a group migrates to another place (tour guide, National Museum of African Art, March 1988). Biebuyck reports that the BaLega judge pieces "to be 'good'" only when "they fulfilled their function" in a specific dance or ritual (*Tradition and Creativity*, 17); Fernandez finds the same thing true among the Fang ("Principles"). What Western eyes judge "beautiful" or "finely crafted" can, in these terms, be no better than an object judged "mediocre" in technique. Since their role in performance counts more than their appearance in repose, masks, for example, could not (for traditional Africans) be judged at all in typical Western contexts—on a wall in a museum or gallery—but only as they were perceived and experienced in a performance, in specific kinds of light, from specific angles, and from within a group's set of traditions (Thompson, *African Art in Motion*).

Many of the values we can extract from the Baule carvers' comments depend on the traditional African artist's role as a conduit of his culture. The term *artist* itself is often a misnomer since some African societies merge the function of "artist" with that of the blacksmith or diviner, and in some the position is hereditary rather than dependent on extraordinary skill. Even among the Yoruba, who professionalize the role of "artist" more than many other groups do and who have preserved the names of their most valued sculptors,[10] the sculptor still works within defined traditions and does not generally fit post-Romantic stereotypes of individualism and nonconformity (Brain, *Art and Society in Africa,* 261–62).[11]

The modern West has great difficulty understanding the traditional African artist's role. Ironically, even the *Perspectives* volume, with its celebration of difference, could not resist distorting the collective nature of the Baule sculptors' comments. It presented the comments of several men as those of a single man, Lela Kouakou— the carver who was, apparently, the most willing to talk to interviewers and to have his picture taken. The distortion may seem trivial but is not: it reflects unwillingness to ask the kinds of questions about masks and sculptures that would have made the Baule carvers willing to talk long enough to fill a section of the volume and unwillingness to accept what was, apparently, indifference to the kinds of questions that *were* being asked. The distortion tallies utterly with Western ideals of artistic individualism but slights the collective production and experience of art central to the Baule and many other African groups.

For his section of the *Perspectives* volume, Rubin did not really select pieces similar to those chosen by the Baule carvers. But let us compare his commentary on a Pende mask with their comments on the mask of the Dye god. The mask in question resembles that in figure 6.2, but omits the scarification marks, broad nose, and open mouth; in fact, the mask Rubin chose (of which I was unable to obtain a reproduction) looks like an African version of Kiki's head in Man Ray's *Kiki,* with eyes, nose, and mouth abstracted into a series of diagonal lines:

This is quite beautiful. Among the African styles that are essentially depictive, the Pende are unusual in the degree of linear abstraction they get into their work. The edges of the forms in Pende art are always very developed and precise. . . . The play of the convexity of the forehead against certain concave areas at the bottom is something that could be said about hundreds and hundreds of Pende masks. But when they are good, as this one is, these contrasts are more intense. (60)

For Rubin, the mask is a mask to be compared with similar masks and evaluated accordingly—the Western art historian's chronic habit of mind. It is an object with no meaning and no context—it is not part of a costume or dance, though Rubin surely knows (it is very basic knowledge) that all African masks in fact were parts of costumes and dances. Rubin says that he is "much more impressed by the *differences* between any two pieces" than in their reworking of traditional forms (61), and one sees that here: it is the mask's difference from other Pende masks and other African masks in general that makes it "good" for him. In fact, Rubin consistently seems to prefer an object that "sets itself off against African art," almost as though the category "African art" is derogatory (56).

Rubin conceives of the Pende tradition as something that progresses and can (and should) be evaluated against other traditions; the attitude toward tradition duplicates the reaction to single objects, insofar as they too must first be compared (favorably or un-

Fig. 6.2.
"Quite beautiful . . . good."
Mask: Face (Pende mask).
Pende, Zaire. Wood,
pigments. Courtesy the
Metropolitan Museum
of Art, Michael C.
Rockefeller Memorial
Collection. Bequest of
Nelson A. Rockefeller.

favorably) to others and then cut off and isolated for formal analysis. In this way, he could never make the kind of comments made by the Baule carvers, in which objects depicting the same subject merge with each other and can be equally, though differently, good. He could also never make the same kind of strong personal and group investment in the piece that the Baule carvers did: all judgments must, for Rubin, be accompanied by appropriate gravity and aloofness.

Unlike the Baule sculptors, Rubin feels obliged to record not just pleasure, but also displeasure. When African objects displease him, it is often because they are not consistently good in terms of stylistic unity. In a remark very similar to some of Fry's, he notes that "the absence of a concept of art *does* make a difference. . . . No civilization which has a concept of art would make that kind of piece [inconsistent in quality and style]" (58). Here, as in Fry, African objects are caught in a double bind created by Western aesthetics: they are criticized, on the one hand, as "unoriginal," and on the other, as "inconsistent." More, Rubin repeats here Fry's sense that African societies lack any governing "concepts" or aesthetics: like Fry, he purports to supply what African objects lack, a critical "voice" that will supply the criteria that guided their creation and enabled their appreciation.

All recent evidence suggests that Rubin is, quite simply, wrong—as Fry was wrong—in assuming that African masks and sculptures need Western art historians to provide a ruling aesthetics. When asked to discuss what they admire in their work, for example, Yoruba artists stressed nineteen factors, including *jijora* (a moderate resemblance to the subject, what Thompson in *African Art in Motion* calls a "modified mimesis"), *gigun* (an upright posture), *ifarahon* (clearly formed parts, visibility, luminosity), *odo* (a subject in the prime of life), and *tutu* (coolness and composure). Some of these factors (moderate resemblance and clearly formed parts) have equivalents or near equivalents in various Western aesthetic systems. Others, like *odo* and *tutu*, sometimes do not have any near equivalents and in fact correspond to categories that would most often (though not universally) be considered in the West moral rather than aesthetic. In fact, some recent attempts to define an aesthetics that can include the many varieties of African art stress the interconnectedness of criteria for moral probity and beauty, seeing this as a flexible criterion found in many African communities (Vogel, *Aesthetics of African Art*). Thompson agrees that the dual moral/aesthetic implications of "coolness" unite many diverse traditions of

African art: "from the Woloff of Senegal to the Zulu of South Africa
. . . coolness is an all-embracing positive attribute which combines
notions of composure, silence, vitality, healing, and social purifica-
tion" (*African Art in Motion*, 43).[12] There are, then, defined and
understood terms in which African masks and sculptures are traditionally viewed, terms that correspond to what is called in the West
an aesthetics. Western art historians need not supply any "voice"
for Africa; African voices can be heard if Westerners are willing to
listen and willing to respect silences when silences greet questions.

As primitive masks and sculptures moved out of their contexts of
origin and into Western contexts, conflicts between the different
ways that "artists" and "art" and "value" were defined were bound
to arise. Rubin finds such conflicts easy to resolve: he assumes that
because he writes as a Westerner to a Western audience, contexts of
origin (what he calls "ethnographic considerations") are "irrelevant"
to understanding African masks and sculptures. As I see it, probing
the conflicts caused by removing objects from their contexts of origin is a more fruitful direction. Exhibitions that pinpoint and dramatize differences between Western and traditional African (or other)
values should, then, be more a matter of course.[13]

The disjunctions between Western and traditional African aesthetics are strong and in some ways absolute; they should not always
be brought closer together. There is no logical reason why the West
should abandon its systems of artistic production, circulation, and
display, or its understandable desire to experience African, Oceanic,
and Native American objects as art. But there is also no logical reason why the West should judge African objects in terms set by the
West or blunt the fundamental challenges that traditional African
and other traditional pieces offer to European conceptions. In fact, I
would argue that only by stressing the *differences* between contexts
of origin and Western contexts of sale and display will African pieces
and other traditional pieces teach all that they can teach.

The potential to inhabit other views of art does not appear to have
an open-ended lease. Increasingly, in modern Africa and other regions, artists are trained in Western traditions, or operate in Western
systems of sale and display, or both. For the artists most fully within
Western traditions, "success" means recognition, exhibition, and
sale in Europe and the United States, often at prices that make their
work inaccessible to individuals, groups, or museums in their places
of origin (Willett, *African Art*, 264). For artists who still work in
traditional modes, new contexts have also arisen. The *Times* and
Atlantic have described the games implicit in current markets for

African art, in which only "old," "used" pieces have considerable value and yet are too scarce to fill demand; a thriving industry of producing new objects passed off as old has resulted (see chap. 1).

Yet in the terms I am suggesting, we must be careful about accepting too readily concepts like *real* and *fake* and resist the assumption that African and other artists should fully enter Western systems of value. Experts testify that new works currently passed off as "old" have considerable artistic merit; some experts even maintain that "carving for money has actually enhanced the carvers' skill, because it allows them to devote much time to their craft; previously they carved only when new pieces were needed for rituals" (Lemann, "Fake Masks," 34). In many parts of Africa, art is thriving, even with the restriction that it must often pretend to be something it is not (e.g., "old"). What might be possible if Westerners rethought criteria and valued not just "old" pieces but unabashedly "new" ones? More radically, what do designations of "real" and "fake," "authentic" and "inauthentic" mean in these contexts? More radically still, will it be possible to allow the attribution of value to arise from outside the West?

Here again, there are no easy solutions. But we must rethink the questions What is art? and How do we treat it? rather than (as is often the case today) assume that we know the answers to these questions for every possible context. This is especially crucial since the exhibition of African and Oceanic pieces in Western museums is and is likely to remain one of our culture's most accessible official means of representing the primitive.

PART 3

Engendering the Primitive

7

Traveling with Conrad

Here we go, into the heart of the heart of darkness

> We penetrated deeper and deeper into the heart of darkness. It was very quiet there. At night sometimes the roll of drums behind the curtain of trees would run up the river and remain sustained faintly, as if hovering in the air high over our heads till the first break of day. Whether it meant war, peace, or prayer we could not tell. . . . We were wanderers on a prehistoric earth, on an earth that wore the aspect of an unknown planet. We could have fancied ourselves the first of men taking possession of an accursed inheritance, to be subdued at the cost of profound anguish and of excessive toil. But suddenly as we struggled round a bend there would be a glimpse of rush walls, of peaked grass-roofs, a burst of yells, a whirl of black limbs, a mass of hands clapping, of feet stamping, of bodies swaying, of eyes rolling under the droop of heavy and motionless foliage. The steamer toiled along slowly on the edge of a black and incomprehensible frenzy. The prehistoric man was cursing us, praying to us, welcoming us—who could tell? We were cut off from the comprehension of our surroundings; we glided past like phantoms, wondering and secretly appalled, as sane men would be before an enthusiastic outbreak in a madhouse. We could not understand because we were too far and could not remember because we were travelling in the night of first ages, of those ages that are gone, leaving hardly a sign—and no memories. (Conrad, *Heart of Darkness*, 37)

The speaker, of course, is Marlow, telling a crew of fellow sailors about his journey, years before, up the Congo. But his voice has reached a larger audience. *Heart of Darkness* is a staple of college courses—read by practically every freshman as an introduction to great fiction. It has enormous force for students, undergraduate and graduate alike—and they often choose to write about it. In our time, the culturally literate remember it, se-

lectively, as William Rubin does. Its version of the primitive has become a fact despite its fictionality.

When we encounter Conrad in college courses we usually encounter the master stylist, the novelist in the great moral tradition,
the chronicler of "psychological complexity," of the modernist
"void." Style is emphasized over content, and the content is selectively described, with an emphasis on psychology and epistemology
conceived as separate from politics. The introductory section on
Conrad in the widely used *Norton Anthology of British Literature*
captures the general tone. It tells us that life aboard ship and in certain remote settlements—coupled with the manipulation of point
of view—were Conrad's "means of exploring certain profound moral
ambiguities in human experience" (Daiches and Stallworthy, 1809).
Conrad's central point, for the *Norton Anthology*, is "the difficulty
of true communion, coupled with the idea that communion can be
unexpectedly forced upon us—sometimes with someone who may
on the surface be our moral opposite, so that at times we can be
compelled into a mysterious recognition of our opposite as our true
self" (1497).

Profound ambiguities, moral questioning, the complexity of experience, the difficulty of true communion, a mysterious recognition of our opposite as our true self: these have constituted, and still
do, the essential, received version of Conrad. The desirability of certain values such as the individualism inscribed in the *Norton Anthology*'s basic terminology and the processing of the other as a version of "our true self" go unquestioned in formulations like this
one, which is entirely typical of a historically important, and once
a dominant, set of reactions to Conrad's writings.[1] Conrad as modernist master was, for most of this century, the only Conrad. And in
certain places, he is still the only Conrad in town.

In recent years, though, it has become possible to encounter a
different Conrad, especially in Marxist criticism—the imperialist
Conrad, the articulator of racial and class values and prejudices.[2] In
1988, Norton recognized changing views by publishing a new critical edition of *Heart of Darkness*, which features essays on racism
and imperialism, including an important essay on Conrad by Chinua Achebe, as well as more traditional essays by critics like Albert
Guerard and Ian Watt.[3] Today, some critics even say that the only
value in reading Conrad is to expose the rotten Western attitudes he
articulates, the colonialist rhetoric embedded in passages like the
one quoted above.[4] In our reactions to Conrad, we seem to have
come very far, very fast. But one has only to watch the profession to

know that the older image of Conrad as master stylist and sage will be hard to dispel, especially by newer, overwrought images of Conrad as Western demon.[5] At conferences, papers critiquing Conrad as imperialist inevitably provoke indignation among humanists and formalists, who use these high values as a charm against the attackers; the two sides listen to each other with strained civility but remain unconvinced.[6]

The real problem with existing critiques of Conrad as imperialist is not, as the humanists and formalists think, that they pollute art with politics or debase artistic considerations, but that the notion of politics they employ is entirely too circumscribed. Colonialism and imperialism *are* important political issues, but they are not the only ones involved in narratives like *Heart of Darkness* or *Lord Jim*. Conrad engages in a more broadly political description of certain versions of masculinity and femininity, and of certain related ideals, such as "restraint." For all their differences, both the humanist/formalist approaches and existing critiques of Conrad as imperialist operate from within the same system of gender values and notions of the political as Conrad himself. They thus cannot help but ignore important issues raised by the text that are political in a different sense.[7]

Any critique of *Heart of Darkness* must account for the ways that the novella can be read as an affirmation of humanistic values, in ways that make us feel good about its treatment of Africa and the Africans. This was the reading given *Heart of Darkness* by Conrad's contemporary British audience, which saw the tale as an indictment of Belgian colonialism, something quite different, they told themselves with only partial justice, from British rule.[8] The British sent, whenever possible (and it was *not* always possible), *colonists* abroad: farmers to plant crops; ranchers to raise animals; families to "populate" vast territories; administrators to establish mini-Britains abroad. This preference accounts for the typical pattern of British colonialism in Africa: first, but usually only first, an armed assault on the indigenous peoples, then the taxation of land, a maneuver that had all the effect—but none of the literal red bloodiness—of a continued military suppression of African peoples. The Belgians, as popular lore has continued to certify, followed an imperial, not a colonial model. They more or less enslaved native populations when they did not slaughter them and did not send large numbers of

Belgians to "populate" their lands. Belgian imperialism was a more explicitly exploitative venture, more in it for the moment than for the ages, although British colonialism could, on occasion, follow the same patterns—as witness the staggering deaths in South African mines and Cecil Rhodes's cunning slaughter of the Zulus.[9]

Statements both in and out of the fiction show that Conrad used this common distinction between British colonialism and other imperialisms.[10] On the map Marlow sees in Brussels, color-coded by European powers, "there was a vast amount of [British] red—good to see at any time because one knows that some real work is done in there" (13). Elsewhere in his narrative, Marlow invests the word "work" with considerable irony; here, modified by "real," the word does not seem to function ironically. In letters on the Boer War, Conrad wrote that "liberty . . . can only be found under the English flag all over the world" (*Life and Letters*, 286). Even in a passage from *Heart of Darkness* frequently quoted to prove Conrad's fundamental condemnation of colonialism, where one stops quoting in part determines overall meaning: "The conquest of the earth, which mostly means the taking it away from those who have a different complexion or slightly flatter noses than ourselves, is not a pretty thing when you look into it too much," Marlow says. So far, the statement is unequivocally skeptical of imperial ventures. But he goes on to say that "what redeems it is the idea only," presumably the idea of bringing liberty and enlightenment to primitive peoples. Ideas, as Marlow goes on to note, can become dangerously like idols, something to "bow down before, and offer a sacrifice to . . ." (10). Still, the luminous apogee of "the idea" before it becomes idol remains important in "redeeming" colonialism for Marlow.[11]

The Belgian merchants in *Heart of Darkness* are, in accord with British xenophobia, almost (though it is an important *almost*) as much "one of them" as the Africans, and little more individualized. Only occasionally, as in the long passage describing his journey up the Congo with which we began, does Marlow group himself with the Belgians as a "we." *Heart of Darkness* tries very hard to distinguish between British and Belgian colonialism: the "whited sepulchre" is not London; the race for ivory, with its enslavement of men, is not typical of British policies in Africa. That Kurtz began with ideas and intentions in the British mold—that he is part British and part (corrupting?) French, that he wrote an eloquent report for the International Society for the Suppression of Savage Customs—accounts, we know, for Marlow's fascination with him. In the language of *Lord Jim*, Kurtz is "one of us." He has some of the "ideas" that

Marlow believes are the only thing that can redeem imperialism's tendency to take land from one people and to give it to another.

The language of "us and them," like all of Conrad's language, is powerfully, almost infinitely, seductive. Today we seem to have a choice of which "us" is "us": the humanist "us" some see epitomized in Marlow—brooding, tolerant, questioning, always questioning, relations of people and things, always attempting—heroically though futilely—to touch bottom and articulate truth; or the imperialist "us," guilty like Marlow, despite his humanism and liberalism, of gross sins.[12] But we still need to ask what is excluded from the "us" both by Conrad's text and by the critical literature that surrounds it.

Conrad's language points us always toward the mysterious and unknown. "We could not tell . . . who could tell" the meaning of things, and mystery is central in Conrad's world as recorded by traditional critics. Marlow makes the "heart of darkness"—the land of primitives—an extended metaphor for the unlimited depths of the human mind, a mind "capable of anything." Critiques of Marlow as imperialist partially see through the seductive rhetoric and grasp the essential values beneath it: stale values in which (as in the passage with which we began) the primitive becomes a veritable treasure house of primitivist tropes: a "swaying" mass of parts, not wholes; a madhouse; a "prehistoric" place with no proper time of its own, and no "memories," language, or history. Ultimately, the Africa of *Heart of Darkness* is an Africa we have seen before, and not an Africa we can feel good about. We do not really need to make that journey up the Congo, for we have already been there.[13] But neither Conrad's text nor existing criticism directs our attention sufficiently to the way that *Heart of Darkness* uses Africa as the setting for the novella. Nor do they direct our attention to the most sustained representation of Africa's indigenous population, the queenly woman who laments Kurtz's departure.

I have read *Heart of Darkness* many times and always been a bit repelled by it. But I have never been so much repelled as on this reading, specifically focused on its version of the primitive and hence on the African woman. My repulsion has something to do with the celebrated vagueness of Marlow's style—usually praised by critics as the essence of Conrad's vision and greatness or, more rarely, in a fashion established by F. R. Leavis, seen as ruining the

book. My objection is not Leavis's objection that Marlow makes a
virtue out of not knowing what he means. Rather my objection is
that this vagueness can be and has been so often linked to terms like
"psychological complexity" or the "mystery and enigma of things."
The work's language veils not only what Kurtz was doing in Africa,
but also what Conrad is doing in *Heart of Darkness*.

To lift the veils, we need to move in and out of the boundaries
established by the text, maintaining a balance between the narrative's criticism of imperialism and yet lavish, even loving, repetition
of primitivist tropes. We need to talk about what the novella refuses
to discuss except in the vaguest terms—"the horror, the horror"—
what Kurtz was about in Africa. "I don't want to know anything of
the ceremonies used when approaching Mr. Kurtz," shouts Marlow
with passion (58). But we need to know about them or, if we cannot
know, to speculate about these and other things that the novella will
not say.

What, then, has Kurtz done? He has, as is made quite clear in the
novella, corrupted the idea of work and carried it to the extreme of
enslavement. He has taken the mechanics of imperialism and applied them so relentlessly that even the Belgian managers consider
his methods "unsound." Kurtz has allowed himself to be worshiped
by his African followers. As fantasy, this idea of the cream always
rising to the top is perfectly acceptable, indeed almost invariable in
the West; Kurtz's mistake has been only going too far in making the
fantasy a lived fact, loosening the "restraint" Marlow finds necessary in all things.[14]

But Kurtz has done more, a "more" that remains less specified
than his corruption of imperial policy. It is a curious fact that the
novella does not do more than hint, for example, in the most indirect way, at Kurtz's relation to the woman who presides over the
Africans' farewell; it is an even more curious fact that no critic I
have encountered pays much attention to her either.[15] Kurtz has apparently mated with the magnificent black woman and thus vio-
lated the British code against miscegenation, a code backed by the
policy of bringing wives and families with colonists and administrators whenever possible. The woman is decked with leggings and
jewelry that testify to a high position among the Africans—the position, one assumes, of Kurtz's wife. She gives voice to the ineffable
sorrow Marlow hears aboard ship the day before he finds Kurtz, and
she alone of the Africans is so devoted to Kurtz that she remains,
arms outstretched after her lord, when the other Africans disperse
at the sound of Marlow's ship's whistle. Marlow clearly conceives

of her as a substitute for, an inversion of, Kurtz's high-minded, white "Intended." Like the Belgian woman, she is an impressive figure, but unlike the Intended, she is not "high-minded": she is presented as all body and inchoate emotion. The novella cuts from the figure of the African woman with outstretched arms to the Intended: one woman an affianced bride, one woman, all body, surely an actual bride.[16] Yet the novella will not say so. As in the Tarzan novels, miscegenation is simply not within the ken of the narrative; it is a "love which dare not speak its name."

Miscegenation challenges a boundary highly charged in the West, the boundary of race. Kurtz's other actions also assaulted Western boundaries of love and hate, life and death, body and spirit. At this point, we might zero in on details that the novella and its critics pass over quickly, noting, for example, those heads that adorn Kurtz's palisade, and provide the first hints of "Kurtz's methods":

> You remember I told you I had been struck at the distance by certain attempts at ornamentation, rather remarkable in the ruinous aspect of the place. Now I had suddenly a nearer view and its first result was to make me throw my head back as if before a blow. Then I went carefully from post to post with my glass, and I saw my mistake. These round knobs were not ornamental but symbolic; they were expressive and puzzling, striking and disturbing—food for thought and also for vultures if there had been any looking down from the sky; but at all events for such ants as were industrious enough to ascend the pole. . . . I returned deliberately to the first I had seen—and there it was black, dried, sunken, with closed eyelids—a head that seemed to sleep at the top of that pole, and with the shrunken dry lips showing a narrow white line of the teeth, was smiling too, smiling continuously at some endless and jocose dream of that eternal slumber. (57)

The heads connect Africa as primitive locale with all primitive societies (like the Scotland of *Macbeth* and the English prehistory at which Marlow begins his narration) in which the spoliation of the enemy's dead body was a common ritual.[17] Neither the novella nor its critics seem able to say more about the heads on the posts, which seem nonetheless to convey a world of information about Kurtz. What can they mean? We can find some answers by looking at documented instances of head-hunting, and at texts nearly contemporary with *Heart of Darkness* which have an explicit fascination with headlessness.

Documented accounts of head-hunting and cannibalism suggest that the practices had very specific, communal goals in primitive societies: a sense of renewal or "lightening," for example, or the provision of souls for boys at initiation, or the absorption of a slain enemy's courage and power (Rosaldo, *Ilongot Headhunting*; Chenevière, *Vanishing Tribes*). These are, at least, the motivations most frequently found in the Philippines and New Guinea, where the practices survived into the 1960s or 1970s among certain groups and have been studied; the existence of similar practices in Africa is far less reliably documented and remains largely conjectural (Sanday, *Divine Hunger*). In New Guinea, the practice of collecting heads had a clearly defined social value, with none of the idiosyncratic, macabre overtones it acquired in the West. Collected heads were a fact of life, often a familiar element of decor. The heads collected sometimes belonged not just to slain enemies but to cherished ancestors. The Asmat of New Guinea, for example, traditionally sleep on their fathers' skulls as a means of drawing strength from ancestors.[18]

Kurtz, clearly, viewed the collecting of heads from the point of view of individual, not communal, power. In collecting the heads, he acted out a Western fantasy of savagery, with emotions different from those typically found among primitive peoples. Any account of his motivations must be, of course, hypothetical. But roughly thirty years after Conrad's narrative, Leiris helped found a group called Acéphale, the headless ones. The ideas that cluster around headlessness for this group of Kurtz's near contemporaries can be helpful in illuminating a "dark" portion of the European mind. Acéphale's writings suggest that headlessness was, for Europeans like Kurtz, a means of bypassing routine existence and the mediation of language. Above all, it was a means of getting to the essential.

Acéphale was preoccupied with rituals of slaughter and with headlessness as a metaphor. The group's emblem (fig. 7.1) makes its concern with headlessness and with violence as a form of natural energy quite clear: the emblem shows a naked man brandishing a sword and a torch; the figure has no head, but it does have a death's-head, located where the penis should be. This last detail suggests that the erotic and the violent share a common bodily locus and, sometimes, common motivations. The emblem reveals Acéphale's fascination (akin, as we shall see, to Lawrence's) with "lower" sources of psychic energy and with ways to circumvent the Western emphasis on the mind and rationality. Accordingly, the group unblinkingly entertained the possibility that streams of blood, flooding European streets, would be necessary to overcome the stagnation of modernity.[19] Fantasized scenes of primitive ritual appear in Acéphale as sites of boundary transgression and transcendence—as

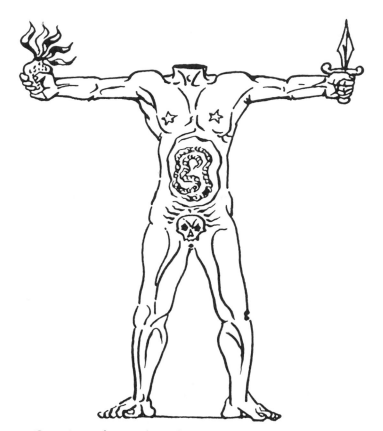

Fig. 7.1. Questions of masculine identity—the erotic, the violent, and a common bodily locus. André Masson. *Acéphale.* Courtesy ARS N.Y./ADAGP, 1989.

precursors and stimulants to revolution at home. This aspect of Acéphale's thought is revealed most clearly in the writings of Georges Bataille.[20]

Bataille was fascinated with human and animal sacrifices in primitive societies and liked to imagine the possibilities such practices might open to the West.[21] "The Pineal Eye," for example, includes a grotesque scene in which a blond Englishwoman cavorts with a number of nude primitive men. At a signal from the Englishwoman, they bind a female gibbon and bury her alive in a pit, allowing only her anus to project from the grave. As the gibbon suffocates, her anus emits a stream of excrement. The ritual is completed when "the mouth of the Englishwoman crushed her most burning, her sweetest kisses" upon the anus of the gibbon (86). The scene is one of several in the collection of Bataille's essays called *Visions of Excess* in which women or little girls are brought pornographically into association with a vision of excrement as both the abject and the transcendent;[22] as in "The Pineal Eye," the connection between the female and the excremental vision of transcendence is usually a form of primitive or animal life (frequently an ape).

In his essay "The Sacred," Bataille maintains that "the creation of forms" and "verbal invention" were just "detours" in "the great 'quest' of what has been given the poor name 'modern spirit'" (*Visions of Excess*, 240). He insists that "long torment and abrupt violence" are the truer elements in the quest and more likely to attain its ends. Conrad has traditionally been associated with "the creation of forms" and "verbal invention": his style is, after all, the reason that traditional critics deem him great. *Heart of Darkness*, however, also alludes to the "long torment and abrupt violence," in its quick, vague glimpses at Kurtz's "methods." In fact, the novella suggests that once the European mind fundamentally doubts the value of "verbal invention," the slide into "abrupt violence" becomes inevitable.

We know from the text that Kurtz's experiences in Africa forced him to look inward and find nothing to sustain him. A "hollow man," he filled himself with his version of the primitive as the brutish yet, potentially, as the sacred. In a sense, language has failed Kurtz, the great "voice" who once mastered language, who once wrote eloquent humanitarian texts; the words have failed to correspond to eternal values, which should be as recuperable in Africa as in European cities. Isolation unhinged for Kurtz the stability of language, making, for example, the phrase "the suppression of savage customs" slide into "exterminate the brutes." The second comment, scribbled in the margin, insidiously doubled and parodied the loftier language officially written into Kurtz's humanitarian text. Kurtz's actions among the Africans may have been his revenge upon language for its fundamental unreliability. His role as killer and collector of heads may have been a frontal assault on the nature and function of language, an attempt to get behind language and to explore the sense in which "the suppression of savage customs" can and does mean "exterminate the brutes." As the Russian Harlequin tells Marlow, Kurtz "made one see things, Things!" Kurtz's actions, whose essentialist goals remain visible in the heads adorning the palisade, literalize some of what we have seen in Fry's version of the primitive: a belief in *perceptual* versus *conceptual* experience; an attempt to recoup for the West the direct, unmediated experience associated with primitive societies. Fry and modern artists like Picasso chose to collect African masks as icons of perceptually conceived form. But the masks were valued, in part, because of their association with magic rituals: owning them, using them as inspiration, the Western artist partook of the diviner's magical power (Lemann, "Fake Masks"). Kurtz chose to collect real heads, dried and shriveled on posts, as dubious conduits to the same sources of spiritual power. In each case, "the primitive" becomes a means of access to "the essential."

Acéphale replaced the penis with the death's-head; its imagery and rhetoric were, as we have seen, fiercely masculinist. To what extent, then, is the nexus of concerns described above specifically tied to questions of masculine identity—a hidden sign of masculinity, as the penis is an outer sign? The answer appears to be "to a considerable extent." We saw in Stanley a ruthless censoring of the self based explicitly on what it meant to be an Anglo-Saxon gentleman. We saw in Tarzan's story the suppression of blacks and women as a way to affirm traditional concepts of masculine identity. We saw in Leiris the identification of violence and suffering with the very fact of manhood. Conrad provides additional testimony to the attraction violence exerts for many men in our culture, perhaps as an outlet for the many alternative values conventionally barred to them: free emotional expression, openness to the "feminine" views of mothers and wives, identification with other men on a basis other than competition.[23] Under such conditions, ritualized enactments of violence and death become flirtations with boundary dissolution; they both test and affirm men's need to maintain separation, difference, and control as attributes of masculinity.[24] They become simulacra of, but also charms against, the loss of self inscribed in the fullest erotic experience.[25] Kurtz's rituals of human sacrifice and cannibalism may thus have been motivated by the same Western mixture of thanatophilia and thanatophobia found in other men of his time.

Bringing these perspectives to bear on *Heart of Darkness* helps us say what the novella will not, and maybe cannot, say. Africa and the Africans became Kurtz's grand fantasy-theater for playing out his culture's notions of masculinity and power through the controlled, borrowed rituals attributed to certain groups within Africa, perverted to Western ends. Kurtz has performed experiments, with human subjects, on the boundaries between life and death, things and words. Those experiments profoundly affected his own view of the world, and threaten Marlow's.

———

When Marlow returns to Brussels after meeting Kurtz, he is at first oppressed by a vision of the emptiness of modern European life. He finds himself "resenting the sight of people hurrying through the streets to filch a little money from each other, to devour their infamous cookery, to gulp their unwholesome beer, to dream their insignificant and silly dreams" (70). Like Kurtz in Africa, he experiences the erosion of conventional European values and the hollowness of the words that correspond to them. But Marlow is gradually able to exercise "restraint" and to explain his hypercritical view of Brussels as the feverish ravings of a diseased mind: "my temperature was seldom normal in these days," he says (70). And he revises his vision of Belgians scurrying meaninglessly about their city to see instead "commonplace individuals going about their business" (70).

Heart of Darkness thematizes the power of words—words like *work* and *business*—to mask the reality of what is happening in the Congo. Language is a euphemism, a saving lie for all the Europeans. The novella thematizes as well the final impotence of words to mask "the horror" just beyond the boundary of language, the horror Kurtz tries but fails to articulate at the end, a horror alternately identifiable as "the void" or as the brutish potential of human nature. But for all its thematization of the deviousness and limitations of language, the novella ultimately falls into the very traps it exposes—the trap that is sprung when pretty phrases obscure ugly facts, facts like how and why those heads got on the palisade, facts like the African woman's relation to Kurtz, facts like her death at the end, which goes unmentioned, so far as I know, in any commentary on the novella.

Heart of Darkness is narrated by Marlow and shares many of his limitations.[26] The narrative is willing to approach, but finally backs away from, really radical themes—about modern Europe, about the human mind in an indifferent universe, about sacrificial and violent rituals as a charm against death, about the degree to which men are driven to affirm their essentiality and identity. Metaphorically speaking, Conrad too learns to accept Brussels and decides that the thoughts that have come to him in Africa are taboo, to be repressed and banished, except as material for a yarn years later.[27] But we should not lose sight of the loathing for certain Western values that flashes through Marlow's vision of Brussels, a loathing Kurtz may have shared in a locale that would seem the antipodes of Brussels, the center of Africa.

In Conrad, as in Bataille, Lawrence, Eliot, and others of their generation, the creation of specific versions of the primitive often depends on and is conditioned by a sense of disgust or frustration with Western values.[28] The primitive becomes a convenient locale for the exploration of Western dullness or degeneracy, and of ways to transcend it, and thus functions as a symbolic entity. As so often in the West's encounters with the primitive, the primitive responds to Western needs, becoming the faithful or distorted mirror of the Western self.[29] This is one reason why in Conrad (as in Lawrence's visions of the Arctic and the African way, the debased extremes of white and black) the hypercivilized and primitive are collapsed and homologous. Not the same thing, they are nonetheless made to point to the same thing: the dire fate of Western man and culture unless values like "restraint" and "work"—the whole set of values that guides the "us" in "one of us"—can be made to hold. Present as sign and symbol, the primitive lacks authenticity in and of itself. It becomes grist for the Western fantasy-mill.

In *Heart of Darkness*, Conrad approaches fantasy sites like miscegenation, ritual slaughter, and head-hunting. But Conrad never touches down for long or makes the fantasy explicit. Instead of withered heads we remember phrases—"the horror, the horror." Real psychological intensity—or, more radically, a remapping of what *constitutes* psychological intensity—is bypassed in favor of Marlow's vaporish posturings. The novella wants to have it both ways: to criticize language and yet to take refuge in the gorgeousness of Conrad's own language. Like Marlow, it "must make its choice of nightmares," and it chooses, finally, the nightmare of language, that sustainer of civilization. But one feels in *Heart of Darkness* the pressure of other narratives, other dreams and nightmares, that Marlow will not and maybe cannot tell. Marlow interrogates the limits of identity through the words of his narration; but the words only begin to fumble at the realities which have produced the narration.

Conrad's version of the primitive is a cheat. It promises much and seems to offer tolerance and sympathy, balance and wisdom, an unlimited and unconditional exploration of experience extreme in its difference from Western norms. But it leaves out too much and is finally unable to transcend the very Western values it attacks. The "gorgeous virility" of Conrad's style in *Heart of Darkness* and related narratives like *Lord Jim*—its maleness and ability to coin

scintillating memorable phrases like "the hollow man," "to the de-
structive element submit," "one of us," "the horror," and "gorgeous
virility" itself—limits, finally, the extent of its vision. The words
are so seductive that, as in the passage recording Marlow's voyage
up the Congo with which we began, it is easy to lose sight of the
ways in which the words repeat a series of clichés. Something cata-
clysmic, transcendent appears to be happening; but really the words
convey only stale, familiar ideas about Africa and the West's relation
to it. The words flirt with a radical critique of certain Western values, but stop short. *Heart of Darkness,* like Marlow, goes only so far.

In my mind, I keep coming back to the African woman who
stalks through *Heart of Darkness:*

> She walked with measured steps, draped in striped and fringed
> cloths, treading the earth proudly with a slight jingle and flash of
> barbarous ornaments. She carried her head high, her hair was
> done in the shape of a helmet, she had brass leggings to the knee,
> brass wire gauntlets to the elbow, a crimson spot on her tawny
> cheek, innumerable necklaces of glass beads on her neck. . . . She
> was savage and superb, wild-eyed and magnificent. (60)

She is the only female in the masculine tale except for Marlow's
aunt, the knitting woman, and the Intended—cameos all. "They—
the women I mean—are out of it—should be out of it," Marlow says
earlier in his narration, apropos of nothing but referring to the Intended (49).[30] But the African woman is manifestly "in it," the tale.
Marlow believes that women need "illusions," and must be protected from the truth toward which characters like Marlow relentlessly grope, "lest our own [men's world] get worse." For Marlow,
women (like primitives) exist outside the circle of rational thought
and do not struggle, as he does, for comprehension; moreover, they
must actively be prevented from doing so. Marlow's aunt and the
Intended may fit this description; as Western women they have been
wrapped in the cottony gauze Victorian Europe spun for women
above the working class. But the knitting woman and the African
mistress need and receive no protection—fall outside, somehow, of
the novella's concept of womanhood, though they are one-half of the
women represented.

That African woman is, for me, the crux of *Heart of Darkness.*
Like Jewel in *Lord Jim,* she is the representative "native," the only

one fully individualized and described in detail, except for the Helmsman, who also dies in the story. She is, the text insists, the symbol of Africa. Once she enters the narrative, she is made to embody the landscape, rendered throughout in the language of pathetic fallacy:

> the whole sorrowful land, the immense wilderness, the colossal body of the fecund and mysterious life seemed to look at her, pensive, as though it had been looking at the image of its own tenebrous and passionate soul.
>
> She came abreast of the steamer, stood still, and faced us. Her long shadow fell to the water's edge. Her face had a tragic and fierce aspect of wild sorrow and of dumb pain mingled with the fear of some struggling, half-shaped resolve. She stood looking at us without a stir and like the wilderness itself, with an air of brooding over an inscrutable purpose. (60)

Why is the woman's sorrow "wild," her pain "dumb," her resolve "half-shaped," her purpose "inscrutable"? Why is she (like the landscape) "fecund and mysterious," "tenebrous and passionate"? Do we not slip here into a prejudiced vocabulary—as Marlow does often when he uses phrases like "fool nigger," "insolent black head," "The man seemed young—almost a boy—but you know with them it's hard to tell" (20). More—why is the woman the embodiment of Africa? What gives Marlow the right (and why does Conrad not challenge his right?) to make this woman so portentous a symbol?

The woman presumably dies when Marlow's ship pulls off and the pilgrims begin their "little fun"—dies because she is unwilling to flinch like the Africans who "broke and ran, they leaped, they crouched, they swerved, they dodged" at the sound of the ship's whistle and hence unknowingly escaped the pilgrims' bullets (67). Her death fulfills her role as emblem of the African landscape and (once recognized) makes explicit the hidden reference of "the feminine" and "the primitive" to death. For the African landscape *is* death in the novella. It is the "white man's grave," "lurking death . . . hidden evil . . . profound darkness." Europeans enter it but leave it either dead or ill or changed and marked forever. Women are uniformly associated with the landscape and with death.[31] Even the eminently white Intended makes Marlow lie, and he "hate[s], detest[s], and can't bear a lie . . . because . . . there is a taint of death, a flavour of mortality in lies" (29).[32]

The same set of associations between women, the landscape, and death functions in *Lord Jim*. What we learn first about Patusan is its association with a woman who "is dead now" and its being "the grave for some sin." When Jim shows Patusan to Marlow, he points out with proprietorial pleasure a moonrise between "the summits of two steep hills very close together, and separated by what looks like a deep fissure, the cleavage of some mighty stroke" (135). Like landmarks such as "Sheba's breasts" in Rider Haggard's *King Solomon's Mines*, and like the use of the African woman in *Heart of Darkness*, the passage proceeds from an axiomatic identification of "primitive" landscape with the female body.[33] When the moon rises, the text tells us that it "rose exactly behind these hills ... as if escaping from a yawning grave" (31). If we complete the gender implications of the metaphor, we are left, once again, with the equation of the grave (death) and the female body.

The nexus of associations here is one we have seen before in Western conceptions of the primitive—women, sex, death, mortality. As in the work of Picasso, Leiris, and other moderns, the associations are not rational but "intuitive," the underside of the rock of Western objectivity and aesthetics. Critiques of Conrad and imperialism, helpful as they have been, have not made this crucial connection. They have not focused on the substitution of one value for another—in this case female for primitive—that is very typical of Conrad's method, typical indeed of Western thinking about the primitive. The ease of substitution here and its implications seem to me the real issues. In some sense, to speak of women in *Heart of Darkness* and to speak of the primitive are, illogically, one and the same thing: fantastic, collective ("women are all alike"), seductive, dangerous, deadly. Until we expose such substitutions, we bypass the stubborn knot of associations hidden *beneath* the text's superficial attention to them both—a yearning for and yet fear of boundary transgression, violence, and death—which may well be the text's real interests.

The circularity between the concepts "female" and "primitive" is so complete in Conrad that it is difficult to tell which set of tropes influenced which. Yet clearly, the feminine is perceived in the same terms used by the West for the primitive—as though all Others, like all gray cats, are alike. Remember, in the passage from *Heart of Darkness* with which I began, the insistence on the primitive as "prehistorical," as ageless and changeless. Compare the circle of feminine life inscribed in this passage from *Lord Jim*, imagining Jewel with her mother, the nameless woman who "is dead now" and whose memory is associated with Patusan:

I cannot help picturing to myself these two, at first the young woman and the child, then the old woman and the young girl, the awful sameness and the swift passage of time, the barrier of forest, the solitude and the turmoil round these two lonely lives, and every word spoken between them penetrated with sad meaning. (169)

I feel in this passage as I do in rooms of nineteenth-century art in which one is surrounded by four paintings depicting the stages of female life, often in seasonal terms.[34] "They are like this, you know," the paintings seem to say, "they are all like this—nature's slaves, part of nature—so much closer than men." In *Lord Jim*, as in *Heart of Darkness*, Marlow goes even further. Real women, he says, "come nearest to rising above the trammels of earthly caution," and their love gives men "an extraterrestrial touch" (169). The terms of his description once again link the feminine to primitive locales, since Marlow compares Patusan to "a distant heavenly body" in his initial description of it (133). Like the primitive for which it substitutes in *Heart of Darkness* and *Lord Jim*, the female is at the mercy of masculine fantasy.

We are not yet ready and in fact may never be ready to tidily sum things up, to firmly state the reasons Western primitivism has made these connections. For they are messy connections, "intuitively" made and rarely examined. They go back to our earliest sense of ourselves among others, to the roots of all our actions and reactions, to the ways the conceptions "self" and "other," "male" and "female," "subject" and "object," "dominant" and "subordinate" first took shape for us, and how they subsequently developed. They are more intensely dangerous than the material traditionally addressed by Freudian psychology, material that has become, over the years, rather tame. In fact, we have only the most rudimentary tools to discuss the phenomena I am describing here.

What is clear now is that the West's fascination with the primitive has to do with its own crises in identity, with its own need to clearly demarcate subject and object even while flirting with other ways of experiencing the universe. Few periods in history have been more concerned than modernity with the articulation of the psychological subject and the cultivation of the individualistic self; yet the fascination with other possibilities, possibilities perhaps embodied in primitive societies, remained acute. "Me Tarzan, you Jane"; "Dr. Livingstone, I presume"—worlds apart grammatically, these tag phrases bespeak dramas of identity. In Marlow's narrations (as in

Livingstone and Tarzan), masculine identity and the need to maintain "masculinity" as something separate, apart, "restrained," and in control are hidden motivators and hidden themes.

We have known for some time—how could we not know—that Conrad's works are about "identity," something achieved through a devious series of identifications and distinctions, through the dialectics of self and other. We have read for some time the structure of *Heart of Darkness* and *Lord Jim* as a series of comparisons and contrasts between one male character and another: Marlow and the Belgians, Marlow and Kurtz; Jim and Marlow and Stein and the French Lieutenant, and the Malay Helmsman, and so on (Van Ghent, *English Novel*). We have tended to pose those dynamics in traditional psychological terms (Freudian or Jungian) or philosophical terms (the "morally responsible" versus the derelict, the "realistic" versus the "romantic"). I am suggesting here that the texts' treatment of primitive societies and their substitution of the female for the primitive are more explosive than these traditional terms allow. More, I am suggesting that the language of the text is deeply political in ways that the humanists and formalists cannot see and that have not interested the Marxists and anti-imperialists enough. Tracking down what Conrad means by "going primitive" means traveling with and beyond Conrad farther than critics have previously been willing to go.

8

Oh, Mexico! D. H. Lawrence's
The Plumed Serpent

.H. Lawrence spent most of his life waiting for "the primi-·
tive" to speak.[1] When it did, a knot of typically Lawrentian
concerns unknotted themselves. Like many moderns, Lawrence freely substituted "the primitive" for other categories
that had obsessed him from the beginning of his career. The main
set of substitutions progressed chronologically in this order:

miners/working-class men
vital masculinity (dependent on the "right" kind of femininity)
phallic power
"the primitive"
natural harmony (attunement with the sun)

At the time he wrote *Women in Love* (1913–19), Lawrence associated the primitive with conventional ideas of the feminine, an association entirely typical of modernism. By the time of *The Plumed
Serpent* (1923–25), the product of his sojourns in Mexico and the
American Southwest, Lawrence associated the primitive with conventional ideas of masculinity.[2] The regendering of the primitive
was crucial; it loosened the Lawrentian knots by facilitating the substitutions charted above, which link late works like *The Plumed
Serpent* with early works like *Sons and Lovers*.

Lawrence's gendered versions of the primitive retell in personal-
ized terms the two major stories about primitive peoples he inher-
ited from the nineteenth century: primitive peoples as dangerous
and irrational, something to be feared; primitive peoples as the
idealized noble savage, something to be emulated. The first, for Lawrence the "feminine" version, is the primitive as degeneration, as a
cautionary tale for the modern West; the second, "masculine" version, is the primitive as regeneration, as the last best hope for the
modern West.

The doubleness in Lawrence's views of the primitive partakes of his culture's general attitudes but adds—as is always true for Lawrence—a personal touch.[3] To Lawrence, the primitive represented, on the one hand, the origin of syphilis. In "An Introduction to These Paintings" (1929), Lawrence saw Western ills as already nascent in the directions Christianity took during the Middle Ages but confirmed by the introduction of syphilis to Europe from the New World during the age of discovery. Once generation became a source of disease and death, the loathing of the body was, Lawrence believed, inevitably accelerated. The association of disease and death with primitive societies was, as we have seen, widespread in the modern period, though Lawrence was unusual in articulating the connection so frankly.

On the other hand, for Lawrence the primitive represented a lost awareness of the body, and hence a potential alternative to Western Christianity's suspicion of sexuality. In fact, in *Fantasia of the Unconscious* (1923) Lawrence articulates the belief that once, before the flood, all civilizations were in dynamic contact, linked by what he calls the sciences of life. His vision has a certain romanticized grandeur: "In that world men lived, and taught, and knew, and were in one complete correspondence over all the earth. Men wandered back and forth from Atlantis to the Polynesian Continent as men now sail from Europe to America. The interchange was complete, and knowledge, science, was universal over the earth" (7). After the flood, these "life" orientations survived in isolated South Sea islands and among what he calls the "savages" of Africa; they survived as well in certain individuals who were misfits in Western civilization, and also in the myths of Western culture. For Lawrence, then, "the primitive" held an important key to alternative social directions; it could recoup for the West possibilities obliterated by the course of history. More personally, it could make the misfit the prophet of change or someone whose values are right at home.[4]

To understand Lawrence's version of the primitive, we need to reimagine the profound linkage in his mind between primitive societies and origins—the origins both of the death of bodily consciousness brought about by the arrival of syphilis from the New World and of the positive "science of life." Traveling with Lawrence to Mexico, we return to origins and get a chance to rewrite mankind's history and future. To make the trip, we must first revisit the "feminine" primitive of *Women in Love*, Lawrence's main point of departure for the "masculine" primitive of *The Plumed Serpent*.

In *Women in Love*, "the primitive" is an important counterpoint to the obsessive modernity of the novel's setting and action. The main characters move in an upper-class artsy set which is doggedly modern—and one of them, Gudrun, is a sculptor whose figures recall primitive carvings. The artsy set—based on Fry's Bloomsbury—champions what Fry called primitive art. They collect it, display it in their homes, and have discussions about it. The chief commentator on primitive art is the primary Lawrence figure in the book, Rupert Birkin. Like Roger Fry, and probably following Fry in *Vision and Design*, Birkin considers all non-Western art "primitive." What we would now call "courtly" art (that is, art from non-Western civilizations with court structures) attracts him: Chinese art tells a tale of the "lotus mystery"; in a scene of sexual fulfillment, Birkin seems Egyptian to Ursula, and she worships the power of his loins. But the true primitive, for Birkin as for Fry, was Africa and Oceania. And the art of these places, while he thinks it "great," frightens Birkin.

Birkin glaringly reads African and Oceanic art according to what we would now call the expressionist misreading;[5] he sees in it the expression of violent emotions and taboo sexuality. And he believes that African and Oceanic statues provide evidence of a slide into imbalanced "mindless sexuality" that happened long ago, among the primitives carving the works. In *Women in Love*, Lawrence presents his formulations about primitive societies axiomatically: it is a given that the Africans and islanders who carved statues *were* mindlessly sensual. The only open questions are whether—and how—Europeans will arrive at the deathliness already writ large in the art of Africa and Oceania. Here, for example, is Birkin's meditation on the African statue of a woman, with all these "givens" in place:

> Her body was long and elegant, her face was crushed tiny like a beetle's, and had rows of round heavy collars, like a column of quoits, on her neck. . . . [She had an] astounding long elegant body, on short, ugly legs, with such protuberant buttocks, so weighty and unexpected below her slim long loins. She knew what he himself did not know. She had thousands of years of purely sensual, purely unspiritual knowledge behind her. It must have been thousands of years since her race had died, mystically; that is, since the relation between the senses and the outspoken mind had broken, leaving the experience all in one sort, mysti-

cally sensual. Thousands of years ago, that which was imminent in himself must have taken place in these Africans; the goodness, the holiness, the desire for creation and productive happiness must have lapsed, leaving the single impulse for knowledge in one sort, mindless, progressive knowledge through the senses, knowledge arrested and ending in the senses, mystic knowledge in disintegration and dissolution, knowledge such as the beetles have, which live purely within the world of corruption and cold dissolution. . . . Is our day of creative life finished? Does there remain to us only the strange, awful afterwards of the knowledge in dissolution, the African knowledge, but different in us, who are blond and blue-eyed from the North? (330–31)

Very dramatically in this passage, as so often in Western versions of the primitive, the primitive is put to the service of the West: its sensuality clarifies through contrast Western rationality; it tells a cautionary tale. It is there, for Lawrence, as for all the moderns, as a convenient symbol. With the freedom from factual grounding that William Rubin approves—but to ends that would probably embarrass him—Lawrence gives an "intuitive" response to African art that, like any "intuitive" response, projects onto the object beheld the deepest, most tangled concerns of the viewer. Lawrence reminds me here of Michel Leiris, and he reads the African statue as Leiris read Cranach's *Lucrece* and *Judith*—as icons of extreme sexuality. Conventions of African sculpture which have nothing to do with sex are sexualized by Lawrence:[6] the woman's scarified face reminds him of a beetle, and beetles of homosexuality, dissolution, and death; her necklace reminds him of bondage rituals and suggests to him her masochistic subjection; her protuberant buttocks suggest to him "taboo" sexual practices, usually (and rightly) identified as the anal intercourse he invokes in his work—at times as "deadly," at times as "liberating"—and which meshes uneasily with his homoerotic fixations; she is to him "purely sensual," though her function probably was not at all "sensual," was probably closer to the "spirituality" he finds foreign to her.

Birkin's theories about the statue, like Lawrence's more general theories about primitives and the West, might—taken in isolation—strike us as idiosyncratic, even crazy. But we know by now that Lawrence's "intuitions" were not utterly his own.[7] They conform to a nexus of associations found elsewhere, even in the radically different temperament of Conrad—associations between women, the primitive, sexuality, death, and, paradoxically, the desire for transcendence. It is very important that the version of the primitive as the degenerate articulated in *Women in Love* hinges on a *female* statue. When, later in his career, Lawrence focuses on male versions of the primitive, opposite, regenerative possibilities become ascendent.

———

In Lawrence's late novel *The Plumed Serpent*, the female protagonist, Kate, receives an education in the regenerative version of the primitive. She begins her education by remaining in Mexico after her American and English friends leave, despite her loathing for the poor Mexican masses and her fear that America was "the great death-continent . . . the great continent of the negation . . . of Godless democracy, energetic negation. . . . The negation which is the life-breath of materialism" (83).[8] Fortyish, the widow of a martyred Irish political leader, Kate feels disgusted with Europe. The same disgust led her creator, Lawrence himself, to travel toward the end of his life in Mexico and the American Southwest, after failed idylls in rural England, Italy, and Australia.[9] To her, Europe "was all politics or jazzing or slushy mysticism or sordid spiritualism. And the magic had gone. The younger generation, so smart and *interesting*, but so without any mystery, any background" (113). Lawrence knew Fry and his Bloomsbury set and loathed them much as Kate hates the young Europeans.[10] And he fled Europe for locales he wished to be as different as possible from England, France, and Germany in his time.[11]

What can Mexico offer Kate that Europe cannot? The Mexico of the colonial heritage can offer little: it is very much like "jazzing" Europe. But the surviving Indian communities are different.[12] Like Conrad's Africa or Patusan, they can offer mystery, "the greater mystery, the higher power that hovered in the interstices of the hot air, rich and potent. It was as if she could lift her hands and clutch the silent, stormless potency that roved everywhere, waiting" (116–17). In Lawrence's primitive, sexuality is everywhere, and "potency" a condition in the very air.[13] Mexico can also offer Mexican men, especially "silent semi-barbarous men" in whom she finds "humility, and the pathos of grace . . . something very beautiful and truly male, and very hard to find in a civilised white man. It was not of the spirit. It was of the dark, strong, unbroken blood, the flowering of the soul" (117). The association now of "the primitive" with masculinity is crucial, I believe, in the turn Lawrence's version of the primitive takes from the degenerate to the regenerative.

Kate eventually finds herself by losing herself in marriage to Cipriano, a pure-blooded Indian general in the Mexican army. Though upper class, Cipriano has chosen to return to his roots and to revive the ancient, primitive Mexican religions. He plays "the Living Huitzilopochtli" in the revival, the god of air and wind, life and death. His close friend and leader, the charismatic Ramon, plays the role of Quetzalcoatl, the plumed serpent of the title, the chief god in the Aztec pantheon.[14] Together, the two men plan to use the religious revival to gain popular support from the peasants and then to isolate all of Mexico from its colonialist past. In the fantastic world of the novel, their plan succeeds; the Catholic church and the government try, but fail, to crush them.

Ramon and Cipriano see themselves as spearheading a worldwide revolution in which Celtic peoples would revive the Celtic gods, Germanic people the Germanic gods, and so on. In all these places, men who have achieved "the greater manhood" would play the male gods, women who have achieved "the greater womanhood," the female gods. Then, their plan goes, these ancient gods would meet together—as emanations of the male and female principles—to make the world a unified, harmonious place quite different from the modern West.[15] The new order would reproduce the global unity Lawrence postulated in *Fantasia of the Unconscious* as existing before the flood through a new understanding of sex as the instrument of spirituality. The novel thus concentrates on Kate's conversion to Ramon and Cipriano's way of seeing things, especially sex.

Kate's attraction to Mexican men is clearly sexual, but—she insists and Lawrence insists—sex is not the point, is no more than a metaphor, a means to an end, an expression of larger, cosmic, unities. As so often in the Western tradition, this ultimate cosmic harmony is imaged in two ways—in terms of smoothly turning wheels (the music of the spheres), with sun and moon in proper balance, and in terms of the regular rhythms of the ocean. Both metaphors structure Kate's impressions of a Mexican dance which constitutes her baptism into the mysteries of "primitive" Mexican life—impressions which fill four full pages in the novel. It is significant that Lawrence chose the dance as an important synecdoche for primitive life, as he later chooses a ritual of human sacrifice; both imputed aspects of primitive societies embody the values of collectivity and proximity to the cosmic that Lawrence found especially mesmerizing.

Lawrence presents the dance as hypnotic and incantatory:

The outer wheel was all men. She seemed to feel the strange dark glow of them upon her back. Men, dark, collective men, non-individual. And herself woman, wheeling upon the great wheel of womanhood. . . . It was sex, but the greater, not the lesser sex. The waters over the earth wheeling upon the waters under the earth, like an eagle silently wheeling above its own shadow.

She felt her sex and her womanhood caught up and identified in the slowly revolving ocean of nascent life, the dark sky of the men lowering and wheeling above. She was not herself, she was gone, and her own desires were gone in the ocean of the great desire. As the man whose fingers touched hers was gone in the ocean that is male, stooping over the face of the waters.

The slow, vast, soft-touching revolution of the ocean above upon ocean below, with no vestige of rustling or foam. Only the pure sliding conjunction. Herself gone into her greater self, her womanhood consummated in the greater womanhood. And where her fingers touched the fingers of the man, the quiet spark, like the dawn star, shining between her and the greater manhood of man. (142–43)

The lapsing of self Kate experiences is the lure of the oceanic—the boundaries of self and other, subject and object dissolve in a feeling of totality, oneness, and unity. In Lawrence's version of this psychological concept,[16] the polarities of male and female do not disappear, but refer to collectivities of maleness and femaleness, not to individual, gendered selves. Lawrence, we should note, is unusual in retaining gender in his version of the oceanic; usually the conception is linked to a state in which this difference, like all others, is obliterated.

The "greater" manhood and womanhood exist as separate oceans, the males in the sky above, the females in the ocean below. In *Women in Love*, as here in *The Plumed Serpent*, Lawrence takes some pains, ultimately futile, to insist that the terms "higher" and "lower" imply no hierarchy subordinating women. Some mystic paradox of surrender making one free pertains (Lawrence never lost his Christian past). At any rate, the passage insists that these two oceans slide effortlessly over one another, merge in purpose, will, and feeling in "the greater, not the lesser sex"—cosmic, frictionless fucking.[17] Other crossings also occur. Kate not only feels identified with all womanhood but with nature and animal life as well.

As a European woman of mature years and independent wealth,

Kate does not always relish immersion in the bath of oneness, *The Plumed Serpent*'s version of the primitive. Her long training in Western individualism resists the experience. Ultimately, its proximity to violence and especially to death repels and frightens her. When Cipriano, in his role of Huitzilopochtli, slays five traitors in an elaborate ritual, "the executions shocked and depressed" Kate, who was "spellbound, but not utterly acquiescent" (423). At times Kate even fears that, as a white woman, her ultimate role in the new religion will be not that of the goddess Malintzi but that of a human sacrifice. (It's a good thing Kate never read Lawrence's "The Woman Who Rode Away," in which a European woman is, literally, made a human sacrifice by Mexican Indians—or all bets might have been off.)

When Ramon, Quetzalcoatl in the Aztec pantheon, marries quiet, submissive Teresa, Kate rebels at Teresa's "self-prostitution" and "slave approach"; the marriage crystallizes her lingering sense that the mutuality of which Cipriano speaks is but another version of the master-slave relation, with herself, as female, destined for the role of slave. She dislikes Teresa's "female power," which consists in glorifying the "blood-male." Her disgust spills over into a general denunciation of "savages, with the impossible fluid flesh of savages, and that savage way of dissolving into an awful black mass of desire" (437). In her anger, Kate forgets the rhetoric of "the greater sex" and follows the more common pattern of linking "savages" with sex, period.

Still, Kate begins "to question whether Teresa was not a greater woman than she" (449). Her questioning leads to her transformation by the end of the novel into Cipriano's wife and Malintzi, the female goddess who is the wife of Huitzilopochtli. That transformation depends first on accepting the violent deaths Huitzilopochtli metes out to others and then on a radical change in her views of sexuality.

To accept violence as part of the life of primitive people—in Lawrence's version of a familiar Western trope, "people who never really changed"—she accepts as well

> the strange reptilian insistence of her very servants. *Blood is one blood. We are all of one bloodstream.* Something aboriginal and tribal, and almost worse than death to the white individual. Out of the dark eyes and the powerful spines of these people, all the time the unknown assertion: *The blood is one blood.* (456; original emphasis)

Once she understands this, Kate loses her sense of racial and class superiority (though never her sense of some more essential kind of superiority) and understands the economy of shared blood which controls the rituals of death she has witnessed. The linking here of racial and class superiority is not, I think, incidental in Lawrence. Somewhere at the periphery of Euro-American versions of the primitive lurk class tensions. To eradicate one set of polarities (male/ female, higher/lower class, civilized/primitive) is to threaten them all.

In a parallel acquiescence, Kate must and does reject "her old love," which "had been frictional, charged with the fire of irritation and the spasms of frictional voluptuousness":

> When, in their love, it came back on her, the seething electric female ecstasy, which knows such spasms of delirium, he [Cipriano] recoiled from her. It was what she used to call her "satisfaction." She had loved Joachim [her dead husband] for this, that again, and again, and again he could give her this orgiastic "satisfaction," in spasms that made her cry aloud.
>
> But Cipriano would not. . . . And succeeding the first moment of disappointment, when this sort of "satisfaction" was denied her, came the knowledge that she did not really want it, that it was really nauseous to her. (463)

In a kind of paradox the novel does not acknowledge, the "primitive" man, Cipriano, rescues Kate from images of sexuality usually associated with the primitive—images of "orgiastic satisfaction." But orgies are not really what this lush repetitive passage—so indiscreet and yet so euphemistic—is about. As Kate Millett pointed out at the dawn of feminist criticism, Kate here renounces female orgasm, a cause and sign, to Lawrence, of the decline of the West. Her renunciation, made equivalent to her adoption of "the greater womanhood," clears the way for what appears to be a happy ending.

Clearly, in *The Plumed Serpent*, the primitive is put to the service of some of Lawrence's strongest obsessions. His female heroine arrives, via her education into the primitive, at conclusions not surprisingly identical to the male author's. Like the primitive itself, the female character is made to serve the author's didactic purposes. Simone de Beauvoir once quipped that Lawrence did not write novels, he wrote training manuals for women. Her comment holds especially true for *The Plumed Serpent*, which weds The Total Woman to many of the primitivist tropes we have examined.

Since Millett's devastating account of Lawrence in *Sexual Politics* (1969), Lawrence has been anathema to feminist critics and, for many women, all but unreadable. He deserves Millett's critique, which cut sharply through the critical pieties that surround

Lawrence's canon.[18] But when we focus on the role the primitive plays in Lawrence's imagination and review Lawrence's career in light of his gendering and regendering of "the primitive," we can modify the anger in Millett's critique to a new understanding of, and even sympathy with, Lawrence. That move is one I want to make in the remainder of this chapter. For it would be too easy merely to hold Lawrence at arm's length as the object of jeers and derision. Like Conrad, he fumbles at ideas he is not quite able or willing to express.

———

Although it has never been one of Lawrence's most respected novels, *The Plumed Serpent* differs from the earlier, "greater" Lawrence mainly in drawing out quite explicitly—and in resolving relatively happily—questions that are muted elsewhere or left unresolved.[19] In the ancient pantheon of the Mexican Indians, complete but sexless love between men, a lifelong goal for Lawrence, becomes possible; Ramon and Cipriano are a successful version of Birkin and Gerald in *Women in Love,* Kate a willing looker-on, quite different from the pugnacious Ursula. Love between women and "forbidden" men (different in race or class) also becomes possible. Unlike the married hell of *Sons and Lovers* or the enforced separations at the end of *Lady Chatterley* and *The Man Who Died,* the union of Kate and Cipriano exists in a never-never land of their own creation and is unchallenged by conventional values. The evils of the clitoris are also defeated in *The Plumed Serpent,* its "corrosive" mode of female sexuality purged, as it will be later in *Lady Chatterley,* with none of the long battles that Birkin wages with Ursula in *Women in Love.* Once the encounter of vital Euro-American male with "modern" Euro-American female is reenvisioned in terms of the primitive, struggle drops out; females recognize masculine phallic power as soon as they feel it. All of these thorny Lawrentian concerns, usually bypassed in criticism in favor of the "moral" categories established by F. R. Leavis, find their fullest resolution in *The Plumed Serpent.* It is the perfect book to understand what "the primitive" could do for D. H. Lawrence.

The Plumed Serpent frees Lawrence because it allows him to integrate the dualities that plagued him. In the Mexican dance, sexual divisions meld, with male and female reenvisioned as two halves of a cosmic whole. Similarly, the novel collapses together the ideas of the primitive as the dangerous and the primitive as the idyllic. Violence seems different once it is seen as loosing the essential stream of "blood" which unifies existence; even death can be "naturalized" as part of this cosmic system. In his affirmation of "blood" and violence, Lawrence resembles here strands of European thought he criticized elsewhere: the proto-fascist Futurists, with their celebration of "war as the sole true hygiene," and Bataille.[20] Yet the story does not repulse readers as much as other works do—"The Woman Who Rode Away," for example, in which the female heroine receives not the primitive phallus but the sacrificial knife, which (as we have seen in the Tarzan stories) can be substituted for it. "The Woman Who Rode Away" is hard to take; *The Plumed Serpent* makes Lawrence's "point" easier by having not death but the death of the female "willful self" the outcome.

In the novel, as in the myth of the noble savage, primitives hold the key to sexual harmony and harmony with nature. They have what the West has lost. In his last works, *Lady Chatterley's Lover* and the novella *The Man Who Died*, Lawrence pursues the possibilities for regeneration inscribed in *The Plumed Serpent*. But both these works back away from the optimistic—albeit highly open-ended—suspension that persists throughout Kate's Mexican idyll, and which is ongoing as the novel ends.[21] In *Lady Chatterley*, Connie and Mellors have been forced to separate, though they promise each other renewed togetherness as Connie awaits the birth of their child. The ending defers that togetherness until an indefinite future: England is too strong an opponent for the two rebellious lovers. The same kind of enforced separation ends *The Man Who Died*, a retelling of the Christ story in which the resurrected Christ meets and mates with a priestess of Isis in Egypt, an "exotic" locale that for Lawrence (as for many moderns) forms a middle ground between "the primitive" and the modern. The "primitive" Mexican setting allows Lawrence a greater freedom than his later settings in England and Egypt do. The primitive lets Lawrence return to origins, rewrite Western history, and imagine a radically different kind of future. The primitive lets Lawrence do what he wants and grants immediate fulfillment—but perhaps not complete fulfillment, or fulfillment of the right kind.

In fact, Lawrence's successive disappointments as a prophet of renewal may have resulted from his failure to identify exactly what he wanted. Lawrence slips—too easily—into using "the primitive" as a shorthand for his terms, or, in one of the substitutions endemic to Western use of the primitive as a generalized whole, to substitute sex or crossing/obliterating class lines instead.

In many of his novels, Lawrence is fascinated with the mythic times when men diverged from gods and male diverged from female (in this, he resembles the poet and painter he admired most among the British, William Blake).[22] In subliminal moments, his novels display a dislike of mankind more fully developed in essays contemporaneous with *The Plumed Serpent*—a wish that human beings would annihilate themselves and give the life-force a different chance for expression.[23] More—and this is always a paradox for a writer—Lawrence yearns at many points for the transcendence of self and language, for a state of perfect quiet and silence such as Kate achieves in her lovemaking with Cipriano. Indeed, this state of utter quiescence, quiescence in which the sense of self dies down, is a repeated locus of idealized values for Lawrence.[24] If we take Kate's dance in *The Plumed Serpent* seriously, as I think we should, Lawrence yearns for what Kate achieves here—a state of cosmic oneness, beyond words because beyond humanity, an utter mixing of things antipodal to language. In *The Plumed Serpent*, Lawrence posits the primitive as a point of entry to this mixing of things beyond language. Others in his time used Eastern myths (T. S. Eliot, for example), or abstract art (Virginia Woolf) to express a vision beyond words, a voyage into silence, a transcendence of the mess in which the modern West found itself.[25]

The primitive both serves Lawrence's needs and—this is what moves me—inevitably disappoints him. He yearns for an idealized primitive state in which man, nature, and eternity are one. That yearning rests on a fundamental paradox. Lawrence wishes to achieve an oceanic state of cosmic oneness, a state beyond subject and object, through the perfect balancing of opposites—male and female, sun and moon, primitive and modern. But to identify such oppositions—to identify an other with which to balance—means that the identification of the self *must already* have occurred.[26] To recognize such oppositions as "primitive" and "civilized" is antithetical to the oceanic state, which recognizes no such coherent boundaries.

We reach here a crucial impasse in Lawrence's work and in modern primitivism more generally. Lawrence's novels (from *Sons and Lovers* forward) are filled with the language and ideas of Freudian psychology, whose texts Lawrence read and sometimes wrote about critically. He was imbued with, and yet often discontented with, the Freudian account of ego development. *Psychoanalysis and the Unconscious* and *Fantasia of the Unconscious* spell out his admiration for, and difference from, Freud. Lawrence liked Freud's kind of scientists best among Western types because they at least acknowledged the importance of sex. But he believed that Freud, like all Western scientists, ignored the religious drive for unities between man and nature—what he calls "the science of life," a form of science he believed existed prior to the rise of the West and still survived in primitive societies. In his account of human development, Lawrence makes all the Freudian stops: infancy, Oedipus complex, "mature" sexuality, and so on. But he emphasizes periods Freud does not, such as the period of the infant's closeness to the mother.[27] In fact, Lawrence gave sustained attention to this relationship long before psychology itself did. His account shares with Freud, however, certain fateful, one might say fatal, assumptions: the mother, in this relationship, is an object (not a subject); the child (when gender is specified) is "a boy."

In his novels, Lawrence repeatedly invokes a state that will transcend individualism—the lapsing of the self in the dance, for example, or the celebrated "sun and star" polarity of male and female, in which two units will merge and yet not merge, but be preserved in a constant tension of mutuality. But Lawrence had no adequate vocabulary for expressing his ideals. He coped in two ways: by repetitiously heightening the vocabulary of Western individualism (with the repetition testing the limits of the concept),[28] and by alluding to a condition of prestate collectivity that categories such as "the primitive" or "the dark male" or "the miners" represented for him. The attraction to "the primitive" depends on a not-quite-realized critique of Western individualism, especially as embodied in Freudian psychology. The critique is not quite realized because the conditions for a genuine receptiveness to the primitive Other do not exist: for Lawrence, as for Conrad, the primitive Other, like all others, must be processed and reprocessed as a potential sign and symbol of the self. More, the desirability of masculinity and phallic power remain axiomatic and unquestioned, despite an inchoate yearning to transgress the boundaries these concepts enforce.

Ironically, given Lawrence's deservedly bad reputation among feminists, recent feminist critiques of Western individualistic philosophies and of the Freudian psychology with which they intermesh might have provided Lawrence with the vocabularies he sought. Lawrence's ideas of male-female relations bear strong comparison to ideas articulated in recent feminist theory.[29] Here, for example, is Jessica Benjamin, writing a psychology of mutuality, in which subject greets subject rather than defines itself against object:[30]

The capacity to enter into states in which distinctness and union are reconciled underlies the most intense experience of adult erotic life. In erotic union we can experience that form of mutual recognition in which both partners lose themselves without loss of awareness. (29)

Feminist theory aims to expand the idea of freedom *to*, offering a view of erotic union as a tension between separation from and attunement to an other . . . that space where subject meets subject. (132)

Anyone familiar with Lawrence's writings will recognize here the outlines of familiar Lawrentian ideas, with a crucial difference. Benjamin writes with a passionate commitment to female subjectivity, to the full recognition of women (as both mothers and lovers) as acting, desiring subjects; indeed, that the mother/infant relation be conceived as the prototype of intersubjectivity rather than object relations is an important turn in recent theory.[31] Lawrence was caught in Freudian systems of thought which articulate only males as desiring subjects, with females as passive actors in masculine plots. Theoretically speaking, Lawrence is "in the middest"—wanting what he cannot yet name, working with ideas and vocabulary drawn from systems of thought fundamentally at odds with his desires. He exists in a world filled with "subjects" and "objects"; what he wants, though he does not fully know it, is a world of harmonious, mutually receptive "subjects." The recourse to "the primitive," with its projected oceanic collectivities, forms a not entirely successful strategy for breaking out of the circles of Western thought. Once we recognize this, it becomes possible to view Lawrence with a sympathy that earlier feminist critiques, like Millett's, could not feel.

From this perspective, the narrative transvestism of some of Lawrence's writing, including *The Plumed Serpent*—the tendency I have noted for him to write third-person prose from within the mind of female characters—may be more significant than incidental. Gregory Bateson suggests that transvestism, when it is not motivated by a desire to be a member of another sex, may express a sense that certain ideas, values, or actions are coded as belonging to another sex by a culture. For someone engaged in those ideas, values, or actions, cross-dressing is a symbolic expression of sharing, temporarily, in matters culturally coded as sexually other.[32] In portions of his work, Lawrence thinks thoughts not traditionally associated with masculinity; he may therefore adopt the feminine voice, strategically, at times. We might compare Lawrence to Henry M. Stanley on this point: when filled with "well-nigh uncontrollable emotions," Stanley identifies his feelings with boyishness and represses them (see chap. 1); when filled with inchoate longings, Lawrence drops into a different kind of otherness—the otherness of what he imagines as the "female" consciousness.

At points, Lawrence loathes outright the white male ethos dominant in his culture. In "Aristocracy," Euro-American manhood is dismissed as a "yelping mongrel with his tail between his legs" who only *thinks* he controls "financial internationalism and industrial internationalism," which themselves "pale upon the hearth of the world" (240). In "The Mozo," Lawrence denounces "the white . . . [as] a sort of extraordinary white monkey that, by cunning, has learnt lots of semi-magical secrets of the universe and made himself boss of the show" (24). As Lawrence was acutely aware in the wake of World War I, "the white monkey" may yet end by bringing the curtain down on the show itself. The white man's self-loathing, so richly expressed in Lawrence's image of the "cunning white monkey," forms one significant basis for certain forms of primitivism: masters of the world, conquerers of themselves and their outer surroundings, self-created "aristocrats," white men like Stanley and Lawrence feel considerable pain, but pain is the one thing they cannot talk about without yielding the essence of what they conceive to be manhood. Filled with the self-loathing Lawrence expresses here, they tend to posit primitive Others who feel no need to master the self or the world—a "them" to counterbalance the repressive, self-repressing "us." But this line of projective thinking has been flawed from the start, as Lawrence's case pressingly indicates.

Lawrence aims at a perfect balancing of self and other. But within traditional European systems of thought and language, to identify "others" is to invoke a "hierarchy"; humans exist in relations of mastery, rather than reciprocity, with other humans and with the world.[33] In studying primitive societies or in inventing versions of them, Westerners pretend to learn about or to create alternative, less oppressive ways of knowing, all the while establishing mastery and control over those other ways of knowing. Primitive societies and systems of thought which might critique Western ones are instead processed in Western terms. Thinkers like Lawrence yearn for, but lack the ground for, radical critique.

Evocations of "the primitive" from within traditional systems of thought, therefore, are all too likely to reaffirm the very conditions that the evoker seeks to deny. They reaffirm Euro-Americans as they are, recoil against them, just as Odysseus' name, flung defiantly at the Cyclops to affirm his identity, came back to him in Polyphemus' curse—which nearly wiped him out. In this sense, Conrad and Lawrence are typical moderns and truly "one of us." They make the primitive enact their dramas of selfhood and consciousness, sexuality and the path of civilization—all conceived in traditional, received terms. Alternately made male and female, sympathetic and frightening, delectable and deadly, "the primitive" does what these authors want it to do. But it strikes back, where it hurts, by exposing the burden "the primitive" is made to bear as excessive. When we stop being seduced by the dazzling language of these modernist masters and examine what they say with regard to "the primitive," the patina of brilliance and wisdom, of innovation and newness, we have been taught to associate with great modernist writers becomes badly, and perhaps irredeemably, tarnished. We cannot protect ourselves with amulets of "humanist" or "formal" values; we need to see the moderns as they were—as needing the primitive and as inventing the primitive that fit their needs. Their truest greatness may lie in their aspiration after ideas and values and alternative modes of being whose time had not yet come.

Mapping the Site of Transcendental Homelessness

9

Adventurers

Their mission is to find territories where primitives have not yet or only sparingly come into contact with Euro-Americans, experience them, and then write about them. Sometimes a television series will follow, since the video camera has become almost as de rigeur as the note pad and camera. Once they would have been professional ethnographers; today they are often outright adventurers. Lorne and Lawrence Blair of the *Adventure* series on Public Television and Arts and Entertainment are two such adventurers. Tobias Schneebaum is another.

Lawrence Blair is an ethnographer of sorts and holds a doctorate in psycho-anthropology; his brother Lorne is a photographer and media expert. Together they have published *Ring of Fire,* an account of their journeys through Indonesia, and produced a television series by the same name. Born British, raised in Mexico, French educated, and based now in Los Angeles, the two confess to being essentially without a culture of their own and to being manifestly greedy for those of others. They go primitive to find "wisdom" conceived in terms of sixties' culture; in fact, Ringo Starr provided their initial funding. Their first trip to Indonesia (ostensibly to film the bird of paradise) lasted (a symbolic?) nine months; they then returned for a ten-year sojourn, self-described as an "odyssey" (ten years also being the length of Odysseus' voyage).

The Blairs structure their adventures and shape their narrative in a way that covers a full range of attitudes toward the primitive. A 20 May 1988 television episode was split down the middle to take in both halves of our culture's dominant images of the primitive. The first half covered life among the swamp-dwelling Asmat tribe of New Guinea (people of the Wood Age who have been headhunters and cannibals) and the second half covered adventures in the "tropical paradise" of Bali. Both groups of Indonesians are renowned artists—the Asmat producing totemic bis poles which house the spirits of ancestors, the Balinese producing batik and religious paintings. But visually and culturally the two groups vividly contrast and provide different kinds of adventures.

The Asmat are dark-skinned and live with far less technology than the Balinese. They wear only penis sheaths or loin cloths, decorate their bodies with white paint and feathers, and frequently wear huge white nosepieces. Their relative isolation has been guaranteed by one hundred miles of coastal swampland at the entrance to their territory, Irian Jaya, where survival is difficult and precarious. Although head-hunting and cannibalism are officially banned in Indonesia, the Asmat are known to have engaged in both activities until quite recently.

The focal point of the Blairs' coverage was a warlike ritual of revenge, in which the Asmat first carve totems and then anoint the poles with the blood of enemies who have killed one or more of their tribesmen. The rules for taking revenge are exquisitely refined and include free notice to the enemy that revenge is coming; the rules are so well defined that the voice-over narration compares them to European codes of chivalry. But the rules also require spine-shivering dances—duly photographed by the Blairs—which end with the capture, beheading, and eating of a member of the enemy tribe (the human brain being a special delicacy).

The real "kick" in the Asmat encounter came by accident when Lorne Blair was told by his best informant, midritual, as it were, that the Asmat, in a recent meeting with whites, had been the consumers of Western culture. The Blairs had come in the early seventies to capitalize on them—to film them and then to sell the films; in the early sixties, another white man, Michael Rockefeller, had come to visit and to purchase bis poles. Rockefeller's visit came at a bad time—a time when some Dutch soldiers had (unbeknown to Rockefeller) killed some Asmat. The logic of Asmat revenge required white blood as atonement, to free the dead warriors' spirits. The Dutch were not available, but Rockefeller was. He was (the voice-over informs us) killed and eaten in the very village the Blairs were photographing. A man of the steel clan had been sacrificed by men of the Wood Age (Blair and Blair, *Ring of Fire,* 189).

No one is really sure what happened to Rockefeller. Many continue to believe he was drowned or killed by alligators during an exploratory mission, despite reports that he was the victim of the people to whose culture, and especially to whose art, he had dedicated years of study. The Asmat themselves stoutly denied the rumors, until Lorne Blair's best confidante among the villagers confessed to the deed in considerable detail. Once Blair was convinced the Asmat had eaten Rockefeller, the news produced uneasy jokes among his companions: perhaps, they feared, despite Asmat "rules," the blood of one white man would not be enough to atone for four Asmat? They began to view their adventure—and Asmat rituals of revenge—with an eye to self-preservation.

The night before the Asmats' proposed journey for revenge (this time supposedly against a neighboring tribe)—with the bis poles ready for the vengeful blood—a thunderstorm engulfed the village; in the longhouse, the Asmat began to smoke and to invoke threatening rituals. Fearful of meeting Michael Rockefeller's fate, Blair fled by plane the next morning. At this point in the television episode, half of our culture's emotions toward the primitive have been evoked. The primitive has revealed depths of violence and the threat of death by decapitation followed by cannibalism; emotions of fear and morbid suspicion have been raised. Lorne Blair had gone beyond the usual bounds of adventure—and he wanted out. Period.

The Blairs' next stop in the episode is Bali. Here the inhabitants are light-skinned, and they wear clothes, build houses, and are devoted to the twin arts of farming and batik. The Balinese, like the Asmat, have violent rituals and customs, but rituals and customs of controlled symbolic and ceremonial violence—the dance of the graveyard spirit and, most of all, the cock fight—in which the cocks serve as animal stand-ins for human sacrifice.[1] Cannibalism here is unthinkable, and the Blairs find themselves infinitely content, visited by lovely Balinese dancing girls and swathed in batiks that reflect the philosophy of the island. That philosophy is communicated by a Balinese sage, filmed for the camera. It's all about the balancing of opposites and the consequent achievement of harmony. This balancing of opposites—sky and ocean, mountain and shore, yin and yang, animal and human life, vegetable and animal life, body and spirit, past and future, reality and dream—proves to be a constant theme in the Blairs' account of primitive Indonesian societies. They encounter numerous rituals designed to preserve the economy of balanced opposites. And they document instances in which the mind harnesses natural energies to perform acts (splitting wood, enduring pain, starting fires without matches) that Westerners often tend to dismiss as circus tricks rather than recognize as a collaboration of the human body and psychic energy. The Blairs are enchanted, indeed committed, to the peaceful version of this wisdom they find in Bali.[2] "We had found a home," the voice-over announces as the episode ends.

So far in my account of the Blairs, I have maintained an edge of cynicism in my tone, a suspiciousness of the factual accuracy of their accounts and of their motives. They deserve this: their historical information is sometimes patently wrong (New Amsterdam was ceded to Britain, they inform us, after the Napoleonic Wars); there are sometimes conflicts of fact between their book and their television series, conflicts created by the need to shape their adventures for the more condensed medium of the hour-long episode. They give (especially in the television series) little sense that the Asmat had ever had white visitors besides Michael Rockefeller and themselves; in fact, Sven Bergman, Pierre-Dominique Gaisseau, Alain Chenevière, and Tobias Schneebaum had all recently visited the region.[3] Yet their work also inspires other feelings in me, feelings of admiration and even (at moments) awe.

These men spent ten years in Indonesia. They endured incredible hardships to reach some of the peoples they encountered—ferocious insects and leeches, month-long treks through uncharted jungles with uncertain chances of success, discomforts beyond imagining. They placed their trust, absolutely, in the coastal Dyak tribesmen who work for timber companies and served as guides to their more isolated ancestral homelands. They risked dying or being permanently lost in the jungle communities to which they were guided. And they came, they authentically persuade me, to find wisdom and to preserve native philosophers and rituals on film. When they found wisdom, it suspiciously matched the kind of drug- or trance-induced mind travel that their sixties background had led them to seek in the primitive; to be sure, their story is another instance of the primitive telling the seeker of "the primitive" what he wants to hear. But at points in the Blairs' adventures, I too want to listen to what their primitive tells them.

Nowhere is this truer than in their journey to the Punans, the Dream Wanderers, a group isolated deep in uncharted Borneo. The Blairs journey for over a month, on a wish and a prayer, before they find the Punans. When they do, we realize with a shock that even these most isolated of peoples own Western clothes (for which they trade, we are told, with other, less-isolated tribes). The book records facts omitted in the television show, and these facts dramatize how little of the primitive remains, even in isolated Borneo: incredibly, the Punans have been contacted, just one week before the Blairs arrive by a long and painful land journey, by missionaries, and forced to build an airfield in the jungle for more missionaries to follow. The fragile isolation of the Punans recalls Lévi-Strauss's encounter with the Tupi-Kawahib, a tribal remnant on its way to join civilization when Lévi-Strauss encountered the group and persuaded its members to spend just a few more weeks with him in the wilderness. In the book, the Blairs leave the Punans via a plane; in the television show, they sail romantically off with Punan guides for the long journey back to Borneo's coast. In one sense the primitive is the same fraud we have found it to be elsewhere: the Blairs falsify the Punans' situation, especially for television. And they omit aspects of Punan life (head-hunting, for example) that do not suit the image of the Punans they wish to convey.[4]

Among the nomadic Punans, the Blairs and their coastal Dyak guides are welcomed, adopted, and loved. Lawrence Blair tells us that love is everywhere among the Punans; they reveal an essential human dependence similar to that eulogized by Lévi-Strauss among the Nambikwara as "the most truthful and moving expression of human love" (*Tristes Tropiques*, 293). The Dyaks and the Blairs respond to the experience by spontaneously wishing to wear Punan tattoos as testimony to the intense emotions they have found; they all carry the tattoos with them back to the coast, the Dyaks as "fresh symbols of their new-found cultural pride," the Blairs as "comforting reminders" that "all life forms are part of a single tree" (254, 257–59).

Although interested in all aspects of Punan life, the Blairs are most curious about the Punan religion and its central god, Aping, associated with the very tallest trees in the jungle. Aping unites man and nature and presides over the individual's multileveled consciousness: the social self, confined to the body, and the "dream wanderer," whose prophetic powers roam at will in nature to "direct our way not only through the forest, but also at the major crossroads of our inner lives" (257). At first, they seek information that the Punans withhold: having met missionaries, they are reluctant to tell any white strangers about their god; and the Blairs have not yet earned the Punans' confidence. Weeks pass. And as the Blairs become friends with the Punans, remarkable films show them at ease with the primitives, really talking—though in what language remains unclear. Once they have earned the Punans' trust, the Blairs are sent to meet the last priest of Aping who will be able to answer their questions.

At this point, familiar motifs thicken: the Punan expedition, like all searches for the primitive, has an urgency about it, an urgency produced by the imminent vanishing of the primitive subjects and their "undiscovered wisdom" (10). This is the last priest of Aping, and he is very old. In fact, the Punans, according to the Indonesian government, no longer exist in their nomadic state, though the Blairs have found proof to the contrary. More, there is a staginess about the affair fully admitted by the Blairs, who allude to their cables and lights and cameras even as the Punans stage a ritual for their spiritual benefit. But the ritual—staged or not—works. Lorne Blair experiences a cosmic dream, a dream of oceanic oneness that is, structurally, the climax of *Ring of Fire*. He is in a tree surrounded by creatures both predatory and friendly. He feels fear and hunger, the desire to escape those creatures who would eat him and the desire to eat other creatures who would normally be his prey. Then he feels, simply, the unity of their lives with his—an oceanic sense of oneness with nature (258–59). This vision is, undeniably, one of the primitive's most attractive gifts. When it comes to us, as via the Blairs (and at times in Lévi-Strauss), it is hard to refuse.

———

Tobias Schneebaum has written three books about encounters with primitive peoples, books that form an autobiographical trilogy: *Keep the River on Your Right, The Wild Man*, and *Where the Spirits Dwell*. In the first, narrated retrospectively and (he confesses in *Spirits*) often fictionalized, he sets out to contact an isolated Peruvian tribe, which had not yet encountered Westerners.[5] He succeeds; they welcome him and make him a member of one of their ambiguous male "sleeping groups." He lodges with men who become intimate friends, mates with women but only on ritual occasions, and then, in the book's climax, accompanies the men on a mission that ends with the slaughter of enemies, male homosexual rituals, and the eating of the slain enemies. Shocked by this encounter with the primitive within himself, Schneebaum returns to the isolated mission that represents "civilization." At the mission, he discovers that his friend Manuelo, who had been (like Schneebaum before he wrote this book) a closeted homosexual, has broken free at last of his guilt about his sexual preferences. He has left the mission and followed Schneebaum into the jungle. He expects to be eaten there by a cannibal tribe, and, Schneebaum later learns, he was in fact eaten. But, Manuelo tells us in a prophetic letter, this will be a happy death (like Celia's in Eliot's *The Cocktail Party*). "They didn't eat him, they loved him," quipped the title of the *New York Times Book Review* essay on Schneebaum's first work; but eating him would have been a form of loving him, the structure of Schneebaum's book declares—male homosexuality and cannibalism are homologous acts.

Schneebaum's *The Wild Man* is deucedly difficult to obtain; it has been out of print since its first edition and was, apparently, pulled from the shelves because of its aggressive endorsement of homosexuality among primitives as the "natural" thing to do.[6] *Where the Spirits Dwell*, published in 1988, sounds some of the same themes. In it Schneebaum meets the Asmat (the same group photographed by the Blairs), who have, incredibly enough, been transported from their village to a nearby mission to see their bis poles in an Indonesian museum. Schneebaum decides to return with them to their village. His white companions joke with him about Michael Rockefeller's fate in the same way that Blair's companions had joked; oddly and yet significantly, the uneasy jokes resemble those men traditionally make about homosexuality. The common response seems to recognize, at some level, the homology that Schneebaum's *Keep the River on Your Right* asserts between male homosexuality and cannibalism. After a brief initial visit with the Asmat, Schneebaum returned to New York, got a degree in cultural anthropology and then a job cataloguing Asmat art which allowed him to spend four of the next ten years (he too describes his journey as an "odyssey") among the Asmat.

Schneebaum writes in the same genres as the Blairs—his book combines the adventure story, ethnography, and autobiography. But he is less given to polarizing his vision of the primitive. It is as though the Asmat and the Balinese are compounded in his narratives, the violent and the harmonic joined—with the lovely dancing girls replaced by Asmat men. The Blairs journey first to film the illusive bird of paradise and then (expressly) to uncover the wisdom of primitive peoples, a wholistic philosophy endangered by the ever-increasing spread of the West. Schneebaum journeys to fulfill his artist soul (he is a painter) and, increasingly in his writings, to justify homosexuality to his Western readers. He shares with the Blairs a fundamental confusion of cultural identity: Jewish by birth, and of Polish Hasidic origins, he lived mostly in New York and was always ill at ease, always, he tells us, "searching for freedom and self-fulfillment without ever knowing what the words meant" (*Where the Spirits Dwell*, 26). Many of his relatives died young, of grim diseases like bowel and brain cancer; he himself has had one operation for cancer by the time he visited the Asmat (19). He remembers at odd moments in the jungle bits of Jewish ritual and Hebrew phrases; as primitives teach him their ways, he hears the Hebrew chants of Hasidic teachers in his ears.

From page one of *Where the Spirits Dwell*, everything is charged with male homosexual energy: bis poles flourish "filigreed phallic wing[s]" and are "powerful affirmation[s] of virility and fertility, as if all the male spirits of the carving were about to explode and ejaculate their life force onto all below." "Just as semen would burst forth from a phallus," Schneebaum writes, "so would the men burst out from the men's house to raid an enemy village" (1). This association of male homosexual energy with acts of physical violence is intended to be affirming of gay male sexuality. But it makes connections between head-hunting and male homosexuality that the Asmats would not necessarily make themselves and thus points to a significant weakness in Schneebaum's work: his need to read Asmat customs in terms of his own history, terms not necessarily appropriate to the Asmats at all.

Poling back to the Asmats' village, Schneebaum experiences the men as "regal, eloquent in movement, one standing behind the other, six, eight, or ten of them paddling easily on," and he watches them with "yearning" (10). He need not worry. For the Asmat, according to Schneebaum, have a tradition of "bond friendship" in which male homosexuality is fully practiced and fully acceptable, with friends reversing freely the active and passive roles (a reversal which contrasts with Schneebaum's experience of Western male homosexuality). Schneebaum first witnesses love between "bond friends" and later acquires one of his own.

Here is Schneebaum on his feelings when the nature of bond friendship was revealed to him:

> Not at all put off by my presence, Kokorai leaned onto the bent back of Amer, pushed his penis into him and pumped away enthusiastically. Within a few minutes, they reversed roles.
>
> The details of the relationship between bond friends in parts of Asmat had been unknown to outsiders. That this one aspect was revealed to me so easily and so directly spoke of something about me that the men recognized, some overt gesture on my part, some restlessness seen in my eyes or filtering through my skin. . . . I no longer felt isolated. . . . I felt for the first time part of a universal clan. . . . Who can know what it meant to me to find myself in a group where I was no different from others in that one way?
>
> Why did I have to go out of my country, out of my culture, out of my family, to find the kind of assurance and companionship necessary to my inner peace? (42–43)

Schneebaum experienced pain and alienation in his native United States, a sense of being irremediably other; we can feel the pain in passages like that above. The revelation of guilt-free male homosexuality among the Asmat gives him much-needed assurance and inner peace. It makes him feel, apparently for the first time, part of a "clan"—a clan willing to adopt him and to replace his original family and culture, neither of which had fully accepted him or made him feel at ease. Among the Asmat, the same desires that make Schneebaum an outcast at home open doors and serve as a passport: Schneebaum discovers details about Asmat life about which other visitors (Bergman, the Blairs, Chenevière) say nothing and may have been entirely ignorant.[7]

As he lives among the Asmat, Schneebaum learns further details of their homosexual customs: a boy's absorption of semen through anal intercourse is considered necessary for his growth into a manly warrior (181). But homosexual bond friendships continue throughout a man's life, even after he has taken a wife. The practices have whole sets of rules and etiquettes that Schneebaum records for us. Very important is the philosophy behind the act, which is the achievement of "balance" ("to balance" with a bond friend is the verb for performing sodomy).[8] Emotionally and physically, Schneebaum among the Asmat (like the stoutly heterosexual Blairs in Bali) finds a home. For him, the feeling of being home is based on the assurance that "homosexual relations existed everywhere, even though, more often than not, they might be underground" (43).

———

The metaphor of finding a home or being at home recurs over and over as a structuring pattern within Western primitivism. Going primitive is trying to "go home" to a place that feels comfortable and balanced, where full acceptance comes freely and easily. It can be a homoerotic paradise (as for Schneebaum) or a place where doubling opposites (life and death, heaven and hell, subject and object) are not constituted in the same way (Lawrence and the Blairs). Whatever form the primitive's hominess takes, its strangeness salves our estrangement from ourselves and our culture.

In a sense, this line of thought about the primitive takes us full circle and returns us to the earliest meanings of the word *primitive* as the original state of something—biological tissue, church organization, social organization. For "going home," like "going primitive," is inescapably a metaphor for the return to origins. In fact, the word *primitive* has been criticized and, sometimes, rejected because it connotes origins and evolutionist beliefs from the nineteenth century.

When evolutionary theory was brought to bear on the existence of racially different primitive peoples after 1850, an attempt was made to follow through on the idea that primitives and Euro-Americans jointly occupy linear time. The attempt led to a conflict between "monogenesis" and "polygenesis"—evolutionary theory bumping up against the Bible. The monogenesists maintained that all races had a common biological origin—and this became the antiracist position. The polygenesists maintained that there had been more than one creation and that the nonwhites were created as inferior to whites (see Curtin, *Image of Africa,* and Stocking, *Victorian Anthropology*). This became the assumption of the racist position. In rejecting it, in rightly letting it die out from intellectual history, we have allowed the doctrine of "common origins" to become a mental delusion: primitives originated at the same time as we did, the delusion says, but did not change; studying them can tell us about earlier versions of human society and about "human nature." What was originally an antiracist position can have racist overtones today, for the idea of the "unchanging primitive" which reveals "our" earlier stages of development helped produce some of the stubborn derogatory tropes for the primitive we have examined (the primitive as the childlike, the irrational, the violent, etc.).

To discard the idea of the primitive as "origin" requires radical measures. Some writers, like the Blairs, challenge the hegemony of linear conceptions of time and express interest in "alternative layers" of reality—a network of branching "times" in which "reality" and "dream" interpenetrate, with one no less "real" than the other.[9] Hans Peter Duerr, in *Dreamtime,* goes so far as to suggest that some anthropological research shows us multiple realities or rather "another part of *the* reality," which the West has persistently either reduced to a homogeneous whole or radically relativized. Duerr sees our denial of this part of "*the* reality" as consistent with a network of boundaries the West has erected between civilization and wilderness.[10] Despite such alternative visions, Western notions of time remain fundamentally evolutionist (Fabian, *Time and the Other*). And the desire that the primitive show us a state before there arose troubling differences—of sexuality, of economic life, of religious beliefs, of humans from nature—has been remarkably consistent.

The primitive's magical ability to dissolve differences depends on an illusion of time and sense in which the primitive is both eternally past and eternally present. For the charm to work, the primitive must represent a common past—our past, a Euro-American past so long gone that we can find no traces of it in Western spaces.

But the primitive must be eternally present in other spaces—the spaces of primitive peoples. Otherwise we cannot get to it, cannot find the magical spot where differences dissolve and harmony and rest prevail. The illusion depends on denying primitive societies "pasts" of their own, their own original states and development (perhaps wholly different from ours). The persistent tendency to elide "history" as a category for primitive groups had its historical usefulness during periods of active colonialism: to see primitives' history as beginning with us meant that we needed to regard them only in terms that suited us.[11] But the trick served psychological needs as well as political ones. If we imagine primitive societies as occupying linear time with us, but as developing in ways of their own to their present state, then they could not be our origin; there would be no time and place for us to "go home" to.

The reverse is also true. If primitive societies resemble our prehistory and exist in contemporary spaces accessible to individuals, then origins remain accessible. Our need for the primitive to be eternally present accounts in part for the anxiety often expressed by anthropologists and adventurers about the speed with which primitive societies vanish. The primitive must be available or our "origins" may no longer be retrievable, re-creatable.

When the primitive equals "origins," then origins transcend family, class, religion, or homeland—potential sites of origin that have become problematic for the Blairs, for Schneebaum, and for many better-known writers on the primitive. "Going home" involves only an individual journey—actual or imaginative—to join with a "universal" mankind in the primitive. There can be no homelessness then.

The condition of exile or cultural estrangement and the consequent desire to "go home"—so marked in the Blairs' and Schneebaum's stories—turn up as grounding conditions for interest in the primitive in a surprising number of important writers. I want to reframe some cameo examples here in the lives and work of figures already discussed; then I turn, in chapters 10 and 11, to more extended examples in Freud and Lévi-Strauss.

Malinowski was a German national caught in Australia during World War I. His revolutionary contribution to ethnography—the idea of living with anthropological subjects for extended periods—depended, absolutely, on the condition of exile from his native Poland. And it made voluntary exile *the* chosen method of the ethnographer. Boas was a German Jew who vacillated about whether to leave Germany but ultimately chose, in 1886, to live in the United States, largely because he "was conscious of anti-Semitic forces in German academic life" (Kuper, *Invention of Primitive Society*, 130).[12] He was especially interested in Eskimos and in Native Americans, whose history was also one of displacement from native lands; in 1911 he published a study on other recent immigrants to the United States. His work was controversial for a number of reasons, among them his assertion of the diversity and complexity of primitive life. By the 1930s, the controversy was deepened by his comparison of the United States's treatment of blacks to Nazi Germany's treatment of Jews—and both to the ways Westerners treat primitives (*Mind of Primitive Man*). His opponents in the thirties (perversely) used his work as a justification for restricting "undesirable" immigrants (Jews and Asians); the argument ran that when you "let in" undesirables like Boas, they cause no end of trouble (Stocking, *Objects and Others*, 115).

We have seen or mentioned other examples: D. H. Lawrence, working-class nomad in search of an idealized community of meritorious aristocratic natures that he never found, and at odds with his own homoeroticism; Conrad; Gide in Africa and Africa in Gide (the locus of forbidden, criminal desires and also of homoeroticism).[13] And we will see others. Freud's Jewishness, for example, was for himself and continues to be for many of his readers a vexed question (Klein, *Jewish Origins of Psychoanalysis*; Gilman, *Jewish Self-Hatred*; Gay, *Godless Jew*). Lévi-Strauss was a French Jew, the grandson of a rabbi, who never thought of himself as specifically Jewish and has spent a lifetime commenting on the religious myths of others.

The list could go on. Is it sheer coincidence that a state of exile—literal or metaphoric—often accompanies an interest in the primitive? I think not. The state of exile is an informing fact and a fundamental condition. It is the most literal sign—but only the most literal—of the site I map in this chapter—the site of transcendental homelessness.

"Transcendental homelessness"—the phrase comes from Lukács.[14] In his theory of the novel, Lukács sees the condition of the modern Western mind, the mind that produced the novel, as "transcendentally homeless": secular but yearning for the sacred, ironic but yearning for the absolute, individualistic but yearning for the wholeness of community, asking questions but receiving no answers, fragmented but yearning for "immanent totality."[15] The site of transcendental homelessness has been the site of much of this century's interest in the primitive, but it is a difficult site to map, except in small bits and pieces.

Leiris began to give us a feel for this site in his portrayal of the self as kaleidoscopic and changeable. His radical autobiographical project, begun in the thirties and continuing into the eighties, conveys a sense of the self as nefarious and evasive—a sense quite at odds with the surehandedness of his ethnographic work (see "The Many Obsessions of Michel Leiris," chapter 5).

Lawrence leads us directly to this site in his evocation of a time when "mankind is destroyed . . . and there is this beautiful evening with the luminous land and the trees" and in his sense that "if mankind passes away, it will only mean that this particular expression [of the life-force] is completed and done" (*Women in Love*, 111). The Lawrence who struggles elsewhere in his work with perfecting human relationships abandons here, rather easily, the very *importance* of things human; he is in that tree, with Lorne Blair, greeting the oceanic. Lurking behind Lawrence's sentiments, though, is a misanthropic sense that the Westerner is, as he puts it in "The Mozo," a "clever white monkey"—and his loathing for contemporary humans is only a step away from indifference to human survival.

Bataille gives us another portion of the map. In his unflagging effort to reveal the irrational baseness of man, he evolved an aesthetics of excrement which shared with the work of his colleague Leiris a fascination for ritual and the sacred, linked to the primitive via rites of animal, but more particularly of human, sacrifice. Bataille's linking of the primitive with human sacrifice makes crystal clear that a connection has been there all along in the West. For "sacrifice" intuitively connects to one of the persistent tropes the West associates with the primitive—cannibalism—evident in Polyphemus' gulping down Odysseus' sailors and in Europeans' obsession with Africans and Pacific islanders as cannibals.[16] Human sacrifice is a symbolic version of cannibalism, in which the human body substitutes for the animal body, and killing for eating. It is a symbolic representation of our normal gustatory acts—but heightened, made less utilitarian, and hence "sacred." Christianity has written some of these connections into its communion rituals—the sacrificed man-God is also the eaten man-God, body and blood.

For Bataille, human sacrifice is also a sacred, transcendental version of suicide, a version in which the voluntary destruction of the self achieves social significance. We might remember here that, for Leiris too, suicide obliterates subject and object, an obliteration that would defy and eliminate all polarities—male and female, rational and irrational, nature and culture, civilized and primitive, self and other—in a perverse version of the oceanic vision the Blairs seek and find in the primitive.

In one of the several essays he wrote on human sacrifice,[17] Bataille reveals the connection between the autobiographic moment and the primitive as a state beyond subject and object:

> *Me*, I exist—suspended in a realized void—suspended from my own dread—different from all other being. . . . But, at the same time, I consider my coming into the world—which depended on the birth and conjunction of a given man and woman, then on the moment of their conjunction. There exists, in fact, a unique moment in relation to the possibility of me—and thus the infinite improbability of this coming into the world appears. For if the tiniest difference had occurred in the course of the successive events of which I am the result, in the place of this *me*, integrally avid to be *me*, there would have been "an *other*." ("Sacrifices," in *Visions of Excess*, 130)

An *other* stands at the gates of being, admitting and yet mocking the self. Bataille's intuition here is Shandyean, but the imagined scene of one's own conception is not humorous as in Sterne's *Tristram Shandy*. It is filled with pain, pain that led Bataille to explore the primitive as a stop on his larger journey to achieve "the transition from discontinuity to continuity," a "lost continuity . . . a primal continuity linking us with everything that is" (*Erotism*, 17, 15).

Bataille yearns for death (even violent death) as a way out of the intolerable uncertainty and limits of being, as a way of affirming the *me*, in its very improbability, with "a space peopled by stars." The paradox resembles the one that allies sacrifice with suicide: the surrender of individuality makes "one"—no longer "one"—part of the cosmic whole. The anxiety of selfhood is transcended, even as the concept of selfhood is both obliterated and affirmed.[18] Transcendental homelessness, a sense of cultural void, a fear of the fragility of the self, sometimes deepening into a loathing of the self or its perceived contexts: how often these seem allied to some of our greatest thinking and thinkers about the primitive.

▬▬▬

The modern anthropologist or adventurer—like the Blairs or Schneebaum or (the best example of all) Lévi-Strauss in *Tristes Tropiques*—launches forth from the modern city, often with the breath of its teeming millions hot on his neck; he enters isolated terrain, already marked by the signs of urban encroachment, like the telegraph lines that (in the 1930s) already bisected Nambikwara territory, or the presence of the anthropologist himself. The lines of the telegraph company and the lines written by the anthropologist presage future openings—tendrils that will spread from the original, opening line and gradually choke off the primitive, making it an outpost of the cities from which the anthropologist and the telegraph workers and the adventurers come and to which they will return. The city, originally Western, becomes a third world phenomenon and grows like Topsy: Nairobi, encroaching on lands once Maasai and Gikuyu, then planter territory, then suburban subdivision; São Paulo, a collection of huts gone wild; Kinshasa—and the list goes on.

Once the city and the jungle could be posed, geographically and imaginatively, as opposite spaces. In the modern age, cities that were loci of imperial power—London, Madrid, Paris, Amsterdam, Brussels, or Berlin—sent forth soldiers, merchants, administraters, explorers, who would enter the jungles (or deserts, imaginatively much the same kind of space) and bring—or attempt to bring—the cultural norms of urban societies to primitive locales. Reciprocally, goods would be exported back to the mother country (really city) and become accessible first to the urban dwellers of the colonial powers. First, tobacco, sugar, corn, spices, gold. Then the "natives" themselves, popular through the nineteenth and early twentieth centuries in freak shows (Fiedler, *Freaks*) as curiosities, as circus performers—or, in larger numbers, in U.S. cities in the South, as slaves. With slavery abolished and the materials of industry and agriculture in mother country and colony thoroughly assimilated (tobacco a normative vice, no longer a curiosity), the "trade" broadened. Part two documents one form that trade later took: the articles unloaded now "valuable" artifacts and masks, as well as foodstuffs and mineral wealth. From the docks or railway stations, the artifacts moved into other urban spaces: the museum, the university, the gallery, the private collection. It is important to grasp this sense of primitive things brought into urban spaces and to realize that the primary sites of primitivism in the West—precisely the museum and the university, the gallery and the private collection—are most often urban spaces, associated with the processes of industrialization and the concentration of population that gave rise to the features of modern culture we know best.[19]

Site of modernism, hotbed of intellectual life, product of industry, the city produces the alienation and crises in identity that fuel the work of many modernists and make them turn their imaginations (in some cases move their bodies) to the alternate space of the primitive—last, desperate, remaining, endangered model for alternative social organizations, for communities that exert communal power and live amid a sense of wonder that transcends the mundane order of modern urban life.

The endangered nature of the primitive produces a common motif of urgency in the Blairs and in Lévi-Strauss and in the work of many anthropologists and adventurers: I can find the jungle now, they seem to say, but in twenty years? Ten years? Next year? Next month? Once it is simply "past," the primitive will lose some of its appeal and function for the West. The tone of urgency and desperation overlooks the fact that primitives, as often as not, do not vanish but change into the urban poor, and thus can no longer serve as a locus for our powerful longings precisely because they have entered our own normative conditions of urban life. The state of transcendental homelessness produces primitivism in its most acute modern forms, with its various desires to go home to something simpler, more comfortable, less urban and chafing and crowded.

Western discourse on the primitive has often been considered a rhetoric of control and domination—its purpose to justify to men the ways of the West with regard to territories we arrogantly call non-Western and, more particularly, with regard to the "lowest" category of the non-Western, the primitive.[20] But this emphasis on *control over others*, while accurate to a point, remains incomplete. That a rhetoric of control and domination exists in Western discourse on the primitive is beyond question. And it exists in at least two senses: control and domination of primitives (and those thought of as like primitives) abroad; and a parallel control of the lower classes, minorities, and women at home, who are linked, via a network of tropes, to the primitive. But the rhetoric of control and domination over others often exists alongside (behind) a rhetoric of more obscure desires: of sexual desires or fears, of class, or religious, or national, or racial anxieties, of confusion or outright self-loathing. Not just outer-directed, Western discourse on the primitive is also inner-directed—salving secret wounds, masking the controller's fear of losing control and power.

The West's versions of the primitive have been remarkably similar from Homer to the present. But their emotional valence—and the degree and direction of their "seepage" to other values (masculine or feminine, black, Jewish, or working class, philosophic, economic, or psychological)—has changed over time. For example, "sexual freedom" has always been a characteristic attributed to primitives; "homosexuality" was not generally mentioned until late in this century. Similarly, "peasants" and, later, "the working class" always shared with primitives in the aristocratic or the bourgeois mind the potential for imminent violence, irrationality, shiftlessness, and promiscuity; but analogies between primitives and the peasantry or the working class were iterated more and more strongly in the late nineteenth and first half of the twentieth century. In fact, the analogy formed the basis for an experiment in Britain called Mass Observation, in which working-class "rituals" were expressly studied as though they *were* primitive rituals.[21] When versions of the primitive show specific historical and cultural variations, they expose different aspects of the West itself. Primitivism is thus not a "subtopic" of modernism or postmodernism: to study primitivism's manifold presence is to recontextualize modernity.

10

Entering Freud's Study

Civilization behaves towards sexuality as a people or a stratum of its population does which has subjected another one to its exploitation.
—SIGMUND FREUD,
Civilization and Its Discontents

This place is familiar to me. I've been here before.
—SIGMUND FREUD,
"The 'Uncanny'"

The photographs are amazing and consistent over the years: Sigmund Freud, first as a relatively young man and then as a very old one, sits in his study or consulting room—alone or with his dog, at his desk or beside it—and gazes at his work or beyond into the distance, but always through a layer of primitive statues. From the title page of *Totem and Taboo* (1913; fig. 10.1) to the archive of Freud's personal space in Engelman's *Bergasse 19* (1938, 1967), Freud looks out at us, surrounded by the objects he collected and loved. The sense of groundedness conveyed, the sense of possessing the space and things around him, is strong. For most of his life, then, Sigmund Freud did not seem to be the victim of homelessness. He seemed rooted to his native Vienna, at home in the city and apartment where he lived and worked.

But there are many kinds of homelessness. And Freud was always, metaphorically, homeless by virtue of being Jewish in a city gripped by alternating periods of virulent persecution and relative tolerance of Jews.[1] If we enter the place where Freud lived and worked, we can find the idea of homelessness and exile both represented and denied in the very decor.

In Freud's study and consulting room, statues abounded, overabounded, astonishing Freud's patients and visitors—Egyptian statues, Greek and Roman statues, African and Asian statues.[2] They formed a border on the desk, lined the cabinets and walls, filled every available inch for storage or display. Freud's friend and colleague Lou Andreas-Salomé commented on how "the archeologist had created the psychoanalyst" in Freud. The reverse is also true: Freud purchased his amazing collection of ancient and primitive artifacts solely from the proceeds of his psychoanalytic practice, other

Fig. 10.1.
Always, a layer of primitive statues. Freud on the title page of the 1913 Hugo Heller edition of *Totem and Taboo*. Courtesy Bettman Archive.

Fig. 10.2. A display alluding to Freud's great themes. Freud's consulting (treatment) room, wall with couch. To the right, the *Gravida*; to the left, "Freud's corner." Copyright Edmund Engelman.

monies (from teaching, for example) being reserved for the family.³
For Freud these statues were more than mere decor or possessions.⁴
They were containers of myth and clues to human nature, collabo-
rators in the stories Freud told about men and women, morality and
sexuality, civilization and the forms of life that came before it.⁵ They
spoke to Freud of his deepest obsessions.

Lying on Freud's couch, the analysand viewed a similarly controlled but motley display alluding to many of Freud's great themes
(fig. 10.2.). At the foot of the couch hung Ingres's painting of Oedipus with the Sphinx. Above it hung the photo-portrait of one of
Freud's teachers, bearded and fatherly. Larger in scale and seeming
to tread over Oedipus and over the patient was a classical bas-relief
of a walking woman, called the *Gravida* (walking or pregnant
woman). So at the analysand's feet, pictorially enacted, was the
same Oedipal drama that would be unfolded on the couch: father
hovering above son, mother looming large, sphinx posing riddles
that would be unraveled in time and precipitate Oedipus's simulta-
neous self-knowledge and self-banishment. The theories preceded
the arrangement, but, in time, the arrangement validated the theories: no patient lying on Freud's couch could have been entirely innocent of the root-drama he was required to enact to produce his
cure.⁶

At the head of the couch were fragments of drawings and etchings
of mythological creatures half man/half animal; among them were
cartoons by Wilhelm Busch, including one of a rhinoceros confronting a frightened African (left side, fig. 10.2). These drawings and
etchings surrounded the Roman head of a man, mounted on a classical column. This was "Freud's corner" of the consulting room, and
he would have sat directly below the Roman bust, backed by the
classical column, his head beneath the carved head. Rita Ransohoff,
who wrote the captions for Engelman's photographs of Freud's study
and consulting room in *Bergasse 19*, reads the symbolism of
"Freud's corner" as the opposition of the "civilized" (the rational,
male, Roman citizen) and the "primitive" (mythological creatures,
animals, and "natives"):

> Here, above the chair where Freud sat listening to his patients,
> are two large framed fragments of Pompeiian-style wall paintings
> dominated by mythological figures: a centaur (half man–half
> horse) and Pan (half man–half goat). They represent aspects that
> are primitive, phallic, and pleasure-seeking in human nature. Be-
> low these large framed fragments, on a pedestal, sits a dignified
> Roman portrait head. . . . It is "the Roman citizen," symbol of a

nation dedicated to the rule of law. . . . Here in Freud's corner the
mythological figures from Pompeii and the head of the Roman
citizen illuminate contrasting aspects of man: his impulsive animal nature and the civilizing influence of conscience and law.
Here is a suggestion of the images of the id and the superego, two
aspects of Freud's hypothesis of the structure of the mind. (59)

Ransohoff's account of the decor enacts a drama of the primitive
and the civilized that echoes the narrative on the couch. Like the
decor itself, her description enforces the roles in that drama rigidly.
The analysand would work down and through various "primitive"
states of mind to share the "civilized" outlook of the powerful doctor. Although hierarchies usually express themselves in terms of the
"high" and "low," the reversal here justifies itself by the coalescence
of the analysand's story and the analyst's master plot under the sign
of the Roman head, masculine symbol of order and law. If ambivalence existed in Freud's mind about the relation of the primitive and
the civilized—and we know it did from his writings—that ambivalence has no place in Freud's consulting room. In "Freud's corner,"
the arrangement of objects fits traditional Western paradigms on the
primitive, which assume that the primitive is prior to the civilized
and can be subordinated by it.

In his essays and books, public events made Freud increasingly
willing to entertain the disturbing thought that civilization was not
a stable category and that civilized man could always, under pressures like war, become with impunity a murderer who shows less
remorse than primitive man. Such thoughts found expression, for
example, in an essay written during World War I called "Thoughts
for the Times on Life and Death" (1915).[7] In this essay, Freud perceived that "the great ruling powers among the white nations upon
whom the leadership of the human species had fallen" persecute
nonwhite societies in order to civilize them (206–7). He also perceived that "white nations" require of their citizens "renunciation
of instinctual satisfactions" (215). He wrote in 1915, however, with
confidence that "the great ruling powers among the white nations"
should wield power over others and with the hope that Germany
(despised as "barbaric" by its enemies in World War I) would be re-
habilitated by virtue of its previous "magnificent co-operation in the
work of civilization" (211).

By the time of *Civilization and Its Discontents* (1930), Freud felt
compelled to stress his growing ambivalence about the relation
of the primitive and the civilized. "Civilization behaves towards
sexuality as a people or a stratum of its population does which has

subjected another one to its exploitation," Freud wrote in 1930, reckoning one cost of the protection that civilization offers us from nature and from human violence (57). The great colonizer of psyches now balked at any unqualified endorsement of the imperial state. What had erupted into the model of the primitive and the civilized in "Freud's corner" was nothing less than the course of history.

In Freud's early writing, he explored the normal and the deviant in the human psyche and methods through which, by revisiting the scenes of our childhood, we can cure neurosis and take our rightful place in society. In his late writing, in part under the pressure of the grim public events that led from World War I to World War II, Freud turned from the evolution of the individual psyche to the evolution of cultures: he needed a broader canvas than the individual psyche to explain what had gone wrong in modern times. While it would be wrong to trace Freud's thinking about culture exclusively to his historical situation, specifically to his Jewishness during the rise of Naziism, it would be equally wrong not to recognize how the historical realities of being a Jew in this time fed into Freud's thinking about Western civilization.

Freud conceived of himself as an imaginary citizen of Rome; the Nazis conceived of him as a prize Jew whom they reluctantly spared the death camp.[8] By 1938, when the photographs of Freud's study and consulting room in *Bergasse 19* were taken, the disjunction between these perceptions had become painfully clear. That year saw Austria annexed by Germany, Jews vilified and beaten in the streets of Vienna, Anna and Martin Freud brought in for questioning by the Gestapo (an event for which they prepared by acquiring a powerful poison), long lines of desperate Austrian Jews at visa offices, the excesses of Die Kristallnacht.[9] In June of 1938 Freud and his family went into exile in England, after the Nazis yielded to international pressure that they be allowed to leave the country of their birth.[10] In fact, we have the archive of Freud's personal space in *Bergasse 19* because his Viennese followers correctly perceived that Freud's apartment was a doomed place, and that theirs was a subculture on the eve of extinction.[11]

All of these terrible things could happen in Freud's beloved Vienna in part because of the Nazis' processing of Jews as primitives. As we have seen, the arrangement of objects in Freud's consulting room and study made distinctions between Freud as the civilized man and the animal-like primitive. Anti-Jewish propaganda portrayed Jews in the same terms Freud and his culture routinely used for primitives. Although he rarely acknowledged its existence, this kind of propaganda, which the Nazis manipulated so skillfully and brought to a new level of explicitness, may have motivated Freud's insistent need to see himself and Jews who were like him as civilized beings antithetical to the primitive, even as it heightened his suspiciousness about the benefits of civilization itself.

A persistent Western fantasy saw the Jews as needing to drink Christian blood, much as primitives were conceived, frequently, as cannibals. Jews from Eastern Europe were frequently represented (by assimilated Jews as well as gentiles) as "primitive"—ritualistic, collective, superstitious, alien, and distasteful. Their odd dress and odd language (Yiddish) reinforced the impression of their Otherness.[12] In infamous propaganda films, shots of *shtetl* Jews would be intercut with cartoonlike caricatures of Jewish features or with shots of swarming insects and rats, and hence Jews were perceived as an undifferentiated mass liable to extermination.

To prepare occupied populations for anti-Jewish measures, the Nazis frequently mounted exhibitions in which Jewish "Otherness" would be displayed visually and palpably; they resembled European expositions and circuses that displayed primitive peoples and their objects as freaks and curiosities.[13] The Nazi exhibitions often included posters and photographs denouncing Jews prominent in European intellectual life, including Freud himself, whose books were burned by the Nazis as early as 1933. Freud arranged the objects in his study and consulting room to suggest an alliance between himself and civilization; Nazi propaganda used visual display to make opposite suggestions, aligning Freud, by virtue of his Jewishness, with the expendable primitive.

Sander Gilman has shown, in a study of Jewish "self-hatred," that Freud was, like many assimilated Germanic Jews, fundamentally secular. He shared the sense of superiority, and even "vehement contempt," many Germanic Jews felt toward provincial Jews from Eastern Europe (Klein, *Jewish Origins of Psychoanalysis,* 49). He felt he had "excelled" (his word) his Hasidic father.[14] He changed his name from the Jewish Sigusmund (used in anti-Semitic jokes) to the Germanic Sigmund (46). He repressed Yiddish as a spoken language in his own life and repressed its importance in early cases, like Anna O.'s, which produced his theories of hysteria.[15] If Gilman is right that Freud repressed certain aspects of the category "Jewishness," the repressed had begun a forced return by the late twenties and early thirties. During these decades, Freud defiantly emphasized more and more the fact that he was Jewish, though he repeatedly treated the question of what it meant *to be* Jewish.[16] His definitions intersect with the dialectic of the civilized and the primitive and reflect his increasing and yet ambivalent need to identify himself as a civilized man, a claim that rested on his status as a man of science.

By 1930 it was abundantly clear to Freud that worsening economic conditions had revived the most violent forms of anti-Semitism. He could no longer gaze on the processes of history as a distressed but clearly "civilized" man; he was now put in the position of the threatened Other, declared "inferior and degenerate."[17] In that year, *Civilization and Its Discontents* alludes quite directly to Freud's concern over increased persecution of the Jews as scapegoats during the Great Depression: "the Devil would be the best way out as an excuse for God [insofar as he has failed to eliminate evil from the world]; in that way he would be playing the same part as an agent of economic discharge as the Jew does in the world of the Aryan ideal" (75). Also in 1930, in a preface he added to a new edition of *Totem and Taboo*, Freud both hints and denies that Jewishness colors his renewed interest in the transition between primitive and civilized social life.[18] He declares in the preface that his "essence" is Jewish, despite his nonbelief in Jewish lore, and that he "has no desire to alter" that essence. But he does make a few suggestions for updating Judaism—and not necessarily in minor ways.

In this preface, Freud describes his own work as "unprejudiced science" which "adopts no Jewish standpoint" (xi). He urges what he calls the "new Jewry" to follow his example and to embrace "unprejudiced science."[19] Freud thus distinguishes between an "old" (unassimilated, religious) Jewry and a "new" (assimilated, secular) Jewry to which he himself belongs (xi). Under the impact of Aryan rhetoric, Freud fights against the identification of the Jew with the primitive by expressly redefining the Jew as a being who conforms to the secular, scientific spirit of the modern age—in his own case, typifies it. He evades the question of what a Jewish "essence" consists of, stripped of any religious sense; in fact, he proposes that science may one day illuminate this vexing question (xi). He similarly evades the question of whether distinctions like that he suggests between an "old" and "new" Jewry play the Nazis' own damnable game of self and Other.

Freud once felt sure that Europeans like the Germans and Austrians were civilized and that primitive life belonged to the past. But by Freud's last years in Vienna, the categories of the "primitive" and the "civilized"—once, for Freud, so clearly separate in time and so arranged in hierarchical order—had become fundamentally more unstable under the pressure of Naziism.[20] Political events made Freud more and more willing to reckon civilization's costs as well as benefits and to entertain the idea that Western civilization had gone, inexorably, wrong—that is the burden of *Civilization and Its Discontents*. But Freud still ultimately saw himself as an apologist for civilization.[21]

Given the material he had to work with, Freud might have arrived at a radical critique of the very ideas of "hierarchy" and "mastery" in the political contexts of the late twenties and the thirties: the Nazis had, after all, given both concepts a bad name. Instead Freud continued to lay siege to the top level of power. Freud's picture of himself as a man of science (and the gender is important) allowed him to believe that he wrote from within the system of European civilization; it sustained his sense of himself as European (Roman) citizen rather than Jewish Other. Ironically, like many in his day, Freud was unable to perceive how science itself could be perverted into a pseudoscience that served the Nazis' genocidal ends through a rhetoric of "race" and "eugenics," and through the safeguarding of Aryan stock at death camps manned by honored doctors.[22]

Freud's desire to write the history of civilization from within the system, to mitigate the intense form of alienation and homelessness that was part and parcel of being a Jew in Christian Europe, appears as early as *Totem and Taboo*, published in 1913.[23] Freud himself conceived of *Totem and Taboo* as initiating the themes of his later work: "As early as the year 1912, at the height of psychoanalytic work," he wrote, "I had made the attempt in *Totem and Taboo* to exploit the newly won analytic insights for an investigation of the origins of religion and morality."[24] That investigation led to the roots of civilization in primitive "prehistory."

Totem and Taboo raises all the interconnected themes to which Freud would return often in the remaining decades of his life, most dramatically in *Civilization and Its Discontents*. *Totem and Taboo* enjoys less critical esteem than the later *Civilization and Its Discontents:* too fanciful and ungrounded, critics call it, too motivated by his feuds with Jung, having as much relation to primitive societies (A. L. Kroeber quipped) as Kipling's *Just-So* stories. But *Totem and Taboo* remains an important work, important most of all for its ideas about the primitive—ideas vividly imagined, but utterly without proof.

As Freud's collection of statues suggests, he possessed an intense visual imagination, and he dramatizes his ideas about the primitive by writing a scene (a "spectacle" he calls it) from human "prehistory."[25] That "spectacle" encodes some of the same ideas and hierarchies we have seen embodied in Freud's consulting room and study. The setting is a primeval landscape. A large rock looms in the background; a primeval horde cowers in the foreground before the entrance to its cave, from which comes the reassuring brightness and warmth of fire. The leader of the horde is the father, who mates indiscriminately with all the women of the horde, his wives and daughters. The other, younger, men are excluded from mating and fiercely jealous. They remain at the mercy of the tyrant until they decide one day to band together and kill the father. They do kill him, instituting, as penance, law, exogamous sexual relations, and religions in which the slain father becomes first the totem animal and then the Father god among gods, and finally the God of monotheism among the Jews.

From this imagined scene of primal Oedipal murder in *Totem and Taboo* would come Freud's explanation for Western anti-Semitism in *Moses and Monotheism* (1939): Christians, Freud believed, acknowledged guilt for the murder of the primal father by accepting Christ the son's sacrifice as atonement; by refusing to acknowledge Christ as Lord, Jews fueled Christian resentment by declining to share mankind's guilt for the murder of the father.[26] This connection between the murder of the father and anti-Semitism is not yet present in *Totem and Taboo*. But *Totem and Taboo* makes utterly clear how Freud's version of the primitive both depends on and supports a traditional, patriarchal model of culture, with Oedipal patterns concerning the father as the central psychological mainspring.

In *Civilization and Its Discontents*, Freud writes a sequel to the story he told in *Totem and Taboo* about the transition between the primitive and the civilized. Like the original, the sequel tells the story of a primeval society ruled by men which became a civilized society, also ruled by men. *Civilization and Its Discontents* revisits the primal rock of *Totem and Taboo*, with primal fire and primal horde, to imagine a different scene than the murder of the father. This time, men and women hover around the comforting fire. Suddenly, the men begin to urinate on the fire, something the women are physiologically prevented from doing. One man, destined to become a man of power, refrains from urinating and commands the others to do so as well. He henceforth controls the fire and becomes the horde's leader and guardian.

This scene—as silly in the original as in the retelling—is a bizarre fantasy which typifies how Freud's theories of the development of individuals and cultures are parallel and male-based.[27] Freud imagines (and is comfortable with) a version of the primitive in which women are excluded from primal moments and unable to seize power; he evolves his script of prehistory in accord with his culture's gender assumptions.[28] He divides history into the categories female/male and primitive/civilized. He then allies himself with the "triumphant" categories—civilized male.

Magically, and at odds with his social realities, Freud becomes one of "us," not one of "them." It was a comforting pattern which reproduced the arrangement of objects we have seen in Freud's study, with Freud rigidly aligned with the head of the Roman citizen atop a classical column. It was the same pattern of mastery and control that Freud, sitting at his desk or in "Freud's corner," communicated to his patients and to the viewers of photographs like that on the title page of *Totem and Taboo* (fig. 10.1). Freud's control over his environment—his ownership and mastery of statues and paintings, his ability to make them tell the stories he wants to hear—echoes and reinforces his control over his patients and over the psychoanalytic process, especially as recorded in Freud's case histories. Ultimately, it prefigures his ideals of self-control and self-mastery, ideals he has bequeathed to us in his influential theories. It is surely significant that Freud's model of the mind depends on rooting out portions of the psyche that frustrate our lives as good citizens—depends, indeed, on a life of fragmentation, conflict, and exile from wholeness, which it is then the goal of psychoanalysis to make liveable. These are the prerogatives available to men of science.

But Freud's version of the primitive was something less than purely scientific—as he himself was aware when he called it a "scientific myth."[29] It was, in fact, produced more by personal and professional needs than by the ideal of scientific observation. From *Totem and Taboo* through *Civilization and Its Discontents*, Freud imagines primitive prehistory in terms of his own psychological theories. He concludes, for example, that "obsessional neurotics behave exactly like savages" on the basis of "submit[ting] the recorded facts [about primitive taboos] to analysis, as though they formed part of the symptoms presented by neurosis" (*Totem and Taboo*, 56, 46). The procedure is entirely circular and self-generating, yielding not "results" based on observation, but axioms based on metaphors.

Freud relies absolutely on the imaginary union of children, primitives, and neurotics in developing his crucial parallel between the origins of civilized institutions and of individual neuroses. He does this *despite* repeated notations in his footnotes that should have prevented metaphor from slipping into fact. Freud says, for example, that primitives have an unknown past of their own which makes their present state an uncertain parallel to our own (the West's) past, only *metaphorically* analogous to what is usually called the "childhood of man" (*Totem and Taboo*, 4). He also says, quite clearly, that primitive customs are collective, while neuroses are individual (71). Strictly speaking, it should thus have been impossible for Freud to compare the traditions and institutions of primitive societies with the beliefs of children or the oddities of the individual neurotic. Indeed, primitive societies might have provided Freud with examples of collective forms of social existence to serve as radical alternatives to Western individualism.[30] But Freud could not stop his powerful analogy-making machine: it was too slickly oiled by his need to be the Roman citizen, a modern man among modern civilized men.

Critics often identify Freud's primitive with the masculine—as when Ransohoff, in her captions to Engelman's *Bergasse 19*, alludes to the "phallic primitive." But this identification of masculinity with the "primitive" id misses a crucial point: for Freud, when societies evolved from the primitive to the civilized after the primal murder of the father, individual men did too. "The primitive" was something left behind, residual, like the "id" within the mature ego. Often (though not exclusively) for Freud, residual "primitive" feelings were associated with the mother and, hence, with femininity. In this sense, it is not surprising that Freud turned, after *Civilization and Its Discontents*, quite explicitly to the questions addressed in "Female Sexuality" (1931) and "Femininity" (1933): the nature of feminine sexual development and the reasons why women (Freud believed) lack a strong ethical sense. In fact, it is possible to read the opening of *Civilization and Its Discontents* as the prelude to the themes developed in these two essays.

In Freud's work, the feminine often functions as the primitive does and as religious Judaism does—as something "the Roman citizen" rejects and controls in his march toward civilization. Sometimes the connection between the female and the primitive in

Freud's mind is hard to miss, as when he compares the female psyche to a "dark continent," with himself as the intrepid explorer Stanley.[31] "Female Sexuality" (1931) is equally clear in aligning the female with the primitive: the period when infants are attached to their mothers (a period Freud believed of paramount importance for women) is described there as like the Minoan past of Greek civilization, "grey with age, and shadowy and almost impossible to revivify" (225).

Sometimes, especially in earlier work, the connection between women and "the primitive" is subtler, though it predicts the associations that we have already seen. In *Beyond the Pleasure Principle* (1920) Freud describes how a little boy's game of "Fort/Da" prepared him for his mother's intermittent departures. He tells how the boy learned to cope with his mother's absences and then, several years later (during which another child had been born into the family), "showed no signs of grief" when his mother died (10). Freud applauds the child's ability to separate from the mother as a "great *cultural* achievement" (9; my emphasis). His language implicitly makes the child's withdrawal from the mother analogous to society's transition from the primitive to the civilized. He makes no comment about the boy's lack of grief: female presence is elided in favor of male development.

In *Civilization and Its Discontents*, Freud addresses the question of the female role in human development in a crucial way, though the book's reference to the female is not immediately apparent. In this work, the female enters the discussion indirectly, through the issue of the infant's attachment to the mother as undifferentiated from the self. Freud's discussion of this phenomenon follows more general attention to a category of experiences in which the individual undergoes "a feeling as of something limitless, unbounded—as it were, 'oceanic'" (11). The prototype of such experiences of boundlessness, Freud will ultimately suggest, is the infant's feeling of oneness with the mother—hence the link between "the oceanic" and the female.[32] Freud treats the "oceanic" in a way that reveals how it was for him, like religious Jewishness and the primitive, a category he wished to suppress and leave behind because it was at odds with the modern city-state and the sense of consummate individualism upon which it depends.[33] But there is something fearful and even erratic about Freud's handling of the "oceanic"; in fact, until he is able to connect it to an infantile state, and hence to associate it with women, he feels distinctly threatened by it.

Freud's discussion of the "oceanic" seems to come out of nowhere at the beginning of *Civilization and Its Discontents.* As the
book begins, Freud considers the idea (urged upon him by his friend
Romain Rolland) that the "oceanic feeling" of being "unlimited,
boundless"—a feeling *not*, at this point, connected to infants and
mothers—is the origin of the religious sense. Freud is intent on refuting this thesis since it discredits the theories elaborated in *Totem
and Taboo* and *The Future of an Illusion*, which trace the religious
feeling to guilt over the primal horde's patricidal act.[34] Since the
"oceanic" stresses feelings of connection and oneness rather than
Oedipal rivalry with the father, it cannot be allowed to stand as an
important factor in human and cultural evolution.

Freud is in some ways surprisingly candid about his need to dismiss the oceanic. Although his friend reports having had this
oceanic feeling and claims that "millions of people" do as well,
Freud himself claims never to have experienced it. Based simply on
his own sensations, Freud decides to remove the "oceanic" from
"the foreground" of attention. He admits that being able to sum-
marily dismiss the "oceanic" is strategic. For the idea of the
"oceanic"—with its emphasis on a "permeable" ego and feelings of
collectivity as something desirable—threatens the very foundations
of psychoanalysis as a discipline.[35] "The 'oceanic,'" Freud says, "fits
in so badly with the fabric of our psychology that one is justified in
attempting to discover a psycho-analytic—that is, a genetic [that is,
neurotic]—explanation of such a feeling" (13). Freud proceeds to tell
the following story to justify the efforts of his lifetime and glorify
the emergence of the sense of self. Although Freud would say that
his story includes both males and females, he was really thinking
about males; though I use neuter nouns, Freud's story demands a
male protagonist for its pattern of heroic exile to be especially clear.

The archetypal moment when the ego fails to perceive its difference from the outside world is that of "an infant at the breast" (14):
this subsequently becomes our culture's dominant image of the
"oceanic" in human experience and portrays the "oceanic" as an
obvious—and "regressive"—extension of the feelings of the child in
the womb. The need to restore the pleasures of the breast and opposite needs to escape pain gradually cause the individual "to learn
a procedure by which, through a deliberate direction of one's sensory
activities and through suitable muscular action, one can differentiate between what is internal—what belongs to the ego—and what
is external—what emanates from the outside world" (15). The

"oceanic" feeling thus eases into the perception of self and other under what Freud calls the "reality principle." The very phrases capture Freud's sense of hierarchy: the oceanic is a "sense," a "feeling"; reality is a "principle."

If the "oceanic" survives this process, it does so, Freud claims, in the way that "Rome" contains past civilizations "buried in the soil of the city or beneath its modern buildings" (18). "The manner in which the past is preserved in historical sites like Rome" resembles the way that "earlier phases of development are in no sense still preserved; they have been absorbed into the later phases for which they have supplied the material" (19). Freud's insistence that the oceanic (like all that existed before Rome) is "in no sense still preserved" but rather "absorbed into the later phases" seems peculiar and overstated. The overstatement denies the continued existence of the "oceanic," yet seems to protest too much. Indeed, Freud's statements in *Civilization and Its Discontents* deny his earlier formulations about the reaccessibility of "primitive" mental formations.[36]

The analogy between the mature ego (below which lie the scattered remains of the id) and the Roman city occupies four of the ten pages Freud devotes to the "oceanic." The analogy is not a casual gesture. In fact, it recapitulates the ideology already encoded in the visual displays we have seen in Freud's study and consulting room. The "oceanic" is identified with the infant at the breast, with "the primitive pleasure principle," and with id forces: the "oceanic" is the primitive and the conjunction of the infantile and the female, none of which conform to "the reality principle."[37] The mature ego is identified with the imperial city-state, which will colonize primitives quite literally and colonize (in the figurative sense) many feelings, including feelings of free sexuality and oceanic oneness. The "oceanic" must be "ousted from a place in the foreground" because it would displace the individualistic paternal line (the Roman line) to which Freud wishes to trace civilization, its benefits, and its discontents. The "oceanic," with its absence of boundaries and divisions, is something we need to be protected *from* if we are to take our places in the "mature" culture of the West: we must fear it as we fear the primitive and separate from it as we separate from "primitive" sexual or aggressive urges and from the bodies of our mothers. That separation has fearful consequences Freud does not pause for long to examine: an alienation from one's past and from one's environment, the establishment and perpetuation of relations of mastery rather than reciprocity, the repudiation of "the feminine" as a source of "primary narcissism" and loss of self.[38] It is a fateful separation, and fateful in the context of Freud's thinking.

It is, in fact, another version of the fall into transcendental homelessness, another form of exile. In "The 'Uncanny,'" Freud refers to the mother's body as "the place where each of us lived once upon a time and in the beginning" and attributes to everyone the utterance "this place is familiar to me, I've been here before" (245). In his repudiation of the "oceanic" sense in *Civilization and Its Discontents*, Freud denies the mother's body, brands it as something that the mature ego must leave behind, as primitive freedom must be left behind by a civilized person. Freud misses here an important, alternative direction. He never fully considers the questions invited by his opening meditation on the oceanic. If there is a state of mind, and potentially a state of culture, that could be derived from the original relationship of our bodies to the bodies of our mothers, what differences in father-centered psychoanalytic theories would follow? What differences in the relation of men and women to the physical world would follow? What political consequences would follow? Might these provide a form of "civilization" with fewer "discontents"? The collectivities of the "oceanic" need not, of course, have led to social utopias.[39] But Freud never even pursued these possible directions of thought. In gynecology, the number of pregnancies a woman has had is designated by the phrase *gravida*, plus a number. The *Gravida* (the woman at the base of the couch in Freud's consulting room) never reaches the point of delivery: she is permanently arrested at gravida one.

In Freud's time, Melanie Klein and Karen Horney charted other possibilities, arguing against the master in different ways for the complexity and validity of infant and female experiences. Klein urged more attention to infancy, though she built upon many of Freud's basic ideas. Horney resented Freud's overemphasis on "penis envy" as women's primary motivation and his subsequent conclusion that women lack a strong moral sense; above all, she urged more attention to cultural factors in women's development.[40] These possibilities have been extended by feminist thinkers in our time, like Nancy Chodorow (*Reproduction of Mothering*) and Jessica Benjamin (*Bonds of Love*).[41] They see a psychology centered around "continuity" and "discontinuity" with the mother's body as a key to our culture's coding of male and female gender roles and as a key to alternative visions of human life and social organization.[42] They propose that alternative visions can benefit both men and women by, for example, getting beyond what seemed to Freud the inevitable need for dominance and articulating instead a psychology of mutuality.[43] Under the sign of the paternal Roman bust, juxtaposed with the statues of primitive Others, Freud made different choices.

11

Remembering with Lévi-Strauss

I t is sometime in the early seventies, 1972 I should think, and a day of rare, because collective, intellectual excitement at Columbia. The gymnasium at Barnard is packed and has been for the past hour. An overflow crowd, unanticipated but eager, has gathered on the pathways adjacent to the gymnasium. Crews have hastily erected speakers so that those outside can hear what goes on inside. Everyone inside feels smug.

The occasion is Lévi-Strauss's visit and a lecture whose title I've long since forgotten. Though I'm a graduate student at Columbia, my experience of Lévi-Strauss is very much secondhand. I know him as a French intellectual associated with Structuralism, but in 1972 I've not read him (much less studied him). But the occasion has more of a political than an academic aura. The audience is young, basically leftist, mostly radical in sympathies. The occasion presents itself as nothing so dry as an introduction to Structuralism. Rather, in a hipper mood, it presents itself as Truth about to descend into the gymnasium at Barnard, some harbinger of the revolution many of those in the audience have not ceased to expect, though the seventies are beginning to seem well established, and ominously bland.

Lévi-Strauss, one of those men who seems to have been old a long time, enters the auditorium. He's frail and small; he looks a little like a Buddhist sage. He begins to talk—a lecture whose particulars I have all but forgotten. But he was working then on *From Honey to Ashes* and presented us with a series of analogies and homologies (not a word current then) that constructed, before our eyes, a house of cards, as elaborately decorated as the faces of the Caduveo about whom he writes in *Tristes Tropiques*. The structure grows taller and taller; I lose the particulars as I try to follow, and I find myself thinking about those outside: how hard they must find it to follow, hearing a voice over a speaker; how disappointed they must be; how easy it would be for them to leave while we, seated in packed splendor in the gymnasium, have no choice but to stay. The talk moves to its conclusion. Ecology is evoked; saving the globe. The audience, bored for a while, begins to stir. Truth begins to descend from the ceiling but then stops, a jammed deus ex machina.[1] What did it all mean? I'm not sure in 1972, but the topic continues to come up, years later, when I'm teaching at Williams, as everyone's still trying to grasp Structuralism, even as Post-Structuralism has arrived on our shores, further to the east and a little south, centered on New Haven. Truth still hovers above us, but refuses to descend.

I remember this scene as I read the beginning of *Tristes Tropiques*, where Lévi-Strauss remembers the conditions under which he left France for New York. It is 1941 after the demobilization of the French army, and France is no longer a safe haven for Jews. Lévi-Strauss has never thought much about himself as a Jew (though he is the grandson of a rabbi), but now he has to think about it. In fact, he has to escape from France to the Americas. He considers returning to Brazil where he had done some research in the 1930s, but then (with great luck and connections) he secures a teaching appointment at New York's New School; like Freud, he was able to find a place ready-made for him outside of threatened Europe. By 1972, Lévi-Strauss would be as famous as Freud and free to travel anywhere he liked; should he be threatened by a new Holocaust, he would be a cultural monument, protected by powerful forces. But in 1941 he is a relative unknown, and he cannot just go into exile after major governments smooth his path through governmental red tape.[2] He has to obtain a visa.

Escape was precarious in the remaining pocket of free France, depending above all on securing, in time, the necessary papers. In Marseilles, the most likely port of exit, Lévi-Strauss pretends to be a teacher going to teach abroad—a mere professional commitment. But he is motivated by his sense of danger as a Jew, and he besieges the visa offices. Lévi-Strauss imagines that the officials he encountered saw him as "a minor ambassador of French culture," but he saw himself "as potential fodder for the concentration camp" (24). This tiny private moment in the text moves me: it captures a sense of the doubleness and duplicity of the self (so typical of modernity in general) and the gap between what we are to ourselves (subjects) and what we are to others—an other, in Lévi-Strauss's case (as a Jew in soon-to-be occupied France) The Other.

Once he was out of France, Lévi-Strauss found life aboard ship uncomfortable and humiliating, especially when contrasted with his memories of earlier voyages, in peace time, traveling first class with just a handful of other passengers. *Then*, he remembers (with an elitism I find painful), he enjoyed "supremacy" and "felt quite at home on board" (22); now he was regarded as "the scum," "the riff-raff as the gendarmes called them," each either "a Jew . . . a foreigner . . . [or] an anarchist" (24). He had lost his distinctiveness and become part of a mass: lower class, "primitive," subject to extermination. His identity was effaced by the overcrowding on board ship in the way that tattooed numbers would far more radically efface the identities of Jews less lucky than he—though he himself does not draw the comparison. On board the ship it was difficult to wash, and the competition for the morning's seat on the privy led to many an early rising. The voyage turned perilous as well as uncomfortable when Lévi-Strauss was almost arrested as a spy (his anthropological writings, in unknown languages, looked suspicious). At this moment, withdrawn from the ship by policemen, Lévi-Strauss was once again threatened by a return to France, where he might meet the fate of other Jews who spoke different "suspicious" languages, like Yiddish.

Lévi-Strauss arrived safely in the United States and began teaching at the New School. His recollections of New York—published in 1985, several decades after *Tristes Tropiques*—evoke many feelings, including a sense of vertigo and amazement produced by the landscape of the city and the unexpected cultural juxtapositions it revealed on every street corner, and especially in locales such as the Northwest Hall at the American Museum of Natural History.[3] As he remembers it in 1985, New York was a "mythical" space "for doorways to open in the wall of industrial civilization and reveal other worlds and other times" (*View from Afar*, 262). The story of Lévi-Strauss's exile is thus one of joyous discovery as well as persistent fears. But the experience of exile and humiliation aboard ship proved a more reliable indicator of the future than the "open doorways" of New York. In fact, Lévi-Strauss believes that the decades between the forties and the eighties closed the doorways still available in the forties in New York: "Losing its old dimensions one after another, this world has pushed us back into the one remaining dimension: one will probe it in vain for secret loopholes" (262). Even his heady experiences in New York contain ominous reminders of the evolving, apocalyptic postmodern condition. He meets a fellow exile, a scientist, who explains to Lévi-Strauss "the principle of the atomic bomb . . . and revealed (this was in May 1941) that the major powers had embarked on a scientific race, the winner of which would be sure of victory" (*Tristes Tropiques*, 34).

The world-weariness which haunts the author in the forties aboard ship and even in the "canyons" of New York persists into the fifties, as he writes *Tristes Tropiques*. Noting the activities of the American FBI and the proliferation of nuclear weapons, he remarks that "everywhere the atmosphere is becoming . . . oppressive" (36). He prepares, like Lawrence before him, to salvage something essential, the life-force, which resides in man but also elsewhere. This salvage operation provides the striking ending to *Tristes Tropiques*:

> during the brief intervals in which our species can bring itself to interrupt its hive-like activity, [let us grasp] the essence of what it was and continues to be, below the threshold of thought and over and above society: in the contemplation of a mineral more beautiful than all our creations; in the scent that can be smelt at the heart of a lily and is more imbued with learning than all our books; or in the brief glance, heavy with patience, serenity and mutual forgiveness, that, through some involuntary understanding, one can sometimes exchange with a cat. (414–15)

Sitting in the heart of a lily exchanging glances with a cat, we seem to have traveled a long way in *Tristes Tropiques:* from the personal memoir of 1941, through four primitive societies in Brazil, through India and Islam, and finally to the philosophical essence of life with the mineral and the lily and the cat. After the personal opening, the scope of the book seems to open out, first to the ethnographer's observations in Brazil and then to a universalist philosophical meditation. We seem to have moved through the story of Lévi-Strauss's exile, to the longer story of his work (his "hive-like activity"?), to an oceanic vista, in which the anthropologist occupies the same level as animal, vegetable, and mineral life.

At one level, the opening-out is surprising. Why, I wondered, would Lévi-Strauss begin with his exile as a Jew only to say nothing more about it? One could say that the memory was too painful for him to pursue, too marked by the fact of difference—and a difference imposed by others, since Lévi-Strauss, like Freud, was a secular, assimilated Jew who thought of himself not as a Jew, but as a citizen of his native land. With equal plausibility, one could see the move away from the personal as determined more theoretically by the Structuralist mind-set with which Lévi-Strauss is so closely associated, which characteristically works from the particular to the universal. But I want to resist opposing these two explanations—the personal and the theoretical—and to uncover the ways in which they overlap, the sense in which *Tristes Tropiques* never does leave behind the fact of exile. Traditional accounts of Lévi-Strauss circle around and around his Structuralism and its historical place in the evolution of twentieth-century thought. I would like to examine a seam in that historical narrative: the role of Lévi-Strauss's refugee status.

Lévi-Strauss's choice to study primitive peoples and his Structuralist inclinations preceded his Otherness as a Jewish exile, but perhaps only superficially. For *Tristes Tropiques*, like other anthropological texts, constructs a notion of "the West" that aligns Lévi-Strauss himself with the dominant norm—makes him no longer a Jewish Other. Indeed, Lévi-Strauss habitually and even elaborately speaks of a Western "us" in *Tristes Tropiques*, despite the opening's radical sense of the Jew as Other. The central impulse of his work as an anthropologist, of structural anthropology in general, is to work through otherness to continuities. Thus, the structure of *Tristes Tropiques* moves Lévi-Strauss out of and beyond history, just as Structuralism (as a discipline) yearned to move out of and beyond history. In touch with deep structures, there can be no alienation, only connections; no homelessness, only an expansive welcome. *Tristes Tropiques* remains enmeshed in Lévi-Strauss's desire to be off the crowded ship carrying him and other refugees from Marseilles to the United States, to be a first-class traveler in the world, "at home on board" once more. But the ship sails on and on, and "being at home" remains an elusive feeling. The movement from the personal to the universal enacted in *Tristes Tropiques* is in a sense delusory: the personal controls the perception of the universal, and the feelings of alienation and exile, of overcrowding and disease that Lévi-Strauss felt aboard ship radiate, outward.

———

Tristes Tropiques punctuates chapters on Amazonian Indians (who represent few people in large spaces) with chapters on crowded, bustling India. These interspersed chapters on India have sometimes been deleted in English translations; but they are crucial to Lévi-Strauss's enterprise, for they establish modern India as a prospective model of what may happen in what are now Western or primitive spaces.[4] The hatred, the wars, the violence of 1941 were, Lévi-Strauss speculates, "outbreaks of stupidity, hatred and credulousness which social groups secrete like pus when they begin to be short of space" (30). The postwar world is faced, Lévi-Strauss believes, by the relentless spread of Western "monoculture" eating away alternative primitive spaces and causing gross ecological consequences. "The first thing we see," Lévi-Strauss notes with sadness, "as we travel round the world is our own filth, thrown into the face of mankind" (38): urban congestion, like that in modern Western cities and in urban India, is invading even the rain forests of the Amazon.

For Lévi-Strauss, India represents "the urban phenomenon, reduced to its ultimate expression" (134). The overcrowding there has blocked what Lévi-Strauss considers the best path for human development—acceptance and mutuality, rather than hierarchization and subordination: "men can coexist on condition that they recognize each other as being all *equally*, though *differently*, human, but they can also coexist by denying each other a comparable degree of humanity, and thus establishing a system of subordination" (149). In India, the development of the caste system followed the second path, "the simple solution of denying one section of the species the right to be considered as human" (149). India's plight foreshadows the situation of mankind in general in the nuclear age, as we move into what Lévi-Strauss acutely calls "a finite world." Mankind has become an endangered species, though we do not cease our "hive-like activity" long enough to realize it.

Lévi-Strauss thus contrasts the ratio of space to population in India and the rain forest; he then establishes a homologous parallel between the scarce space and large population of Europe and large space/small population of the Americas. He fears that, under the pressure of universal urbanization, the possibility of small populations in large spaces will be lost and that overcrowding, with consequent violent discharges, will become a universal condition. The opening of *Tristes Tropiques*, with its evocation of refugee conditions in World War II, should now make perfect sense: those conditions become one possible paradigm of the world's future.

In fact, Lévi-Strauss's central contrast between India and the Amazon repeats his obsession aboard ship with numbers and the spaces in which they live. That obsession repeats, in a different key, the Nazi conception of *Lebensraum*, its justification for the imperial acquisitions that launched World War II. In a sense then, one of the major thematic strands in *Tristes Tropiques*, the theme that motivates its structure, is a projection onto the contemporary world of a scene of personal and historical trauma: on a crowded ship, no

longer a first-class passenger but "riff-raff," Lévi-Strauss has seen an
omen of the future. By the end of *Tristes Tropiques*, in communion
with the mineral, the lily, and the cat, Lévi-Strauss means to get out
of history into the universal life essence. But he reproduces his own
historical situation everywhere he looks.[5] One might even say that
his historical condition *produces* his search for the ahistorical.

The interpretation I am suggesting helps explain some of the odd-
est and most important moments in *Tristes Tropiques*, some of
which have escaped comment in this country because they were,
until recently, omitted from English translations. One such moment
is when Lévi-Strauss throws across the field of his argument, with
crazy curviness, some ideas about Islam as severing East and West.
"It was then," when Islam was born, says Lévi-Strauss, that the West
lost the possibility of blending Buddhism with Christianity, lost a
possible marriage of passive (philosophical) and active (mercantile)
potentialities, "lost the opportunity of remaining female" (409).
Buddhism, for Lévi-Strauss, offers "the unifying reassurance implicit in the promise of a return to the maternal breast"; its fundamental tendency is to abolish differences, as the androgynous garb
of its temple priests and its "radical criticism of life" attest (408).
Islam, by contrast, "has developed according to a masculine orientation" and is a "barrack-room" religion (407, 403). Islam is Germanic, Lévi-Strauss says, and Islam is the future (403). Lévi-Strauss
sees Islam as masculinist, industrialist, and pitiless toward outsid-
ers. The wave of the future is allied to the wave of war that pushed
Lévi-Strauss out of his native France to the United States. Once
again, the present and future are read in terms of a projection of a
past (and personally consequential) historical situation.[6]

But even as I point out (in a way that has perhaps become too fash-
ionable) that Lévi-Strauss "denies history," I feel I am falsifying
some aspects of the text and of my reactions to it.[7] Wild as it is,
produced as it is by the partly unacknowledged facts of personal and
historical trauma, Lévi-Strauss's assertion that the West "lost the
opportunity of remaining female" *interests* me. I need, then, to
question my own critique of Lévi-Strauss and to explore my attraction to him, an attraction partly based on a contrast with Freud, and
perhaps impossible for me without it, given the prejudices that Lévi-
Strauss displays.

Several kinds of prejudice inform *Tristes Tropiques:* the elitism
and class consciousness embedded in his account of incidents
aboard ship, the persistent tendency to view women only as sexual

props, and perhaps, in the unflattering evocation of Islam, suspicions about the Muslims in France's colonies.[8] The work contains more than a few hints of a deep misanthropy or indifference to other humans, including the primitives he studies. At the end of *Tristes Tropiques*, Lévi-Strauss imagines a radiant world filled by a mineral, a lily, and a cat—but not, significantly, any human being other than Lévi-Strauss. Lévi-Strauss cannot be for me, then, an unqualified hero. But he has qualities that I cannot help but admire, especially after having breathed (in the last chapter) the closeted air of Freud's study.

Like Freud, Lévi-Strauss scripts the primitive in an us/them vocabulary that writes himself into the majority "us" of European culture. Once again like Freud, he posits the existence of universal patterns in the human mind—patterns which mean that no time or place is truly alien. But unlike Freud, he is fully aware of his hidden motivations and desperations and has much less faith that what Freud called "unprejudiced science" has much to offer. In fact, he remains convinced that "man never creates anything truly great except at the beginning; in whatever field it may be, only the first initiative is wholly valid" (408). Thus he finds prefigured in Buddhism all of the truths—and knotty dilemmas—of the human situation. His mission as an intellectual—in strong contrast now to Freud—is to seek beginnings as a key to wisdom we can live by, not as something we must reach in order to exorcise. Lévi-Strauss's mineral, lily, and cat are in a sense like Freud's primitive statues—a symbolic representation of some universal essence. But while Freud wants to establish mastery and domination (to *own* and *control* the human mind as he owns and controls the statues), Lévi-Strauss wants to establish communication, reverence, and awe. Despite Structuralism's claim to be science, with its accompanying deluge of facts, charts, and diagrams, some of Lévi-Strauss's goals are unscientific, even unintellectual—hence he reserves the mineral, the lily, and the cat for the very last lines in *Tristes Tropiques*.

Like the adventurers Lorne and Lawrence Blair, Lévi-Strauss is fundamentally attracted to the primitive as a site of alternative possibilities, including the possibility of a world blending male and female, inanimate, animal, and human—a world of oceanic oneness. As we have seen, Freud does not share this mind-set and is manifestly hostile to it: the oceanic must be superseded in the individual just as the primitive must be superseded by civilization. No other possibilities exist for Freud.[9] Other possibilities always and pressingly exist for Lévi-Strauss: that is why he jumps from place to place and reads the human mind, over and over, in light of multiple myths of multiple cultures.

Among the possibilities that Lévi-Strauss considers is the possibility that his "scientific" profession (with the choices and responsibilities it courts or evades) can be variously assessed. Freud believes that the psychologist is the benefactor of human beings and of civilization, someone who helps people live in society and cope with lost possibilities: it is a single-valent evaluation. Lévi-Strauss considers the anthropologist, among other things, a "symbol of atonement" for the West's remorse over lost possibilities (389). In fact, he thematizes the question of the anthropologist's guilt in a crucial portion of *Tristes Tropiques.*

Lévi-Strauss poses the dilemma/shame of the anthropologist in this way: "how can the anthropologist overcome the contradiction resulting from the circumstances of his choice? He has in front of him and available for study a given society—his own; why does he decide to spurn it and to reserve for other societies—which are among the most remote and the most alien—a patience and a devotion which his choice of vocation has deflected from his fellow-citizens?" (383). It is a good, a key, question.[10] He further notes that what he considers the essential attitude of the anthropologist—the attitude that "each society has made a certain choice, within the range of existing human possibilities, and . . . the various choices cannot be compared with each other"—imposes an eternal passivity, refraining from judgment and action (385). His solution to the dilemma, his salve for the guilt, depends on realizing, as did Rousseau before him, that "after demolishing all forms of social organization, we can still discover the principles which will allow us to construct a new form" (390). "Nothing is settled; everything can still be altered," concludes Lévi-Strauss (393). But the alteration depends on discovering a point "beyond thought and beneath society"—a point that may be unreachable, though it is the goal of all of Lévi-Strauss's work. Like the essence of the mineral, lily, and cat, it may also be profoundly nonhuman. It would be a point at which "exile" as Jew or from modernity could no longer exist, would itself be an impossibility; it would be a point at which all human minds—savage and civilized, Western and Eastern—would be open and welcoming to each other and to the natural world in which they live.

There are, then, two kinds of transcendental homelessness in Lévi-Strauss: the undesired but real fact of exile (from France in the 1940s, from the Christian West, from industrial modernity) and the desired but utopian site out of time and place which would allow

Lévi-Strauss to realize his project (Rousseau's project) of "after demolishing all forms of social organization, ... construct[ing] a new form," based on universal communication and respect. Lévi-Strauss has experienced exile in the literal sense (from France) and also in the metaphorical sense—an alienation from modernity which produces "filth" that chokes almost every corner of the globe. He proceeds to write major anthropological texts about vanishing ways of life with the sense that all people may soon vanish from the earth. He writes with a hopefulness and yet an ambivalence about mankind (how often *do* we interrupt our "hive-like activity"?) and his own endeavors as an anthropologist. *Tristes Tropiques,* like the other narratives of the primitive and the modern we have encountered, salves secret wounds.

———

Like *Totem and Taboo* in Freud's canon or *The Plumed Serpent* in Lawrence's, *Tristes Tropiques* was once undervalued among Lévi-Strauss's works. It was written roughly twenty years after the brief fieldwork among Amazonian Indians upon which its longest sections (those set in Brazil) are based, and is, expressly and pervasively, a work of memory.[11] It sends mixed generic signals—now travel book, now ethnography, now Proustian narrative, now philosophic text—signals that confused and in some cases outraged the anthropological community.[12] Although he sometimes takes refuge in the book's ethnographic basis, Lévi-Strauss makes it abundantly clear at points that his fieldwork was very brief and very long ago and that, for him, the "truth" about any particular group is often quite beside the point.

This mixing of generic conventions—like the intercutting between India, the Amazon, Islam, and the modern West—forms a crucial part of Lévi-Strauss's message in *Tristes Tropiques:* we must work backward toward and forward through all prior possibilities to achieve anything truly new. Few people have known exactly what to do with *Tristes Tropiques,* but increasingly it is being recognized as (what I feel it to be) the most subtle and evocative of Lévi-Strauss's texts.[13]

What makes *Tristes Tropiques* so evocative is the way its sentences and sections float like balloons, with other sentences released and floating like parallel balloons. "I knew that, slowly and gradually, experiences such as these were starting to ooze out like some insidious leakage from contemporary mankind," Lévi-Strauss writes of the international catastrophes of 1941, "as if its skin had been irritated by the friction of ever-greater material and intellectual exchange brought about by the improvement in communication" (29). Later on, in the section recounting his travels through Brazil, he writes about his oxen whose backs, irritated by the friction of unaccustomed saddles, break open to reveal a host of maggots, swarming along their spines. Parallel moments, floating balloons. Pus and maggots along the lines of vitality and life. Something in-human erupting from the human: that same sense of the posthuman we have seen being readied in Lawrence and Bataille and that comes forward again in the closing pages of *Tristes Tropiques* where Lévi-Strauss, this French intellectual, imagines himself in profound, wordless communication with a mineral, a lily, and a cat. The text, like the moment at which it ends, has organicist, oceanic yearnings; it wants to embrace speculation and to accept contradictions, as nature does or Buddhism does.

In Derrida's critique of Lévi-Strauss—the single document that made Lévi-Strauss most suspect for my generation—the organicist, Buddhist, oceanic aspirations of the text are overlooked.[14] I approached *Tristes Tropiques* with the Derridean critique in mind and expected to find in it the elaborate and delusory "universal calculus," the attenuated formalism, which poststructuralism has rejected.[15] My writing of this chapter has been, at some level, an attempt to explain why—despite my expectations and despite all my ambivalences about Lévi-Strauss himself—*Tristes Tropiques* moves and impresses me. For all its imperfections and oversights, *Tristes Tropiques* directs our attention to issues of substance, issues that certain forms of poststructuralism do not invite us to contemplate. They are the same issues that stirred the crowd in the gymnasium at Barnard: the quality of life on Earth and the question of how humans can survive in partnership with it, "mastery" having proved a delusion. Lévi-Strauss may scant the truth about individual peoples as much as the other thinkers I have examined, but he makes the scantiness of that local truth both a central topic and the essential condition of his work.

Derrida criticizes *Tristes Tropiques* for its logical flaws; he disassembles it as though it were a machine. He hurts its essence. Derrida is right that Lévi-Strauss "rediscovers a gesture from the eighteenth century" in his "critique of ethnocentrism" which has "often the sole function of constituting the other as a model of original and natural goodness, of accusing and humiliating oneself" (*Of Grammatology*, 114). Lévi-Strauss can often be caught in the vacillating act of denying the Other as an ideal, and then reconstituting it as an ideal of sorts (see *Tristes Tropiques*, 285–92).[16] Derrida is also right that Lévi-Strauss employs an ethnocentric notion of writing ("lines" are not writing but "letters" are) and opposes writing as an instrument of domination and violence to an idealized, romantic "image of a community immediately present to itself in speech" (*Of Grammatology*, 136).[17] Derrida is right again in saying that Lévi-Strauss imposes "a strict separation of the anthropological confession and the theoretical discussion of the anthropologist" (117), even though *Tristes Tropiques* looks, at first, as though it will, precisely, bring these two things together.

But Derrida often misses the *motivation* for separating the personal and the theoretical, and he often misses the spirit of defiance in parts of *Tristes Tropiques*. Although Derrida is aware that Lévi-Strauss's thought "stands on a borderline: sometimes within an uncriticized conceptuality, sometimes putting a strain on the boundaries, and working towards deconstruction," his interpretation emphasizes the first ("theoretically naive") tendency to work "within an uncriticized conceptuality" (105). It is the emphasis necessary for Derrida to make most of his points against Lévi-Strauss. But in fact, Lévi-Strauss seems to anticipate much that Derrida will say about his theoretical limitations but to reject those limitations—willfully and with deliberation. One might say, as Derrida does, that he is "working towards deconstruction" or, with equal validity, that he has seen the possibilities deconstruction articulates and then has willfully looked beyond them. Lévi-Strauss does not care if his catlike book rests on contradiction and paradox, on an illusion of truth; that is what he wants. He says as much in portions of *Mythologiques*, when he asserts that it does not matter whether his mythic system is the product of *his* mind or of those of the peoples he studies (see *Naked Man*).

At times in his career, Lévi-Strauss and his explicators have been guilty of the typically Structuralist reduction of everything to diagrams and mathematical formulas (see, for example, "The Structural Study of Myth," chap. 11 in *Structural Anthropology*). If I downplay that important side of Lévi-Strauss's work, it is to assert something else, equally important, in *Tristes Tropiques*, a work we have had trouble reading sympathetically after Derrida. There is no pure state of nature, Lévi-Strauss says; all men have language, and language implies culture (390). There are more or less rudimentary cultures, but always cultures. For Lévi-Strauss as for Derrida, the binary opposition of nature and culture is a dead letter; all cultures

construct natures. He thus cannot find a "natural" society, an authentic primitive. When he thinks he has found it, among the Nambikwara, he loses sight of the group for the individuals (317). When
he thinks again that he has found it, among the Mundi, he is exhausted and cannot speak their language, so he cannot be sure he
has found it all. When he thinks again he has found it, among the
Tupi-Kawahib, he needs to persuade the group (tribe is too large a
word) to please stay with him for a week or two before joining civilization (they were on their way to a white settlement when he met
them). The structure deliberately signals the failure of the actual
quest, though validating the search via memory. The message is
both clear and obscure. The primitive, like some grail, recedes before the observer. It may not exist and probably does not—but it is
essential to act as though it does (392).

A quotation from Rousseau frequently repeated by Lévi-Strauss
makes just this point: the primitive state "no longer exists, has perhaps never existed, and probably will never exist," yet "it is never-
theless essential to form a correct notion [of it] in order rightly to
judge our present state" (316). As we have seen, Lévi-Strauss builds
on Rousseau's opinions to decide, with Rousseau, "that, after demolishing all forms of social organization, we can still discover the
principles which will allow us to construct a new form" (390). Yet
Tristes Tropiques has no illusions about success in reaching "correct
notions" or "constructing new forms." Lévi-Strauss maintains that
the essential truth is the truth that Buddhism articulated "2500
years ago," a truth similar, up to a certain point, to the assumptions
of deconstruction:

> Every effort to understand destroys the object studied in favour of
> another object of a different nature; this second object requires
> from us a new effort which destroys it in favour of a third, and so
> on and so forth until we reach the one lasting presence, the point
> at which the distinction between meaning and the absence of
> meaning disappears; the same point from which we began. (411)

But, and for Lévi-Strauss it is an important but, "the completed
stages do not destroy the validity of those that went before; they
confirm it" (412).[18] This is the point where Lévi-Strauss stops antic-
ipating the Derridean attack or, rather, defiantly remains open to it:
the point at which meaning and nonmeaning coalesce is not a void,
Lévi-Strauss insists; it is "a lasting presence." Lévi-Strauss's vulnerability to the kind of critique Derrida mounts against him is, absolutely, willed. "Nothing is settled; everything can still be altered.

What was done, but turned out wrong, can be done again" (393): that is the kind of pronouncement which made Lévi-Strauss a cultural hero in the late sixties and early seventies.[19] It all depends, he says, on what has been called his peculiar mix of Freudianism, Marxism, and Buddhism,[20] on "unhitching" from our own societies (and ultimately from all societies, including those we use to "unhitch" from our own) to get to that essence embodied in the lily and the cat. Keeping the spine clear of maggots; reducing the friction that breeds pus out of Western systems of communication. Resisting a commodified monoculture in favor of a varied, harmonious, mystical, maybe mythical, one. That is the true end of the journey in *Tristes Tropiques*, an end point for which the primitive is—as for the adventurers and all the transcendentally homeless—only a sign and a stopping place.

Gone Primitive

12

Physicality

ere is Malinowski, writing in what he imagined would be the privacy of his diary, in 1918, near the end of his field-work in New Guinea:

> At 5 went to Kaulaka. A pretty, finely built girl walked ahead of me. I watched the muscles of her back, her figure, her legs, and the beauty of the body so hidden to us, whites, fascinated me. Probably even with my own wife I'll never have the opportunity to observe the play of back muscles for as long as with this little animal. At moments I was sorry I was not a savage and could not possess this pretty girl. At Kaulaka, looked around, noting things to photograph. (255–56)[1]

The passage captures the multiple layers of repression Malinowski practiced almost every day he spent in the Trobriands. The recorded play of muscles in the young woman's back marks one of the rare moments when Malinowski was willing to use both his eyes and his imagination in a way that may be said to question his own hetero-sexual relations. The yearning gaze with which he envelops the young woman's body and the wistful realization that he will prob-ably never experience his wife's body so fully release an almost pal-pable longing. At the end of the passage, Malinowski takes refuge behind the camera eye, regaining some of his authority as an eth-nographer. But we should savor his unprofessional desires, which have here, momentarily, escaped his vigilance—desires that lead us back, once again, to the site of transcendental homelessness.

For Lukács, who first coined the term, transcendental homeless-ness is a form of absolute (though reversible) alienation from the self, from society, and (the source of all other alienations) from "im-manent totality"—a phrase that denotes the effortless awareness of meaning and purpose, the complete correspondence of personal de-sire and cosmos, the presence of secular grace.[2] The most basic form transcendental homelessness can take is discomfort with the most visible part of the self, the body.

At least three possibilities exist with regard to alienation from the body. Malinowski represents one possibility: learning to live with the fact of alienation, perhaps coming to repress the body as a matter of course and, ultimately, as a matter for pride. Margaret Mead, the other anthropologist I discuss in this chapter, represents a second possibility: protesting against alienation from the body and seeking other ways of relating to the bodily self. Examples of the relations to the body represented by Malinowski and Mead are easy to find in the history of Western primitivism. But much of that history has aspired to a third possibility: overcoming alienation from the body, restoring the body, and hence the self, to a relation of full and easy harmony with nature or the cosmos, as they have variously been conceived.

Within Western culture, the idiom "going primitive" is in fact congruent in many ways to the idiom "getting physical." Freudian theory can help us understand the illogical congruence between the two idioms, though it does not originate with Freud. As we have seen, Freud believed that civilization arose to protect humans from the uncontrolled imperatives of sexuality and aggression.[3] In return, it exacted the repression of sexuality and the control of aggressive impulses. The flip side of this theory was a widely shared, unexamined belief that "uncivilized" people—that is, primitives and certain marginal members of the lower classes—are exempt from the repression of sexuality and control of aggression.[4] On this point, Freudian theory tallies with Lukács's theory of transcendental homelessness. Transcendental homelessness is, for Lukács, the condition of modern societies; it was not, he believed, the condition of Greece in the Heroic Age, before the emergence of the modern state. Within the context of such thinking, "going primitive" and "getting physical" slide together.

Malinowski and Mead reveal their different relationships to the possibility of "getting physical" both in their writings and in the kinds of photographs they took and published of themselves with "their people." For Mead, such photographs are very easy to come by. She left some 50,000 photographs, many of which show her in her fieldwork, in close proximity to her subjects and, sometimes, dressed in local garb. For Malinowski, such photographs are considerably rarer, and no photograph I have seen shows him out of Western dress.[5] For Malinowski and Mead, as for their larger culture, "going primitive" seemed a shortcut to or shorthand for "getting physical" in fuller ways than modern civilization will allow. Mead enjoyed the possibility; Malinowski feared it. I want to probe the sources of that fear in Malinowski, though my target will not be the ethnographer himself, but rather the conceptions of controlled individualism and masculinity that we have seen in Conrad, Lawrence, and Freud—conceptions that made Malinowski love his own repression.

Looking at Malinowski

Malinowski's diary was found by his second wife after his sudden death from a heart attack in 1942. It was published in 1967. Had Malinowski suffered a lingering illness, we have every reason to think that he would have destroyed the diary rather than have risked publication.[6] It was found buried beneath other papers in his desk, at Yale,[7] a fact that tempts me to think it represented his hidden life—the "other" of both his domestic and professional selves.[8]

The *Diary* reveals how Malinowski's eyes and imagination threaten to betray him almost every moment he spent in the Trobriands. Accordingly, he usually treats both as the enemy. He habitually records in his diary the rebellions of his body—in illnesses and depressions, in listlessness and angers, above all in random lusts. He tries to quell his body and his inflamed imagination by doing Swedish gymnastics or by writing down what he calls "moral tenets." Repeatedly, in the *Diary*, he forsakes the reading of novels as an inflammatory source of pleasure that provokes sensual thoughts and a longing for bodily pleasure. To ignore novels will, he believes, make it easier to ignore the existence of bodies.

Malinowski desperately needs to ignore bodies. He tells himself as much, again and again, as he totes up his moral pluses and minuses:

> I sat around until 10:30, making up to Mrs. . . . . , who is not stupid, though quite uncultured. I fondled her and undressed her in my mind, and I calculated how long it would take me to get her to bed. Before then I had lecherous thoughts about. . . . In short, I betrayed [Elsie, his fiancée] in my mind. The moral aspect: I give myself a plus for not reading novels, and for concentrating better; a minus for mentally making love to the matron and for a return to lecherous thoughts. (109)

Or, an even better example:

> I must never let myself become aware of the fact that other women [other than his fiancée] have bodies, that they copulate. I also resolve to shun the line of least resistance in the matter of novels. (249)

Despite Malinowski's efforts, novels he has read and women he has seen or known torment him beneath the mosquito net at night, and he feels, and sometimes submits to, unspecified temptations, one assumes the urge to masturbate. He hates what he calls his characteristically depressed "Dostoevskian state" and the nightly torment under the mosquito net. But life lived against the body is a constant struggle for Malinowski—a struggle he conceives in heroic terms, and sometimes loses.

The need to forget bodies—his own included—is part and parcel of the kind of scientific objectivity Malinowski sought. It is the precondition of the fame he hoped to win once his fieldwork was behind him and he could reside in what he calls the world of "theory," rather than in the "atmosphere created by foreign [Trobriand] bodies" (163; "foreign bodies" appears in English in the Polish text). In fact, Malinowski's goal, as he frankly records it in his *Diary,* was to use this one bit of fieldwork as the basis for sociological theorizing but *to do fieldwork no more* (167). "The life of the natives," he admits, is "utterly devoid of interest or importance, something as remote from me as the life of a dog" (167). But he needs "to collect many documents" to further his ambitions in the university.

"Theory," as he will practice it in his writing and in his life as a professor, represents for Malinowski a high plateau, a place above lusts and temptations, a place of pure mind, above the body. His belief in theory was in no sense naïve; he knew, for example, that "experience in writing leads to entirely different results even if the observer remains the same—let alone if there are different observers" (114). He concludes from the gap between experience and writing, or one observer and another, that "we cannot speak of objectively existing facts; theory creates facts" (114).[9] "Theory" was, then, not absolute and invariable, but a product of the will and a source of empowerment. "Theory" is the equivalent, in the intellectual world, of moral tenets in the life of the body: both attempt to discipline and control phenomena. For Malinowski, "theory" often works better than "moral tenets" because it deals with observations and "facts," not with intractable bodies; as Malinowski agonizingly knew, the stray observation of muscles playing along a back could undo his resolutions, unnerve and cast him back into the world of contingent physicality.

Malinowski wanted his observation of Trobriand bodies in books like *Argonauts of the Western Pacific* and *The Sexual Life of Savages* to be purged of what he calls "elements of worry"—about his body, about his fiancée's, about his fellow expatriates' wives', about the "native" girl's, about various combinations of these (175). Only then would he have a sense of what he calls "the ultimate mastery of things" (175; his phrase, in English, in the mostly Polish original). This "ultimate mastery," achieved through theoretical or "pure" ethnographic writing, will, presumably, move him beyond and compensate for the loss of the muscles playing along the young woman's back. It will reproduce or approximate, in narrow terms of personal intellectual power, a feeling of being completely in control, completely in harmony.

The record of Malinowski's life that the *Diary* provides is mostly one of petty miseries, but it includes moments of sublimity, usually connected to the landscape.[10] Occasionally, Malinowski enjoys the feeling of "letting myself dissolve into the landscape" or the feeling of "moments when you merge with objective reality . . . true nirvana" (73, 120). These feelings seem both analogous to and at odds with his drive to "mastery" and love of abstract theory. Since Malinowski believed that theory *creates* what we call "objective reality," to occupy the theoretical perspective is in some way analogous to "merging with objective reality, true nirvana." It is to get beyond the quotidian and experience the essential. But as Malinowski conceives "theory" in the *Diary*, the forms of totalizing thought it represents are also, paradoxically, a safeguard *against* feelings of merging with the physical world and the surest way to achieve something essentially different from "merging"—that is, professional reputation, the amplified knowledge of the "I."

Between himself and the bodies of the Trobrianders, between himself and the nirvana of merging with the landscape, Malinowski interposes his ethnographic writing and its prerequisites—photographs and theorizing. All are the means of objectifying his feelings, of converting feelings into magisterial observation guided by pure, untainted theory. The Malinowski of the published ethnographies surveys the world with cool authority; it is his home, his oyster, cradling pearls of wisdom. The Malinowski of the *Diary* understands fully the universe of transcendental homelessness—and the furious desire for the primitive it helps to produce.

The *Diary* makes it clear that looking at "natives" was a double act for Malinowski: the scientific act he claims in *The Sexual Life of Savages*, which cannot, he insists, "be pornographic"; and the personal act—replete with longing—that left him night after night in moral agony beneath the mosquito net. The openness of these possibilities, the way that one always existed, hidden, behind the other—two parts of an incomplete whole—intrigued me as I wrote this book.[11] It confirmed my decision to include here a fantasy about Malinowski's body that I originally wrote as a warm-up exercise, to free my prose at a point when it had become strained. The image became a focal point for my meditation on how the West conceives and uses the primitive, a metaphor and symbol of our culture's often fearful yet longing relationship to it. Here, then, is Malinowski's body as I see it in my mind's eye—an image of Western repression of the physicality we see in the primitive, an image that expresses fear of the body and contradictory desires both to preserve and violate its boundaries.

Malinowski's Body

Malinowski's body looks like Lord Jim's. It's cased rigidly in white or beige trousers and shirt, sometimes, but not for long, stained a muddy brown. When this happens, Malinowski summons his servants and has the clothes washed, immediately. For his clothes somehow seem to him an important part of his body, not just a covering for it.

It's a small body, well-fed, but not kindly disposed enough toward itself to put on flesh. It has a narrow chest—pale, with just a few stray hairs and no nipples to speak of. It has thin legs yearning for massive thighs; in fact, if this man does put on weight in later life (and he may) it will begin in his thighs first. The buttocks lie flat, unwelcoming, with maybe a stray pimple. The penis is a center of anxiety for him but is in fact no smaller—and no bigger—than anyone else's. It's one of the few points of identification he can settle on between his body and theirs.

Their bodies—almost naked—unnerve him. His body needs its clothes, his head, its hat. He rarely looks at his body—except when washing it. But he has to look at theirs. The dislike he sometimes feels for the natives comes over him especially when in the presence of their bodies. "Come in and bathe," the natives say from their ponds and rivers. "No thanks," says Malinowski, retrieving the pith helmet and camera he had momentarily laid aside on the grass. He looks at their bodies and makes notes about size, ornamentation, haircuts, and other ethnographic data. He takes photographs. He talks to them about customs, trade, housing, sex. He feels okay about the customs, trade, and housing, but the sex makes him uneasy.

Malinowski has managed to fall in love with an Australian woman, E.R.M. (Elsie), for whom he feels (as he writes in his journal) "a deep passion—based on a spiritual attachment." "Her body" he says, "is like a sacrament of love." His feelings for other women enter his mind (and his loins!) when he's written or thought words like these about his Intended. In his journal he calls these feelings "lechery"; yet he regrets that "Vsich nye per-eyebiosh!" (Russian for "You'll never fuck them all!"). The truth is that despair over never being able to fuck them all has created a peculiar state of mind for Malinowski. Since he can't fuck them all, he may never really fuck any of them. Perhaps not even the sacramental body of the woman from Australia. After all, he wonders, would she understand if he asked her to do it as the natives do, no one on top, no guilt or shame. What would he do if she didn't understand? Even worse, what would he do if she did?

So Malinowski worries about his body and tries to pretend it's not there, that it's just the casing for his intellect. He's not sure it's going to work. So far, he's been reading Conrad and modeling himself on this hero, a fellow Pole exiled in a British world, traveling (in the flesh, in the mind) to exotic places. He tries to pretend he's in a womanless world, like the world of Conrad's novels. And he clings, must cling, to the belief that he knows what "one of us" means, that he is "one of us," like Jim and Marlow. It's been his firm belief that the natives are themselves and he's himself, that they and the landscape exist "out there" to be photographed and observed—that identities have the certainty of Conrad's "us and them." How can he achieve "the ultimate mastery of things" unless he can keep things separate, keep things arranged in levels, with himself at the top? That's why he's bothered by the similarities between the natives' bodies and his body and worries about the similarities of their desires. That's why he needs to articulate and adhere to "moral tenets."

Given his need for us to be us and them to be them, given his dislike for the place in which he finds himself, he has trouble understanding why reading Frazer's The Golden Bough *ever led to his coming to Australia and then to the Trobriands. Someone stranded in the Trobriands should love—more than he even* *wants to—the physical world and the world of bodies he sees everywhere he looks. But of course there's a connection he's been forgetting between the place he finds himself and the needs of his body. He read Frazer during a period of utter rest that his German doctors recommended; his body, unhealthy beggar, made him need a break from work, a change of pace. Later, remembering Frazer and the interest in the primitive Frazer aroused in him, Malinowski chose Australia as the base for his first fieldwork. It was as random as Conrad's sticking a pin in a map and choosing the Congo; and as fateful. Now he's running out of the novels he brought with him—has finished* Vanity Fair *and* The Count of Monte Cristo, *and all the others. And the damn war is keeping him (a German national) in Australia, and hence in the Trobriands, much longer than he intended. In fact, he hates to say it outside of his diary, but he feels "dislike" for the natives ("the niggers" he calls them) and "a longing for civilization." In certain moods his "feelings towards the natives are definitely tending towards 'Exterminate the brutes'"—and he's not sure when he might begin to write such words unironically. Unable to return, trapped in the Trobriands like he's trapped in his body, Malinowski does the next best thing. He's exhausted* Heart of Darkness *and* Lord Jim. *So he orders* The Secret Agent *from Brisbane and wonders whether his Australian fiancée might enjoy reading it too.* *

What I've written about Malinowski's body takes some facts from his life and embroiders upon them: Malinowski really did have advanced degrees in physics, did become interested in primitive societies by reading Frazer, did find himself in Australia at the outbreak of World War I, did bring with him to the Trobriands most of the novels I mention, and did write all the words quoted (except the few in the scene by the river) in his journal. Having invented Malinowski's body from a medley of facts and impressions, I want to stay close to it a little longer.

Imagine that we have before us some actual photos of Malinowski—one from later life, when he was well-known as a founder of modern British ethnography; one from his earlier years in the

---

* In *The Secret Agent*, the wife, Winnie, murders her husband with a meat knife. The novel then juxtaposes her irrational terror of being hanged with a mathematical measure of what being hanged means: "the drop given was fourteen feet."

All material in quotation marks, except the brief comments about bathing in the river, are from Malinowski's journal.

Trobriands. A curious relationship would always exist between the two photos. The satisfactions displayed on the face of the older man, famous now, acclaimed and widely read, would depend on the work done by the younger man, more insecure and troubled. Once he had spent two years there, Malinowski and everyone else thought of the Trobriands as *his* place, *his* inch of ground from which to survey human nature and human culture. He had succeeded in leaving fieldwork and "the atmosphere created by foreign bodies" to breathe the pure air of sociological theory in the university. But his source of authority always remained his work in the Trobriands. This territoriality, a kind of intellectual imperialism, chronically exists in ethnography.[12] Malinowski's authority to speak, his basis for generalization, depended always on his youthful experiences with the Trobrianders, experiences his journals reveal as haunted by lusts, dislikes, and prejudices which he routinely (and perhaps to his credit) tried to filter out of what he wrote for publication. The Trobriands would change, and Malinowski would too. But his authority for theorizing would depend on the pretense that nothing had changed, that the scientist and thinker could reach back into his fieldwork, at will, for an observation to illuminate whatever problem of social life he later addressed.

Malinowski never would escape from the Trobriands—a fact that the *Diary* made manifest, once and for all. He exists there as though preserved in time, in a photograph that never fades and never changes. Unlike many other anthropologists, Malinowski did not routinely publish photographs of himself, either alone or with "his people." He would not have liked for others to consider him an anthropological exhibit, just the man who marshals anthropological exhibits for the inspection of others, just the man who abstracts from the lived experience to the universal truth. It is of the essence in this book that we reverse the ethnographer's traditional gaze and look inward toward the ethnographic authority, not just out at the primitive Other—that we use our eyes and imaginations to make Malinowski an anthropological exhibit as pointed and meaningful as any other.

Looking at Margaret Mead

In a recent edition of *Coming of Age in Samoa*, the first and still the best known of Margaret Mead's more than ten books, an inserted envelope invites the reader to continue Mead's work by contributing to the Museum of Natural History's Margaret Mead Memorial Fund for the Advancement of Anthropology. The hook into this plea for cash is a photo of Mead, the grandmotherly woman I always see in my mind's eye (not the young woman who went to Samoa), peering intently through her glasses at what seem to be a young Balinese mother and her child (fig. 12.1).[13] It was taken in the late fifties, when Mead revisited the sites of her early research after an absence of many years. And it resembles many photographs of Mead in the physical proximity of the ethnographer to her subjects.[14]

Repeatedly in this study, my account of primitivism has led to criticism of masculinity as it has been conceived and enacted in our culture. Often, those most committed to the masculine ethos— Stanley, Burroughs, Leiris, Conrad, Lawrence, Freud, Malinowski— have provided the basis for my critique, as the lure of the primitive turned out to be something that escaped the confines of masculine identity as we know it. The figures I have studied have been male, and this may be inevitable in any account of the main lines of primitivism in the West.[15] But in search of alternative primitivisms, and increasingly interested in photographs of ethnographers with what we usually call "their people," I turned near the end of my study to Margaret Mead. Specifically, I hoped to find her different from Malinowski—with her proximity and alert attention to "foreign bodies" a sign and a symbol of the difference. My hope was both encouraged and disappointed by what I found.

Like Freud and others who journey to primitive societies in fact or via the imagination, Mead went to Samoa to study a problem she felt was too big to grasp at home in a "complex" society like that of the United States; in her case, it was the nature of female adolescence. Boas suggested the problem to her. But she defined its contours and wrote about a "woman's issue" from a woman's point of view. Unlike the male anthropologist (confined to the men's house), she had full access to women's and children's lives and had a primary interest in them. Malinowski had no female confidantes; Mead had many. Hence, in her work the concerns of child rearing and sexuality are presented from female points of view both in the collected data and in the written ethnography. The gender specificity of the information from which these ethnographers worked often could not be helped: in the societies they studied, women anthropologists had to work among women, men among men. But the attitude that motivated Mead is very different from Malinowski's and may be a significant sign of gender differences in their work. Unlike

Fig. 12.1. Peering intently through her glasses, Mead in Bali (1957–58).
Courtesy of Ken Heyman.

Malinowski, Mead did not try to avoid the body; she believed that "through the body, the ways of the body are learned" (*Male and Female*, 77). And she probed every ripple along every back rather than avert her eye or take refuge in the supposed objectivity of the camera eye.

Throughout her career, Mead believed that one of the foremost values of anthropology was to teach us about alternative relations that men and women can establish to their minds and bodies. *Coming of Age in Samoa* treated childhood and adolescence; later work, like *Male and Female* (1949; revised 1967), would cover the entire span of life. *Male and Female* compiles examples of different modes of gender definition in childhood and adolescence, sexual life, child rearing, and the relationship between generations, and then counterpoints what Mead had found abroad with what then existed in the United States. Both *Coming of Age in Samoa* and *Male and Female* sometimes appear to have a radical agenda connected to Mead's ideas about freeing bodies and accepting all forms of sexuality. In the charts that accompany *Coming of Age*, for example, Samoan girls' homosexual experience is recorded along with their heterosexual experience. The charts show that homosexual pairings—

as well as heterosexual—were quite common for Samoan girls. It is important to note, though, that the charts appear in an appendix, and that the text itself makes no mention of lesbian relations: in 1928, Mead, perhaps prudently, avoided any explicit reference to what was then an unmentionable topic.[16]

When, in later life, Mead wrote more directly on homosexuality, she suggests, ambiguously, that "homosexuality is . . . a possibility latent in many children that will never be fully expressed if it is not given social recognition" (*Male and Female*, 107); she repeatedly endorses the goal of making "men and women . . . feel at home with their own bodies, and at home with their own sex and with the opposite sex" (142). Yet in later years, as in 1928, she stops short of explicitly writing against homophobia, and uses terms (like Ellis's term "inversion") that suggest unaccepting views of homosexuality.

Reading Mead, one consistently feels on the verge of new values whose time has not yet come, values at odds with the vocabulary she chooses to use. Mead's reticence on homosexuality matches, for example, her acceptance of essentially Freudian models of female development and matters such as female orgasm. Despite her clear feminist sympathies, Mead, as a good Freudian, refers to the clitoris as a "vestigial phallus" (*Male and Female*, 144). By 1967, when she revised *Male and Female*, this term—like the term "inversion"— had lost currency and any "scientific" basis. Mead wanted to break through certain conventional Western notions and was more willing to entertain unconventional ideas in her published work than Malinowski was. But a curtain of reticence or unwillingness always descends for Mead and prevents her from pressing statements as far as she may have wished to do.

Remembering Mead's own history—shadowed by rumors of bisexuality, and of affairs with Ruth Benedict and others—I think here of another photo of Mead, from her early days in Samoa, in which Mead poses, in a way that seems homoerotic, with a Samoan woman (see fig. 12.2). Did Mead evade what was for her a deeply personal and important topic? The published evidence in the autobiography and standard Howard biography makes it difficult to know. *Blackberry Winter* is a masterpiece of evasion, hiding even the fact of Mead's first marriage;[17] Howard's biography does better but talks around Mead's relationships with women. Among the biographers, only Mead's daughter, Catherine Bateson, openly mentions her mother's love relationships with women.[18] In the sixties and seventies, Mead was popularly thought of as a mother of the sexual revolution. She wrote columns for *Redbook* on subjects like "Bisexual-

Fig. 12.2. A toga party, Samoan style (1928). "Mead with Native Woman in Native Costume, standing in Bushes and Trees." Courtesy the Library of Congress and the Institute for Intercultural Studies, Inc., New York.

ity—What's It All About?" and asserted, ahead of her time, that gender identification is largely a matter of cultural conditioning. *Coming of Age in Samoa* and *Male and Female* both advocate joyous choosing. The freedom to choose homosexuality or bisexuality may have been something she wanted us to read into her writing, though it would not have been prudent (even in the late seventies at the time of her death) to write it into her work more explicitly.

The gaze in Mead's photo thus seems at times to differ from the gaze we have probed in Malinowski and Freud, Leiris and Conrad, Lawrence and Bataille. The gender of the gazer is different, and what she sees is different too. She sees women and children in a woman's way, conceives of them as something separate and complete, as something more than the companions of men; in turn, she is willing to acknowledge that "masculinity" can take different forms under different cultural conditions and within the same culture, and is hence more generous to men than male writers often were to women.[19]

At many points in her work, Mead in fact seems to anticipate themes that have become major in contemporary feminism and in recent revisions of Freudian theory. It is very tempting to think that, had she been born into a later generation, she would have found within contemporary women's studies forms of institutional support to sharpen certain impulses that remain blunted in her work. In *Male and Female*, for example, she maintains the importance of relations between mother and child, especially during the time of breast-feeding, as a key to individual development and cultural norms for interpersonal relations. Her work here anticipates Chodorow's work on mothering, Stern's emphasis on intersubjective relations as prefigured in the nursing couple, and Sagan's attacks on Freud for minimizing the female role in the formation of a moral sense; her work might, in turn, have been furthered by them. Mead speculates that male and female children *may* experience life differently, from birth forward, based on their different anatomies; but she is *sure* that cultural factors in childhood make the ultimate difference in what is considered "male" and what "female."

At times, Mead pinpoints, rather precisely, what the postmodern West seems to want most from the primitive: a model of alternative social organization in which psychological integrity is a birthright, rooted in one's body and sexuality, and in which a full range of ambivalences and doubts can be confronted and defused through the culture's rituals, customs, and play. When Stanley Diamond examined the impetus behind what he calls the West's "search for the

primitive," he reached some of the same conclusions: alienating sta-
tist structures produce the need to find (and emulate) prestate structures, primitive structures, in which work is varied and unalienat-
ing, ambivalence is given full play, and the passage of time assures a
satisfactory entry into maleness or femaleness, as the case may be.
Mead's search for the primitive led to similar beliefs, and, in *Male
and Female*, she urges Americans to conclude, from the diverse
structures found in primitive societies, that American society has
evolved its middle-class notions of sexual conduct too narrowly.

It would be reasonable to criticize Mead for her popularized version of the primitive, a version she re-created over and over again,
years after her active fieldwork. The anthropological establishment
was frequently suspicious of Mead in her lifetime, dismissing her as
a "lightweight" anthropologist, though it rallied around her, in surprisingly positive ways, when Derek Freeman attacked her work in
the early eighties, shortly after Mead died.[20] Certainly, since many
of Mead's generalizations about American society no longer seem
true, what she says about primitive societies seems dubious as well.

But in her popularizing use of primitive societies to comment on
life in the United States, Mead grasped an essential point: whether
"Manu" or "Samoa" or "Bali" ever existed or existed any longer as
she portrayed them mattered less, in a way, than the messages they
conveyed to American society now. "The primitive" could be used
as a source of social and political power—it was repeatedly used in
that way by men—and Mead seized it to further her own ends and
those of causes in which she believed. It is, finally, not only those
who live with primitives who shape themselves against the primitive Other. That shaping occurs for each of us, ethnographer and
non-ethnographer alike. Mead was more honest and, therefore, more
vulnerable than many of her colleagues: she clearly and frankly prescribed for the present and the future on the basis of what she had
learned from societies that supposedly live in the "past." Somebody
would do it—men did it all the time. Why, then, shouldn't she?

But the more one looks at Margaret Mead, the less comfortable it
becomes to oppose *her* relationship to the primitive to that of men
in our culture. The photograph of Mead in Bali with which I began
can lead not just to positive views of Mead, but also to some highly
critical ones. It appears in an edition of *Coming of Age in Samoa*
published after her death by the American Museum of Natural History; yet it shows Mead in Bali, not Samoa. The photograph is thus,
unwittingly I suspect, a monument to the "grab-bag" essentialist

primitive, erected, ironically, by the American Museum of Natural History, which chose this photograph to accompany this edition.

Mead herself deserves some of the same criticisms I have made of Malinowski. She spent, for example, only nine months in Samoa—not a long time, though she claims in a preface that it was enough to get to know a "simple, uncomplex" (her words) culture of this kind.[21] Mead presents herself in *Coming of Age* as living fully among the people she studied. But, we learn in her biography, she (like Malinowski) lived with fellow whites in a Western-style house.[22] And she never fully mingled with the Samoans or with the other peoples she studied. Like some character from Henry James's novels, she never, for example, even on later visits, ate with Samoans, thinking that would be at odds with her dignity as a white woman. In fact, later in her life, she repeatedly warned a young assistant of the need to "keep up white prestige" (Howard, *Mead*, 305).

The entire trajectory of Mead's career testifies to her ability to capitalize on her work among primitive peoples. Like Leiris, Malinowski, Schneebaum, and others, Mead used the primitive for purposes of her own—research, fund-raising, fame, the advocacy of specific goals in the West. Her career testifies to and advances the inexplicable, irrational connections often made covertly between gender, race, and versions of the primitive. Throughout her life, her work in Samoa and New Guinea seemed to Americans to qualify her—quite absurdly when we examine the premise—to pronounce on issues like child rearing, feminism, and civil rights. The record of her pronouncements—in, for example, her "rap on race" with James Baldwin—is often less than cheering. We can find Mead referring routinely to male graduate students as "men" and females at the same stage of professional life as "girls." We can find her, in her conversations with Baldwin, egregiously implying that race prejudice has a "natural" basis in a human preference for light over darkness and that white people look like angels and angels like whites (*Rap on Race*, 31).[23] In her status as what Jane Howard calls an "elder statescreature," Mead could be as embarrassing for liberal and radical causes as she could be (at other moments) inspiring. She was a complicated case, with her final "meaning" impossible to decide, an award of merit impossible to give.

Mead is a classic example of a woman who succeeded largely by virtue of having internalized her culture's dominant and therefore masculine values and attitudes.[24] Mead was a feminist and yet (in her acceptance of Freudian views of women) not a feminist, a radical, and yet not so radical after all, someone who wrote and thought like what her culture called a woman—but also like a man. Mead marks a half-way point, but no more than that, between the figures I have studied and some other relationship to primitive societies or the idea of the primitive that would be fundamentally different. It is not easy to identify in any simple way either "good guys" or "bad guys" in the history of Western primitivism.

Epilogue
Past, Present, and Future

The anthropologist ages but remains tied, always, to the experience of youth, immortalized in a classic text of anthropology. Unlike the face and body of the anthropologist, this classic text—Malinowski's *Argonauts of the Western Pacific,* Mead's *Coming of Age in Samoa*—can never change, since anthropologists resist revision as a process that might falsify original observations. Prefaces and afterwords can be added, but the text itself must remain unaltered. As the conventions of ethnographic writing demand, Mead and Malinowski write in the present tense about cultures receding into the past. The present tense also seems to deny change, to enforce the ethnographer's wish that things stand still long enough to be studied.[1] In a way, the convention is yet another version of the persistent Western tendency to deny a plenitude of time and time-layers to the primitive.

But there is more at stake here than a colonialist denial of the complexity of primitive societies or a nostalgia for the lost simplicity of the past—two motives commonly attributed to anthropological writing and to the idea that primitive societies lack a history.[2] For all of the writers I have discussed—Conrad and Lawrence, Freud and Lévi-Strauss, the Blairs and Schneebaum, Burroughs and Fry—primitive societies or the general idea of the primitive becomes a place to project feelings about the present and to draw blueprints of the future. Sometimes narratives about primitive societies become allegories of modernization that resist seeing themselves or presenting themselves as allegories. The allegories have some basis in the history of primitive societies in the twentieth century. Primitives have been subjected to the advent of Western economic and other value systems; they have been forced to undergo, often in a single generation, processes that took hundreds of years in the West. They are an acute "test case" for processes we are all undergoing. We record their "native" traditions under the pressure of ours. But maybe what we are really doing—though we cannot admit it for a number

244

of reasons—is handling, by displacement, the series of dislocations that we call modernity and postmodernity—handling it by studying places where, supposedly, it does not exist and yet does exist, for instance, in the person of the anthropologist. In the fears and hopes we express for them, the primitives, we air fears and hopes for ourselves—caught on a rollercoaster of change that we like to believe can be stopped, safely, at will.

The primitive has traditionally (by a sleight of mind) been viewed as our beginnings, persisting into the present. But it suggests to us not only beginnings, but endings—desired endings, feared endings. It is no accident that the narratives collected by anthropologists like Lévi-Strauss or linguists like Chenevière often tell creation stories or stories of apocalypse. Our interest in the primitive meshes thoroughly, in ways we have only begun to understand, with our passion for clearly marked and definable beginnings and endings that will make what comes between them coherent narrations.[3] A significant motivation for primitivism in modernism, and perhaps especially in postmodernism, is a new version of the idyllic, utopian primitive: the wish for "being physical" to be coextensive with "being spiritual"; the wish for physical, psychological, and social integrity as a birthright, within familial and cultural traditions that both connect to the past and allow for a changing future; the wish for a view of human relationships as infinitely varied, stretching back into the past and able by inference to adapt to whatever series of cataclysms or boredoms may lie ahead. But we cannot capture these goals by projections onto the primitive or by any of the other routes we have taken thus far.

I began this study with ethnographers and then ranged widely afield, demonstrating two alternating and yet complementary pulsations in our century's involvement with primitive societies and with the idea of the primitive: a rhetoric of control, in which demeaning colonialist tropes get modified only slightly over time; and a rhetoric of desire, ultimately more interesting, which implicates "us" in the "them" we try to conceive as the Other. I returned in the last chapter to the ethnographers, with a sense that their lives, so closely tied for a narrow shaft of time to primitive societies and yet unfolding from that narrow shaft, are an image of all our involvements with the primitive in its full range of meanings.

Primitive societies seem to be so small a part of modernity and postmodernity, to be so distant from our everyday lives—in terms of our omnipresent technologies, to be their virtual antithesis. Yet allusions to them are built into the fashions and styles we live with and into the ways we think about ourselves. The primitive is in our museums and homes, in our closets and jewelry boxes, in our hearts and minds. The primitive is everywhere present in modernity and postmodernity, as impetus or subtext, just as modernity or postmodernity forms the subtext of much ethnological writing and thinking. Interest in the primitive cuts across levels of culture—from the high to the low and vice versa—with the gap between the statements made by "low" culture and those made by "high" culture narrower than we might intuitively expect. A voyeuristic interest in the primitive surrounds us in what we see and hear, what we learn and read, from the cradle to the grave: it is part of our atmosphere, of the culture we live and breathe. We have no need to "go primitive" because we have already "gone primitive" by the fact of being born into our culture. We are all like the writers and thinkers I have studied, imagining "them" in order to imagine "us"—savage intellects leading modern lives.

And yet, as I suggested in chapter 1, this distinction between "us" and "them" is becoming ever more tenuous in the postmodern world. More, as many of my chapters have suggested, something in "us" habitually resists seeing "them" as alien—whether because we project our own concerns onto them, or have oceanic aspirations, or a faith in a universal human nature, or some combination of these factors. Western desires for the primitive have not waned as primitive societies have modified or been forced to modify traditional ways of life. But those desires have become more and more unambiguously tinged with nostalgia as primitive societies ceased to present obstacles to the spread of Western values. The West seems to need the primitive as a precondition and a supplement to its sense of self: it always creates heightened versions of the primitive as nightmare or pleasant dream. The question of whether that need must or will always take fearful or exploitative forms remains pressing.

Throughout this study, I have given hints of more positive forms of Western primitivism lurking behind the forms I have criticized: the potential to reject hierarchies in the original Tarzan story; the possibility of using African aesthetics to rethink the West's systems of art production and circulation; a desire to acknowledge and accept the full range of human sexual possibilities and variations in belief; the intuition that social classes or gender relations have doomed us to structures of mastery rather than mutuality; a reaching out to the natural world as our home and mother, not the exploitation of that world for profit. Each of these possibilities exists within certain forms of primitivism I have examined, though they are, in each case, variously turned aside or undeveloped, often under the pressure of our culture's dominant ideas of selfhood or masculinity.

Western primitivism might have had a different history—a history in which primitive societies were allowed to exist in their own times and spaces, within their own *conceptions of* time and space, not transposed and filtered into Western terms; a history in which primitive societies were allowed to exist in all their multiplicity, not reduced to a seamless Western fantasy; a history in which primitive societies were acknowledged as full and valid alternatives to Western cultures.[4] It may not be too late to bring that history into being. Some disciplines, like ethnography, have begun to explore "dialogic" models as a way of providing the Other a full voice and allowing the mutuality that informs the ethnographic relationship expression in writing.[5] Such first steps are important, though perhaps also largely symbolic. For the telling of alternative stories may open alternative possibilities should—this year or the next—a new and previously unknown people be, miraculously, "discovered."

More concretely, alternative stories can help us rethink political attitudes toward third world nations and their aspirations, attitudes which have been shaped, in part, by confusing *third world* with *primitive,* or by bringing to our relations with nations outside the West attitudes that are demeaningly neocolonial. In a speech during the 1988 U.S. presidential campaign, the soon-to-be-victorious George Bush criticized his opponent Michael Dukakis for thinking that the United States was a country "on the U.N. roll call somewhere between Albania and Zimbabwe."[6] When that kind of statement can make no political points, when the majority of Euro-Americans can accept that our nations—for all their present comforts and power—exist on the same plane with other social or political entities, we will have come a long way toward overcoming the heritage that the West's conceptions of the primitive have left us.

Alternative visions of primitive peoples and of the primitive more generally may depend on an openness to alternative conceptions of knowledge and social reality. It may also depend on using more creatively—probing with our eyes and imaginations—our own traditions rather than inventing a heightened (whether for better or worse) primitive as the screen upon which we project our deepest fears and strongest desires. We have clouded that screen with images much like our own; the task now may be to trace alternative patterns in Western history that will do for us what we have wanted primitive societies to do—to do, even as we helped destroy them: to tell us how to live better, to tell us what it means to be human, to be male or female, to be alive and looking for peace, or to accept death and whatever follows it. This task will require clearing away a lot of traditional notions, debunking a lot of well-known figures in our culture to allow new figures and new patterns to emerge.

The present study has traced, in essence, a male-centered, canonical line of Western primitivism—without question the "major" line in all the senses in which we currently use that term—and has discussed a broad array of intellectual figures. But I can imagine alternative lines of primitivism that would, necessarily, be based on an entirely different selection of texts. Some of those texts would be produced by women; many (whether by men or women) would probe alternative versions of knowledge and social order, including many marginalized in the West. A study of these alternative traditions might produce rather different results.[7] And it might provide an image for my mind's eye different in its implications from those of Malinowski's body: an image that would free us to experience the play of the muscles in our backs and a feeling of harmony with the external world in our own terms—not terms forcibly borrowed from primitive societies or grafted upon the primitive as it has been imagined within the contexts of modern life.

Notes

Chapter 1

1. The best-known expression of the idea of the "noble savage" is in Rousseau's "A Discourse on the Origin of Inequality." Montaigne's classic essay "Of the Cannibals" plays off his favorable impressions of Africans against French ethnocentrism, using cannibalism as a test case. Among his points is that eating men is no more "barbarous" than certain Western practices, such as torture. Hammond and Jablow discuss the eighteenth- and nineteenth-century obsession with cannibalism, concluding that "whites were far more addicted to tales of cannibalism than the Africans ever were to cannibalism. Its prevalence was taken for granted" (*Myth of Africa*, 94). For other views on cannibalism, see note 47 in this chapter.

2. *La mentalité primitive* by Lucien Lévy-Bruhl was first published in 1910; it advanced the idea of the primitive mentality as prerational. *The Mind of Primitive Man* by Franz Boas was first published in 1911 and rebutted Lévy-Bruhl's theories as well as evolutionist perspectives more generally, claiming that primitive language, speech, music, and social customs have great complexity, though, being different, are likely to be misunderstood by Western observers. Other published work from 1911 (on Indian languages and U.S. immigration) expanded the antiracist implications of his findings. I worked with the 1938 revised edition of *Mind of Primitive Man*, in which Boas addressed direct attacks on his book by proponents of racial superiority and wrote with the contexts of Nazi racism and U.S. mistreatment of African-Americans in mind; this edition, reissued in 1963, assumed a special resonance in light of the civil rights movement. *La pensée sauvage* by Claude Lévi-Strauss was first published in 1962 and continued the line of thought begun in the late fifties in *Structural Anthropology*; like Boas and other important anthropologists, such as A. L. Kroeber, Lévi-Strauss argued that savages think ontologically, though in different terms than Westerners. In this country, his work is most often associated with the idea that thinking among primitives is complex, and frequently cited in this connection.

Taken together, the three instances prove two points: first, that Westerners resisted the rebuttal of racial superiority possible through study of primitives, so that Boas's ideas needed to be repeated in 1938 and 1963, and supported by Lévi-Strauss's work, before being generally accepted; second, that even the work of Boas and Lévi-Strauss could use a misleading universal "the" in titles.

3. *Studies of Savages and Sex* by Ernest Crawley was originally published in 1929; Crawley studies primitives in order to illuminate Western chastity customs. *The Sexual Life of Savages* by Bronislaw Malinowski was first published in 1929 and is extensively discussed below. It has been criticized within anthropology, and the limitations of its functionalist approach much debated, but it remains an important formative work.

Coming of Age in Samoa by Margaret Mead (originally published in 1928) is one of the best known of anthropological texts. It recently became a center of controversy after Freeman's *Margaret Mead and Samoa* reversed many of Mead's findings (claiming, for example, that rape and other forms of violence are quite common in Samoa). Generally, Mead's reputation (always tainted by her popularizing work) has survived Freeman's attack, which was seen as bad form and bad anthropology by the profession.

4. These dates of reissue are typical for books on primitives. Interest in the topic (and hence publication or reissuing of books) peaks in the twenties, sixties, and eighties.

5. The distinction I am making between Boasian historical ethnography and the more scientific models advanced by functionalist ethnography is, by necessity, a simplification of lines of influence, though one sanctioned by many experts (see, for example, Stocking, "Introduction," 16–17). Malinowski's functionalist approach is associated with, among others, Radcliffe-Brown and Evans-Pritchard. Boas's theories and methods widely influenced American anthropologists such as A. L. Kroeber, R. H. Lowrie, Ruth Benedict, and Margaret Mead; his work in linguistics was also highly influential.

Boas was not hostile to science (and indeed used compilations of measurements in his work), nor was he hostile to psychoanalysis. But his approach emphasized historical explanations and a range of historically controlled variants rather than an exemplary "average type" as the basis for generalization (Stocking, "Introduction," 3). His sense of the limits of psychoanalysis's usefulness to ethnography was similarly controlled by his belief in "the unique character of historical growth in each area" (Boas, *Race, Language, Culture,* 287). While not denying the validity of psychoanalysis, he thought it became overextended when applied to "the activities of man living under different social forms" (288).

Ethnographers much influenced by Boas and sometimes described as in his "school" (including, most famously, Mead) would, however, be influenced also by Freud. The crisscrossing of lines is indicated by Reo Fortune's complaint to Malinowski that "he was not favorably impressed by the Benedict-Bateson-Mead huddle in pseudo-psychological method" (quoted in Howard, *Mead,* 202). Fortune, one should note, was Mead's second husband, Gregory Bateson her third.

6. The inclusion of miscellaneous myths and magic formulas occurs both in *The Sexual Life of Savages* and, even more notably, in *Argonauts of the Western Pacific*. The direct reporting of materials the ethnographer has been told by informants but does not understand anticipates recent tendencies within ethnography to allow the informant to shape the ethnography and to have a direct, "polyphonic" voice within it (Clifford, *Predicament of Culture*, chap. 1). For recent ethnographies using varieties of the polyphonic method, see Shostak, *Nisa*; Rabinow, *Fieldwork in Morocco*; Rosaldo, *Ilongot Headhunting*; and Crapanzano, *Tuhami*. The technique as used in these volumes is not problem free. And it has a long pedigree. For example, Boas's early work included the verbatim transcription of folktales, with a minimum of scholarly apparatus, a technique based on European methods of narrative analysis (Kuper, *Invention of Primitive Society*, 134).

7. The phrases come from *Argonauts of the Western Pacific*, which is discussed below.

8. See Geertz, *Works and Lives*, and Clifford, *Predicament of Culture*, chap. 1. Like many ethnographers after him, Malinowski used literary devices (such as *le style indirect libre*) to make his narration interesting. See Clifford and Marcus, *Writing Culture*, for a persuasive demonstration of the narrative conventions which rule ethnographic writing, and especially Pratt, whose essay "Scratches on the Face of the Country" questions the dichotomy between "personal narration" and "scientific ethnography" posited by separate publication of memoirs and ethnographic notes, a convention within anthropology.

9. This paperback edition appeared in 1968; Malinowski died in 1942. There is thus no possibility that he was directly responsible for the cover design. My point, though, is that the designer "got it right," and that the cover design mirrors many of the book's premises.

10. Malinowski's diary (found after his death and published in 1967) reveals with unusual candor how difficult, or, rather, impossible, a purely "scientific" state of mind with regard to sexual matters would have been for him during this period. It records numerous illnesses, depressions, and bouts of sexual feelings he tried rigidly, but not always successfully, to repress. See chapter 12 of this study for more on the diary.

11. Havelock Ellis's massive four-volume *Studies in the Psychology of Sex* began appearing in 1906. It depends strongly on Freudian theory and works regularly between three levels of observation: observation of animals, of primitives, of civilized man (pre-and post-Renaissance). The divisions are, in themselves, revealing. For other thinkers, the term *barbarous* often intervened between *primitive* and *civilized* and was identified especially with ancient Greece or Egypt.

12. Malinowski is often considered a revisionist of Freudian theory and indeed proposed to impartially examine Freudian thought. Sometimes he altered Freudian paradigms, as when he suggested that, in matrilineal societies, the Oedipus complex must be modified to include relations between

boys and uncles. But this is not so much a revision of Freudian theory as an extension of it so that matrilineal societies can be processed in terms of the Oedipus complex. For Malinowski, elements of Freudian theory could not be missing, though they could be (as he put it) "elastic" or "misplaced." Programmed by Freudian theory, he could not see that he found what he was looking for—in this case, tension between boys and caretaker males.

13. Linguists concluded that there is no such thing as a primitive language. See Boas's *Handbook of American Indian Languages, Part I.* Bloomfield (*Language*) and Sapir (*Language*) follow Boas on this point. In Sapir, the word *primitive* refers to a quantitatively small number of speakers, rather than to any qualitative factor.

14. Evolutionary paradigms influential in ethnography included both Darwin's and Spencer's; under Spencer's influence, Durkheim, for example, studied the family as a unit in social evolution capable of predicting social change (Kuper, *Invention of Primitive Society*, 121).

It is difficult to fully disentangle evolutionist and antievolutionist lines of influence. In 1909, at Clark University, for example, Boas delivered a lecture attacking evolutionist views of totemism as "a single psychological problem" (*Boas Reader*, 246). Among his auditors was Sigmund Freud, who published *Totem and Taboo* in 1913, seeing totemism as the origin for the religious sense and for civilization itself. Freud's work extended the concept of totemism beyond its original ethnographic contexts and gave it a more enduring life as a principle of social evolution than it enjoyed within ethnography. See Kuper, *Invention of Primitive Society*, 146; Lévi-Strauss in *Totemism* also discusses the uneven progress of the concept within and outside of ethnography.

15. Early in his career, Malinowski defended evolutionist principles; in the foreword to *The Sexual Life of Savages*, he explicitly renounced his early allegiances. In *Sexual Life* and in his most important book, *Argonauts of the Western Pacific*, Malinowski frequently tries to resist the need to translate Trobriand institutions into Western terms, but the resistance often fails. In *Argonauts*, for example, Malinowski's overall argument addresses whether or not the islanders are "communistic" (they are not, he concludes, using the term "communistic" in a very rudimentary sense). Malinowski's weak formulations about "human nature" have been criticized within anthropology, even by those who continued to develop the functionalist methodology. Evans-Pritchard, for example, called him a "futile thinker" with "no idea of abstract analysis" (*History of Anthropological Thought*, 198–99). In Evans-Pritchard's own best-known ethnography, *The Nuer* (1940), he argues for a stronger level of theoretical abstraction, claiming that facts "can only be arranged in the light of a theory" (261).

16. The word *trope* is especially apt for my purposes since it includes images and ideas, and both visual and verbal modes of expression. My use of the term resembles Hayden White's in *Tropics of Discourse*.

17. Primitivist discourse has affinities with the Orientalist discourse de-

scribed by Said, the Africanist discourse described by Miller, and the disciplinary and hegemonic discourses described by Foucault. Said's *Orientalism* has been criticized with some justice for presenting a monologic version of Orientalism (Clifford, *Predicament of Culture,* chap. 11). In the chapters that follow, I try to avoid making either primitive societies or the West seem monologic and try to acknowledge the different accents given primitivist discourse in different countries, and decades, and by different writers. I also try to suggest a variety of motivations beyond the Foucauldian motivations of establishing and preserving hegemonies. Parts two, three, and four cumulatively develop a model of primitivist discourse as yearning for the dissolution of hierarchies and of the binary categories so deeply embedded in Western thought and culture.

18. Distinctions between modernism and postmodernism can be made in various ways. Chronologically, modernism dates from 1885 (or 1900) to 1945, postmodernism from 1945 to the present. In terms of tone and style, most commentators agree that modernism was more serious, more like the Victorianism it itself displaced in articulating moral problems and seeking substitutes for fading religious values in conceptions like "art" or "science." Postmodernism is often more parodic or self-mocking, with diminished faith in either "art" or "science" as saving concepts. Instead of trying, as modernism did, to "make it new," postmodernism embraces, often quite self-consciously, the idea of belatedness, of repetition and reproduction; within certain fields such as architecture, postmodernism is characterized precisely by widespread allusions and borrowings from earlier periods. Economically, modernism can be seen as the triumph of classical capitalism, postmodernism as the era of multinational capitalism. Politically, modernism was a colonialist era; postmodernism witnessed, and often supported, decolonization, but with the maintenance of third world dependency on the first world in relations usually called neocolonial. My study demonstrates more continuities than discontinuities between modernism and postmodernism than are usually recognized. It does not, however, ignore the distinctions made above between modernism and postmodernism, which are real and worth respecting. For various perspectives on the aspects of postmodernism described above, see Jameson, *Political Unconscious;* Newman, *Post-Modern Aura;* Hassan, *Dismemberment of Orpheus* and *Postmodern Turn;* Lyotard, *Post-Modern Condition;* Kiely, *Beyond Egotism;* and Foster, *Anti-Aesthetic.*

19. The term *Euro-Americans* denotes Europeans, Americans of European ancestry, and others of European ancestry who may be citizens of countries outside Europe. This usage corresponds to that common today and is more inclusive than older uses of the term. In adjective form, *Euro-American* denotes the same complex as *Western;* see also note 41 in this chapter.

20. Fascism had both positive and negative versions of the primitive. The aspects listed here, in which the Aryan folk were the vital "primitive,"

formed the positive version. Chapter 10, on Freud, discusses Nazi views of Jews and Gypsies as "primitive" in a negative sense that marked them for death camps.

21. See, for example, Malinowski's *Sex, Culture, and Myth*, 112–23.

22. See Lyotard, *Post-Modern Condition*, and Asante, *Afrocentric Idea*, for recent idealizations of the primitive; see Baudrillard, *Mirror of Production*, for a critique of Marxist thinking with regard to the primitive.

23. The tendency for discussions of the primitive to involve gender and sex roles is of considerable interest below. For a deflationary female rewriting of *In Darkest Africa*, see Manning, *Remarkable Expedition*.

24. The German titles correspond exactly: *Aus den Flegeljahren der Menschheit, Und Afrika Sprach, Das unbekannte Afrika*, and *Atlantis; volksmärchen und volksdichtungen Afrikas*.

25. For the unfortunate history of the Hottentot Venus, see Gilman, in Gates, *"Race," Writing, and Difference*. Her bodily parts, and especially her genitals, were drawn frequently for medical textbooks and, in what may be the ultimate indignity, her labia were surgically removed and preserved in a museum after her death. See also Comaroff and Comaroff's forthcoming book, *From Revelation to Revolution*, parts of which I saw in typescript.

26. See Freud, *Totem and Taboo;* chapter 10, "Entering Freud's Study," discusses Freud in more detail.

27. Malinowski's focus on a single institution (Kula) as a key to social order is typical of many ethnographies. The technique was in part a concession to the relatively short stays ethnographers make in the cultures they study and to their sometimes limited language abilities. It was based on the assumption that reading "parts" would produce a reliable version of the whole, on the sense that a single institution can reveal a people's overall structure of beliefs. Visible here are the lines of influence from Durkheim, to functionalism, to structuralism. The symbolic anthropology associated with later figures like Clifford Geertz extends and heightens the method of "thematic" analysis (Clifford, *Predicament of Culture*, 38).

For a view of gift giving in archaic societies explicitly based on Durkheim's theories, and sometimes preferred (by Evans-Pritchard, for example) to Malinowski's, see Mauss, *Gift;* competition exists in his work too between contextually specific and universal statements (see p. 2).

28. In *Predicament of Culture* (chap. 4), Clifford makes much of the juxtaposition of crown jewels and Kula as an example of what he calls ethnographic surrealism. It is a good phrase and an appealing concept, but a misleading one. Surrealist juxtaposition seeks to evade ethics or hierarchy. This is not true in the juxtaposition of crown jewels and Kula necklaces.

29. I note, in passing, the similarity of the validating terms "indirect" and "complex" to those in New Criticism, whose practices of "close reading" and relating parts to wholes resemble those of functionalism.

Since he is engaged in writing a long and detailed study of Kula, Malinowski's calling the institution "direct" and "lacking complexity" was in a sense self-defeating. His self-deflation belies a different impulse in Malinowski's rhetoric, the impulse of discipline building. Malinowski pointedly invites other ethnographers to find examples of primitive peoples whose lives resemble or contrast with those of the Trobrianders, thus assuring the importance of his books as ones with which other ethnographers can agree or disagree.

30. Jung makes this remark in his journal. I first saw the remark in a cover story on Africa in *Time* (23 February 1987). It is worth noting that these older views of Africa are still quotable and in circulation today.

31. The brochure was available for free at the exhibition. MOMA used the term "misreading," in a sense resembling Harold Bloom's. For more on the MOMA exhibition, see chapter 6, "William Rubin and the Dynamics of Primitivism."

32. Other members of Bloomsbury used monkey-talk to allude to erotic matters, as when Woolf described herself as an "ape" kissing her sister's "most secluded parts" (*Letters*, 124).

33. See Leiris and Delange, *African Art*, 8, and Rubin, "Modernist Primitivism," 35, and my discussion of these texts in chapters 5 and 6. Willett (African Art), Laude (*Arts of Black Africa*), and Fagg and Plass (*African Sculpture*) provide confirmation of how often Western interpretations of primitive objects stress sexuality and horror.

34. *Libido* was the original term, changed to *id* to avoid the association of the word *primitive* with the libidinous. My point is that the change in terminology does not avoid the association.

35. Said's *Orientalism*, Miller's *Blank Darkness*, and Clifford's *Predicament of Culture* are the books I have in mind here. Said's later work—*After the Last Sky* in particular—empathizes more with the feminine imagination and tries at points to imagine things from a female point of view. Clifford, despite his general perspicacity, repeatedly summarizes without comment certain sexist positions in the writers he discusses. He is thereby able to script as heroes figures I write about with much greater ambivalence (see chapter 5 on Leiris). Spivak is the only major critic associated with feminist perspectives on third world cultures and literatures; her approach and concerns are quite different from mine.

36. For examples of how this process worked with regard to Eastern European Jews, see chapter 10 on Freud below; with regard to the working class, see chapter 8 on Lawrence; with regard to African-Americans, see chapter 2 on Tarzan.

37. I used the *Oxford English Dictionary* to trace the basic evolution of the term in English.

38. See Rubin, "Modernist Primitivism," 2–4. Other art historians, and ethnographers who write on primitive artifacts, confirm his usage.

39. Boas's work from the late 1880s contains hints of his relativist position, which nonetheless finds its clearest expression in *The Mind of Primitive Man*. American ethnographers who worked with Native American

cultures, like A. L. Kroeber (Boas's first Ph.D. student at Columbia), also tended to emphasize the specificity of each culture studied; this preference in American ethnography may have been encouraged by the presence of various tribes within the United States' national borders.

But although Boas articulated and followed relativistic principles more fully than ethnographers like Malinowski did, his statements, in *Mind of Primitive Man* and elsewhere, often invoke a version of "eternal truth" that qualifies his relativism. Late in his career, Boas made revisions in the selections for *Race, Language, and Culture* designed to guard against this tendency. For one example, see Stocking, "Introduction," 13.

40. See also note 2 in this chapter. Although available much earlier, these ideas did not achieve true currency until the 1960s; I suspect that they could not be assimilated until the era of decolonization and civil rights. Implicit in my discussion of the word *primitive* is a strong sense that although the term has been attacked and, often, replaced, it continues to inform our imaginations and cultural lives. In *The Invention of Primitive Society*, a new book on anthropology's obsession with "kinship," Kuper reaches the same conclusion.

41. By the West, I mean dominant Euro-American cultures; the discussions that follow differentiate between nationalities, genders, sexual orientations, and social classes within these two large abstractions—categories that are often defined in ways that mesh with definitions of the primitive and with the tropes of primitivist discourse.

Nations such as Japan and the Soviet Union share many features and aspirations of the modern industrial state and might be considered part of the West. Some American views of Japan clarify the usefulness of excluding countries like Japan and the Soviet Union here. Japan has been an imperialist power and is now an industrial one, but stereotypes about Japan often resemble those found in primitivist discourse. The cover of a recent *New York Times* economic report, for example, showed a sumo wrestler hovering over the Manhattan skyline in a possible evocation of King Kong; it is one example of a pattern we shall see repeatedly in this study—the ability for visual juxtapositions to make assertions that would be indignantly rejected if couched in reasoned prose.

I am interested in how nations outside the West are sometimes processed as "primitive," but do not see my topic as the West and the contemporary third world. The West also tends to process nations such as India both as "primitive" and as having an ancient culture and a recognizable history that "distinguish" them from Africa and Oceania; see chapter 4.

42. There are cases in which enclosing *the West* in quotation marks *would* make a political point; for example, in differentiating between U.S., Belgian, and Soviet forms of imperialism, or between the forms that capitalism takes around the globe.

43. I abstract this list of qualities from Diamond's *In Search of the Primitive*, but I do not share all his assumptions. His acceptance of categories

such as "kinship" in romanticized terms remains problematic. His view of primitive societies as conservative and resistant to change is one specific point of difference. I am more persuaded by the general sense that "it is exceedingly improbable that any customs of primitive people should be preserved unchanged for thousands of years" (Boas, *Race, Language, Culture* 286). Within specific fields, such as the history of sculpture, the view of the unchanging primitive is now thought by many art historians to be wrong (Bascom, *African Art in Cultural Perspective*; Willett, *African Art*, 43). Certainly, this study contains many examples of rapid changes following contact with the West; it seems unreasonable to assume that only such contact made change possible, though that view has been articulated, by Malinowski, among others.

44. Benin (in what is now Nigeria) would be one exception to the general absence of cities; the cities of the Aztecs would be another insofar as the Aztecs, as compared to the Spaniards, were technologically primitive (see Montaigne, "Of Coaches").

45. Let me amplify each of these terms. *Savage* and *pre-Columbian* were frequently used in the first decades of this century; but *savage* connotes violence as a characteristic of the primitive, and *pre-Columbian* designates vast territories in relation to a Western explorer. *Tribal* pinpoints the prestate essence of primitive societies but is sometimes (especially among Africans) regarded as a Western invention, designed to downplay the importance and unity of peoples. For a discussion of *tribal*, see Fried, *Notion of Tribe*. For parallel attacks on the idea of "culture" (Western as well as non-Western), see Hobsbawm and Ranger, *Invention of Tradition*; Wagner, *Invention of Culture*; and Clifford, *Predicament of Culture*.

Third world (as its cognate *first world* makes clear) carries with it a pejorative sense, insofar as political power always claims primary, not tertiary, status. The term also confuses the often urban and industrialized third world with surviving forms of technologically primitive life. *Underdeveloped* or *developing* usefully imply a relative lack of technology, but are economic jargon that assumes the modern West as norm. *Archaic man* and *archaic societies* are increasingly used but imply a lack of viability and pastness that duplicate the evolutionary connotations of *primitive*. *Traditional* is too vague and is applicable to societies as diverse as southern Italy and the American South. *Exotic, non-Western* (note that in this word only Western is capitalized), and *Other* beg the question of what defines the norm. *The anthropological record* reinscribes the very circularity that it seeks to avoid—the fact that primitive societies have been repeatedly processed by categories devised within Western anthropology. My occasional use of each of these terms is informed by awareness of its problematic nature.

46. There are other problems with using geographical designations: first, such designations (especially in modern Africa) often notoriously compete with groupings prevalent before statehood and Western mapmaking;

second, some groups, such as the Bushmen, no longer exist in traditional modes of life (see Nixon "Out of Africa," and Ees, "Last in Clan").

47. The most fully documented instances of cannibalism as a social institution come from New Guinea, where head-hunting and ritual cannibalism survived, in certain isolated areas, into the fifties, sixties, and seventies, and still leave traces within certain social groups. But that has not prevented the invocation of the African cooking pot in various popular representations of Africa (including the Tarzan novels). Most scholars agree that cannibalism existed in parts of Africa, but spottily, with neighboring groups often widely diverse in attitudes toward the practice (the same diversity is true in other regions of the world; see Sanday, *Divine Hunger*). Speculation about the motivations for cannibalism can still cause mighty and heated debates. When Harner suggested a material need for protein as the basis for Aztec ritual cannibalism, scholars like Sahlins vigorously objected. The consensus today views cannibalism as "part of the broader cultural logic of life, death, and reproduction" but as varied in motivation (Sanday). It is not generally found in societies "where domination and control are subordinate to accommodation and integration" (Sanday, 26). For different views, see Arens, *Man-Eating Myth* (which suggests, contrary to most experts, that ritual cannibalism is a charge routinely made against "Others" and may never have existed); Tannehill, *Flesh and Blood*; and Sagan, *Cannibalism* (among whose findings is that cannibalism is an "elementary form of institutionalized aggression"). A further twist in scholarly attention to cannibalism is the connection between human sacrifices (including the origins and symbolic rituals of Christianity) and cannibalism; see Girard, *Violence and the Sacred*, and Davies, *Human Sacrifice*.

48. On the identity theme as a key to *The Odyssey*, see Dimock, "Name of Odysseus."

49. Stanley calls Livingstone's book "a book no boy should be without." I think it fair to extend the term to his own books. Edgar Rice Burroughs would surely agree. From boyhood, he was Stanley's avid fan. And he created "boys' clubs" centered on his most famous creation, Tarzan of the Apes.

50. Gide's *Travels in the Congo* and Leiris's *L'Afrique fantôme* use the diary form, for example. Schneebaum's *Keep the River on Your Right* also owes much to Stanley and to Gide.

51. See C. Miller, *Blank Darkness*, 65. I would, however, challenge the priority Miller gives to language in his analysis of Africanist discourse. Conflicts played out in language reflected much larger, and often very complex, issues of epistemology, self-perception, and cultural order.

52. See Pratt, "Scratches."

53. Continuing the dance of fact and fiction, Stanley later published a novel called *My Kavulu*.

54. As previously noted, this matter of being English or being American is rather complicated for Stanley. Born in Wales, Stanley lived his youth in poverty and neglect until he was adopted by a well-heeled Ameri-

can who, report has it, liked his "spunk." Stanley became a U.S. citizen and identified himself as one until late in life, when he married an Englishwoman and resumed British national identity. See Manning, *Remarkable Expedition.*

55. American children intone the phrase "Dr. Livingstone, I presume," in love with its British pomposity. Britons tell me that the phrase, equally popular at home, is held to be proof of American pretentiousness and misconception of "proper English"! Both views are complicated by the snafus of national identity described above.

56. Another drawing in the series, called *Living with Art,* suggests that all collecting is a form of cannibalism which can "eat away" at the collector. In this drawing the same woman sits with the same furniture, in a room denuded of all statues but the female one on the far left in *Gone Primitive,* which glows eerily from overhead spots. The angle of the drawing is very uncomfortable, and the woman diminished in size. Above her head this time hang two abstract paintings, whose designs recall the patterned rug on the floor of the room. She looks bewildered and reduced by the art she lives with.

57. The summer I finished this book, Tom Wolfe's *The Bonfire of the Vanities* was a solid best-seller. Its plot hinges on varied readings of the "urban jungle" motif, a phrase implicit in the Tarzan novels' comparison of cities and jungles, but newly popular in the 1980s. I use the term in this section aware of, and critical of, its vaguely racist implications in suggesting a link between urban and jungle predators. I am expressly interested below in exposing some other political consequences of the identities it facilely establishes.

58. The Philippine Tasaday are suing anthropologists who accuse them of being fake primitives; they are, they insist, quite real, despite their ownership of blue jeans and cheese crackers (Mydans, "20th-Century Lawsuit").

Lawsuits are also being used by groups within the United States. Suits filed by Native Americans have sought to reclaim tribal lands (see Clifford, *Predicament of Culture,* 277–346), to have relics and skeletal remains returned from museums, and to install sweathouses (important in some Native American religions) in prisons. In 1988, the Bureau of Indian Affairs formally recognized what had been a problem for some time: the conflict of interest involved in supplying lawyers for Native American suits against the U.S. government ("All Things Considered," WUNC, National Public Radio, February 1988).

59. James Clifford emphasizes new worldwide input into the dialogue once monologically Western. He sees it as largely positive. See also Naipaul, *Return of Eva Peron,* for a more pessimistic view of the contemporary third world's adoption of first world customs.

60. Examples of contemporary popular culture's appetite for the primitive bombarded me as I wrote this book. The examples were sometimes contradictory in message. The British magazine *I-D,* for example, published

a "Tribal Issue," celebrating the mix of third world cultures into London life, often in terms that used and abused traditional ideas about the primitive as the sexualized (May 1988). A *Newsweek* from the same month reported how London "skinheads" have adopted Maori tattooing; the article was about the violence of this group against the third world "Others" celebrated in *I-D*. *Vogue* ran a feature by Stephen Drucker called "Something Wild" in which Kim Basinger wore safari garb, with "Masai warriors" (a polite fiction) as extras. Banana Republic's catalogue 35 (Spring 1988) offered us an intellectual and sartorial version of the safari that "evokes a store of myth and memories: ours, yours, Africa's" (19). This list could go on and on.

61. For definitions of the carnivalesque, see most of all Bakhtin, *Dialogic Imagination*, and also Castle, *Masquerade and Civilization*. The current emphasis on the carnivalesque and the polyphonic as central features of Bakhtin's thought is to some extent an unfortunate distortion; it is helpful to recognize the carnivalesque and polyphonic as extensions of Bakhtin's theory of subject/subject relations. When brought to bear on interpersonal and intercultural relations, the concepts indeed provide powerful tools for literary and cultural studies. As I suggest below, however, the carnivalesque and the polyphonic can and have been too facilely invoked as positive goods in and of themselves. Juxtaposition, polyphony, and the carnivalesque can serve a politics of liberation; alternatively, they can serve as safety valves that postpone change, or give the illusion of change, where little real change exists.

62. It is worth pointing out, as Mead among others did when the term was first introduced, that "global village" is in a sense a misnomer. It accurately conveys the unities and uniformities made possible by mass media; it downplays the depersonalization of life in cities as compared to traditional village life.

Chapter 2

1. For information about films, sales of books, and other financial ventures associated with Tarzan, see Fenton, *Big Swingers*; Lupoff, *Burroughs*; and Porges, *Burroughs*. The authors, all "fans," may exaggerate statistics a bit, but their numbers are sufficiently large and sufficiently uniform to be convincing.

2. For sample reviews and advertisements, see Heins, *Bibliography*, 34–35, 314–16.

3. In "West of Everything," a book in progress on Westerns, Jane Tompkins notes the same patterns of identification between fictional hero, author, reader, and critic for Zane Grey.

4. The list of ethnographic categories the Tarzan books address could be extended: cannibalism, preferences for raw or cooked food, linguistics (Tarzan crosses Africa to learn new languages), and many other categories used

by ethnographers exist in the novels. The overlap is one of many manifestations of similarities between popular and scholarly views of the primitive. It is significant that the categories are often stated in terms of binary oppositions traditional in the West; such statements guarantee that the primitive occupies an inferior status.

5. On Mead's role as a popular pundit, see Howard, *Mead*, and chapter 12 of this study; see also Mead and Baldwin, *Rap on Race*, and Mead, *Personal Views*.

6. As we saw in chapter 1, cultural relativism was a topical issue with regard to primitive societies, especially associated with work by Boas that is nearly contemporary with Tarzan's birth. For contemporary theories of how context controls perceptions see Fish, *Text*, and Smith, "Contingencies of Value."

7. Tarzan's isolation lasts, in fact, for only one-third of the first novel in the series, *Tarzan of the Apes*.

8. Burroughs asks us to believe that the hereditary instinct for knowledge is enough to keep Tarzan at work deciphering the relationship between letters, words, and pictures in children's books until he teaches himself to read English. That is, at any rate, what happens in the Tarzan plot.

9. Burroughs said that, when he wrote the first Tarzan stories, he "was mainly interested in playing with the idea of a contest between heredity and environment" ("Tarzan Theme"). Then as now, *heredity* and *environment* were terms with strong racial overtones, and much Euro-American debate about race from the nineteenth century on invoked these categories (see Curtin, *Image of Africa*).

Positions we associate with antiracism (like the importance of environment) and those we associate with racism (like inheritable mores) were sometimes not clearly separate in the late nineteenth and early twentieth centuries. One example is the long-standing debate between "polygenesists" and "monogenesists." The "polygenesist" position maintained that there had been separate creations of the races; the "monogenesists" argued for a single creation: both could lend themselves to the support or refutation of racism. See Curtin, *Image of Africa*, 40–43, and Hammond and Jablow, *Myth of Africa*, 96–100.

10. For views that reports of cannibalism are excessive, see Hammond and Jablow, *Myth of Africa*, 94–95, and Arens, *Man-Eating Myth*. For other readings, see chapter 1, note 47.

11. The promise Jane extracts helps link the first five novels in the series, as the villain spared in one novel comes back for revenge in the next. After volume 5, Burroughs made few attempts to link the plots coherently into a chronological development.

12. The term *jungle* is so much a part of the Tarzan story that I use it in my own text repeatedly. I am of course aware that Africa contains forests and savannas, deserts and rain forests and plains. The common use of the term *jungle*, which originally designated the terrain of parts of Southeast

Asia, to describe thickly forested areas in Africa is one example of how the primitive is often a polyglot concept in the West (see chap. I).

13. Miscegenation was a fascination in American popular fiction, including dime novels like *Molesca, or the Indian Wife of the White Hunter*. It also figures in canonical literature like Faulkner's *Light in August*.

14. Tarzan's ideas about African beauty and the hierarchy of African tribes correspond more or less precisely to ideas recorded in nonfiction sources: generalizations are hastily made; European standards of beauty are invoked; the "West Coast savage," the most frequently enslaved, is also the most despised. See Curtin, *Image of Africa*, 408–9, and Hammond and Jablow, *Myth of Africa*, 26, 93, 190–91.

Hammond and Jablow maintain in the preface to their study that "there was no need to treat fiction and non-fiction separately since both are governed by the same tradition"; in fact, they dedicate their book to Lord Greystoke.

15. See C. Miller, *Blank Darkness*, 51, and Hammond and Jablow, *Myth of Africa*, 59–60. See also my discussion of Conrad in chapter 7.

16. Burroughs's portrait of African warfare is often racist: it posits two extremes, a cowardly avoidance of battle and a mindless assault designed to produce casualties but not to win. The racist stereotyping is at odds with the books' assertion at other times that no living creature can be judged as a member of a group and must be judged individually (see, for example, *Tarzan of the Apes*, 216).

17. On the issue of enslavement by nature versus tradition, see *Tarzan and the Golden Lion*, 112. In other Tarzan novels, Africans use euphemism or withhold information to punish abusive masters; the masters in turn misinterpret the blacks' behavior as stupidity.

18. Curtin (*Image of Africa*), C. Miller (*Blank Darkness*), Fabian (*Time and the Other*), Wolf (*People without History*), and Hammond and Jablow (*Myth of Africa*) all discuss this false view of Africa as history-less, which is a specific instance of the more general proposition that primitive societies never change. This view forms the basis for some of the primitivist tropes discussed in chapter 1; it is discussed again in later chapters.

19. Michelet (*African Empires*) and Balandier (*Sociologie de l'Afrique noire*) are others associated, like Davidson (*Lost Cities of Africa*), with resistance within Western scholarship to the idea of a static African past; so is Wolf (*People without History*), who maintains that, before 1400, Africa was more active in world history than Europe was. Mudimbe describes a parallel shift within African scholarship, citing, among others, Kenyatta, Busia, Hazoume, Diop, and Azikiwe (*Invention of Africa*, 88–90).

20. See chapter 1 for more on Frobenius.

21. See, for some examples, *The Return of Tarzan*, *Tarzan and the Jewels of Opar*, *Tarzan the Untamed*, *Tarzan Lord of the Jungle*, *Tarzan and the City of Gold*, *Tarzan and the Lost Empire*, and *Tarzan Triumphant*.

22. Ann McClintock's dissertation (of which I have read a description

though not the text itself) explores these connections between colonial landscape and the female body.

23. For the "racist" label, see Street, *Savage in Literature*, 108, 170–76; Tim Ellis, a graduate student at Duke, consulted me about a paper he wrote on Tarzan and imperialism.

24. This is the premise of volume 4 in the series, *The Son of Tarzan*; volume 3 began by having Jane abducted into the jungle, with Tarzan in pursuit. Obviously, this setup could not be repeated too often; for one thing, it wasted a great deal of time at the beginnings of novels.

25. Heins's bibliography of Burroughs's works is a treasure trove of illustrations from and ads for the Tarzan books.

26. *The Odyssey* and *She* are two examples of fantasy literature more receptive to the idea of matriarchy than the Tarzan books are. Odysseus and Penelope negotiate their reunion in a series of cross-gender images that reinforces other motifs suggesting male and female collaboration in political power (see Foley, "'Reverse Similes' and Sex Roles"). Holly and Leo adore She and are more than willing to live under her power, though the narrative kills her off at the end.

27. See chapter 7 for a similar identification of African landscape with the female body in Conrad.

28. The emphasis on rape is so pronounced in the novels that one wonders how the books were perceived by the boys in Burroughs's audience. Bookstores may be accurate in shelving the Tarzan novels (as they still do—often all twenty-three volumes) in what we might call the male romance section.

29. In addition to misogyny (the topic of an unpublished essay by Burroughs), Burroughs shows at times a distinctly misanthropic strain. It is clearest in his many assertions, both in the novels and in an essay ("Tarzan Theme"), that men are in many ways inferior to animals.

30. The Tarzan series was authentically an international phenomenon. The novels and comics, and films derived from them, appeared all over the world, inlcuding places (the Middle East, India, Africa itself) that might have been expected to object to the novels' portrayal of Arabs as lustful slavers, the British as benign colonialists, and Africans as Tarzan's servants or Tarzan's dupes. While Burroughs sometimes tried to accommodate his European audiences (he tried, for example, to prevent two "anti-Hun" novels from being published in Germany after World War I), the question of how his books would be received outside of Europe and the United States (except in terms of sales and royalties) never seems to have been considered. The books often provoked strong international responses, as when the Nazis burned Tarzan as anti-German and as promoting "racial impurities." See Porges, *Burroughs*, and Fenton, *Big Swingers*, for additional details.

31. Within Africa, Tarzan is being rewritten in an attempt to effect social change. In the "Captain Africa" comics, African heros have replaced the

white hero and typical plots deal with indigenous materials. See Brooke, "Tarzan."

32. In *Tarzan of the Apes*, Tarzan feels no such affection for his step-father. Their relations are Oedipal, and Tarzan kills Tublat in a fight—one of the apes' institutions for male violence.

33. See Burroughs, "Tarzan Theme."

Chapter 3

1. The second half of the nineteenth century was simultaneously the era of museums and department stores; see Bowlby, *Just Looking*, on this point. My analogy is designed to unpack the ideology behind the period style as it was deployed in museums.

2. The Stocking and Williams essays in *Objects and Others* stress the inevitability of aesthetic concerns in display.

3. The use of lifelike statues dates from the mid-nineteenth century in Europe; it became popular in the United States only toward the end of the century. In both Europe and the United States, it was conceived as a way of gaining and controlling the viewer's attention. See Stocking, *Objects and Others*, 81.

4. The mummy's body parallels the African woman's—an iconography explored later in this chapter and in several later chapters.

5. See Torgovnick, *Visual Arts*, and Meisel, *Realizations*.

6. Compare Clifford's metaphor of the "boutique" style in *Predicament of Culture*, chaps. 9 and 10.

7. The exhibition was at the Center for African Art in New York, an institution founded in the 1980s, after the Michael C. Rockefeller Wing at the Metropolitan Museum had drained the collections of what was once New York's Museum of Primitive Art. Some of this energetic institution's exhibitions and publications are discussed below.

8. In *Predicament of Culture*, chap. 9, Clifford's eye was also caught by this photograph; he uses it to make a case for exhibitions that reveal the contiguity of third and first world cultures. He does not comment on the gender issues raised.

9. The debate between universalist and historical approaches has been a recurring feature within my own discipline. New Criticism, Structuralism, and myth criticism have been among the leading formalist or universalizing approaches; Marxism, traditional historicism, and the new historicism have spoken, in different ways, for the need to contextualize.

10. Roger Fry and Georges Hardy represent just such an early contrast between aesthetic and ethnographic approaches. See chap. 4, "The Politics of Roger Fry's *Vision and Design*."

11. See, among art historians, Thompson, *African Art*; among ethnographers Fagg and Plass, *African Sculpture*, and Willett, *African Art*.

12. Compare Grottanelli, "Lugard Lecture," 8; Laude, *Arts of Black Africa*, 177; and Brain, *Art and Society in Africa*, 1–2.

13. In 1988, the Smithsonian returned certain Indian skeletal remains and relics to tribal burial grounds despite protesting the loss to scientific research. The action came in response to a relatively new feature of Native American relations: the use of the law courts to assert traditional tribal rights. In the same year, the Art Institute of Chicago returned an altar piece to Thailand after a complex series of lawsuits and negotiations; the situation was resolved after a private foundation donated a similar piece to the museum.

14. This museum opened on the Mall in Washington in September 1987. It was previously located outside of northwest Washington, and the relocation to the Mall, directly behind the Smithsonian, in itself tells a story. The new museum faces a twin building that houses the Sackler Collection of Asian Art, and this bracketing of Asia and Africa tells a story too, one that can be narrated as a parallel recognition of the United States' diversity or (more cynically) as a confession that Asian and African histories are, somehow, twins in the American imagination.

The building, which is quite beautiful, is also quite unusual; its small surface site required that almost the entire building be located underground, so that entering it is like entering an elaborate tomb or catacomb. The architecture thus reinforces certain primitivist tropes. But the mood at the museum when I have visited it has been optimistic, devoted to African art in its cultural contexts.

15. See Vogel, *Art/Artifact*.

16. Except for some comments near the end of part two, my discussion is limited to masks, sculptures, and other forms of visual expression from technologically primitive groups. Work from the modern, urban third world is excluded, though work from traditional workshops or villages is not. Almost all work from before 1920 can be safely called "traditional"; after 1920—and increasingly as we approach the 1980s—the term must be used selectively and with awareness that even "traditional" art produced after Western influence was widespread may represent significant modifications of earlier practices. Most of my examples come from Africa; the points made are, however, more widely applicable.

Chapter 4

1. On the 1910 exhibition, see Rosenblum, *Bloomsbury Group*, and Woolf, *Fry*.

2. Henry Moore, himself no mean primitivizer, said of Fry's essays, "Once you'd read Roger Fry the whole thing [modernism] was there." Quoted in Spalding, *Fry*, 233.

3. Said's *Orientalism* sees the portrayal of the Other as mass as an important psychological mechanism. See also Curtin, *Image of Africa*.

4. On "tradition" as a nineteenth-century invention useful to the colonial and capitalist enterprises, see Hobsbawm and Ranger, *Invention of Tradition*.

5. See Bascomb, *African Art in Cultural Perspective*, and Willett, *African Art*.

6. Fry resembles E. M. Gombrich in his repeated assertions that conceptions like "reality" are relative, yet his unwillingness to follow through on the full implications of that position. Recently, Gombrich has repudiated the uses others have made of his theories to support relative values.

7. Here, as in some of Malinowski's work, one sees the impulse to build a discipline and enhance its prestige. Fry was wrong about Africans lacking an aesthetics, as chapter 6 discusses.

8. The linking of primitive and children's art is deeply embedded in our systems of learning. For example, both the Dewey decimal and Library of Congress systems of filing sent me to several different sections of the libraries I used; inevitably, in one of these sections, books on primitive art would be preceded by books on children's art (and sometimes the art of the insane).

9. See Goldwater, *Primitivism in Modern Art*, Leiris, *African Art*, and Rubin, *"Primitivism" in 20th-Century Art*, for examples of this habit. Each begins by discussing the importance of African art in the West.

10. Like Fry, Hardy in *L'art nègre* uses "Negro" as his preferred term. I have retained the term in my translations, though it now carries negative connotations, since it is impossible to know whether Hardy would substitute the words *black* or *African* instead. I have also capitalized the term, though Hardy does not.

11. The discovery of drawings in caves at Tassili invalidates Hardy's views. Recent experts have also been inclined to see Africa as containing rich and varied architectural forms (see Willett, *African Art*, chap. 4).

12. An early exhibition at the Center for African Art—"The Aesthetics of African Art"—tried precisely to provide aesthetics based on connections between healthy bodies and moral codes (see Vogel, *Aesthetics of African Art*). A later exhibit at the National Museum of African Art suggested an aesthetics based on the depiction of life and cultural cycles. I return to the issue of African aesthetics in chapter 6.

13. In *Art*, Bell says, "to appreciate a work of art we need bring with us nothing from life, no knowledge of its ideas and affairs, no familiarity with its emotions. Art transports us from the world of man's activity to a world of aesthetic exaltation" (91). Already present are some of the fullest extremes of twentieth-century formalisms.

14. See Krause, "Giacometti," and Maurer, "Dada and Surrealism," for some factual details of Surrealism's encounters with the primitive, though they both accept uncritically the swerve to the pornographic that I believe it essential to expose.

Chapter 5

1. The motivation for this expedition is of interest. The French government believed that housing African objects in French museums would consolidate a sense of belonging to an empire—both for the colonizer and for the colonized. The expedition had trouble encountering the "authentic" Africa, however, since villagers who had met the French before were reluctant to surrender authentic pieces to them. The Mission Dakar-Djibouti found its salvation when it encountered the Dogon, who had not previously been visited by Europeans and who more willingly revealed their most valued objects. See Williams in Stocking, *Objects and Others*.

2. Marcus and Clifford, *Anthropology as Cultural Critique*, and Clifford, *Predicament of Culture*, emphasize different aspects of Leiris's work and, indeed, different texts from those I emphasize in this part of my book. Chameleonlike, Leiris justifies both their view and mine. Readers committed to the view of Leiris as cultural hero may have trouble accepting my reading, which remains, nonetheless, important in forming any adequate assessment of Leiris's contributions to the image of things African in the French- and English-speaking world.

3. See Caillois, "Collège de Sociologie."

4. The Sande society among the Mende of Sierra Leone is a female masking society that forms one exception to the men-only rule in Africa. See Laude, *Arts of Black Africa*, 141.

5. If primitives seem to Westerners more content with their assigned gender roles than many in the West do, that perceived contentment can have various explanations: that the observer is missing something or projecting something, that strong lines of male and female affiliation exist in primitive societies, or that rituals like the dance provide an outlet for ambivalence. Mead's *Male and Female* suggests at some length the importance of having generations of role models; Diamond (*In Search of the Primitive*) suggests that primitive dance allowed full expressions of ambivalence discouraged in the modern state (hence one source of Plato's hostility to artists).

6. Lawrence's *Women in Love* speculates on a utopian period before the division into sexes; its speculations recall Blake's mythological systems.

7. Leiris's concern with the evanescence of self implies a contingency of values that makes ethnography one genre of narrative, even of fiction. See Clifford and Marcus, *Writing Culture*, Geertz, *Works and Lives*, and Shweder, "Storytelling among Anthropologists," for recent expansions of this view. My discussion depends on the gap between the first-person form of *Manhood* and the third-person form of *African Art*. While I put the two together, Leiris does not.

Chapter 6

1. Varnedoe's contributions to *"Primitivism" in 20th-Century Art* were more favorably received than Rubin's, in part because Varnedoe wrote sympathetically about contemporary forms of primitivism, often practiced by women, including sculpture and earthworks (his wife is, in fact, involved in these movements). Glueck hints that Rubin's early retirement may not be entirely unconnected to negative publicity.

2. What goes on the label becomes key for African pieces created after about 1925. Often, after that date, both artists' names and precise dating were available. There appears to be wide inconsistency, however, in whether museums use any labeling other than the vague "post-1925" in identifying pieces that can be placed more precisely, though specific labeling is becoming more common. Price's *Primitive Art in Civilized Places*, which I read in manuscript as my own book was in press, provides additional evidence for many of my points about the West's treatment of what we call primitive art.

3. The point at which museums become common and art moves out of the aristocratic home has much to do, for example, with the empowerment of the bourgeoisie (Malraux, *Museums without Walls*; Williams, *Long Revolution*). Expeditions to collect art frequently espoused political aims, such as the need to prevent "black bolshevism." The latter slogan appears in an application for funding filed by Franz Boas, even though it conflicts with his overall philosophy (Stocking, *Objects and Others*, 126).

4. The need for experts to emphasize certain points of view to overturn others raises, of course, the possibility of overstatement in a good cause. It is more than clear, however, that early commentators vastly exaggerated African sculpture's sexual content and reference and that most African art has no overt sexual content or reference.

5. The phrase "white cube" appears in the title of a recent book on museum spaces by O'Doherty.

6. How long this region will foster traditional art seems questionable. It is currently witnessing construction of a massive and costly replica of St. Peter's Cathedral in Rome, an ironic gesture in a region still largely animist in religion. It seems likely that once the cathedral is completed, a new tourist trade will urge "traditional" carvers to produce Christianized objects.

7. Compare Brain, *Art and Society in Africa*, 1. Thompson (*African Art in Motion*) stresses how—contrary to the assumption of Western museum displays—the mask would not have been the paramount element in the dance.

8. Willett notes that Africans tend "to repeat forms until they are perfected" while Westerners desire "new" forms (*African Art*, 250-51).

9. The evidence on this point is not entirely consistent. Reports of Africans criticizing each other's work do exist (see Laude, *Arts of Black Africa*, 100; Willett, *African Art*, 211). Thompson suggests that reports of noncri-

ticism may result from the tendency to ask artists to criticize their own work—which they are unwilling to do ("Esthetics in Traditional Africa," 44). Here again, as I suggested in note 4, it is often hard to perceive which position best guards against racism and hard to decide whether positions have been overstated in order to avoid racist implications. Overall, reports based on research among groups (as opposed to reports of random individual comments) seem to support the generalization that most traditional Africans are more reluctant to negatively evaluate pieces than most Westerners are. It is also clear that couching questions in positive terms (for example, what do you admire in this piece?) produces more response from traditional African sources.

We need in this matter (as in many others) to recognize differences between African groups, even those close to each other geographically or those sharing origins as indicated by language families.

10. Fagg has contributed substantially to our knowledge of individual artists' names. Olowe of Ise and Arowogon are two of the best-known Yoruba artists. It is becoming more common to see attributions to a specific artist or workshop in museum exhibitions.

11. Here again, some contradictory evidence exists. Herskovits (*Dahomey*) reports that Dahoman artists are often nonconformists; Laude (*Arts of Black Africa*) believes Herskovits was writing from within Western perceptions.

12. The impulse to define a pan-African aesthetics is understandable but can result in oversimplification or in idealization. For a more troubling idealization than Thompson's, see Asante, *Afrocentric Idea*, on the ideal of *nommo* in the verbal traditions of Africa, with its goal, which he describes as transcendence through harmony. His version of what he calls Afrocentrism invokes direct speech as an essentialist ideal in a way criticized by Derrida among others in the West. Asante would respond by saying that the very critique is Eurocentric. Still, one feels that *nommo*, as Asante uses it, is seductive but idealized.

13. Two recent exhibits that do stress the differences were "African Art in Motion" at the University of California at Los Angeles, and "Art/Artifact," at both the National Museum of African Art and the Center for African Art. See Thompson, *African Art in Motion*, and Vogel, *Art/Artifact*.

Another such exhibition in 1988 was "Exotic Allusions: What Do We Really Mean by Primitive Art?" at the Heard Museum in Phoenix, Arizona. At a related conference, some museum directors reportedly protested against the kinds of changes I am urging here. Complicated questions came to the surface, including various questions about where museums' responsibilities rest: with the groups whose work they exhibit? or with some larger idea of full and accurate representation? The questions would include, for example, the issue of whether uses of certain objects that would seem sensational in the West ought, or ought not, be mentioned in museum notes and exhibitions.

Chapter 7

1. For some classic discussions of Conrad, see Leavis, *Great Tradition*; Watt, *Conrad in the Nineteenth Century*; Guerard, *Conrad the Novelist*; and Van Ghent, *English Novel*; a host of other critics follow the humanistic and/or formalist paths they represent. The *Norton Anthology* from which I quote is the 1988, revised edition (ed. Abrams et al.). Among recent critics concerned with colonialism, Darras (*Conrad and the West*) gives a deconstructionist reading; other critics who find Conrad's attitudes toward colonialism highly ambivalent and who share at least some of the humanist/formalist assumptions are Fleishman, *Conrad's Politics*; Mahood, *Colonial Encounter*; McClure, *Kipling and Conrad*; Meyer, *Fiction and the Colonial Experience*; and Raval, *Art of Failure*.

2. See, among the Marxists, Jameson, *Political Unconscious*; Parry, *Conrad and Imperialism*; and Sprinker, *Imaginary Relations*. Achebe ("Image of Africa") wrote a denunciation of Conrad as racist that provoked strong reactions; see, for example, Hawkins, "Racism." Some of the recent studies cited in note 1 are also critical of aspects of Conrad's attitudes toward imperialism, though they find redeeming values. Conroy (*Modernism and Authority*) discusses how rhetoric provides forms of authority challenged by the rupture of imperialist values.

3. The 1988 Norton critical edition follows Achebe's devastating piece with rebuttals by Wilson Harris and C. P. Sarvan, identified proudly, though vaguely, as "third world" critics. The pairings reveal how deeply divisions go in critical views on Conrad and how unlikely either side is to reach the other. Harris condescendingly begins by saying he read Achebe's piece "with much interest and some sympathy"; he goes on to chastise Achebe for missing "the pressures of form that engaged Conrad's imagination" (262–63). The old formalist defenses are set in motion, with Achebe cast as a barbarian at the gates.

Sarvan is equally dense. One of Achebe's central points (a point with which I agree) is that Conrad makes the condition of single European minds (Kurtz's and Marlow's) of greater interest than the life of a whole continent. Sarvan reminds Achebe that *Heart of Darkness* is an allegory—as though the literary category absolves anything. He further notes that "the reference in *Heart of Darkness* is not to a place (Africa) but to the condition of European man; not to a black people but to colonialism" (282). The formulations seem very precisely to repeat Achebe's point—right down to the parenthetical status of Africa and the narrowness of "man." But Sarvan thinks he has scored real points.

My position is distinct from Achebe's insofar as, unlike him, I see no real use in labeling Conrad as "racist" or in proposing that we no longer teach him (the ultimate bugaboo of the "traditionalist" reaction). I believe we will and should continue to teach him but also (borrowing Gerald Graff's phrase) should "teach the conflict," which says a great deal about the current state of literary studies.

4. Without taking so harsh a position (which belongs to Sprinker), Blake ("Racism and the Classics") addresses a question which logically follows the critique of Conrad as holding imperialist attitudes: should we still teach him. She concludes we should, but always with a highlighting of the racial and political problems his works raise. See note 3, above.

5. One measure of Conrad's relative invincibility is that critics who write what is commonly called political criticism—some, like Edward Said and Abdul Jan Mohammed, born in the third world—continue to exempt Conrad from severe criticism. See, for example, C. Miller's discussion of Conrad, which sees him as constructing "allegories of Africanism," rather than writing from within the tropes of Africanist discourse. At work here, I think, is the tacit association of canonical status with moral vision.

Said's position has been evolving in recent years, perhaps under his now strong identification with Palestinian causes. "Through Gringo Eyes" is more critical of Conrad than his early book on the writer or than the sections on him in *The World, the Text, and the Critic*.

6. At the Narrative Poetics conference in 1986, Michael Sprinker, speaking for the Marxists, took on Ralph Rader, representing the humanists. The event was billed as "the fight of the century" and had some of the same atmosphere.

7. The surge in Marxist or more generally political attention to Conrad has not been matched by feminist attention of the kind I give the text. A few recent articles discussing women's roles in Conrad proceed from entirely humanistic assumptions about Conrad's ultimate wisdom and his links to a Western great tradition; see Brodie, "Conrad's Feminine Perspective," and Cleary and Sherwood, "Women in Conrad's Epic," for two examples. In *Fetishism and Imagination*, Simpson makes some illuminating comments about Jim's perceptions of Jewel, but does not give a sustained feminist reading. The need for a feminist rereading of this text is so pressing that I would not be at all surprised if several are in progress; we will need many.

The need for feminist readings was underscored for me at the 1988 meeting of the Modern Language Association, at which I participated in a panel called "The Political Novel." My paper, substantively the chapter on Lawrence that follows, exploded (or so I would have thought) the unsavory basis for the association of "the primitive" with "the feminine." The next two speakers blandly discussed Conrad in terms that fit my paradigm and were manifestly offensive. William Bonney noted that Conrad associates femininity with "mud"; he felt no need to question the association, since he found its origins in Nietzsche's allusions to "the stinking pudenda." Ian Watt then discussed Conrad's *Chance*, where Marlow asserts that he sees through the romantic view of women since he has a little of the female in him. Rightly noting that to be a "little female" is not to be "feminist," Watt then rehearsed Marlow's various derogatory views of women, praising them as realistic rather than romantic. That such papers could be given in 1988, in the context of a panel called "The Political Novel," reinforces my point that "political approaches" can still be sexist.

8. Writing about British colonialism in Kenya, Ngugi, in *Decolonising the Mind*, makes some devastating points about the British suppression of the Gikuyu language that counter the popular image of "benevolent" British rule. Suppression of the Gikuyu and their traditional rivals, the Masai, continues in modern Kenya, often through the manipulation of land.

9. Basil Davidson's television series *Africa* and the book on which it is based are helpful on the subject of British colonialism and Cecil Rhodes.

10. Several critics have demonstrated Conrad's condemnation of Belgian colonialism but mixed attitudes toward the British. Hawkins chronicles Belgian atrocities and sees Conrad's attitudes as marked by them ("Exploitation" and "Critique"); Mahood sees the portrait of Marlow as an indication of the man Conrad might have been had he been born British (*Colonial Encounter*); Lee seems to share the attitude that while Belgian imperialism was damnable, British colonialism was very different (*Conrad's Colonialism*).

11. Marlow is himself described as like a Buddhist idol. The extent to which Marlow speaks for Conrad is, of course, a vexed question and is addressed more fully below.

12. Humanist in impulse, Marlow tries consistently to understand everyone he encounters. While he does not understand the Africans, he tries to save their lives. He is revolted by the life and death of Africans "contracted" to the mines by the company he serves, and he gives an unforgettable portrait of the "grove of death" near the mines. (Melo)dramatically, he sympathizes with the hunger of his supposedly cannibal crew and marvels at their restraint in not eating him. His tolerance, frequently pointed to by sympathetic critics, almost makes us forget that cannibalism was no routine method of satisfying hunger, was, rather, a complex rite usually involving conquered enemies and was unlikely in any event to be practiced by the Africans Marlow encountered. Conrad's emphasis on cannibalism tallies with Western versions of the primitive from Homer's Polyphemus on, but not with the actualities of African history.

As I note below, Marlow is given to racial epithets; in *Lord Jim* his hatred of what he calls "half-caste croakers" is almost pathological, and at odds with what he intends to be a sympathetic attitude toward Jewel. The plot of *Lord Jim* may, however, act out his hostility: Jewel remains childless and is reduced by the narrative's end to the status of pathetic waif; earlier, she is a woman of energy and power.

13. African critiques of Conrad stress the racism implicit in these primitivist tropes. See Achebe ("Image of Africa") and Knipp ("Black African

Literature"), who urges black Africans to produce countermyths; he draws on the African leader L. S. Senghor's idea of an African "cultural inventory."

The same set of tropes operates in *Lord Jim*, where Patusan is described as the opposite of civilization, civilization being where "events move, men change" (200). Given the events chronicled in *Lord Jim*, the persistent assertion of changelessness in Patusan is perverse and illogical.

14. The fantasy of the white man adopted as leader by "natives" is fully realized in the Tarzan novels, in films such as *A Man Called Horse*, and in Conrad's own *Lord Jim*, for example.

15. Achebe excited a flurry of interest in the African woman by contrasting the attention accorded the white Intended with neglect of the African woman ("Image of Africa"). Comments have, however, been brief.

16. This juxtaposition of the white woman and black primitive woman was fascinating to the Surrealists and Dadaists (see chap. 4).

17. McLauchlan in the 1988 Norton critical edition of *Heart of Darkness* correctly notes the element of human sacrifice suggested by the presence of the heads. She accepts all too willingly the idea that Kurtz has erred only in allowing the sacrifices to be directed to him; that is, she does not examine the gap between African rituals and Western versions of African rituals.

18. Although the Asmat no longer collect the heads of slain enemies, the use of ancestral heads apparently continues and has been assimilated into the group's tenuous form of Christianity. On the Asmat practice of using fathers' skulls as pillows, see Schneebaum, *Where the Spirits Dwell*, and Chenevière, *Vanishing Tribes*.

19. Acéphale was a secret society closely linked to the public forum called the Collège de Sociologie. Its "main goals were the rebirth of myth and the touching off in society of an explosion of the primitive communal drives leading to sacrifice," although its programs did not really address mainstream politics (Stoekl, "Introduction," xix). The images of headlessness derive, no doubt, from the particularities of French revolutionary history, but they tally with Lawrence's images and with a more broadly Euro-American interest.

20. Bataille is a very complex figure, whose writing about the primitive was engaged also with economic notions of expenditure and waste. He is of enormous importance in the French tradition. I use him here because he so perfectly illustrates my point; but I do not claim to exhaust the meaning of his texts. My discussion serves, however, the useful function of calling attention to the distasteful nature of his fantasies. Many contemporary discussions of Bataille tend to overlook the content of his writings, focusing with admiration on their abstract meanings instead.

21. Bataille's special interest was Aztec society, which had elaborate rituals for mass sacrifices of humans. He moved freely in his allusions from the Aztecs to primitive groups.

22. On this connection between the abject and the transcendent, see also

Girard, *Violence and the Sacred*, and Kristeva, *Powers of Horror*. Kristeva's work on the abject is useful in showing how certain drives toward the transcendent have been connected with excrement; certainly this linkage is present in Bataille. But Kristeva does not adequately challenge the source of connections between the mother's body, excrement, and "the abject." Although she is frequently cited by those who wish to claim "a feminist perspective," the usefulness of her work for feminists remains for me highly problematic.

23. See Belenky et al., *Women's Ways*, and Gilligan, *Different Voice*, for differing modes of male and female interpersonal relations. See Chodorow, *Reproduction of Mothering*, for how males and females react differently to the figure of the mother in our culture.

24. Freud's equation of regressive narcissism with the mother is one factor that supports men's fear of identification with the mother. For a fine revisionist account, see Benjamin, *Bonds of Love*.

The approach sketched here can clarify Marlow's obsessive love-hate relationship to the dynamics of male bonding. He routinely identifies with other men, but hates himself for doing so. Marlow and the humanist critics emphasize the "universal" dimension of what the *Norton Anthology* calls "true communion." I think we would do well to emphasize the gender specificity of the plots. On male homosociality, see Sedgwick, *Between Men*; *Heart of Darkness* contains a hint of homoerotic dalliance between Kurtz and the Russian Harlequin.

25. See Bataille's *Erotism* for some connections between loss of self in erotic experience and in death. See Benjamin, *Bonds of Love*, for a discussion of pornography as a form of controlled erotic expression.

26. In my remarks, I have been preserving the canonical distinction between "Marlow" and "Conrad," yet I must admit that I find it pious and often impossible to justify. I also find Marlow's auditor in *Heart of Darkness* too vague a figure to function as narrator, as is sometimes proposed. We can find both racist and sexist language in third-person sections of Conrad's texts—language that fully echoes Marlow's own. See, for one example, the famous passage describing the pilgrims streaming aboard the *Jeddah* in *Lord Jim*. In this passage, the pilgrims are grouped and described in terms that are both racist and sexist; our ability to feel superior to the German skipper when he calls them "cattle" is in part delusory, since we have acquiesced to the stylistically beautiful, but racist and sexist, description of the pilgrims.

Marlow's statements are not adequately challenged within the text; indications of irony or distance are lacking. There is no sustained qualification or undercutting of Marlow's racist or sexist moments in the narratives—just a mixture of irony toward certain Western ideas and a serious use of them. Achebe, in "An Image of Africa," makes this point persuasively but his rebutters remain unconvinced.

From experience in teaching Conrad, I know that males are especially likely to raise the distinction between Marlow and Conrad whenever the critique of imperialism merges—as I insist it must—with feminist perspectives. They also frequently invoke the idea that we should let Conrad off as simply expressing "the prejudices of his time" with regard to women. I must reject that appeal, since Conrad continues to be cited as a source of moral wisdom and power.

27. Conrad's wicked late novel *The Secret Agent* literalizes my statement here; I find in it a much more radical critique of Western values than in the earlier, and more famous, *Heart of Darkness* and *Lord Jim*.

28. I do not have the space to say much about Eliot here, though much could be said, using both general notions of the primitive as the non-Western in *The Wasteland* and more specific allusions to primitive peoples in "The Hollow Men," some of the Sweeney poems, and *The Cocktail Party*. In a much-quoted line, Sweeney describes how a fellow really must kill a girl, and the line follows, in the poem, a set of joking remarks about cannibalism. *The Cocktail Party* develops the same trope of death by cannibalism, making it the climax of an otherwise inactive play—when Celia's "happy death" among the cannibals is reported. The association of women, blood, and death is of much interest for Eliot's recent critics; the association of these ideas with the primitive is typical of his era. See the discussion of Schneebaum in chapter 9 for a recent rewriting of death by cannibalism as a "happy death."

29. Achebe ("Image of Africa") sees the role of Africa as helping to affirm the West's sense of superiority by its availability as an image of the "savage." While this is true, it is only half the story. The West's image of Africa allows Westerners to play out their sense of the *West*'s degenerate condition and to use "Africa" or other sites of "the primitive" as fantasized locales for transcendence and renewal.

30. Even defenders of Marlow recognize that his interjection at this point in the novel is erratic.

31. The Tarzan novels similarly identify the African landscape with the female body; the rhetoric of "penetration" for "exploration" conveys the same idea. See Chapter 2 and my comments on Stanley in chapter 1.

32. Garrett Stewart is interested in the lying/dying connection, but does not pay much attention to the African woman ("Lying as Dying in *Heart of Darkness*").

33. As we shall see, the same set of associations exists in psychoanalytic theory, in which the mother's body is seen as the locus of a "primitive" lack of the infant's sense of self. The set of metaphoric associations here and the tendency for metaphor to slide into identification run deep in Western culture.

34. One such room exists in the Clark Art Institute in Williamstown, Massachusetts, where I spent many dark winter afternoons. The exhibition "Cézanne: The Early Years" at the National Gallery of Art also featured such a room, whose seasonal women were among the painter's first efforts.

Chapter 8

1. Lawrence plays fast and loose with the concept of the primitive, rarely grounding it in any extensive ethnographic knowledge or specific society. After this initial instance, the quotation marks are omitted when the context makes it clear that we are dealing with a version of the primitive or with the primitive as a generalized whole.

2. Rossman ("Lawrence and Mexico") provides an impeccable chronology of Lawrence's three trips to Mexico between 1923 and 1925 and his vacillating moods during this period.

3. As almost all critics of Lawrence acknowledge, the lines between Lawrence's life and fiction are fluid and it is impossible to ignore biographical data. The standard biography remains Moore's; many important memoirs by Lawrence's associates exist, including a memoir by Mabel Dodge Luhan (who first invited him to Taos); a good single source drawing on these sources is Nehls, *Lawrence*. Lawrence's letters also contain frequent references to his experience of Mexico. I do not often cite the letters below, relying instead on evidence from *The Plumed Serpent* itself; Rossman includes most of the important references to Mexico in the letters, citing the collection edited by Moore. (See also the Cambridge edition, edited by Boulton and Vasey.) For my purposes it is sufficient to say that the letters support all the various evaluations of Mexico I attribute to Lawrence in the novel.

4. In his first version of an essay on Melville's travels to the South Pacific, Lawrence "identifies intimately with Melville's quest" (Rossman, "Lawrence and Mexico," 181), noting that Melville found "a perfect home among timeless, unspoiled savages" (Lawrence, *Symbolic Meaning*, 202). I amplify on the metaphor of home and homelessness in chapter 9.

5. See chapter 6 for a definition and discussion of the expressionist misreading.

6. The tendency in the West to sexualize the conventions of African sculpture is discussed more fully in chapter 6.

7. At the opening to *Fantasia of the Unconscious*, Lawrence warns readers and critics that his ideas are his own and he does not care whether others share them or not. His emphasis on the solar plexus (as opposed to the head) as the seat of consciousness and on the mythic exposure of the solar plexus to the sun found powerful echoes in Bataille and the members of the Acéphale group in France.

8. We can see here, in Lawrence, some of the same stimuli that Jameson (*Political Unconscious*) attributes to Conrad: a desire to escape the pervasive mercantile values of the West.

9. As critics generally recognize, Lawrence frequently identifies with one or more of his characters so that Kate's ideas and Lawrence's (or Birkin's) are very similar. Kate resembles Frieda Lawrence physically, but her ambivalent

reactions to Mexico echo Lawrence's own as recorded in letters from the period.

10. For more on Lawrence's relations with Bloomsbury, see his *Letters;* Rosenblum, *Bloomsbury Group;* Nehls, *Lawrence;* and Torgovnick, *Visual Arts,* 50–58.

11. Lawrence was not alone in exploring Mexico as an alternative to Europe. Aldous Huxley, Graham Greene, and Malcolm Lowry all did so as well; Artaud visited Mexico and wrote about the experience. For Bataille, the Aztecs were a central locus of "the primitive," chiefly because of their rituals of human sacrifice.

12. In *The Plumed Serpent,* colonized Mexico is linked with the feminine, the Mexico of the surviving Indian culture with the masculine. The bullfight that opens the novel features, for example, feminized matadors; its circular arena anticipates the circular dance in which Kate first fully experiences the ability of the primitive to give what one of my students called "mystical pit-stops." In general, the opening chapters of *The Plumed Serpent* seem designed chiefly to establish a contrast between Mexico City with its colonial heritage and the more vital Indian countryside.

13. Mexico is, of course, a very different kind of locale than either Africa or Oceania, its social systems not primitive in any strict sense. Lawrence, however, clearly treats Mexico in a way that justifies my discussion of *The Plumed Serpent* as an example of primitivism, even if the designation "primitive" for the social conditions Lawrence describes is debatable. Rossman gets it right when he says that Lawrence creates in this novel "a Chapala/Sayula that did not exist outside the novel" ("Lawrence and Mexico," 197).

14. The novel's working title was "Quetzalcoatl." The translation "The Plumed Serpent" may admit the sense in which the novel is ultimately a European version of ancient Mexico rather than an attempt to re-create it faithfully.

15. The world meetings Lawrence imagines seem to parody the League of Nations.

16. See Freud's *Civilization and its Discontents* for a hostile account of the oceanic and for an association between the phenomenon of boundlessness it designates and women; for feminist meditations on the oceanic, see Benjamin, *Bonds of Love.* Chapter 10 is more specifically concerned with Freud's relation to the oceanic.

17. The rejection of "friction" tallies with Lawrence's rejection of female orgasm. Lawrence's fascination with the primitive may, like Leiris's, stem in part from the idea of clitoral extirpation, as practiced by some primitive groups, though not Mexican Indians. The extirpation of the clitoris would, after all, remove the physical ground for the conflicts often played out in Lawrentian love relations.

18. Lawrence's reputation has been subject to greater vacillations than

Conrad's, which, as I discussed in chapter 7, is almost untouchable. For critics of prose fiction, however, writing on Lawrence has been an important touchstone of professional competence, almost a rite of passage. For traditional and basically admiring views of Lawrence, see Leavis, *Great Tradition*; Ford, *Double Measure*; Kermode, *Lawrence*; and Balbert and Marcus, *Lawrence*.

19. *The Plumed Serpent* culminates many of Lawrence's lifelong literary and personal obsessions. It shares all of Lawrence's most typical attitudes toward European society. It includes his most typical themes, including the theme of rebirth after destruction. Its imagery repeats motifs from earlier fictions, and characters like Cipriano have a long pedigree: the Gypsy, the Captain, Birkin, and (in a later work), Mellors. Perhaps most important for my purposes, it repeats Lawrence's mix of fascination and repulsion with the lower classes, replaced here by the Mexicans. As in a contemporary essay, "Aristocracy," Lawrence defines the "natural aristocracy" as those who possess the most life-force. Lawrence qualifies, as do the Mexicans. It is worth remembering that Bloomsbury scorned Lawrence as "underbred"; Lawrence's view of primitives as natural aristocrats thus served as a personal vindication.

20. For Lawrence's reactions to the Futurists, see *Letters* (Zytaruk and Boulton, ed.) 2: 180–81.

21. Kate continues to vacillate through the novel's last pages about the question of whether to leave Mexico. She responds to Cipriano's half-Spanish, half-English expression of liking for her (and hence desire that she stay) with the mixture of attraction, yet repulsion, that has marked all her encounters with Mexicans. The novel's last line ("'You won't let me go!' she said to him.") can be read as desperate and trapped, but is more plausibly read as the wish that Cipriano will want her to stay and, in fact, a decision to stay; that reading would, at least, fit the pattern established by the novel, in which Kate rebels but submits to Cipriano's will and comes to share it. When compared to the endings of *Women in Love, Lady Chatterley*, and "The Man Who Died," the ending is, as I say above, relatively happy—though Lawrence certainly does not leave matters completely unambiguous.

22. Blake's "Vala or the Four Zoas" contains an ample mythology of sexual division and is one source for Lawrence's central idea that human faculties must exist in a harmonious balance. Blake, like Lawrence, deplored the dominance of rationality in the Western tradition (embodied in the character Urizen).

23. See "Aristocracy," in *Reflections on the Death of a Porcupine*, and "Corasmin and the Parrot," "The Mozo," and other essays in *Mornings in Mexico* for these ideas, which appear also at moments in *Women in Love*. Ironically, when he revised his essay on Melville and the South Pacific for publication, Lawrence saw Melville as finally marked by a hatred of man-

kind (Rossman, "Lawrence and Mexico," 188). This may be one of many instances in which Lawrence projected his own feelings outward.

24. Compare moments when Birkin and Ursula cuddle together, without sexual desire, beneath the night sky in *Women in Love*, 479–80.

25. For a discussion of Woolf's relation to abstract art, see Torgovnick, *Visual Arts*.

26. The dynamics here were identified by Hegel as part of the master-slave dialectic. In Hegelian (and later Freudian) formulations, one party in any relationship must occupy the master's role. Lawrence, however, had a will away from mastery that his culture had no vocabulary to express, as I discuss below. J. Hillis Miller, in *Disappearance of God*, explores a similar paradox in the perception of self and other at the heart of *Wuthering Heights*.

27. Female psychologists like Karen Horney vigorously disagreed with Freud during his lifetime, precisely over his neglect of female development and too simple use of "penis envy" as an explanatory mechanism in women's development. Many recent attacks on Freud have focused on Freud's views of the mother-infant relationship, which are more fully discussed in chapter 10. While this period is sometimes called "pre-Oedipal," I resist that label, since I see it as surrendering in advance to Freudian paradigms.

28. This desperate technique accounts for something I have frequently noticed in classes or lectures on Lawrence when quotations are read aloud: the audience's irresistible temptation to giggle. What has happened, I believe, is that the concepts Lawrence alludes to have become so familiar that his heavy-handedness in evoking them seems silly.

29. In addition to Benjamin, *Bonds of Love*, see Dinnerstein, *Mermaid and Minotaur*; Chodorow, *Reproduction of Mothering*; Gilligan, *Different Voice*; and Keller, *Gender and Science*.

30. Benjamin, like Chodorow before her, remains vulnerable to the critique that she proceeds from an unexamined essentialist notion of how the subject is constructed or at least begs the question by conceiving of the subject as created through interpersonal relations. I cannot tackle this issue in any depth here. But her point that we can conceive of subjects and objects or subjects and subjects nonetheless remains valid. Benjamin's ideas bear some relation to Bakhtin's theories of polyphony and the dialogic imagination, which were themselves based on his theory of subjectivity.

31. See Stern, *Interpersonal World of the Infant*, and chapter 10, notes 42 and 43.

32. Bateson was working with the Iatmul ritual Naven; his example in the West (which he candidly admits made him rethink his fieldwork as he wrote it up into an ethnography) was women's adoption of masculine attire in the riding habit.

33. Benjamin (*Bonds of Love*) correctly notes that Freud assumes both hierarchy and dominance/submission to be inevitable in human relations.

For a perspective within anthropology that questions the possibility of avoiding hierarchical thinking, see Dominguez, "Other Peoples."

Chapter 9

1. Geertz has written a classic essay on the Balinese cockfight as symbolic action ("Deep Play," in *Interpretation of Cultures*).

2. See Belo (*Traditional Balinese*), Geertz (*Interpretation of Cultures*), Mead (*Male and Female*), and Mead and Bateson (*Balinese Character*) for alternative interpretations of Balinese culture. Mead reportedly disliked the Balinese as "an excessively dirty people" who are averse to representations of heterosexual love (Howard, *Mead*, 198).

3. Despite their geographic isolation, the Asmat had also encountered, and needed to accommodate in various ways, the Portuguese, the Indonesian government, and Catholic missionaries. The group is a good example of how rare an untouched example of a primitive society really is.

The year 1988 was, in many ways, the year of the Asmat in publishing and media circles. In addition to the books by Blair and Schneebaum that I discuss, Chenevière's *Vanishing Tribes* includes a section on them, and Eric Hansen's *Stranger in the Forest* covers similar material (both published in 1988). The Public Television and Arts and Entertainment networks also broadcast (in June 1988) a segment of *National Geographic Explorer* which showed footage of the Asmat now and during Bergman's visit; the segment stressed how Christianity has transformed Asmat traditions, at least superficially.

4. Chenevière (*Vanishing Tribes*) reveals the Punans as feared headhunters, although he points out that their head-hunting has restricted and well-defined social roles, such as acquiring a "soul" for a woman about to be married from the head of the slain enemy. Other head-hunting rituals (among the Asmat) seek "souls" and courage from the slain enemy's head for youths being initiated into manhood (Schneebaum, *Where the Spirits Dwell*). The Blairs do not fully trust their own materials; they intuit that "head-hunting" will seem wildly violent and unspiritual to Western audiences; understood within the network of Punan beliefs, it need not. The falsification seems to indicate the extent to which Westerners process "the primitive" in terms of clusters of values that correspond to idealizing or fearful versions.

5. In form, Schneebaum's first narrative (published in 1969) resembles the Gidean *récit*: he takes us back in time, through his adventures, which explain how he has become the man we meet as narrator.

6. Recent academic histories of homosexuality make the same assertion, positing eras before the Christian Middle Ages with broad acceptance of male homosexual relations. See Greenberg, *Construction of Homosexuality*.

7. Anthropological reports on the extent and motivation for homosexuality in primitive societies vary considerably. Lévi-Strauss encounters at least one tribe that practices male homosexuality, though he describes it as a response to the scarcity of women. Some other anthropologists do not mention homosexuality at all, or marginalize their accounts. Mead's *Coming of Age in Samoa*, for example, includes statistics on female homosexual experience in the charts included in the appendix, but she does not mention this aspect of Samoan life in her text. Motivations for what anthropologists do or do not say probably vary: some may wish to "protect" the people they study; some may wish to protect themselves or their readers; some may simply not pay attention to this issue at all.

8. There is an interesting comparison here to Lawrence's ideas about the primitive and male friendships.

9. Similar interests in branching or layered time appear in writers exposed to Native American or South American Indian myths, like Carlos Castaneda, Borges, and other mainstream Latin American writers sometimes called Magical Realists. Castaneda's work, which presents itself as anthropology, has been controversial within the discipline.

10. Duerr traces many parallels between accounts of witches' activities and the myths of what he calls "archaic peoples." Both were opposed and persecuted in the interest of "civilization" (*Dreamtime*).

11. The political usefulness of denying non-Western peoples a history has been the dominant theme in writing on the subject, both in the West and outside it. See Said, *Orientalism*, Fabian, *Time and the Other*; Wolf, *People without History*, and Mudimbe, *Invention of Africa*, for a few examples.

12. No respected full-scale biography of Boas currently exists. Kuper's interpretation (*Invention of Primitive Society*) matches that of Stocking (in *Boas Reader*) and Boas's own account of his early life, reprinted in *Boas Reader*.

13. See both *Journey up the Congo* and fictions like *The Immoralist*.

14. Specifically from the early, Hegelian, *The Theory of the Novel*. The concept, as Lukács develops it, depends on an immense nostalgia for an "integrated totality" in the past, when men's souls and desires were equivalent, through a kind of natural grace, to the essence of the world. For Lukács, this period of essential grace existed among the Greeks; for others, it exists among primitive peoples. The concept of "transcendental homelessness" is not, then, above the phenomena I describe, though it is an apt summary of them.

The phrase is proving evocative these days for other critics, including Edward Said, who sees in it a metaphor for the state of distance and skepticism he believes essential to the critic's vocation.

15. In Lukács's *The Theory of the Novel*, the mind-set of the novelistic world is contrasted with that of the classical Greek world that produced the epic. Lukács shares with Freud, Lawrence, and the Frankfurt school the

tendency to interpose the ancient, classical world between the primitive and the modern.

16. I discuss the status of cannibalism in chapter 1, and in note 47 to that chapter.

17. See the collection *Visions of Excess* and "Extinct America" and "Sacrifice" in *October*.

18. Bataille's willingness to explore these issues makes him, as we have seen in chapters 7 and 8, an interesting figure with whom to compare writers like Conrad and Lawrence.

19. One of my graduate students, Richard Dienst, pressed me to think about this connection between primitivism and the city; I thank him for it and for some of the above images.

20. See Said, *Orientalism*, and C. Miller, *Blank Darkness*; see also chapter 1.

21. For connections between fear of the working class and colonial politics, see Hobsbawm and Ranger, *Invention of Tradition*. For an example of a "working-class" custom processed as ritual, see "The Lambeth Walk" in *Britain* by Mass Observation.

Mass Observation's connections to primitivism were present from the start. The idea of studying Britain's reactions to the sexual implications of the abdication crisis apparently motivated its founder, Charles Madge. A letter to the *New Statesman* started the process. The letter said: "Anthropologists and psychologists all over the world are studying the reactions of primitive tribes to sexual situations. There have been concentrated within the last ten days the reactions of the people of the British Empire to a sexual situation. Here in a relatively limited form is some of the material for the anthropological study of our own civilization of which we stand in such desperate need." Madge's reply was printed next to a poem about cannibals by Mass Observation cofounder T. H. Harrison. See Hynes, *Auden Generation*, and Cunningham, *British Writers*, for additional information.

In its various publications, Mass Observation recruited members of its observation team: this was a grass-roots movement, though directed by academics. In the post-Munich volume of Mass Observation's findings, the application of anthropological methods to the "common man" is seen, expressly, as a way of countering the growing political tendency to generalize "the Voice of the Nation" as located in heads of state. The "common man" was seen as the last best hope for avoiding the war into which Europe was drifting.

Chapter 10

1. Anti-Semitism emerged as a movement in Austria after 1860, peaked in the 1880s, again around 1900, and once again after the Great Depression and the rise of Hitler. During the first three periods, large numbers of Jews from Eastern Europe entered Vienna. Freud was sensitive to the changes.

During periods of calm, Freud made significant assimilationist gestures. He tended to affirm his identity as a Jew (but as a secular Jew) during periods of intense anti-Semitism. See Klein, *Jewish Origins of Psychoanalysis*, 42–55.

2. All these statues—African and Egyptian, Asian and Roman—would have been called "primitive" during the years Freud collected them. By the mid-twenties, art historians routinely singled out African, Native American, and Oceanic art for the designation *primitive,* using other terms (such as *court art*) to describe Asian and classical art. The arrangement of objects in Freud's study suggests that Freud conceived of the ancient world as a boundary between the primitive and the civilized; still, for him, the term *primitive statue* would have applied to most of his collection. See Rubin, *"Primitivism" in 20th-Century Art,* 1: 2–3.

3. Ransohoff quotes Lou Andreas-Salomé and provides this information about Freud's finances in Engelman, *Bergasse 19,* 57.

4. One measure of how important his collection was to Freud was his insistence that the statues accompany him into exile in England, an event discussed below. Some visitors to Freud in England, like Leonard and Virginia Woolf, felt, correctly, that the rooms resembled museums (Gay, *Freud,* 639–40).

5. In using the terms *story* and *drama* to describe Freud's narratives, I continue a recent tendency to stress the fictional and creative, rather than scientific, quality of Freud's work. See Marcus, Brooks, and Fish in Meltzer, *Trials of Psychoanalysis.*

6. Freud's methodology depended on working from the verbal narratives his patients composed with the help of their analyst to a generalized account of human psychological development. But behind the verbal narratives, as shaping forces, were systems of visual display. For Freud and his contemporaries, the habit of reading action against the background would have been a pattern well established by traditions of nineteenth-century narrative painting. See Meisel, *Realizations.*

7. This essay in fact anticipates several of the ideas and formulations developed in the better-known *Civilization and Its Discontents.* His remarks on primitive man's remorse over slaying occur on p. 230.

8. It is an interesting fact that as a child and in his daydreams Freud recognized his alienation from the "Roman" line. When, as a child, he witnessed the humiliation of a Jew, he imagined himself as the Semite avenger Hannibal; Rome at this point represented for Freud the Catholic church. He reports this boyhood identification with Hannibal and a consequent obsession with Rome in a letter to Wilhelm Fleiss in 1897. His first visit to Rome in 1901 represented, for Freud, conquest of the city his boyhood hero had failed to conquer; after this visit, Rome's ancient past was paramount in Freud's mind, rather than its status as the seat of Catholicism. See Gay, *Freud,* 20, 132, and 139–40.

9. The Freud children planned to use their poison to commit suicide should questioning lead to deportation; see Gay, *Freud,* 625.

10. *Anschluss* was the term for Germany's annexation of Austria; it occurred in March 1938 and was followed by savage expressions of anti-Semitism in Austria, exceeding even those that had occurred to that point in Germany. Freud was at first reluctant to consider leaving Austria; his reluctance was overcome, in part, by the arrest and questioning of his children. Final negotiations for Freud's departure, in June 1938, were facilitated by the Nazis' desire to look reasonable in the months following the takeover of Austria; Hitler met with Chamberlain in Munich the following September, still giving false promises of goodwill. For the details of Freud's exile and the complicated negotiations that preceded it, see Gay, *Freud*, 616–29.

11. The photographs in *Bergasse 19* were taken, secretly, to preserve Freud's apartment and offices on film, once it was known that he would have to leave this shrine of the psychoanalytic movement. A camera had to be smuggled into Bergasse 19, since the SS had established surveillance some time before; the negatives themselves had to be left behind when the photographer, Edmund Engelman, decided it was time for him to seek exile after the excesses of Die Kristallnacht. (See Engelman's memoir in *Bergasse 19*).

The existence of this cocktail-table book celebrating Freud's personal space reminds me, ironically, of many recent books filled with pictures of primitive peoples who have often vanished or changed by the time the book sees publication; see, for example, Chenevière, *Vanishing Tribes*, and Blair and Blair, *Ring of Fire*.

12. See Gilman, *Jewish Self-Hatred*, and Kaplan, "Anti-Semite and Jew," for more on forms of anti-Semitic propaganda.

13. See Kaplan, *Reproductions of Banality*, and "Anti-Semite and Jew," for some striking reproductions of these exhibitions.

14. Freud's father and mother, who was an Orthodox Jew, were themselves relatively secularized by the experience of moving to Vienna; nonetheless, their religious origins remained, and Jacob Freud was his son's sole teacher until 1865, when Freud entered the gymnasium (Klein, *Jewish Origins of Psychoanalysis*, 42). "A Disturbance of Memory on the Acropolis," written in 1936 when Freud was an old man, describes how, when he visited the Acropolis in 1904, shortly after Jacob Freud's death, he repressed his sense of having "got further" and "excelled" his father.

15. Gilman, *Jewish Self-Hatred*, 260–70. Anna O., whose real name was Bertha Pappenheim, went on to become an important figure in the women's movement, with a special interest in ending child abuse and the white slave trade; Ernest Jones revealed her identity, wishing to give her credit for her role in establishing the psychoanalytic method. See Dianne Hunter, "Hysteria, Psychoanalysis, and Feminism: The Case of Anna O.," in Garner, Kahane, and Sprengnether, *(M)other Tongue*.

16. His assertions and qualifications during these years fit the patterns of a lifetime, since Freud apparently never felt as Jewish (and yet as much

of an atheist) as when anti-Semitism was on the rise in his native Austria. See Gay, *Freud*, 597–99. Klein (*Jewish Origins of Psychoanalysis*) records Freud's intermittent assertions of his Jewishness and agrees that Freud tended to espouse his Jewish identity most vociferously when anti-Semitism peaked in Austria; see also note 1 in this chapter.

17. The terms "inferior and degenerate" come from Freud's 1915 essay "Thoughts for the Times on War and Death," where he uses them to describe how "white nations" view "non-whites." While Freud disapproved of the derogatory adjectives in 1915, and declared himself "disillusioned" by recent history about the "white nations'" ability to work together for human enlightenment, he did not take the terms of racial disparagement so very seriously or so very personally. In fact, he seemed to accept the "white nations'" leadership as a given fact of history.

18. The preface was added on the occasion of *Totem and Taboo*'s publication in a Hebrew translation. Despite a recent flurry of attention to Freud's Jewishness, this preface has not received the attention it deserves.

19. "Unprejudiced science" will, presumably, be ample enough to accommodate Christian and Jew alike.

20. The instability was multidirectional: "civilized" Germans had slid into the violence Freud associated with the primal horde at the same time that they imaged Jews as "primitive." Other thinkers, like members of the Frankfurt school, similarly reconsidered (in light of events of the thirties and forties) the relation of the primitive to the civilized, and the ancient Greek world as a transition between the two. The fundamental questions asked in Horkheimer and Adorno's *Dialectic of Enlightenment* resemble the question motivating *Civilization and Its Discontents:* was "civilization" (enlightenment) the best path for human development, given the world's slide into a new barbarism? The book uses the Odysseus myth as the basis for its theorizing about culture very much in the way that Freud used the Oedipus myth.

21. Even in 1932, in an open letter to Albert Einstein called "Why War?" Freud was capable of maintaining that "whatever fosters the growth of culture works at the same time against war" (287).

22. On the historical role of doctors in Nazi Germany, see Lifton, *Nazi Doctors*. Although they do not treat Freud's works per se, feminist critiques of the philosophy and methodology of science in the West as andocentric are relevant to my argument; see Keller, *Gender and Science;* Longino and Doell, "Body, Bias, and Behavior"; and Harding, *Science Question*. None of these feminist writers means to denounce all of science, and my remarks here pertain only to certain abuses of science.

23. To be Jewish in the modern Christian West was, in a sense, to be doubly "transcendentally homeless" or, as an exile from Hitler's Europe, triply so.

24. The quotation is from Freud's "Postscript" to "Autobiographical Study," 72.

25. The phrases come from *Totem and Taboo*; the scene occurs on pp. 140–46.

26. This argument appears in *Moses and Monotheism*, which begins from the premise that Moses was an Egyptian; Freud originally thought of it as "an historical novel," though he published it as a historico-philosophical essay.

27. It is tempting to see the scene as a piece of political satire on leaders of hordes. But there is nothing in the text to suggest that Freud intended for it to seem either silly or satiric. The scene has been important evidence in feminist reactions against Freud. See Millett, *Sexual Politics*; G. Rubin, "Traffic in Women"; Benjamin, *Bonds of Love*; and note 41 in this chapter.

28. There is an interesting contrast to be drawn here to Jean Auel's recent Earth's Children series (*The Clan of the Cave Bear, The Valley of the Horses, The Mammoth Hunters*) in which primal moments and moments of power belong to females. Freud's version and Auel's are sheerly imaginary. But the real directions the imagination can take are clearly marked by cultural assumptions about gender.

29. It is probably no accident that the problem of genre classification arises for Freud more explicitly in connection with his writing on the primitive than elsewhere.

30. In the teens, when he wrote *Totem and Taboo*, Freud might not have wanted to pursue this line of thought; although he had begun to speculate about cultural origins, his main concern was still the individual psyche. By the thirties, his interest in primitive societies as alternative social forms would have been logical, but complicated. Nazi rhetoric joined the vocabulary of the civilized Reich to primitivist images of "blood" and "folk" and to the ritualized mass rally; it is clear, then, that collectivities need not, in and of themselves, be politically desirable. But Nazi reliance on scientific rhetoric in racist policies made Freud's use of "science" as his chosen counterweight to Naziism equally problematic.

31. In *The Question of Lay Analysis*, 212. The phrase "dark continent" in reference to women occurs in English in the original; Freud may have imbibed it from his early reading of Henry M. Stanley's accounts of journeys through Africa.

32. At one striking point, Freud suggests, illogically, that children depend most not on their mothers, but on their fathers: "I cannot think of any need in childhood as strong as the need for a father's protection" (*Civilization and Its Discontents*, 20). Sagan rightly sees this observation as belied by Freud's own experience of nursery relations in bourgeois households; he suggests that fear of women's power motivates Freud's demoting of the mother's importance.

33. It is worth remembering (though I do not, in psychoanalytic fashion, want to build my argument on it) that Freud's own mother was an Orthodox Jew from the East, a member of the "old Jewry" Freud thinks has had its day.

34. Differences about the validity of "oceanic" feelings were one of many disagreements between Freud and his one-time disciple Carl Jung, with whom Freud broke decisively in *Totem and Taboo*. Freud hated to lose Jung's adherence: a Swiss Protestant, Jung could (Freud believed) dispel the image of psychoanalysis as a "Jewish" science.

35. The phrase "permeable ego" as used here comes from Chodorow, *Reproduction of Mothering*, where it is applied to women's sense of themselves and of community in our culture.

36. Compare Freud, "Thoughts for the Times," 219. Even within *Civilization and Its Discontents*, Freud wonders, "Perhaps we are going too far in this. Perhaps we ought to content ourselves with asserting that what is past in mental life *may* be preserved" (20).

37. The primitive need not be identified with the mother's body and with the oceanic, just as civilization need not be identified with the father's body (or, in the Lacanian rewrite, name). These are just the choices, and images, Western culture has made.

38. The Freudian repudiation of the mother as a danger to selfhood is surely one reflection of, and in turn source of, the linkage of women and death that recurs so often in Western primitivism.

39. That the cultivation of "oceanic feelings" in rituals of social collectivity would not guarantee in any straightforward way social systems free of hierarchy and the urge to mastery can be demonstrated in part by fascism. Fascist rituals in Nazi Germany evoked, as I have noted, "primitive" slogans of "blood" and "folk." In their versions of "the primitive," however, fascists duplicated Freud's sense of the female as a subordinate principle. On the complex role that fear of women and the oceanic played in fascism, see Theweleit, *Male Fantasies*. I do not mean to suggest here a romantic version of the oceanic as social ideal or of females as inevitably experiencing the oceanic sense.

40. See Horney, *New Ways in Psychoanalysis*, 104–13. It seems to me significant that Horney's work is much harder to obtain than Freud's in bookstores and is rarely written about extensively. See also Sagan, *Freud*, for a critique of Freud's view of women and morality.

41. For other feminist revisions of Freudian theory, see Garner, Kahane, and Sprengnether, *(M)other Tongue*. See also Millett, *Sexual Politics*, and Kofman, *Enigma of Woman*. The essays by Moi, "Representation of Patriarchy," and Hertz, "Dora's Secrets," in Bernheimer and Kahane, *Dora's Case*, are also useful. Masson's recent book, *Assault on Truth*, suggesting Freud falsified girls' reports of sexual molestation also fueled recent controversy about Freud's perceptions of women. Feminist critiques of science are also relevant in a general way to feminist revisions of Freudian theory; see note 22 in this chapter.

42. See Chodorow, *Reproduction of Mothering*. Although Chodorow remains a relatively orthodox Freudian, both Chodorow and Benjamin move several steps beyond the clinical documentation of mother-infant relations

along orthodox Freudian lines; see, for clinical examples, Mahler, Pine, and Bergman, *Psychological Birth*, and Winnicott, *Playing and Reality*. Jessica Benjamin's work is especially helpful in demonstrating how males, as well as females, have suffered as a result of too simple a resolution of problems in object relations.

43. Within psychology, the last fifteen years have seen an explosion of attention to infant development that has advanced the idea of a psychology of mutuality, including a turn toward the view that infants actively participate in social relationships. In this view, infants do not perceive themselves as one with the mother, though they do perceive themselves as in mutual relationship with her. See Stern, *Interpersonal World of the Infant*.

Chapter 11

1. Compare the metaphor of the incomplete play here to Lévi-Strauss's "The Apotheosis of Augustus" in *Tristes Tropiques*.

2. The path into exile Lévi-Strauss describes is identical to that followed by Freud's photographer, Edmund Engelman, who left Europe from Marseilles.

3. For Lévi-Strauss's recollections of New York, see *View from Afar*, 258–67. He wrote about locales such as the Northwest Hall earlier, in 1943.

James Clifford has recently discussed Lévi-Strauss's writings about New York (in *Predicament of Culture*, 236–46), seeing in the New York experience both the proper setting for the evolution of structural anthropology and evidence of how (in, for example, the short-lived Surrealist journal *VVV*) "anthropology was part of the decor of avant-garde art and writing" (243). Our mutual and independent interest in the Lévi-Strauss of the New York years is one of several instances in which Clifford and I cover, in different ways, the same territory. In this instance, as on the prevailing mood of the encounter between "the third world" and "the postmodern," our emphasis differs: Clifford stresses juxtaposition as liberation; I stress an acute core of anxieties beneath the "dialogic" moment (see chap. 1). Our similar interest in figures like Leiris and Lévi-Strauss and in issues such as art collecting are more, finally, than mere coincidence. They point to the peculiar value "the primitive" holds for the postmodern.

4. I first read *Tristes Tropiques* without the chapters in question (14, 15, 16, and 39) and can testify that they make a radical difference. The full translation first appeared in 1984.

5. I want to suggest in the next chapters that the nascent analogy Lévi-Strauss uses here (the endangered primitive as a substitute for endangered mankind) informs much modern primitivism. For Lévi-Strauss, the endangered Jews (in part because of Nazi propaganda like that discussed in chapter 10) form an intervening term in the analogy.

6. Somewhere in the background of Lévi-Strauss's critique of Islam—his prejudices coming through again—lurks the sense that, within France, Mus-

lims from French colonies are forming a minority population, with the potential to spread. He alludes to the French colonial experience, and consequent immigration, but not very directly.

7. The issue of how Structuralism fails to include diachronic perspectives has been one of the most important in criticism of Lévi-Strauss, even among writers basically sympathetic to Structuralism. See, for important statements, Sahlins (*Historical Metaphors* and *Islands*) and Tambiah (*World Conqueror*). Also of interest with regard to the construction of "history" as a concept equivalent to "Western history" is Wolf (*People without History*).

Frank Lentricchia is among the important commentators within my own field, literary criticism, to criticize Structuralism for its evasion of history; an article by David Simpson ("Literary Criticism and Return to 'History'") indicates that a counter-reaction may be growing against the invocation of "history" as a magic charm.

8. Lévi-Strauss's account of the voyage from Marseilles omits, as we have seen, a sense of the parallels between his situation and that of Jews trapped in Europe. The terms of his description certainly invite comparison, but Lévi-Strauss stresses his own discomforts. That account also includes a number of offensive remarks (which he intends to be cute) about the potential seduction of women. At a rather unintentionally amusing moment in *Tristes Tropiques*, Lévi-Strauss very casually mentions that his wife accompanied him most of the way through Brazil; except at this moment, he presents himself as the heroic white man, enduring alone the discomforts of the jungle.

9. In *The Jealous Potter*, Lévi-Strauss criticizes Freud for his monovalent, hedgehog ways of thinking. He sees the central flaw of psychoanalysis as its reliance on a single strand of myths, and he elevates instead Structuralism's polyvalent readings of multiple myths.

10. Sontag isolates this quotation in her essay on Lévi-Strauss ("Anthropologist as Hero").

11. Lévi-Strauss is notorious for having done very little actual fieldwork. He has often been criticized for practicing a form of armchair ethnography in the nineteenth-century tradition.

12. On the use of multiple genres see Leiris, "A travers *Tristes Tropiques*," and Geertz, *Works and Lives*.

13. Geertz's *Works and Lives* sees *Tristes Tropiques* as a coda for all of Lévi-Strauss's work.

14. See chapter 4 of Derrida's *Of Grammatology*.

15. Lukács uses the phrase *universal calculus* in *History and Class Consciousness*. It has been used in poststructuralist critiques of Structuralism.

16. Tobin Siebers in *Ethics of Criticism* discusses Derrida's reading of Lévi-Strauss, pointing out that the two share certain unacknowledged utopian goals and a too-easy assumption that writing (language) is the source of violence.

17. Compare Lukács, *Theory of the Novel*, and Asante, *Afrocentric Idea.*

18. We should note in passing how different this is from the role assigned past states—the pre-Roman, the oceanic—in *Civilization and Its Discontents.*

19. Anyone who forgets Lévi-Strauss's status in the 1960s and 1970s, before the poststructuralist reaction, should see the anthology edited by Hayes and Hayes, *Lévi-Strauss.* It is filled with essays that appeared in the popular press, all attempting to explain Lévi-Strauss to a breathless American public.

20. See Paz, *Lévi-Strauss.*

Chapter 12

1. The passage continues: "Then walked to the beach, admiring the body of a very handsome boy who was walking ahead of me. Taking into account a certain residue of homosexuality in human nature, the cult of the beauty of the human body corresponds to the definition given by Stendhal." ("Taking into account" appears in English in the Polish text.) The move from the body of the young woman to the boy's is of interest. In part, it stems from Malinowski's interest in Freudian theories. Given Freud's beliefs concerning bisexuality, it is hardly surprising that Malinowski seems comfortable with a "residue" fleeting attraction to the boy's body, just as he seems comfortable with the dream he records on one of his first nights in the Trobriands: "strange dream; homosex., with my own double as partner" (12). He similarly juxtaposes, with a Freudian knowingness, allusions to his fiancée and his mother.

But there may be more to it than this. Although it is not clearly mentioned in studies of Malinowski available in this country, a visiting Polish scholar, Eva Kurlyk, tells me that Malinowski is frequently discussed in Poland as a gay man and that portions of the *Diary* will remain unavailable to scholars for the next ten to fifteen years. Some of the suppressed entries are said to involve a visitor to Malinowski in the Trobriands: the painter Stanislaus Ignacy Witkiewicz (Witkacy), who followed him there after Witkacy's fiancée committed suicide. Malinowski's possible homosexual impulses would, of course, be of great interest in this study. But the exact nature of those impulses currently remains a matter of conjecture. In fact, recent discussions sensitive to gay issues vary considerably in assessing the material available on Malinowski's friendship with Witkacy. Stocking discusses the ethnographer's friendship with Stás (Witkacy) but does not suggest that it was homoerotic (*Malinowski*, 18); Pilling believes that Stás was, for the period 1904–14, emotionally Malinowski's "significant other" ("Homosexuality," 19). It seems quite likely that his friendships with men fit certain patterns of male bonding and homoeroticism; it remains uncertain whether they included genital contact. In this chapter, I treat Malinowski as what he clearly was, whatever the nature of his involvement with men:

as a yearning heterosexual, engaged in various scriptings and editings of his heterosexual desires.

2. Lukács ends *The Theory of the Novel*, written in 1915, before his turn to Marxism, with an evocation of a potential return to the world of "immanent totality." His nostalgia for the past implies, absolutely, utopian hopes for the future and a belief that the processes of transcendental homelessness can be reversed. This early form of utopian thinking anticipates his later turn to Marxism.

3. Freud wavered throughout his career over which component to emphasize—sexuality or aggression. In general, he emphasized sexuality in his early work, aggression in his later work. See Sagan, *Freud*, 120.

4. Freud shared his culture's identification of primitives with members of the lower class; see Sagan, *Freud*, 123.

5. After some searching, I found a photograph of Malinowski (in Young, *Ethnography of Malinowski*). Malinowski, identified in the caption only as "the ethnographer," looked very much like the image I had constructed in my mind's eye.

6. At least one reviewer, I. M. Lewis, suggests quite the contrary: that Malinowski, had he lived longer, might have published the diary himself. See Young, *Ethnography of Malinowski*, 14. I find that likely only in the event he had lived into the late sixties, when the mood of truth-questioning and self-exposure might well have allowed him to consider publishing the journal.

7. Malinowski was persuaded to remain at Yale, where he was a visiting professor, for the duration of World War II. This "exile" to the United States curiously echoes his earlier "exile" in Australia during World War I.

8. At the time of publication, numerous reviewers commented on issues of privacy, as well they might, for the *Diary* is frank in ways that the work Malinowski published during his lifetime is not. It includes a fuller expression of personality than the published ethnographic and sociological writing. It gives us a sense of the man, while the ethnographies and essays try to give us a sense of the scientist only. The *Diary* hit hard at the Malinowskian myth of the ethnographer as hero. Among those glad to see the myth bite the dust, Geertz gets the award for the harshest characterization: he describes Malinowski as a "crabbed, self-pre-occupied, hypochondriacal narcissist, whose fellow-feeling for the people he lived with was limited in the extreme" ("Beneath the Mosquito Net," quoted in Young, 12).

9. Compare the positions of Knapp and Michaels, "Against Theory," and Fish, *Text*.

10. Like Henry M. Stanley, Malinowski identifies the landscape with certain feelings of sublimity, derived from Burke and Romanticism (see chap. 1). Like Stanley as well, he finds these feelings of sublimity, or of emotion more generally, at odds with his conception of masculinity and the "white man's dignity."

11. It is too simple to see the *Diary* as revealing the "truth" about

Malinowski's fieldwork hidden by the published ethnographies. The interaction of the two is essential.

12. From a different angle, this is the disjunction Geertz explores between "being there" and "writing here" in *Works and Lives.*

13. It of course makes little sense that a picture taken in Bali should accompany a book about Samoa, but that appears to be the case. It is, as I say below, another example of how the "composite" primitive can operate even in anthropological circles. The photograph that appears in *Coming of Age* is a slightly cropped version of the original, which is reproduced here.

14. In *Balinese Character*, Mead and Bateson pioneered the extensive use of photography to record what we today call "body language" as a key to reading a culture's institutions and symbolism. Mead was familiar with the camera's potential value to ethnography and also with its usefulness in making her own image an extension of her work.

15. Perhaps the best-known women writers on the subject are Mary Kingsley, Elspeth Huxley, and Isak Dinesen. A mixture of motives and effects is discernible in their versions of the primitive. In *Travels in West Africa* and *West African Studies*, Kingsley opposes the traditional views of missionaries and colonialists, insisting that Africans were different from, but not inferior to, Europeans. In *The Flame Trees of Thika* and *Out in the Midday Sun*, Huxley writes from a commitment to animal rights and to the proposition that male supremacy (both among the Africans and the white colonists) is a ridiculous institution. To my surprise, many of my male students found her work extremely offensive, much more offensive than the work of figures like Leiris or Bataille. Dinesen's *Out of Africa* imagines Africa in terms of an idealized feudal order. Each of these women projects a version of the primitive congruent to male versions of the primitive we have examined, but with real differences that should not be underestimated, for example, a willingness to learn indigenous customs and to question Western norms on the basis of what has been learned.

I expect to say more about these women and others who write about exotic cultures or the primitive as they conceive it in a sequel to the present study.

16. Ruth Benedict, Mead's friend (and, by many reports, lover), once was tempted to publish work that would reveal her lesbianism. Mead and other friends were highly alarmed at the prospect, fearing it would cost Benedict her job at Columbia (Howard, *Mead*).

17. Mead was in fact married three times, the last two to fellow anthropologists Reo Fortune and Gregory Bateson. Bateson appears to have been the great love of her life. They had one daughter (Mead's only child) together.

18. The Howard biography hints that Benedict and Mead were lovers, and notes that Mead lived, toward the end of her life, longer with a female roommate than with any of her husbands. It is difficult to make much of such statements—so coy and yet so vague. Catherine Bateson revealed her moth-

er's attachments to women in her biography of Mead and calls Benedict and Mead lovers (115–27).

19. Schneebaum (chap. 9) is of course very frank in using primitive societies to make a case for male homosexual relations as normative. Yet he shares the tendency to pretty much ignore women (even women as lesbians) in his writing. On one occasion, Schneebaum suggested to his Asmat friends that women may have an equivalent form of homosexual bond friendship. He reports that the Asmat collapsed in laughter, unable to conceive the possibility.

20. See chapter 1, note 3.

21. The "nine month" period recurs too often in these pages to be accidental. Symbolically, it is the period of gestation. The alternative most-popular time span seems to be the equally symbolic ten years of *The Odyssey*.

22. Both Mead's Samoa and Malinowski's Trobriands were societies already exposed to Westerners and Western values at the time the ethnographers studied them. The published works downplay Western influences and present themselves as studying the "pure" primitive.

23. Baldwin was clearly taken aback by Mead's assertions with regard to the "universal" value of light and dark, and refers ironically to them several times (*Rap on Race*, 202, for example). He was also taken aback by Mead's amazed allusions to blacks who cannot dance (32).

24. Mead's field, anthropology, was relatively friendly to women in the academy. But that "relatively" must be stressed. Even today, conferences in anthropology frequently exclude "gender studies" from the realm of "theory," which enjoys the greatest prestige in the profession.

Epilogue

1. As an "eternal present," the choice of the present tense by anthropologists and sociologists also suggests the impossibility of social change and hence reinforces, at the level of style, certain conservative impulses. In my own discipline, literary studies, the conventional use of the present tense when discussing literature reinforces the same sense of universal and timeless values.

2. See Fabian, *Time and the Other*, Curtin, *Image of Africa*, Mudimbe, *Invention of Africa*, and Wolf, *People without History*, for varied statements of this position.

3. My first book, *Closure in the Novel*, was on narrative endings. I did not fully realize how my early interest in the relation of beginnings and endings in fiction anticipated my interest in primitive societies until a chance conversation with Mikael Parsons. He asked whether there were any connections between my earlier work on closure and my work in progress. Answering him gave me some answers I had been looking for about the sources of Western primitivism.

4. As has been true throughout this study, I do not mean here to idealize primitive societies or to imply that they would be incapable of doing to Western nations what the West has done to them. Within certain parts of the non-West that are viewed through the tropes of primitivist discourse (Iran under Khomeini, for example), the West has been both generalized and demonized: both sides can participate in this dance.

5. See chapter 1 and ethnographies by Shostak (*Nisa*), Crapanzano (*Tuhami*), and Rosaldo (*Ilongot Headhunting*). Their ethnographic strategies are often based on a certain reading of polyphony as liberating, a reading whose virtues and dangers I address at the end of chapter 1.

6. The comment was part of Bush's acceptance speech at the 1988 Republican National Convention, a speech generally praised by the media. No commentator I encountered singled out this aspect of the speech for special notice or criticism, though it is in fact true that the United States does come, alphabetically, somewhere between Albania and Zimbabwe. Reprinted in *New York Times,* 19 August 1988, A14.

7. I have begun to investigate writing a study of such alternative traditions, as a sequel and response to this one.

Reference List

Achebe, Chinua. "An Image of Africa." *Massachusetts Review* 18 (1977): 782–94.

Arens, W. *The Man-Eating Myth.* New York: Oxford University Press, 1979.

Asante, Molefi Kete. *The Afrocentric Idea.* Philadelphia: Temple University Press, 1987.

Azikiwe, Nnamdi. *Renascent Africa.* 1937; rpt., London: Cass, 1969.

Bakhtin, M. M. *The Dialogic Imagination: Four Essays by M. M. Bakhtin.* Ed. Michael Holquist. Trans. Caryl Emerson and Michael Holquist. Austin: University of Texas Press, 1981.

Balandier, Georges. *Sociologie actuelle de L'Afrique noire.* Paris: Presses universitaires de France, 1955.

Balbert, Peter, and Phillip L. Marcus. *D. H. Lawrence: A Centenary Consideration.* Ithaca: Cornell University Press, 1985.

Bascomb, William. *African Art in Cultural Perspective: An Introduction.* New York: Norton, 1973.

Bataille, Georges. *Erotism: Death and Sensuality.* Trans. Mary Dalwood. 1957; rpt., San Francisco: City Lights, 1986.

———. "Extinct America." *October* 36 (Spring 1986): 4–10.

———. "Sacrifice." *October* 36 (Spring 1986): 61–74.

———. *Visions of Excess: Selected Writings, 1927–39.* Ed. and trans. Allan Stoekl. Theory and History of Literature, no. 14. Minneapolis: University of Minnesota Press, 1985.

Bateson, Gregory. *Naven: A Survey of the Problems Suggested by a Composite Picture of the Culture of a New Guinea Tribe Drawn from Three Points of View.* Cambridge: Cambridge University Press, 1936.

Bateson, Mary Catherine. *With a Daughter's Eye: A Memoir of Margaret Mead and Gregory Bateson.* New York: Morrow, 1984.

Baudrillard, Jean. *The Mirror of Production.* Trans. Mark Poster. St. Louis: Telos, 1975.

Beier, Ulli. *Contemporary Art in Africa.* New York: Praeger, 1968.

Belenky, Mary Field, Blythe McVicker Clinchy, Nancy Rule Goldberger, and Jill Mattuck Tarule. *Women's Ways of Knowing: The Development of Self, Voice, and Mind.* New York: Basic Books, 1986.

Bell, Clive. *Art.* London: Chatto and Windus, 1914.

Belo, Jane. *Traditional Balinese Culture.* New York: Columbia University Press, 1970.

Benjamin, Jessica. "The Bonds of Love: Rational Violence and Erotic Domination." In Hester Eisenstein and Alice Jardine, eds., *The Future of Difference.* Boston: G. K. Hall, 1980.

———. *The Bonds of Love.* New York: Pantheon, 1988.

Bergman, Sten. *My Father the Cannibal.* London: R. Hale, 1959.

Bernheimer, Charles, and Claire Kahane, eds. *In Dora's Case: Freud-Hysteria-Feminism.* New York: Columbia University Press, 1985.

Biebuyck, Daniel. *Tradition and Creativity in Tribal Art.* Berkeley: University of California Press, 1969.

Blair, Lawrence, and Lorne Blair. *Ring of Fire: Exploring the Last Remote Places of the World.* Toronto and New York: Bantam, 1988.

———. *Ring of Fire.* Adventure. Six episodes. Public Television (WUNC), 1988.

Blake, Susan L. "Racism and the Classics: Teaching *Heart of Darkness.*" *College Language Association Journal* 25 (1982): 396–404.

Blake, William. "Vala or the Four Zoas." In *Works,* 263–82. Oxford Standard Authors. New York: Oxford University Press, 1966.

Bloomfield, Leonard. *Language.* New York: Holt, Rinehart, 1933.

Boas, Franz. *A Franz Boas Reader.* Ed. George W. Stocking, Jr. Chicago: University of Chicago Press, 1974.

———. "Introduction," in *Handbook of American Indian Languages.* 1911; rpt., Lincoln: University of Nebraska Press, 1966.

———. *The Mind of Primitive Man.* Rev. ed. 1938; rpt. New York: Collier, 1963.

———. *Race, Language, and Culture.* New York: Macmillan, 1940.

Bowie, Malcolm. *Freud, Proust, and Lacan: Theory as Fiction.* Cambridge: Cambridge University Press, 1987.

Bowlby, Rachel. *Just Looking: Consumer Culture in Dreiser, Gissing, and Zola.* New York: Methuen, 1985.

Brain, Robert. *Art and Society in Africa.* New York: Longman, 1980.

Brodie, Susan Lundvall. "Conrad's Feminine Perspective." *Conradiana* 16 (1984): 141–54.

Brooke, James. "Faced with a Shrinking Supply of Authentic Art, African Dealers Peddle the Illusion." *New York Times*, Arts and Leisure, sec. 2, 17 April 1988, 27.

——. "Goodbye to Tarzan, Meet Captain Africa." *New York Times*, 27 September 1988, C22.

Brooks, Peter. *Reading for the Plot: Design and Intention in Narrative*. New York: Knopf, 1984.

Burroughs, Edgar Rice. *Jungle Tales of Tarzan*. 1915, 1916; rpt., New York: Ballantine, 1963.

——. *The Return of Tarzan*. 1913; rpt., New York: Ballantine, 1963.

——. *The Son of Tarzan*. 1915, 1916; rpt., New York: Ballantine, 1963.

——. *Tarzan and the Ant Men*. 1924; rpt., New York: Ballantine, 1963.

——. *Tarzan and the City of Gold*. 1932; rpt., New York: Ballantine, 1964.

——. *Tarzan and the Golden Lion*. 1922, 1923; rpt., New York: Ballantine, 1963.

——. *Tarzan and the Jewels of Opar*. 1916; rpt., New York: Ballantine, 1963.

——. *Tarzan, Lord of the Jungle*. 1927, 1928; rpt., New York: Ballantine, 1963.

——. *Tarzan of the Apes*. 1912; rpt., New York: Ballantine 1963.

——. *Tarzan the Invincible*. 1930, 1931; rpt., New York: Ballantine 1964.

——. "Tarzan Theme." In Henry H. Heins, *A Golden Anniversary Bibliography of Edgar Rice Burroughs*. West Kingston, R.I.: Donald M. Grant, 1964.

——. *Tarzan the Terrible*. 1921; rpt., New York: Ballantine, 1963.

——. *Tarzan the Untamed*. 1919, 1920; rpt., New York: Ballantine, 1963.

——. *Tarzan Triumphant*. 1931, 1932; rpt., New York: Ballantine, 1964.

——. *Tarzan's Quest*. 1935–1936; rpt., New York: Ballantine 1964.

Busia, Kofi Abrefa. *The Challenge of Africa*. London: Pall Mall, 1962.

Caillois, Roger. "The Collège de Sociologie: Paradox of an Active Sociology." *SubStance* 11–12 (1985): 61–64.

Castaneda, Carlos. *Journey to Ixtlan: The Lessons of Don Juan*. New York: Simon and Schuster, 1972.

———. *A Separate Reality: Further Conversations with Don Juan.* New York: Simon and Schuster, 1971.

———. *The Teachings of Don Juan: A Yaqui Way of Knowing.* Berkeley: University of California Press, 1968.

Castle, Terry. *Masquerade and Civilization: The Carnivalesque in Eighteenth-Century English Culture and Fiction.* Stanford: Stanford University Press, 1986.

Caws, Mary Ann. "The Poet at the Sword's Point." *SubStance* 11–12 (1985): 110–15.

Chenevière, Alain. *Vanishing Tribes: Primitive Man on Earth.* New York: Dolphin/Doubleday, 1988.

Chodorow, Nancy. *The Reproduction of Mothering: Psychoanalysis and the Sociology of Gender.* Berkeley: University of California Press, 1978.

Cleary, Thomas R., and Terry G. Sherwood. "Women in Conrad's Ironical Epic: Virgil, Dante, and *Heart of Darkness.*" *Conradiana* 16 (1984): 183–94.

Clifford, James. "Of Other Peoples: Beyond the 'Salvage' Principle." In Hal Foster, ed., *Discussions in Contemporary Culture,* vol. 1. Seattle: Bay Press, 1987.

———. *The Predicament of Culture.* Cambridge: Harvard University Press, 1988.

Clifford, James, and George E. Marcus, eds. *Writing Culture: The Poetics and Politics of Ethnography.* Berkeley: University of California Press, 1986.

Coe, Ralph. *Lost and Found Traditions: Native American Art, 1965–1985.* Seattle: University of Washington Press, 1986.

Comaroff, John, and Jean Comaroff. "Africa Observed." Chapter of book-in-progress, "From Revelation to Revolution."

Conrad, Joseph. *Heart of Darkness.* Robert Kimbrough, ed. Norton critical edition. New York: Norton, 1988.

———. *Life and Letters.* Vol. 1. Ed. G. Jean-Aubry. Garden City, N.Y.: Doubleday, 1927.

———. *Lord Jim.* Thomas C. Moser, ed. Norton critical edition. New York: Norton, 1968.

Conroy, Mark. *Modernism and Authority: Strategies of Legitimation in Flaubert and Conrad.* Baltimore: Johns Hopkins University Press, 1985.

Crapanzano, Vincent. *Tuhami: Portrait of a Moroccan.* Chicago: University of Chicago Press, 1980.

Crawley, Ernest. *Studies of Savages and Sex.* Landmarks of Anthropology series. 1929; rpt., London: Methuen, 1969.

Cunningham, Valentine. *British Writers of the Thirties*. New York: Oxford University Press, 1988.

Curtin, Philip D. *The Image of Africa: British Ideas and Action, 1780–1850*. Madison: University of Wisconsin Press, 1964.

Daiches, David, and Jon Stallworthy. "Joseph Conrad." In *The Norton Anthology of English Literature*, 1808–10. 5th ed. General ed. M. H. Abrams. Vol. 2. New York: Norton, 1986.

Darras, Jacques. *Joseph Conrad and the West: Signs of Empire*. Trans. Anne Lyat and Jacques Darras. New York: Barnes and Noble, 1982.

Davidson, Basil. *Africa* series. Public Television (WUNC), 1986.

———. *The Lost Cities of Africa*. Boston: Little, Brown, 1959.

Davies, Nigel. *Human Sacrifice in History and Today*. New York: Morrow, 1981.

Deleuze, Gilles, and Felix Guattari. *Anti-Oedipus: Capitalism and Psychoanalysis*. Trans. Helen R. Lane, Robert Hurley, and Mark Seem. New York: Viking, 1977.

Derrida, Jacques. *Of Grammatology*. Trans. Gayatri Chakravorty Spivak. Baltimore: Johns Hopkins University Press, 1974.

Diamond, Stanley. *In Search of the Primitive: A Critique of Civilization*. New Brunswick, N.J.: Transaction (Dutton), 1974.

Dimock, G. E. "The Name of Odysseus." In George Steiner and Robert Fagles, eds., *Homer: A Collection of Critical Essays*, 106–21. Englewood Cliffs, N.J.: Prentice-Hall, 1962.

Dinesen, Isak. *Out of Africa*. 1937; rpt. New York: Vintage, 1985.

Dinnerstein, Dorothy. *The Mermaid and the Minotaur*. New York: Harper, 1976.

Dominguez, Virginia. "The Marketing of Heritage." *American Ethnologist* 13, 3 (August 1986): 546–55.

———. "Of Other Peoples: Beyond the 'Salvage' Paradigm." In Hal Foster, ed., *Discussions in Contemporary Culture*, vol. 1. Seattle: Bay Press, 1987.

Drucker, Stephen. "Something Wild: On Safari in Kenya with Kim Basinger." *Vogue*, April 1988, 304–20, 401.

Duerr, Hans Peter. *Dreamtime: Concerning the Boundary between Wilderness and Civilization*. Trans. Felicitas Goodman. Oxford: Blackwell, 1985.

Ees, Erik van. "Last in Clan Seek 'Bit of Land.'" *Chicago Tribune*, 5 April 1987, 6.

Eisenstein, Hester, and Alice Jardine, eds. *The Future of Difference*. Boston: G. K. Hall, 1980.

Elgar, Frank. *Picasso: A Study of His Work*. New York: Praeger, 1956.

Ellis, Havelock. *Studies in the Psychology of Sex*. 4 vols. 1906; rpt., New York: Random, 1936.

Engelman, Edmund. *Bergasse 19: Sigmund Freud's Home and Offices, Vienna 1938; The Photographs of Edmund Engelman*. New York: Basic Books, 1976.

Evans-Pritchard, Sir Edward. *A History of Anthropological Thought*. Ed. André Singer. New York: Basic Books, 1981.

———. *The Nuer*. Oxford: Oxford University Press, 1940.

Fabian, Johannes. *Time and the Other: How Anthropology Makes Its Object*. New York: Columbia University Press, 1983.

Fagg, William, and Margaret Plass. *African Sculpture*. London: Dutton, 1964.

Fenton, Robert W. *The Big Swingers*. Englewood Cliffs, N.J.: Prentice-Hall, 1967.

Fernandez, James W. "Principles of Opposition and Vitality in Fang Aesthetics." *Journal of Aesthetics and Art Criticism* 25,1 (Fall 1966): 53–64.

Fiedler, Leslie. *Freaks: Myths and Images of the Secret Self*. New York: Simon and Schuster, 1978.

Fish, Stanley. *Is There a Text in This Class?* Cambridge: Harvard University Press, 1980.

———. "Withholding the Missing Portion: Psychoanalysis and Rhetoric." In Françoise Meltzer, ed., *The Trials of Psychoanalysis*. Chicago: University of Chicago Press, 1988.

Fleishman, Avrom. *Conrad's Politics: Community and Anarchy in the Fiction of Joseph Conrad*. Baltimore: Johns Hopkins University Press, 1967.

Foley, Helene P. " 'Reverse Similes' and Sex Roles in *The Odyssey*." *Arethusa* 11, 1–2 (1978): 7–26.

Forbath, Peter. *The Last Hero*. New York: Simon and Schuster, 1988.

Ford, George H. *Double Measure: A Study of the Novels and Stories of D. H. Lawrence*. New York: Holt, Rinehart, 1965.

Foster, Hal. "The 'Primitive' Unconscious of Modern Art." *October* 34 (Fall 1985): 45–70.

———, ed. *The Anti-Aesthetic: Essays on Post-Modern Culture*. Port Townsend, Wash.: Bay Press, 1983.

Frazer, Sir James. *The Golden Bough*. 1890; abridged ed., New York: Mentor/NAL, 1964.

Freeman, Derek. *Margaret Mead and Samoa: The Making and Un-*

making of an Anthropological Myth. Cambridge: Harvard University Press, 1983.

Freeman, Lucy, and Herbert S. Stream. *Freud and Women*. New York: Continuum, 1988.

Freud, Sigmund. "Autobiographical Study." In *Standard Edition*, vol. 20.

———. *Beyond the Pleasure Principle*. Trans. James Strachey. New York: Norton, 1961.

———. *Civilization and Its Discontents*. Trans. James Strachey. New York: Norton, 1961.

———. "A Disturbance of Memory on the Acropolis." In *Collected Papers*, vol. 5. Ed. James Strachey. London: Hogarth, 1950.

———. "Female Sexuality." In *Standard Edition*, vol. 21.

———. "Femininity." In *New Introductory Lectures in Psychoanalysis*. Trans. and ed. James Strachey. 1939; rpt., New York: Norton, 1965.

———. *The Future of an Illusion*. Trans. James Strachey. New York: Norton, 1961.

———. *Moses and Monotheism*. Trans. Katherine Jones. New York: Vintage/Random House, 1955.

———. *The Question of Lay Analysis*. In *Standard Edition*, vol. 20.

———. *Standard Edition of the Complete Psychoanalytic Works of Sigmund Freud*. Trans. James Strachey. 24 vols. London: Hogarth, 1953–74. Referred to throughout as *Standard Edition*.

———. "Thoughts for the Times on War and Death." Rpt. in Benjamin Nelson, ed., *On Creativity and the Unconscious*. 1915; rpt., New York: Harper, 1958.

———. *Totem and Taboo*. Trans. James Strachey. 1913; rpt., New York: Norton, 1950.

———. "The Uncanny." In *Standard Edition*, vol. 17.

———. "Why War?" In *Collected Papers*, vol. 5. Ed. James Strachey. London: Hogarth, 1950.

Fried, Morton. *The Notion of Tribe*. Menlo Park, Calif.: Cummings, 1975.

Frobenius, Leo. *African Nights: Black Erotic Folk Tales*. Trans. Peter Ross and Betty Ross. New York: Herder and Herder, 1971. Translation of *Atlantis*.

———. *Atlantis; Volksmärchen und volksdichtungen Afrikas*. 12 vols. Munich: Veroffentlichungen d. Forschungsinstituts für Kulturmorphologie, 1921–28.

———. *The Childhood of Man: A Popular Account of the Lives,*

Customs, and Thoughts of the Primitive Races. Trans. Augustus Henry Keane. Philadelphia: Lippincott, 1909.

———. *Das unbekannte Afrika* (The unknown Africa). Munich: Beck, 1923.

———. *The Voice of Africa: Being An Account of the Travels of the German Inner Africa Expedition in the Years 1910–1912.* 2 vols. London: Hutchinson, 1913.

Fry, Roger. *The Letters of Roger Fry.* Ed. Denys Sutton. 2 vols. New York: Random House, 1972.

———. *Vision and Design.* New York: Brentano's, 1920.

Garner, Shirley Nelson, Claire Kahane, and Madelon Sprengnether. *The (M)other Tongue.* Ithaca: Cornell University Press, 1985.

Gates, Henry Louis, Jr., ed. *"Race," Writing, and Difference.* Chicago: University of Chicago Press, 1986.

Gay, Peter. *Freud: A Life for Our Time.* New York: Norton, 1988.

———. *A Godless Jew: Freud, Atheism, and the Making of Psychoanalysis.* New Haven: Yale University Press, 1987.

Geertz, Clifford. "Being There Writing Here." *Harper's,* March 1988, 33–38.

———. "Deep Play: Notes on the Balinese Cockfight." In *The Interpretation of Cultures.* New York: Basic Books, 1973.

———. *Works and Lives: The Anthropologist as Author.* Stanford: Stanford University Press, 1988.

Gide, André. *Travels in the Congo.* Trans. Dorothy Bussy. New York: Modern Age, 1937.

Gilligan, Carol. *In a Different Voice: Psychological Theory and Women's Development.* Cambridge: Harvard University Press, 1982.

Gilman, Sander L. "Black Bodies, White Bodies: Towards an Iconography of Female Sexuality in Late Nineteenth-Century Art, Medicine, and Literature," *Critical Inquiry* 12, 1 (Autumn 1985): 223–61.

———. *Difference and Pathology: Stereotypes of Sexuality, Race, and Madness.* Ithaca: Cornell University Press, 1986.

———. *Jewish Self-Hatred: Anti-Semitism and the Hidden Language of the Jews.* Baltimore and London: Johns Hopkins University Press, 1986.

Girard, Réné. *Violence and the Sacred.* Trans. Patrick Gregory. Baltimore: Johns Hopkins University Press, 1972.

Glueck, Grace. "The Modern Prepares for the Twenty-first Century." *New York Times,* Arts and Leisure, sec. 2, 6 March 1988, 1.

Goldwater, Robert J. *Primitivism in Modern Art.* 1938; rpt., New York: Random House, 1967. Originally published as *Primitivism in Modern Painting.*

Gombrich, E. M. "Representation and Misrepresentation." *Critical Inquiry* 11, 2 (December 1984): 202–25.

Gordon, Donald E. "German Expressionism." In William Rubin, ed., *"Primitivism" in 20th-Century Art,* 369–404. New York: Museum of Modern Art, 1984.

———. *Modern Art Exhibitions, 1900–1916.* Munich: Prester-Verlag, 1974.

Greenberg, David F. *The Construction of Homosexuality.* Chicago: University of Chicago Press, 1988.

Grottanelli, Vinig L. "The Lugard Lecture of 1961." In Daniel F. McCall and Edna G. Bay, eds., *African Images: Essays in African Iconology.* New York: Africana Publishing, for African Studies Center, Boston University, 1975.

Guerard, Albert. *Conrad the Novelist.* Cambridge: Harvard University Press, 1958.

Haggard, H. Rider. *She* and *King Solomon's Mines.* New York: Modern Library, 1957.

Hammond, Dorothy, and Alta Jablow. *The Myth of Africa.* New York: Library of Social Science, 1977. Originally published as *The Africa That Never Was.*

Hansen, Eric. *Stranger in the Forest: On Foot across Borneo.* Boston: Yolla Booly/Houghton, 1988.

Harding, Sandra. *The Science Question in Feminism.* Ithaca: Cornell University Press, 1986.

Hardy, Georges. *L'art nègre: L'art animiste des noirs d'Afrique.* Paris: Henri Laurens, 1927.

Hassan, Ihab Habib. *The Dismemberment of Orpheus: Towards a Post-Modern Literature.* Madison: University of Wisconsin Press, 1982.

———. *The Postmodern Turn: Essays in Postmodern Theory and Culture.* Columbus: Ohio State University Press, 1987.

Hawkins, Hunt. "Conrad and the Congolese Exploitation." *Conradiana* 13 (1981): 94–100.

———. "Conrad's Critique of Imperialism in *Heart of Darkness.*" *PMLA* 94 (1979): 286–99.

———. "The Issue of Racism in *Heart of Darkness.*" *Conradiana* 114 (1982): 163–71.

Hayes, E. Nelson, and Tanya Hayes, eds. *Claude Lévi-Strauss: The Anthropologist as Hero.* Cambridge: MIT Press, 1970.

Heins, Henry Hardy. *A Golden Anniversary Bibliography of Edgar Rice Burroughs*. West Kingston, R.I.: Donald M. Grant, 1964.

Hemming, John. *Amazon Frontier: The Defeat of the Brazilian Indians*. Cambridge: Harvard University Press, 1988.

Herskovits, Melville Jean. *Dahomey: An Ancient African Kingdom*. New York: J. J. Augustin, 1938.

Hertz, Neil. "Dora's Secrets, Freud's Techniques." In Charles Bernheimer and Claire Kahane, eds., *In Dora's Case: Freud-Hysteria-Feminism*, 221–42. New York: Columbia University Press, 1985.

Hobsbawm, Eric, and Terence Ranger, eds. *The Invention of Tradition*. Cambridge: Cambridge University Press, 1983.

Holtzmark, Erling B. *Tarzan and Tradition*. London: Greenwood Press, 1981.

Homer. *The Odyssey*. Trans E. V. Rieu. Baltimore: Penguin, 1946.

Horkheimer, Max, and Theodor W. Adorno. *Dialectic of Enlightenment*. Trans. John Cumming. 1944; rpt., New York: Herder and Herder, 1972.

Horney, Karen. *New Ways in Psychoanalysis*. New York: Norton, 1939.

Howard, Jane. *Margaret Mead: A Life*. New York: Simon and Schuster, 1984.

Huxley, Elspeth. *The Flame Trees of Thika*. 1959; New York: Penguin, 1987.

———. *Out in the Midday Sun*. 1985; New York: Penguin, 1987.

Hynes, Samuel Lynn. *The Auden Generation*. London: Bodley Head, 1976.

I-D. "The Tribal Issue." 56 (March 1988).

Jameson, Frederic. *The Political Unconscious: Narrative as a Socially Symbolic Act*. Ithaca: Cornell University Press, 1981.

Kaplan, Alice Yaeger. *Reproductions of Banality: Fascism, Literature, and French Intellectual Life*. Theory and History of Literature, no. 36. Minneapolis: University of Minnesota Press, 1985.

———, ed. "Anti-Semite and Jew: The Aesthetics and Politics of Ethnic Identity." *SubStance* 15, 1 (1986).

Keller, Evelyn Fox. *Reflections on Gender and Science*. New Haven: Yale University Press, 1984.

Kenyatta, Jomo. *Facing Mount Kenya*. 1938; rpt., New York: Vintage, 1962.

Kermode, Frank. *D. H. Lawrence*. New York: Viking, 1973.

Kiely, Robert. *Beyond Egotism: The Fiction of James Joyce, Virginia Woolf, and D. H. Lawrence*. Cambridge: Harvard University Press, 1980.

Kingsley, Mary H. *Travels in West Africa.* London: Macmillan, 1897.
———. *West African Studies.* 1899; New York: Barnes and Noble, 1964.

Klein, Dennis B. *Jewish Origins of Psychoanalysis.* Chicago: University of Chicago Press, 1985.

Knapp, Steven, and Walter Benn Michaels. "Against Theory." In *Critical Inquiry* 8 (1982): 723–42.

Knipp, T. R. "Black African Literature and the New African State." *Books Abroad* 44 (1970): 373–79.

Kofman, Sarah. *The Enigma of Woman: Woman in Freud's Writings.* Trans. Catherine Porter. Ithaca: Cornell University Press, 1985. Original volume published in French in 1980.

Kramer, Hilton. "The 'Primitivism' Conundrum." *New Criterion* 3, 4 (December 1984): 1–7.

Krauss, Rosalind. "Giacometti." In William Rubin, ed., *"Primitivism" in 20th-Century Art,* 503–34. New York: Museum of Modern Art, 1984.

Kristeva, Julia. *Powers of Horror: An Essay on Abjection.* Trans. Leon S. Roudiez. European Perspectives. New York: Columbia University Press, 1982.

Kuper, Adam. *The Invention of Primitive Society: Transformations of an Illusion.* London: Routledge, 1988.

Lacan, Jacques. *Feminine Sexuality.* Trans. Juliet Mitchell and Jacqueline Rose. Basingstoke: Macmillan, 1982.

Laude, Jean. *The Arts of Black Africa.* Trans. Jean Decock. Berkeley: University of California Press, 1971.

Lawrence, D. H. "Aristocracy." In *Reflections on the Death of a Porcupine and Other Essays.* Philadelphia: Centaur, 1925.
———. *The Collected Letters of D. H. Lawrence.* 2 vols. Ed. Harry T. Moore. New York: Viking, 1962.
———. "Corasmin and the Parrot." In *Mornings in Mexico.* London: Heinemann, 1956.
———. *Fantasia of the Unconscious* and *Psychoanalysis and the Unconscious.* 1923; rpt., London: Heinemann, 1971.
———. "An Introduction to These Paintings." In *Phoenix: The Posthumous Papers of D. H. Lawrence.* Ed. Edward D. McDonald. New York: Viking, 1936.
———. *Lady Chatterley's Lover.* 1928; reprint, New York: Grove, 1957.
———. *The Letters of D. H. Lawrence.* Five volumes, Cambridge: Cambridge University Press, 1982–1989.

———. *The Man Who Died*. Published with *St. Mawr*. New York: Vintage/Random House, 1953.

———. "The Mozo." In *Mornings in Mexico*. London: Heinemann, 1956.

———. *The Plumed Serpent*. 1926; rpt., New York: Vintage, 1959.

———. *The Symbolic Meaning*. Ed. Armin Arnold. New York: Viking, 1964.

———. "The Woman Who Rode Away." In *The Complete Short Stories of D. H. Lawrence*, vol. 3. New York: Viking, 1961.

———. *Women in Love*. Ed. Charles Ross. 1920; rpt., Baltimore: Penguin, 1982.

Leavis, F. R. *The Great Tradition*. 1937; rpt., New York: New York University Press, 1967.

Lee, Robert F. *Conrad's Colonialism*. The Hague: Mouton, 1969.

Leiris, Michel. "A travers *Tristes Tropiques*." In *Brisées*, 199–209. Paris: Mercure de France, 1966.

———. *L'Afrique fantôme*. 1934; rpt., Paris: Gallimard, 1981.

———. "L'ethnographe devant le colonialisme" In *Brisées*, 125–45. Paris: Mercure de France, 1966.

———. *Les règles du jeu*. 4 vols. Paris: Gallimard, 1948–76.

———. *Manhood: A Journey from Childhood into the Fierce Order of Virility* [*L'age d'homme*]. Trans. Richard Howard. San Francisco: North Point Press, 1984.

Leiris, Michel, and Jacqueline Delange. *African Art*. Trans. Michael Ross. Arts of Mankind series. 1967; rpt., London: Thames and Hudson, 1968.

Lela, Kouakou. Commentary, "Lela Kouakou" section. In Susan Vogel, ed., *Perspectives: Angles on African Art*, 145–160. Referred to in *Gone Primitive* as the "Baule Carvers'" section.

Lemann, Nicholas. "Fake Masks." *Atlantic*, November 1987.

Lévy-Bruhl, Lucien. *How Natives Think* [*La mentalité primitive*]. Trans Lillian A. Clare. New York: Washington Square Press, 1966.

Lévi-Strauss, Claude. "The Art of the Northwest Coast at the American Museum of Natural History." *Gazette des beaux arts*, September 1943, 145–82.

———. *From Honey to Ashes*. Vol. 2 of *Mythologiques*. Trans. John Weightman and Doreen Weightman. New York: Harper, 1973.

———. *The Jealous Potter*. Trans. Benedicte Chorier. Chicago: University of Chicago Press, 1988. Originally published in French in 1985.

———. *The Naked Man*. Vol. 4 of *Mythologiques*. Trans. John

Weightman and Doreen Weightman. New York: Harper and Row, 1981.

———. *The Raw and the Cooked.* Vol. 1 of *Mythologiques.* Trans. John Weightman and Doreen Weightman. New York: Harper, 1969.

———. *The Savage Mind* [*La pensée sauvage*]. Chicago: University of Chicago Press, 1966.

———. *Structural Anthropology.* Trans. Clair Jacobson and Brooke Grundfest Schoepf. New York: Basic, 1963.

———. *Totemism.* Trans. Rodney Needham. Boston: Beacon, 1963.

———. *Tristes Tropiques.* Trans. John Weightman and Doreen Weightman. New York: Atheneum, 1984.

———. *The View from Afar.* New York: Basic, 1985.

Lifton, Robert Jay. *The Nazi Doctors: Medical Killing and the Psychology of Genocide.* New York: Basic, 1986.

Longino, Helen, and Ruth Doell. "Body, Bias, and Behavior: A Comparative Analysis of Reasoning in Two Areas of Biological Science." *Signs* 9:2.

Luhan, Mabel Dodge. *Lorenzo in Taos.* New York: Knopf, 1932.

Lukács, Georg. *The Theory of the Novel.* Trans. Anna Bostock. Cambridge: MIT Press, 1971. Originally published in German in 1920.

———. "Reification and the Consciousness of the Proletariat." In *History and Class Consciousness.* Trans. Rodney Livingstone. Cambridge: MIT Press, 1988.

Lupoff, Richard A. *Edgar Rice Burroughs: Master of Adventure.* New York: Canaveral, 1965.

Lyotard, Jean-François. *The Post-Modern Condition: A Report on Knowledge.* Trans. Geoffrey Bennington and Brian Massumi. Theory and History of Literature, no. 10. Minneapolis: University of Minnesota Press, 1984. Originally published in French in 1979.

McClintock, Ann. "Mines, Maps, and Maidens: Race and Gender in British Imperial Literature (1860–1914)." Ph. D. diss. in progress, Columbia University.

McClure, John A. *Kipling and Conrad: The Colonial Fiction.* Cambridge: Cambridge University Press, 1981.

McLuhan, Marshall. *Understanding Media.* New York: McGraw-Hill, 1964.

Mahler, Margaret S., Fred Pine, and Anni Bergman. *The Psychological Birth of the Human Infant: Symbiosis and Individuation.* New York: Basic, 1975.

Mahood, Molly Maureen. *The Colonial Encounter: A Reading of Six Novels.* London: Collings, 1977.

Malinowski, Bronislaw. *Argonauts of the Western Pacific*. 1922; rpt., Prospect Heights, Ill.: Waveland Press, 1984.

——. *A Diary in the Strict Sense of the Term*. Trans. Norbert Guterman. London: Routledge, 1967.

——. *Sex, Culture, and Myth*. New York: Harcourt Brace Jovanovich, 1962.

——. *The Sexual Life of Savages: An Ethnographic Account of Courtship, Marriage, and Family Life among the Natives of the Trobriand Islands, British New Guinea*. New York: Harcourt Brace and World, 1929; rpt., 1987.

Malraux, André. *Museum without Walls*. Trans. Stuart Gilbert and Francis Price. Garden City, N.Y.: Doubleday, 1967.

A Man Called Horse. Produced by Sandy Howard. Directed by Elliot Silverstein. Cinema Center Films, 1969.

Mandel, Paul. "Tarzan of the Paperbacks." *Life*, 29 November 1963, 11–12.

Manning, Olivia. *The Remarkable Expedition: The Story of Stanley's Rescue of Emin Pasha from Equatorial Africa*. New York: Atheneum, 1985.

Marcus, George. *Anthropology as Cultural Critique*. Chicago: University of Chicago Press, 1986.

Marcus, Steven. *Freud and the Culture of Psychoanalysis*. Boston: Allen and Unwin, 1984.

Marinetti, Tommaso Filippo. "The Founding and Manifesto of Futurism." In *Marinetti: Selected Writings*. Ed. R. W. Flint. Trans. R. W. Flint and Arthur A. Coppotelli. New York: Farrar, 1971.

Mass Observation. *Britain*. 1941; rpt., London: Hutchinson Cresset, 1986.

Masson, J. L. *The Assault on Truth: Freud's Suppression of the Seduction Theory*. New York: Farrar, 1984.

Masters, William H., and Virginia Johnson. *Human Sexual Response*. Boston: Little, Brown, 1966.

Maurer, Evan. "Dada and Surrealism." In William Rubin, ed., *"Primitivism" in 20th-Century Art*, 535–94. New York: Museum of Modern Art, 1984.

Mauss, Marcel. *The Gift: Forms and Functions of Exchange in Archaic Societies*. Trans. Ian Cunnison. New York: Norton, 1967.

Mead, Margaret. *Blackberry Winter: My Earlier Years*. 1972; rpt., New York: Pocket Books, 1975.

——. *Coming of Age in Samoa*. 1928; rpt., New York: American Museum of Natural History, 1973.

————. *Male and Female: A Study of the Sexes in a Changing World.* 1949; rpt., New York: Morrow, 1968.

————. *Some Personal Views.* Ed. Rhoda Metraux. New York: Walker, 1979.

Mead, Margaret, and James Baldwin. *A Rap on Race.* Philadelphia: Lippincott, 1971.

Mead, Margaret, and Gregory Bateson. *Balinese Character: A Photographic Analysis.* New York: New York Academy of Sciences, 1942.

Meisel, Martin. *Realizations: Narrative, Pictorial, and Theatrical Arts in Nineteenth-Century England.* Princeton: Princeton University Press, 1983.

Meltzer, Françoise, ed. *The Trials of Psychoanalysis.* Chicago: University of Chicago Press, 1988.

Meyer, Jeffrey, *Fiction and the Colonial Experience.* Ipswich, England: Boydell, 1973.

Michelet, M. *African Empires and Civilisations.* London, 1945.

Miller, Christopher. *Blank Darkness.* Chicago: University of Chicago Press, 1989.

Miller, J. Hillis. *The Disappearance of God: Five Nineteenth-Century Writers.* Cambridge: Harvard University Press, 1963.

Millett, Kate. *Sexual Politics.* New York: Avon, 1969.

Mitchell, Juliet, and Jacqueline Rose. "Introduction I and II." In Jacques Lacan, *Feminine Sexuality,* 1–57. Basingstoke: Macmillan, 1982.

Mohammed, Abdul Jan. *Manichean Aesthetics.* Amherst: University of Massachusetts Press, 1983.

Moi, Toril. "Representation of Patriarchy: Sexuality and Epistemology in Freud's Dora." In Charles Bernheimer and Claire Kahane, eds., *In Dora's Case: Freud-Hysteria-Feminism,* 181–99. New York: Columbia University Press, 1985.

Montaigne. "Of Coaches." In *The Complete Essays of Montaigne.* Trans. Donald M. Frame. Stanford: Stanford University Press, 1958.

————. "Of the Cannibals." In *Selected Essays of Montaigne.* Trans. John Florio. Ed. Walter Kaiser. Boston: Houghton-Mifflin/Riverside, 1964.

Morrow, Lance. "Africa: An Essay." *Time,* 27 February 1987.

Mount, Marshall Ward. *African Art: The Years since 1920.* Bloomington: Indiana University Press, 1973.

Mudimbe, V. Y. *The Invention of Africa: Gnosis, Philosophy, and the Order of Knowledge.* Bloomington: Indiana University Press, 1988.

Mydans, Seth. "20th-Century Lawsuit Asserts Stone-Age Identity." *New York Times,* 29 October 1988, 4.

Naipaul, V. S. *The Return of Eva Peron.* New York: Knopf, 1980.

Nazareth, Peter. "Out of Darkness: Conrad and Other Third World Writers." *Conradiana* 14 (1982): 173–87.

Nehls, Edward. *D. H. Lawrence: A Composite Biography.* Vol 1. Madison: University of Wisconsin Press, 1957.

Newman, Charles. *The Post-Modern Aura: The Act of Fiction in an Age of Inflation.* Evanston, Ill.: Northwestern University Press, 1985.

Ngugi, wa Thiong'o. *Decolonising the Mind.* London: James Currey, 1986.

Nixon, Rob. "Out of Africa." *Grand Street,* Summer 1986, 216–227.

Ohmann, Richard. "The Shaping of a Canon: U.S. Fiction 1960–1975." *Critical Inquiry* 10 (September 1983): 199–223.

Parry, Benita. *Conrad and Imperialism: Ideological Boundaries and Visionary Frontiers.* Topsfield, Mass.: Merrimack, 1984.

Paudrat, Jean-Louis. "From Africa." In William Rubin, ed., *"Primitivism" in 20th-Century Art,* 125–78. New York: Museum of Modern Art, 1984.

Paz, Octavio. *Claude Lévi-Strauss: An Introduction.* Trans. J. S. Bernstein and Maxine Bernstein. Ithaca: Cornell University Press, 1970.

Pearce, Roy Harvey. *The Savages of America: A Study of the Indian and the Idea of Civilization.* Rev. ed. Baltimore and London: Johns Hopkins University Press, 1965.

Peterson, Iver. "Looting of Tribal Sites Grows as Illicit Profits Rise in the West." *New York Times,* 8 December 1984, 6–7.

Pilling, Arnold R. "Anthropology's Culture and Personality School and Homosexuality." *Society of Lesbian and Gay Anthropologists Newsletter* 2, 1 (February 1988): 19–22.

Porges, Irwin. *Edgar Rice Burroughs: The Man Who Created Tarzan.* Provo, Utah: Brigham Young University Press, 1975.

Praise Poems: The Katherine White Collection. Seattle: Seattle Art Museum, 1984; distributed by University of Chicago Press.

Pratt, Mary Louise. "Scratches on the Face of the Country, or, What Mr. Barrow Saw in the Land of the Bushman." *Critical Inquiry* 12, 1 (Autumn 1985): 119–43.

Price, Sally. *Primitive Art in Civilized Places.* Chicago: University of Chicago Press, 1989.

Rabinow, Paul. *Reflections on Fieldwork in Morocco*. Berkeley: University of California Press, 1977.

Rader, Ralph. Talk on Conrad. Narrative Poetics Conference, Columbus, Ohio, 1986.

Raval, Suresh. *The Art of Failure: Conrad's Fiction*. Boston: Allen and Unwin, 1986.

Rosaldo, Renato. *Ilongot Headhunting, 1883–1974: A Study in Society and History*. Stanford: Stanford University Press, 1980.

Rosenblum, S. P., ed. *The Bloomsbury Group*. Toronto: University of Toronto Press, 1975.

Rossman, Charles. "D. H. Lawrence and Mexico." In Peter Balbert and Phillip L. Marcus, eds., *D. H. Lawrence: A Centenary Consideration*. Ithaca: Cornell University Press, 1985.

Rousseau, Jean-Jacques. "A Discourse on the Origin of Inequality." In *The Social Contract and Discourses*. New York: Dutton, 1950.

Rubin, Gayle. "The Traffic in Women: Notes on the 'Political Economy' of Sex." In Rayna Reiter, ed., *Towards an Anthropology of Women*. New York: Monthly Review Press, 1975.

Rubin, William. "Modernist Primitivism: An Introduction." In William Rubin, ed., *"Primitivism" in 20th-Century Art*, 1–84. New York: Museum of Modern Art, 1984.

———. "Picasso." In William Rubin, ed., *"Primitivism" in 20th-Century Art*, 241–344. New York: Museum of Modern Art, 1984.

———. Commentary, "William Rubin" section. In Susan Vogel, ed., *Perspectives: Angles on African Art*, 49–64. New York: Abrams/Center for African Art, 1987.

———, ed. *"Primitivism" in 20th-Century Art*. 2 vols. New York: Museum of Modern Art, 1984.

Sagan, Eli. *Cannibalism: Human Aggression and Cultural Form*. London: Psychohistory Press, 1974.

———. *Freud, Women, and Morality: The Psychology of Good and Evil*. New York: Basic, 1988.

Sahlins, Marshall. *Historical Metaphors and Mythical Realities*. Ann Arbor: University of Michigan Press, 1981.

———. *Islands of History*. Chicago: University of Chicago Press, 1985.

Said, Edward. *After the Last Sky*. New York: Pantheon, 1986.

———. *Orientalism*. New York: Pantheon, 1978.

———. "Through Gringo Eyes: With Conrad in Latin America." *Harper's*, April 1986, 70–72.

———. *The World, the Text, and the Critic*. Cambridge: Harvard University Press, 1983.

Sanday, Peggy Reeves. *Divine Hunger: Cannibalism as a Cultural System*. London: Cambridge University Press, 1986.

Sapir, Edward, *Language: An Introduction to the Study of Speech*. 1921; rpt., New York: Harcourt, Brace, World, 1949.

Schneebaum, Tobias. *Keep the River on Your Right*. New York: Grove, 1969.

———. *The Wild Man*. New York: Viking, 1979.

———. *Where the Spirits Dwell*. New York: Grove, 1988.

Sedgwick, Eve Kosofsky. *Between Men: English Literature and Male Homosocial Desire*. New York: Columbia University Press, 1985.

Seelye, John. "Tarzan Was a Problem." *New York Times Book Review*, 26 October 1975, 36–37.

Shostak, Marjorie. *Nisa: The Life and Words of a !Kung Woman*. Cambridge: Harvard University Press, 1981.

Shoumatoff, Alex. *The River Amazon*. San Francisco: Sierra Club, 1978.

Shweder, Richard A. "Storytelling among the Anthropologists." *New York Times Book Review*, 21 September 1986, 1.

Siebers, Tobin. *The Ethics of Criticism*. Ithaca: Cornell University Press, 1988.

Simpson, David. *Fetishism and Imagination*. Baltimore: Johns Hopkins University Press, 1982.

———. "Literary Criticism and the Return to 'History.'" *Critical Inquiry* 14, 4 (Summer 1988): 721–47.

Smith, Barbara Herrnstein. "Contingencies of Value." *Critical Inquiry* 10,1 (Fall 1983): 1–36.

Sontag, Susan. "The Anthropologist as Hero." In *Against Interpretation*, 69–81. New York: Farrar, 1966.

Spalding, Frances. *Roger Fry: Art and Life*. Berkeley: University of California Press, 1980.

Spivak, Gayatri Chakravorty. *In Other Worlds: Essays in Cultural Politics*. New York: Routledge, 1988.

Sprinker, Michael. *Imaginary Relations: Aesthetics and Ideology in the Theory of Historical Materialism*. New York: Verso, 1987.

———. Talk on Conrad. Narrative Poetics Conference, Columbus, Ohio, 1986.

Stanley, Henry M. *The Congo and the Founding of Its Free State: A Story of Work and Exploration*. 2 vols. New York: Harper, 1885.

———. *How I Found Livingstone: Travels, Adventures, and Discoveries in Central Africa*. 1874; rpt., New York: Scribner's, 1899.

———. *In Darkest Africa, or the Quest, Rescue, and Retreat of*

Emin, Governor of Equatoria. London: Sampson, Low, Marston, 1897.

———. *My Kalulu, Prince, King, and Slave: A Story of Central Africa.* London: S. Low, Marston, and Searle, 1893.

Stern, Daniel. *The Interpersonal World of the Infant: A View from Psychoanalysis and Developmental Psychology.* New York: Basic Books, 1985.

Stewart, Garrett. "Lying as Dying in *Heart of Darkness.*" In Joseph Conrad, *Heart of Darkness,* Norton critical edition, 358–74. New York: Norton, 1988.

Stocking, George W., Jr. "Introduction." In Franz Boas, *A Franz Boas Reader.* Chicago: University of Chicago Press, 1974.

———. *Victorian Anthropology.* New York: Free Press, 1987; London: Macmillan, 1987.

———, ed. *Malinowski, Rivers, Benedict and Others: Essays on Culture and Personality.* History of Anthropology, no. 4. Madison: University of Wisconsin Press, 1986.

———, ed. *Objects and Others: Essays on Museums and Material Culture.* History of Anthropology, no. 3. Madison: University of Wisconsin Press, 1985.

Stoekl, Alan. "Introduction." In Georges Bataille, *Visions of Excess: Selected Writings, 1927–39.* Minneapolis: University of Minnesota Press, 1985.

Street, Brian V. *The Savage in Literature: Representations of "Primitive" Society in English Fiction, 1858–1920.* London and Boston: Routledge and Kegan Paul, 1975.

Tambiah, Stanley J. *World Conqueror, World Renouncer.* New York: Cambridge University Press, 1976.

Tannehill, Ray. *Flesh and Blood: A History of the Cannibal Complex.* New York: Stein and Day, 1975.

Theweleit, Klaus. *Male Fantasies: Women, Floods, Bodies, History.* Vol 1. Trans. Stephen Conway, in collaboration with Erica Carter and Chris Turner. Minneapolis: University of Minnesota Press, 1987.

Thomas, John-Jacques, ed. *SubStance* 11–12 (1985). Special issue on Michel Leiris.

Thompson, Robert Farris. *African Art in Motion: Icon and Art in the Collection of Katherine Coryton White.* Los Angeles: University of California, 1974.

———. "Esthetics in Traditional Africa." *Art News* 66, 9 (January, 1968): 44f.

Todorov, Tzvetan. *The Conquest of America.* Trans. Richard Howard. New York: Harper, 1984.

Tompkins, Jane. "West of Everything." Book in progress.

Torgovnick, Marianna. *Closure in the Novel.* Princeton: Princeton University Press, 1981.

————. *The Visual Arts, Pictorialism, and the Novel: James, Lawrence, and Woolf.* Princeton: Princeton University Press, 1985.

Trowell, Margaret. *Classical African Sculpture.* 1954; rpt., New York: Praeger, 1970.

"Twelve Masterworks from North Carolina Collections." Exhibition notes. Chapel Hill, N.C.: Ackland Museum of Art, 1985.

Vallentin, Antonina. *Picasso.* London: Cassell, 1963.

Van Ghent, Dorothy. *The English Novel: Form and Function.* New York: Rinehart, 1953.

Vidal, Gore. "Tarzan Revisited." *Esquire,* December 1963, 192–93.

Vogel, Susan. *The Aesthetics of African Art: The Carlo Monzino Collection.* New York: Center for African Art, 1986.

————, ed. *Art/Artifact.* New York: Abrams/Center for African Art, 1988.

————, ed. *Perspectives: Angles on African Art.* New York: Abrams/Center for African Art, 1987.

Vogel, Susan, and Francine D'Diaye. *African Masterpieces from the Musée d'Homme.* New York: Abrams/Center for African Art, 1985.

Wagner, Roy. *The Invention of Culture.* Rev. ed. Chicago: University of Chicago Press, 1980.

Watt, Ian. *Conrad in the Nineteenth Century.* Berkeley: University of California Press, 1979.

White, Hayden. *Tropics of Discourse: Essays in Cultural Criticism.* Baltimore and London: Johns Hopkins University Press, 1978.

Willett, Frank. *African Art: An Introduction.* New York: Praeger, 1971.

Williams, Raymond. *The Long Revolution.* Rev. ed. New York: Harper and Row, 1966.

Winnicott, D. W. *Playing and Reality.* New York: Basic, 1971.

Wolf, Eric R. *Europe and the People without History.* Berkeley: University of California Press, 1982.

Wolfe, Tom. *The Bonfire of the Vanities.* New York: Farrar, 1987.

Woolf, Virginia. *The Letters of Virginia Woolf: The Question of Things Happening.* Vol. 2, 1912–22. Ed. Nigel Nicolson and asst. ed. Joanne Trautmann. London: Hogarth, 1976.

————. "Modern Fiction." In *The Common Reader*. Ed. Andrew McNeillie. 1925; New York: Harcourt Brace Jovanovich, 1984.

————. "Mr. Bennett and Mrs. Brown." In *The Essays of Virginia Woolf*, 3:384–89. Ed. Andrew McNeillie. 1923; New York: Harcourt Brace Jovanovich, 1988.

————. *Roger Fry: A Biography.* New York: Harcourt, Brace, and World, 1925.

Young, Michael W., ed. *The Ethnography of Malinowski: The Trobriand Islands, 1915–18.* London: Routledge, 1979.

Index

Acéphale, 148–49, 151, 276 n.7, 273 n. 19
Achebe, Chinua, 270 n. 3, 272 n. 13, 273 n. 15
Adorno, Theodore, 285 n. 20
Advertising: 21; of Tarzan, 44, 45, 260 n. 2
Aesthetics: African, 135–37; Western art historians and, 78–84, 87–88, 136–37. *See also* Art
Africa: colonization of, 10, 14, 57–58, 60–62, 76–77, 88–89, 91, 94, 96, 98, 267 n. 1; history of, 60, 98–99, 104, 262 n. 18, 19; 272 n. 12, 293 n. 2; in *Heart of Darkness*, 141, 143, 150–51, 270 n. 3; cannibalism/head-hunting in, 14, 22, 50, 147–48, 151; peoples of, 22, 257 n. 45, 260 n. 60; South Africa, 40, 62, 144; Stanley and, 10, 26–27, 30–33, 34, 58, 61; Tarzan novels and, 23, 44, 45, 47, 48, 50, 52, 55–58, 60–62, 75, 77, 262 n. 14, 16; television and, 13–14; Western perceptions of, 29, 30, 60, 160–62; Zaire (Congo) 50, 61–62, 75–77, 261 n. 127, 275 n. 29
African art: aesthetics of, 94, 96, 98–99, 135–37, 266 n. 7, 269 n. 9, 12; and artists, vs. Western critics, 90, 91–92, 94, 98–99, 130–37; contemporary developments in 38, 136–37, 265 n. 16; dating of, 90–91, 268 n. 2; in art criticism/history, 80–84, 85–87, 92, 97–99, 133–36, 161–62; mis-

readings of, 12, 15–17, 102, 126–28, 161–62, 255 n. 33, 268 n. 4; modern art and, 85–87, 99–104, 119–22, 151; noncontextual approach to, 78, 83, 264 n. 10. *See also* Museums; Museum exhibitions; Primitive art
—drawings: Bushman, 94–96; cave, 90, 266 n. 11; Fry's "Art of the Bushman," 85–86, 87, 89, 94–96;
—masks, 35, 92–93, 102, 131–33, 267 n. 4, 268 n. 7; hermaphroditic, 116–17; in modern art, 34–35, 102, 151; in Picasso's work, 104, 128, 151; in Western sexual imagery, 102, 104, 117; J. Coatmellac's suicide and, 14–17, 104, 126;
—sculpture/statues: Freud and, 194–97, 203; Lawrence and, 12, 117, 161–63; misread as pornographic, 102, 104, 110, 113–14, 116–17, 162, 268 n. 4; Oceanic, 9, 136, 161; R. Fry's "Negro Sculpture" on, 86, 87–88, 89–92, 93–94, 96; Western consumption of, 37–39, 136, 161
Amazon/Amazonian Indians, 14, 22, 40–41, 214–15, 219
Anthropology, 7, 8, 10, 21, 45, 190–92, 218, 219, 244, 250 n. 5, 251 n. 8, 254 n. 27, 282 n. 21, 293 nn. 1, 24; "being there/writing here" in, 231, 234–35, 251 n. 8, 293 n. 1; dialogic/polyphonic method in, 23, 247, 251 n. 6, 294 n. 5; ethnography and, 3, 7, 250 n. 5, 251

317